Anniversaries and Holidays

Anniversaries and Holidays

Fourth edition

by
Ruth W. Gregory

American Library Association　　Chicago　　1983

Composed by Modern Typographers Inc.
  in Linotron 202 Times Roman and Helvetica
Printed on 50-pound Antique Glatfelter, a pH-neutral
  stock, by Malloy Lithographing, Inc.
Bound in B-grade Holliston cloth by
  John H. Dekker & Sons

Library of Congress Cataloging in Publication Data

Gregory, Ruth W. (Ruth Wilhelme), 1910–
  Anniversaries and holidays.

  Bibliography: p.
  Includes index.
  1. Holidays. 2. Anniversaries. 3. Fasts and
feasts. 4. Holidays—Bibliography.
5. Anniversaries—Bibliography. 6. Fasts and feasts—
Bibliography. I. Title.
GT3930.G74 1983   394.2′6   83-3784
ISBN 0-8389-0389-4

Contents

Preface

This volume of ANNIVERSARIES AND HOLIDAYS is the fourth edition of a book of days originated in 1928 by the late Mary Emogene Hazeltine, former director of the Library School of the University of Wisconsin. The second edition was published in 1944, and a third edition in 1975. The cut-off date for the fourth edition was November 15, 1982.

The purpose of ANNIVERSARIES AND HOLIDAYS is to provide a quick identification of notable anniversaries, holy days, holidays, and special events days, and to link outstanding days to books for further information or background reading.

This book is designed to serve as an information tool for use by public and school librarians, research specialists in system reference centers, teachers, writers in the communication fields, public relations personnel planning programs and exhibits for special days, and the individual reader curious about holidays as one aspect of world history.

The fourth edition enlarges the international scope established in 1975. It includes the holidays and days of observance of 183 nations as compared with 153 in the third edition. However, even though multiple holidays of the world at large are listed, the observances of the United States predominate.

The text of the fourth edition includes 2,637 entries and follows the pattern of earlier editions in including holy days and religious festivals, holidays and civic days, and days that commemorate the achievements of outstanding men and women or a memorable event.

The fourth edition has been brought up to date in recognition of the changes in the status of nations since the publication of the third edition in 1975. Newly independent nations have selected names for their holidays which are symbolic of the culture of their people and are purposefully removed from any association with earlier colonialism. Several dozen holidays have disappeared in the last few years because of changing political conditions. In addition, the interests of industrial society have brought about a trend toward a planned limitation on the number of holidays and free-time festivals. The most vulnerable holidays are those honoring contemporary leaders and those celebrating revolutions superseded by later revolutions. The most stable holidays are the great religious holidays which have been celebrated for centuries.

Organization of the Fourth Edition

The text of ANNIVERSARIES AND HOLIDAYS is divided into three parts: the Calendar of Fixed Days, the Calendars of Movable Days, and the bibliography of books related to anniversaries, holidays, and special events.

Part 1, Calendar of Fixed Days, is arranged by the months of the Gregorian calendar. There are three possible categories for each day of the month: Holy Days and Feast Days, Holidays and Civic Days, and Anniversaries and Special Events Days. However, not every day of the year includes all three categories. Since this is not a book of saints or a book on religion, the Holy Days are limited to 271 of the most prominent of the religious days and feasts. Although there are holidays in every month of the year, there were seventy days, as of 1982, on which no country observed a holiday. Consequently, the number of categories varies under specific dates.

The category Holidays and Civic Days includes not only holidays which are observed universally but also the civic days which commemorate historic events and may be observed only by a region, by governmental agencies, or by schools but do not affect the normal operation of business and industry.

The entries within each category in the Calendar of Fixed Days are alphabetically arranged by the names of saints, holidays and civic days, persons, and special events. Holidays outside the United States are entered under the name of the country which is the locale for the celebration.

The modern trend toward moving fixed holidays to a weekend creates difficulties in assigning exact dates to some holidays. A c (meaning "circa") before a date, such as Washington's actual birth date, indicates that the birthday is observed at a time near that date. Many days of observance have been shifted slightly from the date of establishment. This edition enters those days, such as Mother's Day or Boy Scout Day, under the founding date with a c to indicate that the observance is not fixed to the date of establishment but remains within the same time period.

Part 2, Calendars of Movable Days includes the Christian Church Calendar, the Islamic Calendar, the Jewish Calendar, and a Calendar of Movable Feasts, Festivals, and Special Events. The Christian Church Calendar includes the important days which are observed by many denominations within Christian society. The Islamic and the Jewish calendars are unique to those faiths. The Calendar of Movable Feasts, Festivals, and Special Events includes religious festivals which vary in time observance because of the date of Easter or because of a nation's use of the lunar calendar. This section also describes selected secular events of prominence enjoyed in various parts of the world.

The Calendars of Movable Days, with the exception of the Islamic calendar (see page 170), are arranged to allow for a parallel column which indicates the approximate time relationship to the Gregorian calendar.

Part 3 is an annotated bibliography of books and other materials related to anniversaries and holidays. The bibliography carries out one of the original purposes of ANNIVERSARIES AND HOLIDAYS by providing suggestions for reading for enjoyment or for information about a holiday or about people or happenings associated with a particular day.

The bibliographies are of varying lengths depending upon the popularity of a holiday or in some cases upon the availability of material. The longest is the bibliography on Christmas, which includes 125 titles. The shortest relates to Mother's Day for which there is a paucity of good material.

The bibliographies include books for all age groups, with one exception. Holiday picture books written for very young readers are excluded, unless the text of a particular book goes beyond a few words and many pictures to contribute to an understanding of the origins and customs of a holiday. This scheme admittedly excludes some very attractive picture books useful in work with small children and a number of colorful volumes suitable for display. However, for the purpose of this edition, the books that have been included were selected because of the treatment of the text rather than the beauty of the illustrations. The titles included in the bibliographies are not graded, since a designation of a reading level often creates barriers to the examination and use of printed material.

The major criteria for the inclusion of a title were quality and usefulness. The bibliography does not constitute a selection of best books on any holiday subject, although a check of reviews indicated an affirmative approval for each title from one or more critics. To apply a "best books" criterion to books related to holidays is not feasible. There are more than five thousand books written about Abraham Lincoln, for example, and many would be valuable in preparing programs for Lincoln's Birthday. Every expert in Lincolniana could quarrel over an omission on a "best books" list. The suggestions of titles on individuals associated with holidays about whom much has been written cover various aspects of their lives simply as reminders of the diversity of approaches that are possible in planning holiday observances.

The titles in the bibliography are numbered. Where appropriate, these numbers have been correlated with the entries in Parts 1 and 2 to suggest readings related to a holy day, holiday, person, or event as cited in a main entry.

The Index

ANNIVERSARIES AND HOLIDAYS concludes with an index which is the key to the date of a feast, a holiday, an anniversary of the birth or death of a notable person, or a special event in either Parts 1 or 2. The prime index entries for holidays are the unique or specific names, as in the case of the holiday called the Assassination of the Hero of the Nation day, in order to expedite the search for data on a holiday with an unusual name. Holidays are listed in the index under a country only in the case of the use of a name, such as Revolution Day, which is common to many nations. Feast days are entered alphabetically under the names of saints. People are entered under their proper names and events under their popular or official names. The index entries list dates for Part 1 and pages for referral to the introductory material, to Part 2, and to the bibliography.

Introduction

Holidays and the Calendar

A calendar is a device for reckoning the beginning, length, and divisions of a year and for locating a holiday or any other particular day. It is one of the essential tools of daily life and one that is taken for granted. It seems simple. However, upon examination, a calendar is found to be an ingenious and complicated system of reckoning and recording time.

The major problem in determining the date of a holiday is that there are three basic kinds of calendars in use in the twentieth century: the solar, the lunar, and the lunisolar. In addition, there are local or regional variations of these calendars.

The solar calendar is based on the solar or seasonal year, the time taken by the earth to go once around the sun. It consists of 365.2425 days, divided into twelve months of unequal length. To compensate for the quarter-day differential between the ordinary and the astronomical years, it is necessary to introduce a year with 366 days every fourth year. The Gregorian calendar, utilized by the Western nations for public and private purposes and by world nations for civil or commercial purposes, is a solar calendar.

A lunar calendar represents a year composed of twelve months determined by complete cycles of phases of the moon. Each month totals approximately the time required for the moon to wax and wane from a new moon to a full moon and back again to a new moon. The Islamic calendar (see page 170) is a modern example of a lunar calendar.

The lunisolar calendar is well illustrated by the Jewish calendar, in which the months are reckoned by the moon and the years by the sun. A month is reckoned as the time from the period when the moon is directly between the sun and the earth to the next period when this phenomenon occurs. (See also the Jewish Calendar, page 171).

The solar calendar allows for fixed days, which may be identified by a recurring date, year after year, within the same time frame. New Year's Day, for example, is always January 1 in the Gregorian calendar, although the day of the week upon which it falls may vary slightly from one year to another.

The lunar and lunisolar calendars consist of movable days and dates. A specific festival in a lunar calendar moves into all months within the established cycle of lunar years. This is called "wandering through the calendar." In a lunisolar calendar, the movement of a festival is confined within a season, since the lunar cycles are adjusted to the solar agricultural seasons.

The Sumerians of Babylonia have been credited with the creation of the first lunar calendar, and the Egyptians with the first solar calendar. In 46 B.C., Julius Caesar established the calendar that has been known for centuries as the Julian calendar. That year, 46 B.C., has been described by some historians as "the year of great confusion." Nevertheless, the Julian calendar became the calendar of the early Western world and is still used by the Eastern Orthodox churches.

There were weaknesses in the Julian calendar. Consequently, in 1582, Pope Gregory XIII promulgated a calendar for the purpose of reconciling the civil and church calendars. Pope Gregory decreed that the day following Thursday, October 4, 1582, was to be Friday, October 15, 1582, thus advancing all dates in the calendar by eleven days. The Gregorian calendar came to be known as the New Style calendar, and the Julian calendar as the Old Style calendar.

If it is true, as some historians say, that the Julian calendar created a year of confusion, then the Gregorian calendar bears responsibility for generations of confusion in the recording of births, deaths, and historic dates because of the advancing of all dates by eleven days back in the sixteenth century. The confusion would not have occurred had the Gregorian calendar been immediately acceptable in all of the Western world.

The Gregorian calendar was adopted by Roman Catholic countries in 1582. However, it was not adopted by England and the British Empire, including the American colonies, until 1752. Russia started with the Gregorian calendar in 1918, then experimented with a calendar of its own at the end of the Bolshevik Revolution, and did not return to the use of the Gregorian calendar until 1940. The Chinese had made use of the Gregorian calendar for governmental purposes as early as 1912 but did not enforce its use in public life until 1930. It was not until after the end of World War II that the Gregorian calendar took a dominant position among world calendars, and its widespread use has facilitated world trade and intergovernmental relations. However, it has not replaced the lunar and lunisolar calendars for domestic and religious date calculations on a worldwide basis. This means that many nations use both the Gregorian calendar and their own time-honored calendars, and holy days and holidays are tied to local or national time-measurement customs.

Holidays in History

Centuries ago, the word *holiday* was written as *holy day*, signifying, and limited to, a religious commemoration. In the course of history, the meaning of *holiday* broadened to encompass civic and secular as well as religious observance. It even came to be used to designate a vacation period, days of individual freedom from routine obligations. In the strictest sense, holidays are those days set aside by nations, or groups within nations, for the purpose of religious, civil, or secular observances on a universal or optional free-day basis.

A compilation of holidays provides an insight into life situations that humankind has considered important enough to cherish with carefully preserved customs and continued recognition. Holidays evolved through the centuries as a human response to at least six distinct factors: the mysteries of nature; the inherent awareness of the existence of a supreme deity; respect for the dead; hero worship; the growth of a tribal or national spirit; and an unusual event.

Nature and the mystery of the changing seasons were responsible for the most ancient of celebrations, especially at the time of the equinoxes. The favorite period was the spring equinox, which brought into being the welcome-to-spring festivals that are observed even in a sophisticated twentieth century. Gratitude for a good growing season was, and still is, expressed with harvest festivals and thanksgiving days. The modern communication media engage in seasonal commentaries on the ancient weather-prediction days, such as Groundhog Day or Saint Swithin's Day, even though the prophecies associated with such days are predictably inaccurate.

The veneration of nature by primitive people merged with their worship of deities, at least in terms of the calendar. Many early religious festivals coincided with seasonal observances. However, religious holy days and festivals came to be a visible affirmation of the beliefs and traditions of all faiths. A large proportion of the holidays observed throughout the modern world are related to religious customs and practices. For example, Corpus Christi is a holiday in 24 nations, Good Friday is a holiday in 104 nations, and Ascension Day is a holiday in 40 nations. Each community in the Roman Catholic countries of Europe and Latin America has its own special saint's day, which usually is a local holiday. A noteworthy example of the dominance of religion in holiday observances is to be seen in the Islamic nations, where relatively few civic days are observed and the most important holidays are those directed by the tenets of the Moslem faith.

Holiday festivals honoring the dead are an ancient and universal custom. Days of tribute to ancestors have carried over through generations into the festivals of the modern nations of the Far East. Every country in the contemporary world has some kind of a memorial day as a separate observance, combined with a religious festival, or centered around a day of commemoration for a single individual.

Important days have been added to the world calendar by the United Nations. These include World Literacy Day, World Health Day, and others that confirm the importance of the goals that all people hold in common. The United Nations days have become holidays in many new nations and are observed in other parts of the world as special-events days.

Special-events days ordinarily are not holidays in the usual sense. They are days of recognition or commemoration of events that have significance in the history of a nation, an organization, a profession, or a technological development. Some, such as Moon Day, occur only once in history as a first-time day. However, there are special-events days that have become holidays in some parts of the world. An example is Arbor Day, which has its counterpart in the tree-planting days in various countries of Africa where restoration is not only essential but also a matter of national pride.

Anniversaries and holidays have a history of varied life spans. Some, like Christmas, are a basic part of the fabric of life. Others, such as civic holidays, are vulnerable to changes in government and may be wiped off the calendar or completely altered in purpose in any one year. Still others diminish in public interest until some event or major anniversary recalls their significance. Although the fact remains that holidays are generally popular, a particular holiday will last only as long as people want it to last. This may be for a decade or it may be for hundreds and even thousands of years.

Calendar of Fixed Days

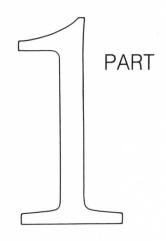

January

January, the first month in the Gregorian calendar, begins with the most popular civil day of the entire year. At least 162 sovereign nations and their territories celebrate New Year's Day as a public holiday.

The name *January* was derived from the Latin *Januarius Mensus*, or the month of Janus. In the old Roman year, it was a festival month honoring Janus, the god of gates and doorways. Janus is depicted on coins and works of sculpture as a deity with two faces, one looking into the past, the other into the future. Janus is associated in mythology with new beginnings for all human enterprises. January, consequently, is one of the most appropriately named months of the year.

January has thirty-one days and two official flowers. The chief flower is the carnation and the snowdrop is the alternate. The January birthstone is the garnet.

Holy Days and Feast Days

1 Feast of Saint Basil, fourth-century archbishop of Caesarea, defender of the faith, doctor of the church, and patriarch of Eastern monks, celebrated by Eastern Orthodox churches on January 1. 9.

1 The Circumcision of Our Lord Jesus Christ is the major feast observed by the Western church on January 1, a holy day of obligation celebrating Christ's submission to Jewish law. 5, 7.

1 Solemnity of Mary, Mother of God, a holy day of obligation in the Roman Catholic church honoring Mary's divine maternity and celebrating the Marian role in the commemoration of the octave day of Christmas. 1, 5.

1 Feast of Saint Odilo, the eleventh-century Cluniac abbot who inaugurated All Souls' Day as an annual commemoration of the faithful departed. 4, 9.

Holidays and Civic Days

1 Liberation Day in Cuba, a national holiday, celebrating the end of Spanish rule on January 1, 1899. 875.

1 Haiti Independence Day, a public holiday honoring Jean Jacques Dessalines, the nation's founder, who proclaimed a state of independence on January 1, 1804, and restored the original Indian name *Haiti*, "land of mountains," to the country. 868, 875.

1 New Year's Day, the first day of the first month in the Gregorian calendar, a holiday in 162 nations of the world, and in all of the fifty states of the United States. 254, 269, 270, 572, 582, 606, 607, 866.

1 Sudan Independence Day, a nation-wide celebration with major events held at Khartoum in honor of Sudan's sovereignty, established on January 1, 1956. 868, 875.

1 Taiwan Foundation Days, celebrated as holidays in Taiwan on January 1 and 2, in commemoration of the founding of the Republic of China on January 1, 1912. 868, 875.

1 Independence Day for Western Samoa, consisting of the South Pacific islands of Savaii, Upolu, Manono, and Apolino; honors with Polynesian enthusiasm the declaration of independence from New Zealand, which occurred on January 1, 1962. 868, 875.

Anniversaries and Special Events Days

1 Birthday of William Henry Harrison Beadle (January 1, 1838–November 13, 1915). American educator, superintendent of public schools in the Dakota Territory. Represents South Dakota in a Statuary Hall sculpture done by H. Daniel Webster. 870.

1 Colonial Flag Day, the anniversary of the official formation of the Continental Army under Washington on January 1, 1776, and of the raising of the first flag of the united colonies known as the Grand Union flag. The site of the first raising is marked by a memorial tower and observatory at Somerville, Massachusetts. 268, 281.

1 Coon Carnival, a traditional holiday festival held on January 1 and 2, in Cape Town, Union of South Africa; famed for colorful dancing, music, and revelry; an attraction comparable in style to the Mardi Gras in the United States.

1 Emancipation Day, the anniversary of the January 1, 1863, Emancipation Proclamation issued by President Abraham Lincoln; a special United States postage stamp was issued in 1963 to honor the proclamation. Emancipation Day is commemorated annually by various organizations and in school programs. 268.

1 First-Foot Day, a continuance of an old custom of introducing the New Year in Britain and in scattered areas of the United States. First-Foot, or Lucky Bird, traditionally a man, crosses the threshold of a home in the early hours of New Year's Day to bring symbolic tokens of good fortune or just words of good wishes for the New Year. 256.

1 Granddad Frost Day in the USSR, sometimes called Daddy Frost, or Jack Frost, Day. Celebrated with the customs of the New Year; of particular importance to children since it is Granddad Frost who brings their presents. A day of family gatherings, special foods, games, and gift or card exchanges.

1 Mobile Carnival, in Mobile, Alabama, starts off the New Year with an elaborate fun-making celebration that has a history dating back to 1831. 268.

1 The Mummers Day parade held on January 1 in Philadelphia is an event dating back to 1876 and characterized by unusual costuming, string bands, clowns, and mummers. 268.

1 Anniversary of the baptism of Bartolomé Esteban Murillo (January 1, 1618–April 3, 1682). Spanish painter, the first to become famous outside his own country. His great creations are the depiction of the Immaculate Conception and the portrayal of Christ and Saint John as children. 5.

1 Polar Swim Day, an annual event carried out since 1920 by swimmers plunging into the frigid waters of Vancouver's English Bay on New Year's Day. Called "a rite of lunacy" by some observers, the custom has been picked up by American Polar Bear Clubs using Lake Michigan and other frigid waterways in the United States for the annual event.

1 Birthday of Paul Revere (January 1, 1735–May 10, 1818). American patriot and craftsman whose famous ride in the spring of 1775 placed him among the immortals in the American tradition. 268, 673, 707.

1 Birthday of Elizabeth (Betsy) Ross (January 1, 1752–January 30, 1836). American colonial woman who is reputed to have made the first American flag. On January 1, 1952, a three-cent postage stamp was issued by the United States government in commemoration of her two-hundredth birthday. 268.

1 Birthday of Manuel Roxas y Acuña (January 1, 1892–April 15, 1948). Philippine statesman and first president of the Philippines, which came into being as an independent republic on July 4, 1946. 864.

1 The Tournament of Roses, Pasadena, California, has been held annually since January 1, 1886, with flower-decorated floats forming processions that are hours—and miles—long. The climax of the day is the Rose Bowl football game held annually since January 1, 1902. The Rose Bowl preceded the other well-known annual American bowl games by three decades. 268.

1 Birthday of Anthony Wayne (January 1, 1745–December 15, 1796). American Revolutionary War officer whose brilliant action in storming an almost impregnable fort at Stony Point, New York, lifted the hearts of his countrymen; known as "Mad Anthony." 864.

Holy Days and Feast Days

2 Feast of Saint Macarius, patron saint of pastry cooks and confectioners, famous for sugarplums. 9.

2 Feast of the Martyrs for the Holy Scriptures, commemorating the slaughter of an English community that refused to surrender the New Testament to Diocletian's men. 20.

Holidays and Civic Days

2 Georgia Ratification Day, commemorating Georgia's entry into the Union, January 2, 1788, as the fourth state among the original thirteen. 268, 856, 862.

2 Ancestry Day, a holiday in Haiti, honoring the founders of the nation and the heroes of the country. 875.

2 Berchtoldstag, a holiday in many cantons of Switzerland honoring the twelfth-century Duke Berchtold V, who founded the city of Berne with a promise to name it for the first animal killed in a hunt. Thus a bear provided not only the city's name but also its coat of arms. 875.

Anniversaries and Special Events Days

2 Birthday of Count Folke Bernadotte (January 2, 1895–September 17, 1948). Swedish statesman, Red Cross official, United Nations mediator in Palestine, May 20 to September 17, 1948, when he was assassinated by terrorists. 864.

2 Granada Day in Spain, commemorates the recapture of the city from the Moors in 1492.

2 Shigoto Hajime, or Beginning of Work Day, observed in Japan with belief in good omens for work begun on this day.

2 Birthday of James Wolfe (January 2, 1727–September 13, 1759). English general who died on the Plains of Abraham at the hour of victory against Montcalm, in a battle that assured the future of Canada as a member of the English family of nations. 864.

Holy Days and Feast Days

3 Feast Day of Saint Geneviève, patron saint of Paris, and of secretaries, actors, lawyers, and the Woman's Army Corps. 4, 14.

Holidays and Civic Days

3 Alaska Admission Day, statehood celebration held throughout Alaska to commemorate the admission of Alaska as the forty-ninth state on January 3, 1959. 268, 856, 862.

3 Upper Volta Revolution Day, a holiday in the Republic of Upper Volta, commemorating a change in government leadership on January 3, 1966, following a general strike and street demonstrations protesting waste and corruption in government. 868, 875.

Anniversaries and Special Events Days

3 Anniversary of the death of Joy Adamson on January 3, 1980, in Kenya; the royalties from her books *Born Free, Living Free*, and *Forever Free* were given to conservation causes in her lifetime. 874.

3 Birthday of Joseph Damien de Veuster (January 3, 1840–April 15, 1889). Belgian Roman Catholic missionary who, as Father Damien, brought hope to the leper colony on Molokai Island. 5.

3 Birthday of Larkin Goldsmith Mead (January 3, 1835–October 15, 1910). American sculptor who executed the Lincoln Monument in Springfield, Illinois, completed in 1883. 347.

3 Birthday of Lucretia Coffin Mott (January 3, 1793–November 11, 1880). American abolitionist and advocate of woman's rights who, with Elizabeth Cady Stanton, organized the convention at Seneca Falls in 1848, a major factor in the growth of the feminist movement in the United States. 268, 738.

3 Anniversary of the Battle of Princeton, which forced Cornwallis to return to New York on January 3, 1777; commemorated at Princeton, New Jersey. 268.

3 Birthday of J. R. R. Tolkien (January 3, 1892–September 2, 1973). Oxford professor, linguist, author of *The Hobbit* and *The Lord of the Rings*, honored by Tolkien societies and student groups. 864.

Holy Days and Feast Days

4 Feast of Elizabeth Ann Bayley Seton, first American-born saint; founder of the Sisters of Charity; pioneer leader of the American Catholic school system; canonized by Pope Paul VI on September 14, 1975. 4, 9, 268.

Holidays and Civic Days

4 Burma Independence Day, a public holiday in Burma commemorating its establishment as a free nation on January 4, 1948. 868, 875.

4 Utah Admission Day. Utah entered the Union on January 4, 1896, as the forty-fifth state. 268, 856, 862.

4 Zaire Martyrs' Day, a holiday honoring the memory of the sacrifices of the martyrs of independence. 875.

Anniversaries and Special Events Days

4 Birthday of Louis Braille (January 4, 1890–January 6, 1852). French educator of the blind who originated the Braille system of printing and writing. 5, 864.

4 Birthday of Jacob Grimm (January 4, 1785–September 20, 1863). German philologist and writer who, with his brother William, published the famous *Grimm's Fairy Tales*. 864.

4 Birthday of Sir Isaac Newton (January 4, 1643–March 31, 1727). Physicist and mathematician; leader in the seventeenth-century scientific revolution; discoverer of the law of gravity. 775.

Holy Days and Feast Days

5 Feast of Saint John Nepomucene Neumann, the first American male saint; a superior of the American Redemptorists and fourth bishop of Philadelphia; canonized by Pope Paul VI on June 19, 1977. 4, 9.

Anniversaries and Special Events Days

5 Befana Fair, held on the eve of Epiphany in many communities in Italy; a celebration for children greeted by a little old woman, with a broom and a gift-laden basket, bringing to life the legend of Befana who refused to accompany the Three Kings to Bethlehem and afterwards could not find them or the Christ Child. 98, 627.

5 Bird Day, anniversary of the incorporation of the National Association of Audubon Societies on January 5, 1905, with the purpose of protecting bird life. Bird Day is frequently observed with Arbor Day, which has varying dates of observance. 477–92.

5 Anniversary of the death of George Washington Carver on January 5, 1943. American chemist noted for his research in the industrial uses of vegetable crops; founder of the Carver Foundation for Research at Tuskegee. 268, 796.

5 Birthday of Stephen Decatur (January 5, 1779–March 22, 1820). American naval officer who is remembered for his proclamation "My country—may she ever be right, but right or wrong, my country." 867.

5 Epiphany Eve, or Twelfth Night, has a history of centuries of merrymaking. Shakespeare's play *Twelfth Night* was specifically written for this celebration, and some ceremonies, such as cutting the Baddeley, or Twelfth Night, cake at the Theatre Royal in London are still carried on. 256.

5 The Glastonbury Thorn in England blooms an Old Christmas Eve, January 5, and is an occasion for pilgrims to go to Glastonbury, Somerset, to see the thorn and to visit the cradle of Christianity in England.

5 Birthday of Cyrus Hamlin (January 5, 1811–August 8, 1900). American educator and missionary who helped establish and administer Robert College in Turkey.

5 Birthday of Zebulon Montgomery Pike (January 5, 1779–April 27, 1813). American general who commanded an early exploring expedition into the West. Pike's Peak, one of the highest summits in the Rockies, is named in his honor. 864.

5 Nellie Taylor Ross became the first woman governor in the United States with her installation as governor of Wyoming, Janurary 5, 1925. 268.

Holy Days and Feast Days

6 Feast of the Epiphany of Our Lord, one of the oldest of Christian feasts, commemorates the manifestation of the divinity of Christ in the homage of the Magi, the wise men from the East; Epiphany may be celebrated on January 6 or on a Sunday between January 2 and 8. It is honored as a Solemnity in the Roman Catholic church. 5, 7, 259.

6 Feast of Peter Baptist, sixteenth-century Franciscan missionary martyred near Nagasaki; one of the patron saints of Japan. 4, 9.

Holidays and Civic Days

6 Army Day, a holiday in Iraq, a day of parades and patriotic events. 875.

6 New Mexico Admission Day. New Mexico entered the Union on January 6, 1912, as the forty-seventh state. 268, 856, 862.

6 Children's Day, a holiday in Uruguay celebrated with special programs and events for boys and girls. 875.

6 Three Kings' Day or Twelfth Day, or Day of the Three Wise Men, or Old Christmas, or Epiphany, the oldest festival on the church calendar; a religious and national holiday in fifteen nations of the world; observed with religious services followed by the enjoyment of traditional customs and festivities usually centered around children and young people. 258, 268.

Anniversaries and Special Events Days

6 Blessing of the Waters Day, a tradition celebrated on Epiphany on the shores of the Bosporus in Turkey with the traditional blessing of the waters and the diving for golden or wooden crosses; a tradition observed by many Greek Orthodox communities throughout the world. 268.

6 Crown of Saint Stephen Day, the anniversary of the January 6, 1978, return to Hungary of the ancient crown of Stephen, secured at Fort Knox since World War II. 874.

6 Four Freedoms Day, commemorating Franklin Roosevelt's message to Congress of January 6, 1941, which defined the national goals of the United States as "Four Freedoms: Freedom of Speech, Freedom of Worship, Freedom from Want, and Freedom from Fear." 268.

6 The Greek Cross Day as observed at Tarpon Springs, Florida, is one of the most beautiful events of the Epiphany season in the United States. It includes mass at the Greek Orthodox Church of Saint Nicholas, a solemn procession, and ceremonies on the banks of the bayou from which symbolic doves are released and a gold cross is cast into the water to be recovered by divers. 268.

6 Birthday of Joan of Arc, the Maid of Orleans (January 6, 1412–May 30, 1431). The national heroine of France whose life is commemorated on her birthday, or on May 30 when she was burned at the stake, or on May 16, 1920, when she was named a saint. 1, 20, 764.

6 Birthday of Carl Sandburg (January 6, 1878–July 22, 1967). American poet, historian, folklorist, and biographer of Abraham Lincoln. 351, 864.

c6 "Birthday" of Sherlock Holmes, fictional detective in the works of Sir Arthur Conan Doyle. Celebrated on or near this date by the Baker Street Irregulars, a society of Holmes enthusiasts, and other afficionados. 268.

Holy Days and Feast Days

7 Feast of the Nativity of Our Lord, the commemoration of the divine liturgy of Christmas, is celebrated on January 7 by Eastern churches, including the Russian Orthodox, which use the Julian calendar. 268.

7 Feast of Saint Raymond of Penafort; Spanish Dominican famed for his preaching and for codifying papal decrees which became the cornerstone of canon law until the revision of 1917; the patron saint of medical record librarians. 4, 9.

Holidays and Civic Days

7 Ganna, or Christmas Day, a holiday in Ethiopia with special events for children. 169, 869.

Anniversaries and Special Events Days

7 Birthday of Millard Fillmore (January 7, 1800–March 8, 1874). English ancestry; New York lawyer; thirteenth president of the United States, 1850–53. Episcopalian. Buried at Forest Lawn, Buffalo, New York. 359–66, 370–72, 374, 378, 379.

7 Pioneers' Day, a commemorative day and a one-time holiday in Liberia honoring the pioneers who came, mostly from the United States in the nineteenth century, to establish a black nation in Africa. 868.

7 Saint Distaff's Day, reportedly named by a medieval wit for a nonexistant saint, a patronness of the spinning wheel, to create a day when housewives resume normal routines after the rush of the Christmas season. 20.

Holy Days and Feast Days

8 The Feast of Saint Gudula, patron saint of Brussels, celebrates with great solemnity the anniversary of the seventh-century saint who is always portrayed in the company of an angel who is lighting her lantern. 4, 9.

Holidays and Civic Days

8 Battle of New Orleans Day, or Old Hickory's Day, or Jackson Day. A legal holiday in Louisiana commemorating the historic battle with the British won by Andrew Jackson, commander of the United States forces, in 1815; as Jackson Day, January 8 is observed by the Democratic party in the United States with banquets and speeches. 268.

Anniversaries and Special Events Days

8 Birthday of Jacob Collamer (January 8, 1791–November 9, 1865). United States senator from Vermont and postmaster general in 1849–50. Represents the state of Vermont in a Statuary Hall sculpture by Preston Powers. 870.

8 Anniversary of the first State of the Union message, delivered by President Washington on January 8, 1790. 371.

Holy Days and Feast Days

c9 Plough Sunday, a day of religious services for a bountiful harvest with blessings upon the plough and the workers in the fields; observed in Britain on the Sunday following January 6. 7, 20.

Holidays and Civic Days

9 Connecticut Ratification Day. Connecticut entered the Union as the fifth state on January 9, 1788. 268, 856, 862.

Anniversaries and Special Events Days

9 Birthday of Carrie Lane Chapman Catt (January 9, 1859–March 9, 1947). American suffrage reformer, founder of the National League of Women Voters in 1919. She was a moving force behind the adoption of the Nineteenth Amendment to the United States Constitution. On July 17, 1982, she was inducted into the National Women's Hall of Fame. 268, 738.

9 Birthday of Richard Milhous Nixon (January 9, 1913–). English-Scotch-Irish ancestry. Quaker. Thirty-seventh president of the United States, January 20, 1969–August 9, 1974. 360–66, 369, 371, 374, 379.

9 Birthday of John Broadus Watson (January 9, 1878–September 25, 1958). American psychologist, founder of the behaviorist school of psychology in the United States.

Holy Days and Feast Days

c10 Feast of the Baptism of the Lord, a commemoration of the baptism of Christ by John the Baptist marking the beginning of Christ's public mission; celebrated on the Sunday after Epiphany except at those times when the observance coincides with the celebration of Epiphany. 5, 7.

Anniversaries and Special Events Days

10 Anniversary of the first session of the General Assembly of the United Nations, held on January 10, 1946, in London. 754.

10 Anniversary of the establishment on January 10, 1429, of the Order of the Golden Fleece, celebrated order of knighthood in Austria-Hungary and Spain. 285.

10 Anniversary of the founding of the League of Nations on January 10, 1920, in a worldwide movement toward peace and cooperation between nations. 268.

c10 Volunteer Fireman Day, observed in New Jersey on the second Sunday in January to express appreciation of the contributions and the sacrifices of those who volunteer for fire duty. 647, 668.

10 Anniversary of the death on January 10, 1957, of Laura Ingalls Wilder, author of the Little House stories. First recipient of the Wilder Medal Award named in her honor to recognize an author or illustrator whose books, published in the United States, have made an important contribution to children's literature. 858, 867.

Holidays and Civic Days

11 Albania Proclamation of the Republic Day, a holiday commemorating January 11, 1946, when Albania was established after years of resistance against foreign interests. 868, 875.

11 Prithvi Jayanti, a holiday in Nepal, honoring the eighteenth-century founder of the kingdom, King Prithvinarayan Shah. 875.

11 Hostos Day, a holiday in Puerto Rico, commemorating the birth of Eugenio Maria de Hostos on January 11, 1839; a Puerto Rican philosopher and outstanding nineteenth-century patriot. 868, 875.

Anniversaries and Special Events Days

11 Birthday of Ezra Cornell (January 11, 1807–December 9, 1874). American capitalist and philanthropist who established and endowed Cornell University. His birthday is observed as Founder's Day at Cornell. 864.

11 Birthday of Phillipp la Renotiere Von Ferrary (January 11, 1848–May 20, 1917). Internationally renowned philatelist honored by collectors and stamp clubs.

11 Birthday of Alexander Hamilton (January 11, 1755–July 12, 1804). First United States secretary of the treasury; birthday observed by the United States Department of the Treasury. He was elected to the Hall of Fame for Great Americans in 1915. 744, 773, 791.

11 Birthday of William James (January 11, 1842–August 26, 1910). American psychologist and philosopher. His most noted work is *Pragmatism*. 864.

11 Birthday of Sir John Macdonald (January 11, 1815–June 6, 1891). First prime minister of Canada. 864.

Holidays and Civic Days

12 Tanzania's Zanzibar Revolution Day, a holiday in Tanzania to commemorate the successful Zanzibar revolt against the Sultan on January 12, 1964. 868, 875.

Anniversaries and Special Events Days

12 Anniversary of the election on January 12, 1932, of Hattie Caraway of Arkansas as the first woman senator in the United States. 861.

c12 Meitlisunntig, a Swiss festival held on the second Sunday of January in the Seetal district of Aargau, Switzerland, featuring a military procession of girls re-enacting the roles of women in the Villmergen War of 1712. 857.

12 Birthday of Johann Heinrich Pestalozzi (January 12, 1746–February 17, 1827). Swiss educational reformer whose beliefs and system laid the foundations for elementary education. 864.

12 Printing Ink Day, a commemorative day instituted by ink manufacturers to honor the contributions of printing inks to the educational, publishing, communication, and graphic arts fields. 857.

12 Birthday of John Singer Sargent (January 12, 1856–April 15, 1925). Distinguished American portraitist and muralist. A series of Sargent's decorative panels was executed for the Boston Public Library. 867.

12 Birthday of John Winthrop (January 12, 1588–March 26, 1649). American colonial leader; first governor of the Massachusetts Bay Colony. 268.

Holy Days and Feast Days

13 Feast of Saint Hilary of Poitiers, a fourth-century theologian called "the Athanasius of the West" through his defense of the divinity of Christ against the Arians; proclaimed a doctor of the church in 1851. 4, 9.

Holidays and Civic Days

13 Liberation Day, a holiday in the Republic of Togo. A new constitution went into effect on January 13, 1980, and the Third Togolese Republic was proclaimed. 868, 875.

Anniversaries and Special Events Days

13 Birthday of Salmon Portland Chase (January 13, 1808–May 7, 1873). American lawyer and statesman, secretary of the treasury under Lincoln; sixth chief justice of the Supreme Court. 268.

13 Anniversary of the death of George Fox (July 1624–January 13, 1691). English founder of the Society of Friends; honored by all Quaker societies. 20.

13 Old New Year's Day, the official New Year's Day for the people of the Gwaun Valley in Wales who maintain an allegiance to the Julian calendar.

13 Saint Knute's Day, the twentieth day after Christmas, January 13, the occasion for the dismantling of Christmas trees in Sweden and for celebrating with dances. 169.

13 Stephen Foster Memorial Day, commemorating the anniversary of Foster's death, January 13, 1864; permanently established as a memorial by presidential proclamation in 1952; observed by the Stephen Foster Memorial Association and musical organizations. 268.

13 Birthday of Charles Perrault (January 13, 1628–May 16, 1703). French lawyer and author; famous for *Les Contes de Perrault*, through which he gave immortality to the folk tales *Cinderella, Sleeping Beauty, Little Red Riding Hood*, and others. 864.

13 Anniversary of the death of Edmund Spenser, January 13, 1599. English poet best known for *The Faerie Queene*. 864.

13 Tyvendedagen, the twentieth day after Christmas, January 13, the official end of Yuletide in Norway, observed in some regions with the traditional Christmas race on sleighs, which carries out the old folk saying "Saint Knute drives Christmas away."

Anniversaries and Special Events Days

14 Birthday of Matthew Fontaine Maury (January 14, 1806–February 1, 1873). American hydrographer and naval officer. He was the first to give a complete description of the Gulf Stream and to chart specific routes for Atlantic crossings. He was elected to the Hall of Fame for Great Americans in 1930. 864.

14 Maryland Ratification day, the anniversary of the January 14, 1784, ratification by the Continental Congress of the Treaty of Paris officially ending the Revolutionary War and establishing the United States of America as a sovereign nation. The ratification took place at the Maryland State House where the act is honored annually with special ceremonies. 268.

14 Birthday of Albert Schweitzer (January 14, 1875–September 4, 1965). Author, organist, theologian, and medical missionary who established hospitals at Lambaréné, now in Gabon; recipient of the 1952 Nobel Peace Prize for his work for the brotherhood of nations. Among his writings are *The Quest for the Historical Jesus* and *Out of My Life and Thought.* 864.

14 Feast of Saint Sava, a children's festival in Serbia in honor of Saint Sava, a king's son, who built schools and monasteries all over Serbia and died on January 14, 1237. The day is observed in schools and by communities with feasting, music, and dancing.

Holy Days and Feast Days

15 Feast of Christ of Esquipulas, the Black Christ Festival, observed on January 15 at Esquipulas in Guatemala, named for the famous figure of Christ carved out of dark-brown balsam.

Holidays and Civic Days

15 Adults Day, or Seijin-No-Hi, a holiday in Japan honoring young men and women who have reached adulthood; observed by families and organizations with special programs and events. 875.

15 Martin Luther King, Jr., Day, birthday of Martin Luther King, Jr. (January 15, 1929–April 4, 1968). Black champion of civil rights, minister, author, Nobel Peace Prize winner in 1964, proponent of nonviolence; a legal holiday in Connecticut, the District of Columbia, Florida, Illinois, Kentucky, Louisiana, Maryland, Massachusetts, New Jersey, Pennsylvania, South Carolina, and the Virgin Islands; observed with special programs in schools, state agency and school closings, and commemorations by civic and civil rights organizations. 269, 270, 310–22, 759, 866.

Anniversaries and Special Events Days

15 Anniversary of the death of Mathew B. Brady on January 15, 1896. American photographer who made the first photographic war records on the battlefields of the Civil War. 864.

15 Historic Fraunces Tavern Day, a tribute to the 1762 purchase by innkeeper Samuel Fraunces of the DeLancey mansion; twentieth-century Manhattan's oldest building.

15 Birthday of Sonya Kovalevski (January 15, 1850–February 10, 1891). Russian mathematician who pioneered in a field that was hostile to women; received the Prix Bordin of the Paris Academy for her achievements. 864.

15 Anniversary of the baptism of Molière (Jean-Baptiste Poquelin) on January 15, 1622. French dramatist recognized as the greatest French writer of comedy. His finest comedy is considered to be *Le Misanthrope.* 864, 866.

15 Teachers' Day, Dia Del Maestro, observed annually in Venezuela on January 15; a national day of tribute to educators.

15 Birthday of Ella Flagg Young (January 15, 1845–October 26, 1918). American educator, superintendent of the Chicago school system, first woman president of the National Education Association. 864.

Anniversaries and Special Events Days

16 Prohibition Day, the anniversary of January 16, 1920, when the Eighteenth Amendment to the Constitution of the United States became law and the sale of alcoholic beverages became illegal. 268.

Holy Days and Feast Days

c17 World Religion Day, observed on the third Sunday of January to promote unity among the peoples of the world through demonstrating the truth in the concept of oneness in all revealed religion; a day of meditation and prayer sponsored by the Baha'is. 857.

Anniversaries and Special Events Days

17 Battle of Cowpens Day, the anniversary of the battle of January 17, 1781, near Spartansburg, S.C., which thwarted the plans of General Cornwallis to move into the middle of the Carolinas.

17 Birthday of Benjamin Franklin (January 17, 1706–April 17, 1790). American printer, statesman, inventor, and diplomat who was America's first world citizen. It has been customary for schools in some areas to start Thrift Week on Franklin's birthday. He was elected to the Hall of Fame for Great Americans in 1900. His birthday is observed annually by the city of Philadelphia, the Franklin Society, and other organizations. 268, 302, 791.

17 Birthday of David Lloyd George (January 17, 1863–March 26, 1945). British statesman, one of the great figures in twentieth-century British history. 766.

17 Birthday of Glenn Luther Martin (January 17, 1886–December 4, 1955). American pioneer aviator and airplane manufacturer who developed several of the most famous military planes; awarded the aeronautics industry's highest award, the Collier Trophy, in 1933, and the Guggenheim Medal of the Institute of Aeronautical Science in 1944. 864.

17 Nautilus Day, anniversary of the launching of the United States submarine *Nautilus*, the world's first atomic-powered vessel, on January 17, 1955. 268.

Holidays and Civic Days

c18 Martin Luther King Jr., Day, a holiday in Michigan and Ohio commemorating the birth on January 15, 1929, of the civil rights leader; observed on the third Monday of January in Michigan and on the Monday nearest January 15 in Ohio. 269, 270, 310–22, 759, 866.

c18 Robert E. Lee Day, a holiday in Alabama and Mississippi, celebrating the January 19, 1807, birth of Robert E. Lee, commander of the southern forces in the American Civil War; observed on the third Monday in January. 269, 659, 758.

c18 Lee-Jackson Day, a holiday in North Carolina and Virginia, observed on or near the third Monday of January to honor Robert E. Lee and Stonewall Jackson. 268.

18 Santa Prisca Day in Taxco, Mexico, a holiday honoring the village saint and climaxing one of the most colorful fiestas in Latin America; features the dance of the Moors and the dance of the shepherds in costumes of the Moors and Christians. 259.

18 Tunisia National Revolution Day, a holiday in Tunisia, the smallest country of North Africa, honoring the nationalist movements of the 1930s and 1940s that led to independence in 1956 and the abolishment of the monarchy in 1957. 868, 875.

18 Wellington Day, a provincial anniversary holiday celebrated in Wellington, the capital of New Zealand, a city established in 1840. 875.

Anniversaries and Special Events Days

18 Birthday of Rubén Dario (January 18, 1867–February 6, 1916). Nicaraguan poet and short-story writer recognized as one of the outstanding poets of Latin America. 864.

18 Birthday of Alan Alexander Milne (January 18, 1882–January 31, 1956). English poet and playwright who is best known for his volumes of verses and prose for children, including *Winnie-the-Pooh*. 867.

18 Birthday of Peter Mark Roget (January 18, 1779–September 12, 1869). English physician, author of books on physiology, remembered for the famous *Thesaurus of English Words and Phrases*. 864.

18 Birthday of Daniel Webster (January 18, 1782–October 24, 1852). American statesman, lawyer, and orator whose birthday is observed in Massachusetts. He was elected to the Hall of Fame for Great Americans in 1900. 268.

Holy Days and Feast Days

19 Feast of Saint Canute, king of Denmark; supporter of the clergy and missionaries; a patron saint of Denmark. 4, 9.

19 Greek Epiphany, or Greek Cross Day, observed by the Greek Orthodox churches that use the Julian calendar; a commemoration of the baptism of Jesus in the River Jordan and the witness of his divinity as the Holy Spirit descended in the form of a dove. A traditional day for the blessing of the waters in many parts of the world. 268.

19 Feast Day of Saint Henry of Uppsala, patron saint of Finland. 9.

Holidays and Civic Days

19 Confederate Heroes Day, observed in Texas in memory of the Confederate forces of the American Civil War. 875.

19 Robert E. Lee Day, birthday of Robert Edward Lee (January 19, 1807–October 12, 1870). American soldier and educator; commander of the Army of Northern Virginia; president of the college known today as Washington and Lee University. He was elected to the Hall of Fame for Great Americans in 1900, and he represents the state of Virginia in Statuary Hall in a sculpture done by Edward Virginius Valentine. Lee's birthday is observed as a holiday in Arkansas, Florida, Georgia, Kentucky, Louisiana, and South Carolina. 268, 269, 659, 758.

Anniversaries and Special Events Days

19 Anniversary of the January 19, 1980, death of William O. Douglas, colorful and controversial Supreme Court Justice remembered for his unflagging support of individual liberties and intellectual freedom. 730, 746.

19 Birthday of Edgar Allan Poe (January 19, 1809–October 7, 1849). American poet, short-story writer, and critic whose influence upon poetry and fiction has been extensive. Elected to the Hall of Fame for Great Americans in 1910. Edgar Allan Poe awards are presented annually by the Mystery Writers Association for the best mystery novel written by an American author, for the best mystery novel published in America, and for radio, motion picture, and television writing in the field. 268, 858.

19 Birthday of James Watt (January 19, 1736–August 25, 1819). Scottish engineer and inventor who developed a separate condensing vessel for the steam engine. The watt and the kilowatt units of power are named in his honor. 864.

Holy Days and Feast Days

20 Feast Day of Saint Sebastian, patron saint of archers, soldiers, and athletes; a holiday celebrated in Rio de Janeiro with church services, colorful religious processions, and festivities. 9, 20.

Holidays and Civic Days

20 Heroes Day, a national holiday in the Republic of Cape Verde commemorating all of the courageous and sacrificial citizens of the islands. 875.

20 Mali Army Day, a national holiday in Mali, formerly the French Sudan. 875.

20 Rio de Janeiro Foundation Day, a holiday in Rio de Janeiro celebrating the long history of the beautiful Brazilian city which began with the establishment of a settlement in 1555 by the French. 875.

20 Presidential Inauguration Day, observed in the capital of the United States every fourth year; a legal holiday in the District of Columbia. 269, 866.

Anniversaries and Special Events Days

20 Birthday of André Marie Ampère (January 20, 1775–June 10, 1836). French physicist, mathematician, and discoverer of Ampère's law. 5.

20 Babin Den, Grandmother's Day, observed in Bulgaria. Festivities include ducking of girls by boys in anticipation of good health.

20 Hostage Freedom Day, the anniversary of the release on January 20, 1980, of 52 Americans held in hostage for 444 days by Iranian militants in Teheran. 710.

Anniversaries and Special Events Days

20 Birthday of Johannes Vilhelm Jensen (January 20, 1873–November 25, 1950). Danish novelist and lyric poet whose series of epic novels describing the northern peoples from the Ice Age to the fifteenth century brought him the Nobel Prize in literature in 1944. 864.

20 Anniversary of the announcement of the Point Four program in President Truman's January 20, 1949, inaugural address extending the benefits of American scientific advances to the underdeveloped areas of the world. 371.

Holy Days and Feast Days

21 Feast Day of Saint Agnes, patron saint of Girl Scouts, patroness of chastity and young girls. It is the day the Pope blesses two lambs whose wool is used to make circular bands called "pallia," which the Pope sends to his archbishops. 4, 9.

21 Feast Day of Saint Meinrad, hermit martyr, celebrated at the Hermitage of Einsiedeln in Switzerland, attracting pilgrimages from all parts of Europe. 9, 34.

Holidays and Civic Days

21 Altagracia Day, a holiday celebrated in the Dominican Republic on January 21 with a pilgrimage to the Saint Altagracia shrine. 875.

21 Birthday of Ethan Allen (January 21, 1738–February 12, 1789). American Revolutionary commander, organizer of the Green Mountain Boys. Represents the state of Vermont in a Statuary Hall sculpture done by Larkin Goldsmith Mead. 268, 870.

21 Birthday of John Charles Frémont (January 21, 1813–July 13, 1890). American surveyor and army officer who made official expeditions into the American West; frequently called "the Pathfinder." 268.

21 Birthday of Thomas Jonathan Jackson (January 21, 1824–May 10, 1863). American Confederate general known as Stonewall; famous for strategy and tactics in the Civil War. He was elected to the Hall of Fame for Great Americans in 1955. 864.

21 Anniversary of the death on January 21, 1924, of Lenin, revolutionary leader of Russia; observed on January 21 in Moscow with processions before the Lenin mausoleum, military displays, and speeches. 864.

Holy Days and Feast Days

22 Feast Day of Saint Vincent of Saragossa, patron saint of winegrowers; celebrated in Europe with processions, prayers, and weather-omen ceremonials. 9.

Holidays and Civic Days

22 St. Vincent Discovery Day, a holiday in St. Vincent, one of the Windward Islands in the Lesser Antilles; a celebration of the discovery of St. Vincent by Columbus in 1498. 875.

Anniversaries and Special Events Days

22 Birthday of Francis Bacon (January 22, 1561–April 9, 1626). English essayist, philosopher, and jurist who developed the inductive method of inquiry. 864.

22 Birthday of George Gordon Byron (January 22, 1788–April 19, 1824). English poet famous for *Childe Harold*. 867.

22 Ukrainian Day, marks the January 1918 proclamation of the free Ukrainian Republic, now a part of the Union of Soviet Socialist Republics.

22 Birthday of Beatrice Potter Webb (January 22, 1858–April 30, 1943). English economist who collaborated with her husband Sidney Webb on many works on economics. 738.

Holy Days and Feast Days

23 Feast day of Saint Ildephonsus, doctor of the church, archbishop of Toledo, for whom the New Mexican pueblo of San Ildefonso is named and whose feast day is celebrated there with the buffalo dance and other ceremonial dances combining pagan rites and Christian ceremonies. 4, 9.

Anniversaries and Special Events Days

23 Anti-Poll Tax Day, the anniversary of the final ratification of the Twenty-fourth Amendment to the Constitution of the United States forbidding the collection of a poll tax as a requirement for voting in national elections. 268.

23 Birthday of John Hancock (January 23, 1737–October 8, 1793). American Revolutionary patriot, signer of the Declaration of Independence, whose name has become synonymous with the word *signature* because of his distinctive handwriting on that document. 307, 309.

23 Handwriting Day, a day of encouragement of legibility in handwriting, appropriately observed on John Hancock's birthday. 866.

Holy Days and Feast Days

24 Feast of Saint Francis de Sales, author of *Introduction to the Devout Life* and *Treatise on the Love of God*, seventeenth-century classics that are widely used in the twentieth century; known in his lifetime as the "gentle Christ of Geneva"; declared a doctor of the church in 1877; named the patron saint of the Roman Catholic press and of journalists in 1923. 4, 5, 9.

Anniversaries and Special Events Days

24 Alacitis Fair, an annual celebration of the Aymara Indians of Bolivia. It has been held at La Paz for hundreds of years in honor of their god of prosperity, to whom miniature replicas are offered of all the goods the Aymaras would like to have.

24 California Gold Rush Day, the anniversary of the discovery of gold in northern California on January 24, 1848. The anniversary is commemorated with an annual Gold Discovery celebration at the Marshall Gold Discovery State Historical Park in Coloma on the weekend nearest January 24. 268, 686, 866.

24 Birthday of Edith Newbold Wharton (January 24, 1862–August 11, 1937). American novelist whose *Ethan Frome* has become an American classic. Her *Age of Innocence* received the Pulitzer Prize in 1921, and *The Old Maid* the Pulitzer Prize in drama in 1935. Edith Wharton was the first woman to receive an honorary degree from Yale University. 738.

Holy Days and Feast Days

25 Feast of the Conversion of Saint Paul, commemorating the transformation of Saul of Tarsus, enemy of the Christians, into Paul, the apostle and dedicated leader of the Christians. 7.

25 Feast of Saint Ananias of Damascus, who baptized Paul and brought him into the church.

Holidays and Civic Days

25 Auckland Day, a provincial anniversary holiday observed in Auckland, New Zealand, a city established in 1841. 875.

Anniversaries and Special Events Days

25 Birthday of Robert Boyle (January 25, 1627–December 30, 1691). Irish physicist and chemist who set forth the famous Boyle's law. 864.

25 Burns Day, commemorates the birth on January 25, 1759, of Robert Burns, with celebrations in Scotland, England, and Newfoundland. The Scottish-Americans of Minneapolis, St. Paul, and other sections of the United States gather on this date to honor the national poet of Scotland. 268, 866.

25 The Burns Supper, honoring the ploughman poet, held annually by Burns societies in Scotland, Tokyo, Moscow, Vancouver, Mauritius, and other places in the world; a supper with special menus and programs.

Holy Days and Feast Days

26 Feast of Saint Timothy, bishop of Ephesus; disciple and companion of Paul; martyr. 5, 14.

26 Feast of Saint Titus, ordained bishop of Crete by Paul in the first century; patron of Crete. 9.

Holidays and Civic Days

c26 Australia Day, or Foundation Day, a public holiday in commemoration of the landing on the Australian continent of Captain Arthur Phillip and his company of men and women on January 26, 1788; celebrated on the 26th or on the first Monday after the 26th. 875.

26 Duarte Day, a holiday in the Dominican Republic honoring Juan Pablo Duarte, a founder of the republic and a leader in its fight for liberation from Haiti. 875.

26 India's Republic Day, Basant Panchmi, celebrated in commemoration of the proclamation of the republic on January 26, 1950. It is observed at Delhi with several days of pageantry and military parades. 868, 875.

26 Michigan Day, commemorates Michigan's admission to the Union as the twenty-sixth state on January 26, 1837. 268, 856, 862.

Anniversaries and Special Events Days

26 Birthday of Roy Chapman Andrews (January 26, 1884–March 11, 1960). American natural scientist, explorer, and author famous for his finding of dinosaur eggs, new geological formations, and the remains of the largest mammal known to have existed. 864.

26 MacArthur Day, observed in Arkansas in tribute to the January 26, 1880, birth of Douglas MacArthur, five-star general and commander of the U.S. forces in the Far East during World War II and Arkansas's most famous son. 268.

Holy Days and Feast Days

27 Feast of Saint Angela Merici, founder of the Ursuline Order in 1535, the first teaching order of nuns in the Roman church. 9.

Holidays and Civic Days

27 Saint Devota Day, a holiday in Monaco, honoring with colorful festivities the country's patron saint who was saved on a perilous voyage by a dove which directed the boat bearing the saint to the shores of Monaco. 875.

Anniversaries and Special Events Days

27 Birthday of Charles Lutwidge Dodgson (January 27, 1832–January 14, 1898). English mathematician and author who wrote under the pseudonym Lewis Carroll; the author of the classic *Alice's Adventures in Wonderland*. 858, 864.

27 Birthday of Samuel Gompers (January 27, 1850–December 13, 1924). American labor leader, first president of the American Federation of Labor. 864.

27 Birthday of Jerome Kern (January 27, 1885–November 11, 1945). American composer who composed almost exclusively for the theater and whose most popular achievement was the score for the musical version of Edna Ferber's novel *Show Boat*. 820.

27 Birthday of Wolfgang Amadeus Mozart (January 27, 1756–December 5, 1791). Austrian concert pianist and world-renowned composer. In appreciation of his work, Mozart's birthday is celebrated by musical societies in all nations. The annual Salzburg Festival, held in late July through August in Salzburg, honors Mozart. 864.

27 Vietnam Day, the anniversary of the official signing, on January 27, 1973, of the peace agreements to terminate the Vietnam War. 866.

Holy Days and Feast Days

28 Feast of Saint Thomas Aquinas, a thirteenth-century Dominican teacher and theologian; author of *Summa Theologiae* and other classics; known as Doctor Communis, Doctor Angelicus, and "the great synthesizer"; proclaimed a doctor of the church in 1567; patron saint of students. 1, 4, 9.

Holidays and Civic Days

28 Rwanda Democracy Day, a holiday in Rwanda, which is called the African Switzerland; a civic day concerned with equality for all peoples in the nation. 868, 875.

Anniversaries and Special Events Days

28 Saint Charlemagne's Day, an annual French college celebration, honoring the great emperor at a speechmaking, champagne-drinking breakfast. 20.

28 Anniversary of the death on January 28, 1596, of Sir Francis Drake, sixteenth-century English navigator, the first Englishman to circumnavigate the world. He frequently is a central figure in modern-day pageants and plays related to commemorative events. 823.

28 Birthday of Charles George Gordon (January 28, 1833–January 26, 1885). British soldier and military hero known as Gordon Pasha, Gordon of Khartoum, or Chinese Gordon. 864.

28 Anniversary of the death of John McCrae on January 28, 1918. Canadian physician and poet best remembered for the poem "In Flanders Fields," frequently used in Veterans Day observances. 864.

28 Birthday of Sir Henry Morton Stanley (January 28, 1841–May 10, 1904). Anglo-American explorer remembered for his fulfillment of the mission to find the explorer David Livingstone. 866.

Holidays and Civic Days

29 Kansas Day, a commemorative day honoring the admission of Kansas as the thirty-fourth state in the Union on January 29, 1861. The anniversary of statehood has been a special day of celebration by the Republicans of Kansas since 1892 and is a popular day for political meetings. 268, 856, 862.

Anniversaries and Special Events Days

29 Canada's Rescue-Mission Day, the anniversary of January 29, 1980, when Canadians boldly and successfully aided six members of the U.S. Embassy to escape from Teheran where they were being held hostage. 874.

29 Birthday of Anton Pavlovich Chekhov (January 29, 1860–July 14, 1904). Russian dramatist and short-story writer. 864.

29 Birthday of William McKinley (January 29, 1843–September 14, 1901). Scotch-Irish ancestry; Ohio lawyer; Civil War officer; twenty-fifth president of the United States, 1897–1901. Methodist. Buried at Canton, Ohio. Carnation Day, January 29, was created in honor of President McKinley, and a William McKinley banquet is held annually at Canton, Ohio, on his birthday. 359–66, 370–72, 374, 378, 379.

29 Thomas Paine Day, the anniversary of the birth on January 29, 1737, of the American Revolutionary propagandist and author of *Common Sense, The Rights of Man*, and *The Age of Reason*. Elected to the Hall of Fame for Great Americans in 1945. January 29 was named Common Sense Day in his honor to encourage the use of good sense in appreciating and protecting the rights of all people. Thomas Paine Day is honored by the Hugenot–Thomas Paine Historical Society with annual meetings on a Sunday nearest his birthday on January 29. 268.

29 Anniversary of the institution by Queen Victoria of the Victoria Cross, the most coveted of all British orders, on January 29, 1856, to reward individual acts of bravery.

Holy Days and Feast Days

30 Saint Charles Day, observed by Anglican churches in commemoration of King Charles the martyr. The Society of Charles the Martyr holds an annual service on January 30 commemorating the execution of King Charles I on the scaffold site in the courtyard of the Royal United Services Museum; commemorative services are held at the Church of Saint Martin-in-the-Fields and in Trafalgar Square in London on or near February 2. 14.

30 Holiday of the Three Hierarchs, an Eastern Orthodox holy day commemorating Saint Basil, Saint Gregory, and Saint John Chrysostomos.

Holidays and Civic Days

30 Franklin D. Roosevelt's Day, a holiday in Kentucky, commemorating the birth on January 30, 1882, of the thirty-second president of the United States, the only man elected to four terms in the executive office. 268.

Anniversaries and Special Events Days

30 Anniversaries of the purchase on January 30, 1815, of Thomas Jefferson's library for use by the Library of Congress. 678.

30 Birthday of Franklin Delano Roosevelt (January 30, 1882–April 12, 1945). Dutch ancestry; lawyer; New York governor; statesman; assistant secretary of the navy under Wilson; thirty-second president of the United States, 1933–45. First president to be elected to a fourth term. Episcopalian. Buried at Hyde Park, New York, where his house and library are under the jurisdiction of the federal government. 359–67, 369–72, 374, 378, 399.

30 Birthday of John Henry Towers (January 30, 1885–April 1, 1955). American naval officer and avaitor who, in 1912, established a world's record for endurance in a seaplane; commander of the *Langley*, the first American aircraft carrier; the first naval aviator to reach the rank of admiral. 864.

30 Woman Peerage Day, anniversary of the passage of a bill by the House of Lords on January 30, 1958, and by the House of Commons on February 13, 1958, establishing lifetime peerages for both men and women, thus admitting women into the House of Lords for the first time in its six-and-a-half-century history.

Holy Days and Feast Days

31 Feast Day of Saint John Bosco; founder of the Salesians; friend of boys; patron saint of editors. 9.

Holidays and Civic Days

31 Nauru Independence Day, a holiday in Nauru, an island in the Pacific Ocean, commemorating the achievement of independence on January 31, 1968. 868, 875.

Anniversaries and Special Events Days

c31 Dicing for the Maid's Money Day, a ceremony held near the end of January in Guildford, Surrey, England, to fulfill the terms of a seventeenth-century will providing for the casting of lots by two maidservants for the interest from a trust. 256.

31 Birthday of Irving Langmuir (January 31, 1881–August 16, 1957). American chemist who is credited with the development of the basic scientific principle and discoveries that have been applied in the atomic age. He received the 1932 Nobel Prize in chemistry for his many contributions to science. 864.

31 Birthday of Robert Morris (January 31, 1734–May 7, 1806). American merchant, financier of the American Revolution, and signer of the Declaration of Independence. 292, 294.

31 Birthday of Jackie Robinson (January 31, 1919–October 24, 1972). First black man to play in major-league baseball; recipient of the Spingarn Medal in 1956. Elected to the Baseball Hall of Fame in 1962. 761.

31 Birthday of Franz Peter Schubert (January 31, 1797–November 19, 1828). Austrian composer, famous for *The Unfinished Symphony* and for such songs as "Who Is Sylvia?" 864.

c31 Up-Helly-Aa, an old Norse fire festival, observed with all the old ceremonials at Lerwick in the Shetland Islands on the last Tuesday of January. 256.

February

February, the second month of the Gregorian calendar, gets its name from *Februarius* through the verb *februare*, meaning "to purify." It is the shortest month, with twenty-eight days, except in leap year when it has twenty-nine. In ancient Rome it was the month of purification, with special ceremonies of repentance held at the festival of Februa on February 15. In the twentieth century, it is a period for many Christians of preparation for Easter. It is frequently, but depending upon the date of Easter, the month of Mardi Gras and other pre-Lenten carnivals. It is also the month of great sports events. In the United States, February is sometimes called "Presidents' Month" because of the observance of the birthdays of two great American presidents, Washington and Lincoln.

The flowers for February are the violet and primrose. The birthstone is the amethyst.

Holy Days and Feast Days

1 Feast Day of Saint Brigid, or Bride, patroness of Irish nuns, dairy workers, and of Ireland, Wales, Australia, and New Zealand. 4, 9, 20.

Holidays and Civic Days

c1 Lincoln's Birthday, a holiday in Delaware and in Oregon celebrating Abraham Lincoln's birthday; observed on the first Monday of February. 875.

Anniversaries and Special Events Days

1 Birthday of Sir Edward Coke (February 1, 1552–September 3, 1634). English jurist, an eminent legal specialist on the supremacy of the common law. 864.

1 National Freedom Day, commemorates the signing by President Lincoln on February 1, 1865, of the Thirteenth Amendment to the Constitution, which abolished slavery. A presidential proclamation of 1949 established the perpetuity of this observance. 268.

1 Birthday of Granville Stanley Hall (February 1, 1844–April 24, 1924). American psychologist, an authority on child and educational psychology; first president of the American Psychological Association. 864.

1 Birthday of Victor Herbert (February 1, 1859–May 26, 1924). American composer and conductor whose operettas *Babes in Toyland, Naughty Marietta*, and others are a part of the musical heritage of the United States. 268.

1 Birthday of Langston Hughes (February 1, 1902–May 22, 1967). Black American poet; innovator in the interpretation of the black experience in the United States. Known also for his anthologies *The Poetry of the Negro* and *The Book of Negro Folklore*, compiled with Arna Bontemps. 815.

1 Khomeini Day, the anniversary of the February 1, 1979, return of Ayatollah Khomeini to Iran as its spiritual leader and governmental strong man after fifteen years of exile. 874.

1 Robinson Crusoe Day; anniversary of the rescue of a Scot, Alexander Selkirk, from an uninhabited island on February 1, 1709; an event which inspired Daniel Defoe in his writing of *Robinson Crusoe*. 857.

Holy Days and Feast Days

2 Candlemas, or the Feast of the Presentation of the Lord, or the Feast of the Purification of Mary, observed by the Roman Catholic, Episcopal, Lutheran, and most Eastern Orthodox churches on February 2. Eastern Orthodox churches using the Julian calendar observe the feast on February 15. The blessing of the candles is one of the great traditions of the feast day. 5, 7.

Holidays and Civic Days

2 Candlemas Day, a religious holiday in Porto Alegere, Brazil, and in Liechtenstein commemorating the Presentation of the Lord and the blessing of candles. 857.

Anniversaries and Special Events Days

2 Birthday of Christian Gauss (February 2, 1878–November 1, 1951). American educator and writer in whose name Phi Beta Kappa presents an annual award for an outstanding book published in the United States on literary scholarship or criticism. 864.

2 Groundhog Day, a traditional day of observance. According to folklore, if the groundhog, or woodchuck, comes out of his burrow on this day and sees his shadow, he will go back for another six weeks. In Canada, the bear is sometimes substituted for the groundhog. 20, 269, 572, 866.

2 Birthday of James Joyce (February 2, 1882–January 13, 1941). Irish poet and novelist, author of *Ulysses*, considered to be a masterpiece in world literature. 833.

2 Anniversary of the death of Giovanni Palestrina on February 2, 1594. Italian composer celebrated for his masses and other sacred music. 5.

2 Anniversary of the signing of the Treaty of Guadalupe Hidalgo, ceding Texas, New Mexico, Arizona, and California to the United States; signed by Mexico and the United States, February 2, 1848. 268.

Holy Days and Feast Days

3 Feast Day of Saint Anskar, or Ansgar, missionary to Denmark, Sweden, Norway, and Northern Germany; patron saint of Denmark. 9.

3 Feast Day of Saint Blaise, patron saint of people who suffer from sore throats, of wool combers, and of waxchandlers. Throats are blessed on this day. 9, 20.

Holidays and Civic Days

3 Saint Blas Day, a holiday in Paraguay that begins with religious services for the blessing of throats; a special devotion derived from the tradition that the saint saved the life of a boy choking on a fishbone. The religious services are followed by holiday festivities centered around old customs. 875.

3 Martyrs Day, a holiday in the Democratic Republic of São Tomé and Principe honoring the victims of the Batepa Massacre of 1953. 875.

Anniversaries and Special Events Days

c3 The Bean-throwing Festival, or Setsubun, observed in Japan on or near February 3 with good fortune bean-throwing ceremonies that have come down from ancient times to the present. Setsubun marks the last day of winter in the lunar calendar. 22, 251.

3 Birthday of Elizabeth Blackwell (February 3, 1821–May 31, 1910). First woman doctor in the United States, founder of the New York Infirmary for Women and Children, and lecturer on hygiene and preventive medicine. An American Women's Medical Association Award for distinguished service has been named in her honor. 738, 788.

3 Four Chaplains Memorial Day, honoring Alexander Goode, Jewish chaplain; Father John P. Washington, Roman Catholic chaplain; and George L. Fox and Clark V. Poling, Protestant chaplains, who gave up their life jackets to others and went down with the *Dorchester* on February 3, 1943. 857.

3 Anniversary of the death of Johann Gensfleisch Gutenberg on February 3, 1468. German inventor of movable type; publisher of the Gutenberg Bible, "the finest example of printer's art ever known." 855.

c3 Homstrom, a Swiss festival celebrating the end of winter with the burning of straw men as a symbol of the departing Old Man Winter; observed on the first Sunday in February. 857.

3 Birthday of Sidney Lanier (February 3, 1842–September 7, 1881). American poet, musician, and critic. Elected to the Hall of Fame for Great Americans in 1945. 864.

3 Birthday of Felix Mendelssohn-Bartholdy (February 3, 1809–November 4, 1847). German romantic composer famous for piano and violin concertos, oratorios, and chamber music. 864.

3 Birthday of Gertrude Stein (February 3, 1874–July 27, 1946). American author whose *Making of Americans* led to a heated literary controversy over style and meaning. *The Autobiography of Alice B. Toklas* is actually Gertrude Stein's autobiography. 738, 864.

Holy Days and Feast Days

4 Feast Day of Saint Andrew Corsini, bishop of Fiesoli, mediator between quarrelsome Italian states; a saint invoked to compose quarrels and discords. 4, 9.

Holidays and Civic Days

4 Commencement of the Armed Struggle Day, a holiday in Angola honoring the insurrection against Portuguese rule that began with organized armed resistance on February 4, 1961, at the São Paulo fortress and police headquarters in Luanda. 868, 875.

4 Sri Lanka Independence Day, a national holiday commemorating the granting of independence on February 4, 1948, to the former British colony which changed its name in 1972 from Ceylon to Sri Lanka. 868, 875.

Anniversaries and Special Events Days

4 Anniversary of the death of Miguel Covarrubias on February 4, 1957. Mexican painter and illustrator of such books as *The Eagle, The Jaguar*, and *The Serpent*. 864.

4 Birthday of Mark Hopkins (February 4, 1802–June 17, 1887). American educator and moral philosopher who served as president of Williams College. He was elected to the Hall of Fame for Great Americans in 1915. 268.

4 Kosciuszko Day, observed by Polish-American communities in the United States to honor the February 4, 1746, birth of Tadeusz Kosciuszko, who fought with the colonists in the American Revolutionary War. 306.

4 Birthday of Charles Augustus Lindbergh (February 4, 1902–August 26, 1974). American aviator known as the Lone Eagle for his pioneering solo flight across the Atlantic on May 20–21, 1927; the first American private citizen to become a public hero. 470, 473.

4 Anniversary of the incorporation of the National Institute of Arts and Letters on February 4, 1913, with the objective of furthering literature and the fine arts in the United States.

4 Anniversary of the founding of the United Service Organizations (USO) on February 4, 1941, to serve the social, educational, religious, and welfare needs of the United States armed forces. The February 4 anniversary is observed annually at service centers. 268.

Holy Days and Feast Days

5 Feast Day of Saint Agatha, patron saint of Malta; patroness of nurses, bell founders, jewelers, and fire fighters; invoked for protection against fire in homes. 4, 5, 9, 738.

Holidays and Civic Days

5 Mexican Constitution Day, a legal holiday in Mexico honoring the anniversaries of the constitutions of 1857 and 1917. 868, 875.

5 Saint Agatha's Day, a religious and national holiday in San Marino honoring the nation's patron saint and patron of nurses. 875.

5 Chama Cha Mapinduzi Day, a holiday in Tanzania honoring the birth of CCM, the revolutionary party, on February 5, 1977. 868, 875.

Anniversaries and Special Events Days

5 Japanese Martyr Day, memorializing Saint Peter Baptist and his companions, who were killed by the Emperor Tagosama in 1597. 20.

5 Birthday of Hiram Stevens Maxim (February 5, 1840–November 24, 1916). Anglo-American inventor whose most important invention was the automatic single-barrel rifle; honored by gun and rifle societies. 864.

5 Birthday of Dwight Lyman Moody (February 5, 1837–December 22, 1899). American evangelist who built the first YMCA building in America in Chicago; conducted revivals all over the world with Ira Sankey, organist; and founded the Chicago Bible Institute, now known as the Moody Bible Institute. 268.

5 Birthday of Robert Peel (February 5, 1788–July 2, 1850). English prime minister, nineteenth-century orator, advocate of liberal reforms. The British police became known as "bobbies" as a result of his interest in public safety and criminal-investigation reforms. 867.

5 Runeberg's Day, observed in Finland to honor Johan Ludvig Runeberg, Finland's leading poet, on the day of his birth, February 5, 1804. 849.

5 Birthday of Adlai Ewing Stevenson (February 5, 1900–July 14, 1965). Lawyer; governor of Illinois; United States representative to the United Nations. 864.

5 Roger Williams Day, observed by American Baptists to celebrate the arrival of Roger Williams, their American founder, on the North American continent on February 5, 1631. Roger Williams represents Rhode Island in a Statuary Hall sculpture done by Franklin Simmons. 20, 870.

5 Weatherman's Day, the anniversary of the birth on February 5, 1744, of John Jeffries, a Boston doctor, who for many years kept the continuous daily records of weather. 866.

Holy Days and Feast Days

6 Feast of Saint Amand, seventh-century monk and missionary who established many monasteries in Belgium; known as "the apostle of Belgium." 5, 9.

6 Feast of Saint Dorothy, fourth-century Christian martyr. Legends tell of the appearance of an angel with a basket of three roses and three apples at her execution; patron of brides and gardeners. 4, 9.

Holidays and Civic Days

6 Massachusetts Ratification Day. Massachusetts entered the Union on February 6, 1788, as the sixth state of the original thirteen. 268, 856, 862.

6 New Zealand Day, or Waitangi, commemorates the signing of the 1840 Waitangi Treaty between the Maori and the Europeans; a national holiday in New Zealand. 868, 875.

Anniversaries and Special Events Days

6 Anniversary of the accession of Elizabeth II to the British throne on February 6, 1952, recognized annually by the royal salutes fired by the Queen's Troops of the Royal Horse Artillery. 874.

6 Birthday of Sir Henry Irving (February 6, 1838–October 13, 1905). English actor-manager who made his reputation in the role of Hamlet. He was knighted in 1895, the first actor to receive this honor; buried in Westminster Abbey. 864.

6 Birthday of Károly Kisfaludy (February 6, 1788–November 21, 1830). Hungarian romantic poet and dramatist who inspired his fellow Hungarians to voice their national cultural heritage. 864.

6 Birthday of Ronald Wilson Reagan (February 6, 1911–). English-Scotch-Irish ancestry. Fortieth president of the United States, January 20, 1981– . 361, 371–72, 374.

6 Birthday of George Herman (Babe) Ruth (February 6, 1895–August 16, 1948). American baseball player whose home-run record was not exceeded until 1974 with the triumph of Henry Aaron of the Atlanta Braves. 867, 864.

Holidays and Civic Days

7 Grenada Independence Day, a holiday in the Caribbean island of Grenada honoring the attainment of complete independence on February 7, 1974. 868, 875.

Anniversaries and Special Events Days

7 Birthday of John Deere (February 7, 1804–May 17, 1886). American inventor and manufacturer of the steel plow. 864.

7 Birthday of Charles Dickens (February 7, 1812–June 9, 1870). English novelist whose major works, which include *Oliver Twist, David Copperfield*, and *A Tale of Two Cities*, are still popular. Dickens is buried in Westminster Abbey. 743.

7 Birthday of Frederick Douglass (February 7, 1817–February 20, 1895). Leader in the abolition movement and first black to hold high rank in the United States government, as a consultant to President Lincoln and United States minister to Haiti. 268.

7 Birthday of Sinclair Lewis (February 7, 1885–January 10, 1951). American novelist and playwright. The first American to receive the Nobel Prize in literature; presented to him in 1930. 864.

7 Birthday of Sir James Augustus Henry Murray (February 7, 1837–July 26, 1915). Scottish philologist and lexicographer whose lifework was the *New English Dictionary on Historical Principles*, now known as the *Oxford English Dictionary*. 864.

7 Birthday of John Rylands (February 7, 1801–December 11, 1888). English merchant and philanthropist whose memorial is the treasure-rich John Rylands Library in Manchester, England. 864.

7 Anniversary of the authorization on February 7, 1936, of a flag for the office of the vice-president of the United States. 281.

Holy Days and Feast Days

8 Feast of Jerome Emiliani, founder of the Clerks Regular of Somascha, devoted to the care of orphans and the education of children; named the patron saint of orphans and abandoned children in 1928. 5, 9.

Holidays and Civic Days

c8 Lincoln Day, a holiday in Arizona celebrating Abraham Lincoln's birthday; observed on the second Monday in February. 875.

8 Iraq's February Revolution, a holiday commemorating the revolution of February 8, 1963, known as 8th February Revolution. 868, 875.

Anniversaries and Special Events Days

c8 Boy Scouts Day, commemorates the incorporation of the Boy Scouts of America on February 8, 1910. A Boy Scouts of America Sabbath is usually scheduled for a Sunday near this date. Boy Scouts Day is scheduled annually near the date of the organization's founding and is followed by week- or month-long activities. 268.

c8 Inventors Day, a day of recognition of the contributors of inventors; a day of induction of outstanding inventors into the National Inventors Hall of Fame; observed around February 8. 857.

8 Kite Flying Day, a contest day in Korea, preserving age-old traditions through encouraging children to develop skills in the art of kite flying. 615.

8 Narvik Sun Pageant Day, celebrates the return of the sun after its winter absence; observed on February 8 at Narvik, Norway.

8 Birthday of William Tecumseh Sherman (February 8, 1820–February 14, 1891). American Union general remembered as the leader of the march through Georgia during the Civil War and famous for the phrase "War is hell." Elected to the Hall of Fame for Great Americans in 1905. 721.

8 Birthday of Jules Verne (February 8, 1828–March 24, 1905). French novelist famous for *Twenty Thousand Leagues under the Sea*; an author whose writing stimulated the development of science fiction. 867.

Holy Days and Feast Days

9 Feast Day of Saint Apollonia, patron saint of dentists; invoked against toothaches and all dental troubles. 9, 20.

9 Feast of Saint Maron, the seventh- and eighth-century founder of the Maronite church, a Syrian community in communion with the Roman Catholic church since the twelfth century. 1.

Holidays and Civic Days

9 Saint Maron Day, a holiday in Lebanon commemorating the founder of the Maronite church; observed not only by the Maronite Christians in Lebanon but also by Maronites in North and South America. 875.

9 Hobert Regatta Day, a holiday in southern Tasmania, celebrated with two-day aquatic carnivals and sailing races. 875.

Anniversaries and Special Events Days

9 Birthday of George Ade (February 9, 1866–May 16, 1944). American playwright and humorist who was famous for his *Fables in Slang*. 864.

9 Birthday of Mrs. Patrick Campbell (February 9, 1865–April 9, 1940). English actress and great friend of George Bernard Shaw, who wrote *Pygmalion* as a vehicle for her talents. 864.

9 Anniversary of the proclamation of the Confederate States of America on February 9, 1861. Jefferson Davis became the provisional president on February 18, 1861. 268.

9 Birthday of William H. Harrison (February 9, 1773–April 4, 1841). English ancestry. Ohio lawyer and soldier; congressman; ninth president of the United States, 1841. Died in the White House after one month in office. Episcopalian. Buried at North Bend, Ohio. 359–66, 370, 374, 378, 379.

9 Birthday of Amy Lowell (February 9, 1874–May 12, 1925). American poet, biographer, and critic; a leader among the imagist poets; author of a monumental life of Keats. 864.

9 Birthday of Samuel Jones Tilden (February 9, 1814–August 4, 1886). American politician and philanthropist whose will established the Tilden Foundation, one of the integral components of the New York Public Library. 864.

Holy Days and Feast Days

10 Feast of Saint Paul's Shipwreck off the coast of Malta in A.D. 60, commemorated in Malta.

10 Feast Day of Saint Scholastica, sister of Saint Benedict and special patroness of the Benedictine nuns; patron saint of children in convulsions. 9.

Anniversaries and Special Events Days

10 Birthday of Charles Lamb (February 10, 1775–December 27, 1834). English essayist and critic whose works include a variety of material, from *Tales from Shakespeare* to the miscellaneous *Last Essays of Elia*. 864.

10 Birthday of Boris Leonidovich Pasternak (February 10, 1890–May 30, 1960). Russian poet, novelist, and translator who was awarded the 1958 Nobel Prize in literature but was forced to refuse it because of political opposition; the author of *Doctor Zhivago*. 864.

10 Birthday of William Allen White (February 10, 1868–January 29, 1944). American journalist and author, editor of the Emporia *Gazette*, who was known as "the sage of Emporia." Among the editorials for which he was noted were "To an Anxious Friend," which won a Pulitzer Prize, and the one on his daughter Mary at the time of her accidental death. The William Allen White Children's Book Award is given annually for a children's book chosen by Kansas school children. 858, 864.

Holy Days and Feast Days

c11 The Feast of Our Lady's Miraculous Apparitions to Saint Bernadette Soubirous at Lourdes, a major religious weeklong celebration at Lourdes. The Philippine Catholics observe the anniversary of the apparition with a spectacular fete including religious rites, long processions, and a fiesta. 5.

Holidays and Civic Days

11 Cameroon Youth Day, a public holiday in Cameroon, a republic on the west coast of Africa, dedicated to the children and young people of the nation. 875.

11 Japanese National Foundation Day, a national holiday in Japan commemorating the founding of the nation of Japan in 660 B.C. by the first emperor. 868, 875.

11 Liberia Armed Forces Day, a public holiday honoring the professional army and navy and the militia of Liberia. 875.

11 Lateranensi Pacts Day, a holiday in the Vatican City State celebrating the conclusion of treaties between the Italian government and the Vatican on February 11, 1929, which, among other settlements, established the sovereignty of the Vatican City State, the smallest independent country in the world. 5.

Anniversaries and Special Events Days

11 Birthday of Thomas Alva Edison (February 11, 1847–October 18, 1931). American inventor who took out over a thousand patents. His best-known inventions are the phonograph and the incandescent lamp. He was elected to the Hall of Fame for Great Americans in 1960. The Thomas Alva Edison Foundation presents four awards annually in honor of Edison: for the best science book for children and youth and for books that contribute to character development and to an understanding of American history. 268, 867.

c11 The Gasparilla Carnival, recreating the days of the pirates, has been held in Tampa, Florida, since 1904. The carnival is held in mid-February and revives the nineteenth-century Gasparilla, the Spanish pirate, his buccaneers, and their three-masted sloop with welcoming ceremonies at the harbor, pirate parades, fireworks, and balls. 268.

11 Birthday of Josiah Willard Gibbs (February 11, 1839–April 28, 1903). American physicist and chemist. Elected to the Hall of Fame for Great Americans in 1950. 864.

11 White Shirt Day, a day of recognition marking the end of the 1937 sit-down strikes at the plants in Flint, Michigan; observed through the wearing of white shirts by "blue-collar" workers as a symbol of the dignity of work. 857.

Holy Days and Feast Days

12 Feast of Saint Julian the Hospitaler, who mistakenly murdered his parents. In penance he established an inn for travelers and a hospital for the poor; the patron of hotelkeepers, boatmen, and travelers. 4, 9.

Holidays and Civic Days

12 Burma Union Day, a public holiday in Burma commemorating the 1947 conference of national and ethnic leaders which led to the formation of the Union of Burma. 868, 875.

12 Birthday of Abraham Lincoln (February 12, 1809–April 15, 1865). English ancestry; Illinois lawyer and debater; sixteenth president of the United States, 1861–65. Assassinated in office. Called the Great Emancipator. No formal religious affiliation. Buried in Oak Ridge Cemetery, Springfield, Illinois. Lincoln was elected to the Hall of Fame for Great Americans in 1900; Lincoln's birthday is celebrated on February 12 as a holiday in Alaska, California, Colorado, Connecticut, Florida, Illinois, Indiana, Iowa, Kansas, Kentucky, Maryland, Missouri, Montana, Nebraska, New Jersey, New Mexico, New York, Utah, Vermont, Washington, and West Virginia. 269, 270, 339–54, 359–66, 370–72, 374, 377–79, 572, 624, 631.

Anniversaries and Special Events Days

12 Birthday of Peter Cooper (February 12, 1791–April 4, 1883). American industrialist and civic leader whose name lives in the Cooper Union for the Advancement of Science and Art, which he founded and endowed. He was elected to the Hall of Fame for Great Americans in 1900. 864.

12 Birthday of Charles Robert Darwin (February 12, 1809–April 19, 1882). English biologist whose theory of evolution by natural selection came to be known as Darwinism. His most-noted work is *On the Origin of the Species by Means of Natural Selection; or the Preservation of Favored Races in the Struggle for Life*. 864.

12 Georgia Day, or Oglethorpe Day, a special day in Georgia commemorating the landing of James Edward Oglethorpe at Savannah on February 12, 1733, and the founding of the state. Major celebrations occur at Savannah with the ringing of bells, processions, an Oglethorpe banquet, and displays of historic memorabilia. 268, 856, 862.

12 Nancy Hanks Lincoln Memorial Day, observed at Booneville, Indiana, on February 12, and at Lincoln City, Indiana, on May 30. 365.

12 Birthday of Cotton Mather (February 12, 1663–February 13, 1728). American colonial minister, man of letters, and author of the most important literary work produced in the colonies, the *Magnalia Christi Americana*, an ecclesiastical history of New England. 20.

12 Anniversary of the establishment of the National Association for the Advancement of Colored People (NAACP) on February 12, 1909. 874.

Anniversaries and Special Events Days

13 Anniversary of the establishment of the American Society of Composers, Authors and Publishers (ASCAP) on February 13, 1914. 874.

13 Fiesta de Menendez, observed in St. Augustine, Florida, to honor the 1565 birthday of the city's founder.

Holy Days and Feast Days

14 Feast of Saints Cyril and Methodius, two brothers known as "the apostles of the Slavs"; patron saints of the Danubian countries and of Eastern and Western church unity. 4, 9.

14 Feast Day of Saint Valentine, patron saint of lovers; invoked against epilepsy, plague, and fainting diseases. 14.

Holidays and Civic Days

14 Admission Day in Arizona, a civic day commemorating February 14, 1912, when President Taft signed the proclamation admitting Arizona to the Union as the forty-eighth state. It is celebrated by schools and patriotic groups. 268, 856, 862.

14 Oregon Statehood Day, commemorates Oregon's entry into the Union on February 14, 1859, as the thirty-third state. 268, 856, 862.

Anniversaries and Special Events Days

14 Birthday of Richard Allen (February 14, 1760–March 26, 1831). American clergyman, founder and first bishop of the African Methodist church. The first black to be regularly ordained in the Methodist Episcopal church. 1, 20.

14 Birthday of Nicolaus Copernicus (February 14, 1473–May 24, 1543). Polish doctor and scientist who is known as the founder of modern astronomy; creator of the Copernican system. 775.

14 Fjortende Februar (Fourteenth of February) is the traditional day for the exchange of tokens and gifts among schoolchildren in Denmark.

14 Selma March Day, the anniversary of a key day in the historic 160-mile civil rights march from Selma to Montgomery, Alabama, led by Martin Luther King, Jr., in 1965. The march, marked by violence, influenced the passage by Congress of the Voting Rights Act signed on August 6, 1965. 314.

14 Birthday of Anna Howard Shaw (February 14, 1847–July 2, 1919). American suffrage leader, physician, and minister, the first woman ordained in the Methodist church. 867.

14 Birthday of Joseph Thomson (February 14, 1858–August 2, 1895). Scottish geologist and naturalist who conducted explorations into Africa that yielded important data on the flora, fauna, and geology of the African continent. Thomson's gazelle, an East African species, was named for him. 864.

14 Valentine's Day, a folk festival, bears the name of the saint and continues the customs of the pagan festival called Lupercalia. The widespread custom of exchanging cards and gifts on this day has no connection with Saint Valentine but is enjoyed by children of all ages. England, France, and, more recently, the United States are among the countries that unofficially celebrate this holiday. 269, 558–65, 567, 572, 588, 607, 614, 623–24, 628, 831, 866.

14 Viticulturists' Day, or Trifon Zarezan, a centuries-old festivity celebrated in Bulgaria with customs based on the cult of Dionysus, god of wine and merriment.

Holidays and Civic Days

c15 Susan B. Anthony Day, the anniversary of the February 15, 1820, birth of Susan Brownell Anthony, American abolitionist; pioneer crusader for women's rights, temperance, and Negro suffrage; author and lecturer. Elected to the Hall of Fame for Great Americans in 1950. Honored with the 1979 Susan B. Anthony dollar; the first American woman to have her likeness on coinage. A holiday linked with Washington's birthday in Florida. 268, 738, 866.

c15 Presidents' Day, a holiday observed on the third Monday of February in the states of Hawaii, Michigan, Minnesota, Nebraska, Wisconsin and Wyoming to honor the presidents of the United States. 359–80.

c15 Washington's Birthday, a holiday in all of the fifty states of the United States, the District of Columbia, Guam, Puerto Rico, and the Virgin Islands; observed on the third Monday of February. 269, 419–29, 430, 624, 631, 791.

Anniversaries and Special Events Days

15 Birthday of Galileo Galilei (February 15, 1564–January 8, 1642). Italian astronomer, mathematician, and physicist, considered to be the founder of the experimental method. 5, 750.

15 Birthday of Cyrus Hall McCormick (February 15, 1809–May 13, 1884). American inventor of the mechanical reaper, industrialist, and philanthropist who endowed the McCormick Theological Seminary. 864.

15 Maine Memorial Day, the anniversary of the explosion in the Havana harbor of the American battleship *Maine* on February 15, 1898; the fate of the ship prompted the use of the slogan "Remember the Maine." The day has been called Battleship Day or Spanish-American War Memorial Day; observed in Connecticut, Maine, and Massachusetts. 268.

15 Anniversary of the establishment of the city of St. Louis, Missouri, by Auguste Chouteau and Pierre Laclede in 1764. 784.

15 Birthday of Alfred North Whitehead (February 15, 1861–December 30, 1947). English mathematician and philosopher. His most distinguished work is *Principia Mathematica*, which he wrote with Bertrand Russell. 864.

Anniversaries and Special Events Days

16 Birthday of Henry Adams (February 16, 1838–March 27, 1918). American historian and philosopher whose best-known works are *Mont-Saint-Michel and Chartres* and *The Education of Henry Adams*; recipient of the Pulitzer Prize in 1919. 864.

16 Lithuanian Independence Day, marks the proclamation of independence for Lithuania in 1918; commemorated by Lithuanian-American communities and organizations with special programs and group observances. 268.

17 Birthday of Dorothy Canfield Fisher (February 17, 1879–November 9, 1958). American novelist of stories dealing with Vermont life, a member of the book selection committee of the Book-of-the-Month Club from 1926 to 1951. A Dorothy Canfield Fisher Library Award has been established by the Book-of-the-Month Club as a memorial, with funds to be used by small libraries for the purchase of books. 816, 858.

17 Birthday of René Théophile Laënnec (February 17, 1781–August 13, 1826). French physician who invented the stethoscope, called "the father of chest medicine." 864.

17 Anniversary of the organization of the National Congress of Parents and Teachers in Washington, D.C., February 17, 1897. The founders are honored annually on this day. 857.

Holy Days and Feast Days

18 Festival of Saint Bernadette and the anniversary of her second vision, celebrated at Lourdes. 34.

Holidays and Civic Days

18 Gambian Independence Day, a holiday in The Gambia, honoring February 18, 1965, when independence within the Commonwealth was achieved. The Gambia became a republic on April 24, 1970. 868, 875.

18 Tribhuvan Jayanti, a holiday in Nepal. On February 18, 1951, the king proclaimed a constitutional monarchy. 868, 875.

Anniversaries and Special Events Days

18 Birthday of George Peabody (February 18, 1795–November 4, 1869). American merchant, financier, and philanthropist. Elected to the Hall of Fame for Great Americans in 1900. 864.

18 Birthday of Solomon Rabinowitz (February 18, 1859–May 13, 1916). Russian author, best known under the pen name Sholom Aleichem. A master of the short story, he is known as the Yiddish Mark Twain. 864.

18 Birthday of Alessandro Volta (February 18, 1745–March 5, 1827). Italian physicist and pioneer in the science of electricity; inventor of the electric battery. 867.

Anniversaries and Special Events Days

19 Birthday of Francis Preston Blair, Jr. (February 19, 1821–July 9, 1875). American congressman from Missouri. He represents Missouri in Statuary Hall in a sculpture done by Alexander Doyle. 870.

19 Birthday of Sven Anders Hedin (February 19, 1865–November 26, 1952). Swedish scientist and explorer whose explorations in central and eastern Asia determined the source of the Indus and the continuity of the trans-Himalayan range. 864.

Anniversaries and Special Events Days

20 Anniversary of the death of Klas Pontus Arnoldson on February 20, 1916. Swedish author, founder of the Swedish Society for Peace and Arbitration; corecipient of the Nobel Peace Prize in 1908. 867.

20 John Glenn Day, commemorating the first orbit of the earth by a United States astronaut; John Glenn orbited on February 20, 1962. 268, 866.

20 Princess Alice Day, the anniversary of the February 20, 1980, death of Alice Roosevelt Longworth, daughter of President Theodore Roosevelt; known as Princess Alice in the White House and as the sharp-tongued dowager-critic of American politics and Washington, D.C., society in her later years. 809.

Holy Days and Feast Days

21 Feast of Saint Peter Damian, an eleventh-century Benedictine noted for his practical pastoral leadership; proclaimed a doctor of the church in 1828; a patron saint of physicians. 4, 9.

Holidays and Civic Days

21 Shaheel Day, a holiday in Bangladesh, observed as a national day of mourning. 875.

Anniversaries and Special Events Days

21 Birthday of Wystan Hugh Auden (February 21, 1907–September 27, 1973). English-born American poet known as a "poet's poet." Awarded the 1948 Pulitzer Prize for his long philosophical poem *The Age of Anxiety*. 864.

21 Birthday of Otto Hermann Kahn (February 21, 1867–March 29, 1934). American banker and philanthropist who organized the Metropolitan Opera Company in 1907. 864.

21 Anniversary of the death of Malcolm Little, known as Malcolm X, on February 21, 1965. Black militant leader; organizer of Muslim Mosque, Inc.; founder of the Organization of Afro-American Unity; and author of an autobiography of widespread interest and influence. 759.

21 Birthday of John Henry Newman (February 21, 1801–August 11, 1890). English cardinal-deacon; author of the hymn *Lead Kindly Light* and the autobiography *Apologia pro Vita Sua*; honored by Newman societies in the United States and Europe. 34.

21 Birthday of Alice Freeman Palmer (February 21, 1855–December 6, 1902). Pioneer American educator. Elected to the Hall of Fame for Great Americans in 1920. 864.

21 Anniversary of the dedication on February 21, 1885, of the Washington Monument in Washington, D.C., designed by Robert Mills. 268.

Holy Days and Feast Days

22 Feast of the Chair of Peter, commemorates the establishment of the see of Antioch of Peter, a liturgical expression of belief in the episcopacy. 5.

Holidays and Civic Days

22 St. Lucia Independence Day, the anniversary of the achievement of independence on February 22, 1979, for an island in the West Indies which had been under British control since 1802. 868, 875.

Anniversaries and Special Events Days

22 Birthday of Sir Robert Stephenson Smyth Baden-Powell (February 22, 1857–January 8, 1941). British major general, founder of the Boy Scouts, and, with his sister, of the Girl Guides. 867.

22 Dalai Lama Consecration Day, the anniversary of the consecrating of the fourteenth Dalai Lama of Tibet on February 22, 1940. The superior one of the Gelugpa Order of Tibetan Buddhism was exiled in 1959 to India, where he is the central figure in work to preserve the cultural and religious heritage of Tibet. 1.

22 Birthday of Eric Gill (February 22, 1882–November 17, 1940). English sculptor, engravor, and typographer who carved the stations of the cross at Westminster Cathedral, executed other important commissions, and illustrated *Canterbury Tales, The Four Gospels*, and other books. Notable among his own writings are *Christianity and Art* and *Autobiography*. 864.

22 Girl Guides Thinking Day, observed by the members of the Girl Guides of England and the British Commonwealth countries; commemorates the February 22, 1857, birthday of their founder, Sir Baden-Powell.

22 Birthday of James Russell Lowell (February 22, 1819–August 12, 1891). American poet, essayist, and diplomat. Remembered for *The Vision of Sir Launfal*. He was elected to the Hall of Fame for Great Americans in 1905. 268.

22 Birthday of Edna St. Vincent Millay (February 22, 1892–October 19, 1950). American poet who made her reputation with the publication of *Renascence* in 1917. She received the Pulitzer Prize for *The Harp Weaver* and wrote the libretto for an opera composed by Deems Taylor. 738, 819.

22 Mother's Day in India, established as a memorial to Mrs. Mohandas K. Gandhi, the wife of India's most famous citizen.

22 Birthday of Arthur Schopenhauer (February 22, 1788–September 21, 1860). German philosopher and man of letters whose greatest work is *The World as Will and Idea*. 864.

22 Virgin Island Donkey Races Day, alternating between Frederiksted and Christiansted and featuring both cart and bareback riding for the sheer entertainment of the public.

22 Birthday of George Washington (February 22, 1732–December 14, 1799). English ancestry; Virginia planter; surveyor; colonel in Virginia militia; member of the House of Burgesses; commander-in-chief of the Continental Army; first president of the United States, 1789–97; Episcopalian. Buried at Mount Vernon, Virginia. Elected to the Hall of Fame for Great Americans in 1900. Washington's birthday has been observed since 1782, while the Revolution was still being fought. Since 1971, Washington's birthday has been observed in all states on the third Monday of February. 419–29.

Holy Days and Feast Days

23 Feast of Saint Polycarp; reputed to be the most influential Christian in Roman Asia in the second century; an important ecclesiastical writer and martyr. 5, 9.

Holidays and Civic Days

23 Guyana Republic Day, commemorating the February 23, 1970, establishment of Guyana as a sovereign democratic state in South America and within the British Commonwealth. 868, 875.

Anniversaries and Special Events Days

23 Battle of Buena Vista, the anniversary of the battle between the United States and Mexico fought at Buena Vista in the Mexican state of Coahuila on February 23, 1847; the American victory over General Santa Anna contributed to the end, in September of 1847, of the Mexican War. 268.

23 Birthday of William Edward Burghardt Du Bois (February 23, 1868–August 27, 1963). American sociologist and author; awarded the 1920 Spingarn Medal for leadership in securing opportunities for blacks. 759, 853.

23 Birthday of George Frederic Handel (February 23, 1685–April 20, 1759). German-born English composer famous for oratorios and operas. Handel's *Messiah* is sung around the world during the Christmas season. 864.

23 Iwo Jima Day, anniversary of the raising of the American flag atop Mount Suribachi in Iwo Jima by United States marines on February 23, 1945. 418.

23 Birthday of Jean-Baptiste Le Moyne, Sieur de Bienville (February 23, 1680–March 7, 1767). French-Canadian explorer and colonizer; founder of New Orleans in 1718. 864.

23 Birthday of Samuel Pepys (February 23, 1633–May 26, 1703). English writer famous for the most frequently quoted diary in the English language. 864.

23 Anniversary of the death of Sir Joshua Reynolds on February 23, 1792. English portrait painter and first president of the Royal Academy. 864.

23 Birthday of Emma Willard (February 23, 1787–April 15, 1870). Pioneer American educator whose major concern was the education of girls and young women. Elected to the Hall of Fame for Great Americans in 1905. 268, 738.

Holy Days and Feast Days

24 Feast of Saint Matthias, a disciple chosen as the apostle to take the place of Judas Iscariot who betrayed Jesus; observed by the Episcopal and Lutheran churches on February 24, and in leap years on February 25; his feast is celebrated in the Roman Catholic and the Eastern Orthodox churches on August 9. 14.

Anniversaries and Special Events Days

24 Birthday of Mary Ellen Chase (February 24, 1887–July 28, 1973). American educator; author of *Mary Peters* and other novels, as well as books on the Bible, including *The Bible and the Common Reader* and *Life and Language in the Old Testament*. 864.

24 Anniversary of the death of Auguste Chouteau on February 24, 1829. American fur trader and cofounder of the city of St. Louis. 784.

24 Estonia National Day, honoring a peace treaty signed on February 24, 1920, confirming Estonian independence; Estonia has since been absorbed by the Union of Soviet Socialist Republics.

24 Birthday of Winslow Homer (February 24, 1836–September 29, 1910). American landscape and seascape painter elected to the National Academy of Design in 1865. 864.

24 Mexican Independence Proclamation Day, a historic day in Mexico; the anniversary of the proclamation of the Iturbide's Plan of Iguala, proclaimed on February 24, 1821, projecting independence from Spain. 397.

24 Vincennes Day, observed in Indiana in commemoration of George Rogers Clark's defeat of the British at Vincennes during the American Revolution.

Holidays and Civic Days

25 Kuwait National Day, a holiday in Kuwait in southeastern Asia celebrating the accession of Shaykh Sir 'Abdallah Al-Salim al-Sabah. 875.

Anniversaries and Special Events Days

c25 Coronado Day, honoring Francisco Vásquez de Coronado's search for the Seven Cities of Cibola in 1540 and his exploration of Mexico and what is now the American Southwest; commemorated with regional festivals.

25 Birthday of Benedetto Croce (February 25, 1866–November 20, 1952). Italian humanist, historian, and editor, the foremost Italian philosopher of the first half of the twentieth century. 864.

25 Birthday of Charles Lang Freer (February 25, 1856–September 25, 1919). American art collector who specialized in Chinese and Japanese painting and Oriental pottery. His collections were presented to the nation, and he endowed the Freer Gallery in Washington, D.C. to house them. 864.

25 Birthday of Carlo Goldoni (February 25, 1707–February 6, 1793). Italian author, founder of Italian realistic comedy. 864.

25 Birthday of José Francisco de San Martín (February 25, 1778–August 17, 1850). Latin American general, liberator of Chile from Spanish control, leader in the wars of independence in Argentina and Peru. Honored in Chile for moral grandeur, military genius, and statesmanship. 5.

Holy Days and Feast Days

26 Ayyam-i-Ha, the intercalary days in the Baha'i calendar, four in ordinary years and five in leap years, which adjust the nineteenth-month calendar to the solar year; the intercalary days extend from February 26 to March 1 and are observed as days of hospitality, charity, the giving of gifts, and rejoicing. 1, 854.

Anniversaries and Special Events Days

26 Birthday of William Frederick Cody, "Buffalo Bill" (February 26, 1846–January 10, 1917). American plainsman and showman who personifies the romance of the Old West. 268, 802, 824.

26 Birthday of Victor Hugo (February 26, 1802–May 22, 1885). French novelist and dramatist known universally for his novel *Les Misérables*. 793.

26 Birthday of John George Nicolay (February 26, 1832–September 26, 1901). American author, secretary to, and biographer of, Abraham Lincoln.

Holidays and Civic Days

27 Independence Day in the Dominican Republic, a public holiday of parades and political meetings honoring the independence secured through the withdrawal of the Haitians in 1844. 868, 875.

27 Statehood Day, a holiday in St. Kitts–Nevis, a part of the West Indies Associated States; a celebration of the achievement of self-government through agreements with Great Britain on February 27, 1967. 875.

Anniversaries and Special Events Days

27 Birthday of Sveinn Björnsson (February 27, 1881–January 25, 1952). First president of Iceland, upon its establishment as a republic in 1944.

27 Birthday of Henry Edwards Huntington (February 27, 1850–May 23, 1927). American railroad executive and philanthropist; founder of the Huntington Library at San Marino, California.

27 Birthday of Henry Wadsworth Longfellow (February 27, 1807–March 24, 1882). American poet famed for *Evangeline* and *The Song of Hiawatha*. He was elected to the Hall of Fame for Great Americans in 1900. 268.

Anniversaries and Special Events Days

28 Birthday of Sir Wilfred Grenfell (February 28, 1865–October 9, 1940). English medical missionary in Labrador who outfitted the first hospital ship for North Sea fisheries. 867.

28 Kalevala Day, a commemorative day in Finland, dedicated to the greatest Finnish epic poem; observed on the anniversary of the dating of the preface to the first edition by Dr. Elias Lönnrot on February 28, 1835. Parades and other fitting ceremonies honor Lönnrot who transcribed more than twenty-two thousand verses from the memories of his compatriots. 849.

28 Birthday of Mary Lyon (February 28, 1797–March 5, 1849). Pioneer American educator; founder and first principal of Mount Holyoke Seminary, which later became Mount Holyoke College. She was elected to the Hall of Fame for Great Americans in 1905. 268, 738.

28 Birthday of Michel Eyquem de Montaigne (February 28, 1533–September 13, 1592). French essayist who was the first to use the term *essay* to describe the literary form he so successfully executed. 864.

28 Birthday of Louis Joseph de Montcalm de Saint-Véran (February 28, 1712–September 14, 1759). French general who was mortally wounded in battle with General Wolfe on the Plains of Abraham near Quebec. 5.

28 Birthday of Sir John Tenniel (February 28, 1820–February 25, 1914). English cartoonist and illustrator remembered as the illustrator of Lewis Carroll's *Alice's Adventures in Wonderland*. 864.

29 Leap Year Day, from tne name given to every year of 366 days; occurs every fourth year; sometimes called Bachelors' Day. 20, 268.

29 Ann Lee Day, the anniversary of the birth on February 29, 1736, of Ann Lee, founder of Shakerism in America; called Mother Ann by her disciples. The Shaker contributions to American crafts and domestic arts are preserved in a number of museums located in Massachusetts, New York, Kentucky, Maine, and Ohio. 268, 738.

29 Birthday of Gioacchino Antonio Rossini (February 29, 1792–November 13, 1868). Italian composer famous for the operas *The Barber of Seville* and *William Tell* and for the sacred composition *Stabat Mater*.

March

March, the third month of the year, was named for Mars, the Roman god of war. In the days of the Julian calendar, March included New Year's Day. New Year's was then March 25 and was the day on which annual leases for homes and farms were signed, a time schedule that has continued in many parts of the world, even though New Year's Day was moved to January with the adoption of the Gregorian calendar.

March was called the "loud or stormy month" by the early Britons. It is the month of the vernal equinox, the official beginning of spring. The young people in the canton of the Grisons in Switzerland are among the first to respond to the season, by wearing herdsmen's costumes with wide belts from which are hung countless cowbells to "ring out the winter."

The most popular March day is the seventeenth, Saint Patrick's Day. It is a major holiday in Ireland, but it is celebrated in New York City, too, with the "wearers of the green" of all nationalities joining in a spectacular Saint Patrick's Day parade, a tradition that began in 1762.

The flowers for the month of March are the jonquil or daffodil, and the birthstones are the bloodstone and the aquamarine.

Holy Days and Feast Days

1 Feast of Saint David, a Welsh monk; founder and restorer of monasteries and first bishop of Mynyw, or Saint David's, in Wales; the patron saint of Wales. 14.

1 Feast of Saint Swithbert, an English-born missionary; the patron saint of angina sufferers and one of the patron saints of Germany. 9, 831, 866.

Holidays and Civic Days

c1 Magellan Day, or Discovery Day, a holiday in Guam honoring the Portuguese navigator, Ferdinand Magellan, and his discovery of Guam in March of 1521; observed on or near March 1 with the sailing of pleasure boat flotillas and with fiestas. 5.

1 Samiljol, or Independence Movement Day, a holiday in the Republic of Korea, honoring the beginning on March 1, 1919, of the passive movement toward freedom from Japanese colonial rule. 868, 875.

1 Nebraska Admission Day, proclaimed annually by the governor as a day of patriotic observance by citizens and by the schools in honor of the state's admission to the Union in 1867 as the thirty-seventh state. 268, 856, 862.

1 Ohio Admission Day; Ohio entered the Union on March 1, 1803, as the seventeenth state. 268, 856, 862.

1 Heroes' Day, a public holiday in Paraguay; also called National Defense Day. 875.

1 Labour Day, a holiday in Tasmania and in Western Australia honoring the achievement of an eight-hour working day in 1871 for all Australians. 875.

Anniversaries and Special Events Days

1 Birthday of Frédéric Chopin (March 1, 1810–October 17, 1849). Polish pianist and composer of well-known preludes, études, nocturnes, songs, and concertos for piano and orchestra. His romance with the novelist George Sand has been the subject of many books. 864.

c1 Cotton Carnival, the anniversary of the first of the annual Memphis Cotton Carnivals held on March 1, 1931; now observed for five days beginning the second Tuesday in May, with a program illustrating life in the Old South, cotton-fabric style shows, parades, and dances. 268.

1 Saint David's Day, a day of music, mirth, and friendship for all Welsh groups throughout the world, honoring the patron saint of Wales with the wearing of leeks or daffodils in hats, with choral singing and festive dinners.

1 Birthday of Dimitri Mitropoulos (March 1, 1896–November 2, 1960). Symphony orchestra conductor and composer. Director of the Minneapolis Symphony, the New York Philharmonic Orchestra, and the Metropolitan Opera; known for his interpretations of twentieth-century musical works. 864.

1 The Peace Corps was established on March 1, 1961, by President John Kennedy to provide youth with the opportunity to help underdeveloped countries.

1 Chalanda Marz, a day of announcing the coming of spring in Engadine, the picturesque valley of the Inn River in eastern Switzerland. Young people wear herdsmen's costumes with wide belts from which are suspended countless cow bells with which they "ring out the winter." 857.

1 Pinzon Day in Bayona, Spain, commemorating the arrival of Martin Pinzon, who brought to Europe the news of the discovery of the New World.

1 Birthday of Augustus Saint-Gaudens (March 1, 1848–August 3, 1907). American sculptor whose works include statues of Abraham Lincoln and General Sherman. Elected to the Hall of Fame for Great Americans in 1920. 864.

1 Whuppity Scoorie Day, a festival day in Lanark, Lanarkshire, Scotland, carrying on an ancient custom of noisemaking to drive away the evil spirits and thus protect the crops of the new season. 256.

1 Anniversary of the establishment of Yellowstone National Park as the first of the great national parks of the United States on March 1, 1872. 681.

Holidays and Civic Days

2 Peasants' Day, a holiday in the Union of Burma, featuring meetings of representatives of the Peasants' Council; a part of a one-week educational and cultural event. 875.

2 Victory of Aduwa Day, a holiday in Ethiopia commemorating the defeat of Italian forces in the Italian-Ethiopian conflict of 1896, which resulted in the treaty of Addis Ababa and the recognition of the independence of Ethiopia. 868, 875.

2 Independence Day in Morocco, a holiday commemorating the termination of the Treaty of Fez and the establishment of sovereignty on March 2, 1956. 875.

2 Texas Independence Day, celebrated in Texas as the anniversary of the declaration of independence from Mexico in 1836; a legal holiday and the first day of Texas Week. 268, 875.

c2 Town Meeting Day, a holiday in Vermont observed on the first Tuesday of March; a day of citizen participation in local government and civic issues. 268.

Anniversaries and Special Events Days

2 Birthday of Samuel Houston (March 2, 1793–July 26, 1863). American statesman; first president of the republic of Texas, governor of the state of Texas, and regional leader for whom the city of Houston is named. He represents the state of Texas in Statuary Hall in a sculpture done by Elisabet Ney. 870.

2 Birthday of Bedřich Smetana (March 2, 1824–May 12, 1884). Czech composer and orchestral leader whose opera *The Bartered Bride* has become popular. The Smetana Society in Prague maintains a museum dedicated to his work. 864.

Holidays and Civic Days

3 Florida Admission Day. Florida entered the Union as the twenty-seventh state on March 3, 1845. 268, 856, 862.

3 Malawi Martyr's Day, a public holiday in Malawi, formerly the British protectorate of Nyasaland in the eastern part of southern Africa; honors the nation's heroes.

3 Throne Day, a national holiday in Morocco, honoring His Majesty King Hassan II who succeeded his father on March 3, 1961, as the sovereign head of the Kingdom of Morocco. 868, 875.

3 Unity Day, a public holiday in Sudan honoring cooperation among the Arab nations. 875.

Anniversaries and Special Events Days

3 Birthday of Alexander Graham Bell (March 3, 1847–August 2, 1922). Scotch-born American physicist, famous for the invention of the telephone. Elected to the Hall of Fame for Great Americans, 1950. 268, 753.

3 Bulgaria Liberation Day, a commemoration of the anniversary of Bulgaria's release from Ottoman domination, secured through the Treaty of San Stefano in 1878.

3 Birthday of William Green (March 3, 1873–November 21, 1952). American labor leader and president of the American Federation of Labor from December 19, 1924, to his death in 1952. 864.

3 Dolls' Festival, Hina Matsuri, an annual Japanese national festival, honors little girls and their dolls. It is also called the Peach Blossom Festival, since that flower symbolizes to the Japanese the attributes of little girls. Dolls are on display on this day, and the little girls are hostesses to their friends and are honored by their families. 251.

3 Star-Spangled Banner Day, the anniversary of the March 3, 1931, passage of federal legislation proclaiming "The Star-Spangled Banner" as the national anthem of the United States. 694, 857.

Holy Days and Feast Days

4 Feast Day of Saint Casimir, patron saint of Poland and Lithuania. 9.

Holidays and Civic Days

4 Vermont Admission Day, a commemoration of the admission of Vermont into the Union on March 4, 1791, as the fourteenth state. 268, 856, 862.

Anniversaries and Special Events Days

4 Charter Day, honored in Pennsylvania in commemoration of the granting by Charles II of a charter on March 4, 1681, to William Penn, the founder of the state. 268.

4 Birthday of Count Casimir Pulaski (March 4, 1747–October 11, 1779). Polish soldier; hero of the American Revolution; organizer of a corps of cavalry and light infantry known as Pulaski's Legion; mortally wounded in the siege of Savannah. A Pulaski Memorial Day is observed on the day of his death, October 11. 268.

4 Birthday of Knute Kenneth Rockne (March 4, 1888–March 31, 1931). American football coach famed for his leadership in the sport and for the development of the "Fighting Irish" and the "Four Horsemen," which are a part of the Notre Dame football legend. 864.

4 Birthday of Johann Rudolf Wyss (March 4, 1782–March 21, 1830). Swiss folklorist and editor of his father's *Swiss Family Robinson*, which has been translated into many languages. 864.

Holy Days and Feast Days

c5 World Day of Prayer, sponsored by Church Women United; observed in over 170 countries on the first Friday of March. 857.

Anniversaries and Special Events Days

5 Boston Massacre Day, the anniversary of the attack by British troops on colonial citizens on March 5, 1770, an event that lives in history as the Boston Massacre. 268.

5 Crispus Attucks Day, anniversary of the March 5, 1770, death of Crispus Attucks, American Revolutionary leader who led the group whose anti-British defiance precipitated the Boston Massacre; honored as the first American black to die for freedom. 857.

5 Birthday of Elisha Harris (March 5, 1824–January 31, 1884). American physician; pioneer in public health and one of the organizers of the American Public Health Association. 864.

5 Birthday of James Merritt Ives (March 5, 1824–January 3, 1895). American lithographer; a partner in the firm of Currier & Ives, publishers of prints showing the historic events, manners, and customs of nineteenth-century America. 864.

5 Mother-in-law Day, first celebrated on March 5, 1934, in Amarillo, Texas; initiated by the editor of the local paper; observed by individuals and families. 857.

5 Birthday of Howard Pyle (March 5, 1853–November 9, 1911). Illustrator, painter, and author, best known for his children's books. 864.

Holidays and Civic Days

6 Ghana Independence Day, a public holiday in honor of the establishment of the former British Crown Colony of the Gold Coast as a sovereign nation on March 6, 1957. 875.

Anniversaries and Special Events Days

6 Alamo Day, commemorates one of the great days in Texas and American history, the end of the siege of the Alamo by the Mexicans on March 6, 1836. 288.

6 Birthday of Elizabeth Barrett Browning (March 6, 1806–June 29, 1861). English poet and wife of the poet Robert Browning. Her best-known work is *Sonnets from the Portuguese*. 738.

6 French Academy Woman's Day, the anniversary of the March 6, 1980, election of Marguerite Yourcenar, French-born, naturalized U.S. citizen, classicist and translator, as the first woman selected to be a member of the select, more than three-centuries-old French Academy. 851.

6 Birthday of Michelangelo Buonarroti (March 6, 1475–February 18, 1564). Italian sculptor, painter, architect, and poet, famous for his statues of David and of Moses, the paintings of the Sistine Chapel, and the famous cupola of Saint Peter's basilica. 864.

6 Birthday of Philip Henry Sheridan (March 6, 1831–August 5, 1888). American soldier who made the famous ride to Cedar Creek and turned a Union defeat into a great victory of the Civil War; known as Little Phil because of his size. 5.

Anniversaries and Special Events Days

7 Burbank Day, commemorating the birth of Luther Burbank on March 7, 1849. American naturalist and plant breeder who introduced over six hundred varieties of plants to America, many of which form the basis of fruit industries. His birthday is observed in California; in some regions Burbank Day is combined with Bird or Arbor Day. 268.

7 Birthday of Alessandro Manzoni (March 7, 1785–May 22, 1873). Italian novelist and poet whose novel *The Betrothed* is considered a model of Italian prose. 864.

7 Birthday of Tomáš G. Masaryk (March 7, 1850–September 14, 1937). Czech patriot called "the father of Czechoslovakia." 864.

7 Birthday of Maurice Joseph Ravel (March 7, 1875–December 28, 1937). French composer whose *Bolero* has been one of the most popular concert selections of the twentieth century. 864.

Holy Days and Feast Days

8 Feast Day of Saint John of God, patron saint of hospitals; patron saint of book- and printsellers. 9.

Holidays and Civic Days

8 International Women's Day, a national holiday in Afghanistan, Cape Verde Islands, Guinea-Bissau, Mauritania, Nepal, and the USSR; a day honoring working women which has its roots in the March 8, 1857, revolt of American women protesting conditions in the textile and garment industries. 866, 875.

8 Labour Day, a holiday in Victoria, Australia, celebrating the establishment of an eight-hour working day in Australia in 1871. 875.

8 Syrian Revolution Day, a holiday in the Arab Republic of Syria, honoring the assumption of political power by the National Council of Revolution on March 8, 1963. 868, 875.

8 Tij Day, or Woman's Day, a holiday in the Kingdom of Nepal celebrated exclusively by women. 868, 875.

8 Women's Day, a holiday in Mauritania enjoyed as a free day by women only. 875.

Anniversaries and Special Events Days

8 Birthday of Frederick William Goudy (March 8, 1865–May 11, 1947). American printer and type designer; honored by printer's guilds and publishing associations. 864.

8 Birthday of Kenneth Grahame (March 8, 1859–July 6, 1932). English banker and author of *The Wind in the Willows*, a children's classic. The book was dramatized by A. A. Milne as *Toad of Toad Hall* and became a popular play for Christmas-tide presentations. 864.

8 Birthday of Oliver Wendell Holmes, Jr. (March 8, 1841–March 6, 1935). American jurist and one of the most famous and revered justices of the United States Supreme Court; known as "the great dissenter." Elected to the Hall of Fame for Great Americans in 1965. 268.

8 Birthday of Joseph Lee (March 8, 1862–July 28, 1937). Pioneer in the development of playgrounds for children; long-time president of the National Recreation Association.

Holy Days and Feast Days

9 Feast Day of Saint Catherine of Bologna, patron saint of artists. 9.

9 Feast Day of Saint Frances of Rome, model for housewives and widows; patron saint of motorists; observed by Italian motorists, who drive to the Colosseum in Rome for the blessing of their cars. 9.

Anniversaries and Special Events Days

9 Amerigo Vespucci Day, honoring the fifteenth-century Italian navigator for whom the Americas were named. 5.

9 Baron Bliss Day, a public holiday in Belize, formerly British Honduras, honoring Baron Bliss, an Englishman, who, for unknown reasons, left his entire fortune to the city of Belize. 875.

9 Anniversary of the Battle of Hampton Roads, the engagement between the *Monitor* and the *Merrimac* on March 9, 1862.

9 Taras Shevchenko Day, a commemorative day honoring the great national poet of the Ukraine born on March 9, 1814.

9 Birthday of Leland Stanford (March 9, 1824–June 21, 1893). American capitalist, politician; one of the builders of the first transcontinental railroad in the United States; the founder of Stanford University, a memorial to his son. 864.

Holidays and Civic Days

10 Decoration Day, a public holiday in Liberia. 875.

Anniversaries and Special Events Days

10 Alexander Bell Day, the anniversary of March 10, 1876, when Alexander Bell transmitted the first message by telephone. 268.

10 Birthday of John McCloskey (March 10, 1810–October 10, 1885). American Roman Catholic prelate; the first president of St. John's College (later Fordham University) and the first United States cardinal of the Roman Catholic church. 5.

10 Anniversary of the arrival of the Salvation Army in the United States on March 10, 1880; officially organized on March 28, 1885. 20.

10 Harriet Tubman Day, the anniversary of the March 10, 1913, death of Harriet Tubman, abolitionist and organizer of Underground Railroad escape routes for nineteenth-century American slaves. 738, 806.

10 Birthday of Lillian D. Wald (March 10, 1867–September 1, 1940). American sociologist; founder of the Henry Street Settlement and the organizer of the first nonsectarian public-health nursing system in the world. Elected to the Hall of Fame for Great Americans in 1970. 767.

Anniversaries and Special Events Days

11 Birthday of Vannevar Bush (March 11, 1890–June 28, 1974). Electrical engineer; developer of the first electronic analogue computer. 864.

11 Johnny Appleseed Day; anniversary of the death on March 11, 1845, of John Chapman, known as Johnny Appleseed, the "patron saint" of American orchards. 20, 268, 583, 866.

11 Birthday of Thomas Hastings (March 11, 1860–October 22, 1929). American architect of the firm Carrère & Hastings, designer of the New York Public Library and the Frick mansion, which houses the Frick Collection. 864.

11 Birthday of Torquato Tasso (March 11, 1544–April 25, 1595). Italian epic poet of the late Renaissance whose masterpiece is *Jerusalem Delivered*. 864.

Holidays and Civic Days

12 Moshoeshoe's Day, a public holiday in Lesotho honoring the nineteenth-century tribal leader who consolidated the Basotho nation, now called Lesotho. 875.

12 Mauritius Independence Day, a public holiday in Mauritius honoring the attainment of independence from Britain on March 12, 1968. 868, 875.

12 Anniversary of the death of Sun Yat-sen on March 12, 1925. Chinese physician and first president of the Chinese Republic; the day is observed on Taiwan and in Chinese-American communities. 713.

Anniversaries and Special Events Days

12 Birthday of Gabriele D'Annunzio (March 12, 1863–March 1, 1938). Italian author and soldier who vigorously promoted Italian patriotism. 864.

12 Fireside Chat Day, the anniversary of the March 12, 1933, radio talk presented to the nation by President Franklin Roosevelt; the first of the famous Roosevelt broadcasts which served as models for succeeding presidents. 866.

12 Girl Scout Day, the anniversary of the founding of the Girl Scouts on March 12, 1912; observed with special ceremonies by the Girl Scouts and their leaders. 268.

12 Jane Delano Day, sponsored by the American Red Cross; recognizes the anniversary of the January 12, 1862, birth of Jane Delano, founder of the American Red Cross Nursing Service. 677.

12 Birthday of Kemal Atatürk (March 12, 1880–November 10, 1938). Turkish military commander and first president of the Turkish Republic. 864.

12 Birthday of Simon Newcomb (March 12, 1835–July 11, 1909). American scientist; one of the greatest mathematical astronomers. He was elected to the Hall of Fame for Great Americans in 1935. 864.

Holy Days and Feast Days

13 Feast Day of Saint Ansovinus, protector and patron saint of crops. 4.

Holidays and Civic Days

13 National Day in Grenada, a holiday commemorating a bloodless revolution led by the Joint Endeavor for Welfare, Education and Liberation (JEWEL) on March 13, 1979. 868, 875.

13 Zambia Youth Day, a holiday in the Republic of Zambia dedicated to the interests and activities of young people. 875.

Anniversaries and Special Events Days

c13 Burgsonndeg, a festival day in Luxembourg celebrated with the burning of bonfires to greet the sun and with the recreation of ancient customs signifying the end of winter. 857.

13 Anniversary of the dedication of *Christ of the Andes*, the bronze statue of Christ on the Argentina-Chile border, on March 13, 1904.

13 Anniversary of the naming of Harvard University, oldest university in the United States, on March 13, 1639, for clergyman John Harvard. 268.

13 Birthday of Percival Lowell (March 13, 1855–November 12, 1916). American astronomer who laid the groundwork for the discovery of the planet Pluto. 864.

13 Birthday of Joseph Priestley (March 13, 1733–February 6, 1804). English discoverer of oxygen. 864.

Anniversaries and Special Events Days

14 Birthday of Thomas Hart Benton (March 14, 1782–April 10, 1858). American congressman known as Old Bullion because of his stand on gold and silver currency. Benton represents the state of Missouri in Statuary Hall in a sculpture done by Alexander Doyle. 870.

14 Birthday of Albert Einstein (March 14, 1879–April 18, 1955). German-Swiss-American theoretical physicist noted for his theory of relativity. Awarded the Nobel Prize in physics in 1921 for his photoelectric law and work in theoretical physics. 268.

c14 Holmenkellen Day, the second Sunday of March, the first day of a winter festival in Norway; held at Holmenkellen Hill outside Oslo and attracting thousands of skiers and spectators. 857.

14 Birthday of Casey Jones (March 14, 1864–April 30, 1900). American railroad engineer immortalized in a ballad originally composed by Wallace Saunders. 857.

14 Birthday of Isadore Gilbert Mudge (March 14, 1875–May 17, 1957). American librarian, author, and bibliographer. Since 1959, a citation has been given annually in her name through the American Library Association to a reference librarian for "a distinguished contribution to reference librarianship."

Holidays and Civic Days

c15 Canberra Day, observed as a holiday in Australia honoring the acquisition in 1911 of the Canberra site for the Australian capital. 875.

15 J. J. Roberts Day, a holiday in Liberia commemorating the birth on March 15, 1809, of the first president of Liberia and the first president of the College of Liberia. 853, 875.

15 Maine Admission Day. Maine entered the Union on March 15, 1820, as the twenty-third state. 268, 856, 862.

Anniversaries and Special Events Days

15 Buzzard Day, the traditional day for the annual return of the buzzards to Hinckley, Ohio, for the mating season. 857, 866.

15 Birthday of Lady Augusta Gregory (March 15, 1852–May 22, 1932). Irish playwright; poet; leader in the Irish literary revival and the Irish National Theatre. 864.

15 Ides of March, commemorating the assassination of Julius Caesar in 44 B.C. 866.

15 Birthday of Andrew Jackson (March 15, 1767–June 8, 1845). Scotch-Irish ancestry; frontiersman and soldier; general in War of 1812; self-taught Tennessee lawyer; seventh president of the United States, 1829–37; a Presbyterian; buried at Hermitage, near Nashville, Tennessee. He was elected to the Hall of Fame for Great Americans in 1910. He represents the state of Tennessee in Statuary Hall in a sculpture by Belle Kinney Scholtz. 359–66, 370–72, 374, 378, 379.

15 Anniversary of the riot of the Watts section of Los Angeles on March 15, 1966, which re-emphasized the problems of the black community unresolved by the riots of 1965.

Anniversaries and Special Events Days

16 Black Press Day, the anniversary of the March 16, 1827, founding of *Freedom's Journal*, the first newspaper in the United States published by and for blacks. 857.

16 Anniversary of the death of Nathaniel Bowditch on March 16, 1838. American mathematician and astronomer famous for *The New American Practical Navigator* and for the discovery of the Bowditch curves, which had important applications for future developments in physics and astronomy. 864.

16 Docking Day, anniversary of the first docking of one space ship with another, accomplished by United States astronauts Neil Armstrong and David Scott on March 16, 1966. 874.

16 Goddard Day, recalls the March 16, 1926, flight of the first liquid-fueled rocket, developed by Robert Goddard. 706, 866.

16 Birthday of Caroline Lucretia Herschel (March 16, 1750–January 9, 1848). Anglo-German astronomer who received a gold medal from the Royal Astronomical Society in 1828 for her discoveries of eight comets and many nebulae. 738.

16 Birthday of James Madison (March 16, 1751–June 28, 1836). English ancestry; Virginia lawyer, known as "the father of the Constitution." Fourth president of the United States, 1809–17; an Episcopalian. Buried at Montpelier, Orange County, Virginia. Elected to the Hall of Fame for Great Americans in 1905. 359–66, 370–72, 374, 378, 379.

16 Mylai Massacre Day, anniversary of the massive killing of noncombatant villagers at Mylai and Mykhe, Vietnam, on March 16, 1968. 857.

16 Birthday of René Sully Prudhomme (March 16, 1839–September 7, 1907). French poet and critic, the first recipient of the Nobel Prize in literature, which was awarded to him in 1901. 874.

16 Anniversary of the establishment of the United States Military Academy at West Point, New York, on March 16, 1802; observed by graduates throughout the country at ceremonial dinners. 268.

16 Saint Urho Tay, a mock Finnish-American day of observance which began in Minnesota as a joke on a store manager who claimed that Finland's Saint Urho rivaled Ireland's Saint Patrick. Fun-loving American Finns in several states have adopted the day as a kind of midwinter frolic. 849.

Holy Days and Feast Days

17 Feast Day of Saint Gertrude of Nivelles, patroness of travelers; invoked for protection and for outdoor garden work. 9.

17 Feast Day of Saint Joseph of Arimathea, the noble counselor who provided the tomb in which the Lord's body was laid after the Crucifixion; patron saint of funeral directors. 9.

17 Feast Day of Saint Patrick, patron saint of Ireland, Ireland's greatest holy day and holiday. 9, 14.

Holidays and Civic Days

17 Saint Patrick's day, a holiday in all of Ireland observed with religious services followed by festivities throughout the country. 875.

17 Evacuation Day, observed in Boston and Suffolk County, Massachusetts; commemorates the British withdrawal from Boston on March 17, 1776. It has been a legal holiday in Suffolk County since 1941. 268.

Anniversaries and Special Events Days

17 Camp Fire Girls Founders Day, commemorating the establishment of the Camp Fire Girls on March 17, 1910. 857.

17 Birthday of Kate Greenaway (March 17, 1846–November 6, 1901). English watercolor artist whose drawings of children provided an exemplary model for book illustration. 756, 858.

17 Saint Patrick's Parade Day, an annual celebration that tremendously enlarges the Irish population, at least for a day. The most famous of the Saint Patrick's parades is held in New York city and has a recorded history that goes back to 1762. 254, 269, 550–57, 588, 624, 631, 866.

17 Birthday of Stephen Samuel Wise (March 17, 1874–April 19, 1949). American reform rabbi and Jewish leader; president of the Zionist Organization of America; founder of the Jewish Institute of Religion; and instrumental in the founding of the World Jewish Congress. 812.

Holidays and Civic Days

18 Day of the Supreme Sacrifice, a holiday in the People's Republic of Congo commemorating the March 18, 1977, assassination of President Ngouabi. 868, 875.

Anniversaries and Special Events Days

18 Birthday of John Caldwell Calhoun (March 18, 1782–March 31, 1850). American statesman; congressman from South Carolina; brilliant exponent of states' rights. He represents the state of South Carolina in Statuary Hall in a sculpture done by Frederic Wellington Ruckstull. 870.

18 Birthday of Grover Cleveland (March 18, 1837–June 24, 1908). English ancestry; New York lawyer; the twenty-second and the twenty-fourth president of the United States. Presbyterian; buried at Princeton, New Jersey. Elected to the Hall of Fame for Great Americans in 1935. 359–66, 370–72, 374, 378, 379.

c18 De Molay Day, observed each year by the Order of De Molay in commemoration of the martyrdom of Jacques De Molay, the last grand master of the Order of Knights Templar, on March 18 or 19, 1314.

18 Birthday of Nikolai Rimski-Korsakov (March 18, 1844–June 21, 1908). Russian composer whose work is representative of the Russian nationalist school. 864.

18 Sheelah's Day, observed in Ireland with shamrocks saved from Saint Patrick's Day to honor Sheelah, who might have been Saint Patrick's wife or his mother. 20.

18 Space Walk Day; the anniversary of the first space walk undertaken by USSR cosmonaut Alekeski Lenov on March 18, 1965. 874.

Holy Days and Feast Days

19 Feast of Saint Joseph, commemorating the husband of the Blessed Virgin Mary; patron of the universal church, of workmen, and of Belgium; a Solemnity in the Roman Catholic church. 4, 9.

Holidays and Civic Days

19 Saint Joseph's Day, a religious and national holiday in Andorra, Colombia, Costa, Rica, Liechtenstein, San Marino, the Vatican City State, Venezuela, and in parts of Brazil, Spain, and Switzerland. 875.

Anniversaries and Special Events Days

19 National Agriculture Day, established by Presidential Proclamation, a day of recognition in the United States in tribute to farmers, ranchers, and growers; observed by farm bureaus, marketing associations, and the Future Farmers of America. 857.

19 Birthday of William Bradford (March 19, 1589–May 9, 1657). American Pilgrim father, author of the *History of Plymouth Plantation*, and governor of the Plymouth Colony for thirty years. 268.

19 Birthday of William Jennings Bryan (March 19, 1860–July 26, 1925). American lawyer and political leader, known as "the silver-tongued orator," whose career ended shortly after the famous Scopes trial involving the anti-evolution law. Bryan gave powerful support to woman suffrage. He represents the state of Nebraska in Statuary Hall in a sculpture done by Rudulph Evans. 268, 726, 870.

19 Birthday of David Livingstone (March 19, 1813–May 1, 1873). Scotch doctor, explorer, and medical missionary who taught the church to develop an overall Christian culture in foreign lands; discoverer of Victoria Falls; the subject of the famous search by Henry Stanley following reports of his death in Africa. 20.

19 Swallows Day, the date on which the swallows traditionally return to the San Juan Capistrano Mission in California. 866.

Holy Days and Feast Days

20 Feast of Saint Cuthbert, seventh-century bishop of Lindisfarne, the Holy Island off the Northumberland coast of England; buried at Durham Cathedral; patron saint of shepherds and seafarers. 14.

Holidays and Civic Days

20 Independence Day in Tunisia, a holiday honoring French recognition of the autonomy of Tunisia under the treaty of March 20, 1956. 864, 875.

Anniversaries and Special Events Days

20 Birthday of Charles William Eliot (March 20, 1834–August 22, 1926). American educator, president of Harvard, and editor of the famous "five-foot shelf of books," the fifty-volume Harvard Classics.

20 Birthday of Mathias Keller (March 20, 1813–October 12, 1875). German-American song and hymn writer who wrote the "American Hymn" (Speed Our Republic, O Father on High).

20 Lajos Kossuth Day, anniversary of the death on March 20, 1894, of Kossuth, the symbol of Hungarian nationalism; commemorated by Hungarians around the world.

Holidays and Feast Days

21 Feast Day of Saint Benedict, patriarch of Western monks, founder of the Benedictine order, patron saint of speleologists. 4, 9.

21 Feast of Naw-Ruz, the Baha'i New Year, commences on the first day of the month of Baha; a holy day observed with prayers and readings from the Baha'i writings, consultation on affairs of the faith, and enjoyment of Baha'i music and fellowship. 1, 854.

Holidays and Civic Days

21 Juárez Day, a holiday in Mexico honoring Benito Palbo Juárez on the day of his birth, March 21, 1806. Juárez was the first Mexican president of Indian descent, a statesman known as "the Mexican Washington." Juárez Day is sometimes called "the day of the Indian chief." 398, 875.

c21 Vernal Equinox Day, a holiday in Japan on either March 21 or 22. The vernal equinox marks the beginning of spring in the northern hemisphere. 875.

Anniversaries and Special Events Days

21 Birthday of Johann Sebastian Bach (March 21, 1685–July 28, 1750). German composer and instrumentalist. A master of counterpoint, Bach is noted as one of the foremost composers of all time. 864.

21 Children's Poetry Day, observed in many nations and in various ways to foster an appreciation of poetry and to encourage expression in poetry.

21 Earth Day, a day of international recognition of the critical need to preserve the earth's resources. 583.

21 Elimination of Racial Discrimination Day, initiated by the United Nations in commemoration of the African demonstrators killed in the 1960 disturbances in Sharpeville, South Africa, and as a memorial to all victims of injustice throughout the world. 866.

21 Marzanna Day, a festival day along the Vistula River in Poland enjoyed by young people. The celebration includes songs, dances, and the placing of a straw figure of a girl in the river to bring to life the old story of a young man's faith in one god which stopped the sacrifice of a girl's life to placate the gods of storms and floods. 869.

21 Anniversary of the first presentation of the Sylvanus Thayer Award, named for the fifth superintendent of West Point, on March 21, 1958. This medal, given annually by the Assocation of Graduates of West Point, is bestowed on "the United States citizen whose record of service to his country exemplifies devotion to the principles expressed in the motto of West Point—Duty, Honor, Country." The first recipient was Ernest O. Lawrence of the University of California. 871.

Holy Days and Feast Days

22 Feast Day of Saint Nicholas von Flüe, patron saint of Switzerland. 9.

Holidays and Civic Days

22 Arab League Day, a holiday in the Kingdom of Jordan commemorating the formation of the Arab League on March 22, 1945, an organization designed to maintain a channel for mediation and cooperation for all Arab countries. 868, 875.

22 Tree Planting Day, a national holiday in Lesotho, formerly Basutoland. 875.

22 Puerto Rican Emancipation Day, or Emancipation of the Slaves Day; a holiday in Puerto Rico marking the abolishment of slavery on the island on March 22, 1873. 875.

Anniversaries and Special Events Days

22 Birthday of Randolph Caldecott (March 22, 1846–February 12, 1886). English artist and illustrator for whom the Caldecott Medal is named; the medal is awarded annually to the artist who has illustrated the most distinguished picture book for American children published in the preceding year. 858, 863.

22 Birthday of Robert Andrews Millikan (March 22, 1868–December 19, 1953). American physicist; specialist in research on cosmic rays. He received the 1923 Nobel Prize for isolating the electron, and the Presidential Medal of Merit for his work on rockets and jet propulsion during World War II. 864.

22 Birthday of Sir Anthony Van Dyck (March 22, 1599–December 9, 1641). Flemish painter of society portraits. One of his most famous is the portrait of Charles I. 864.

Holidays and Civic Days

23 Pakistan Day, a holiday in the Republic of Pakistan, the commemoration of the anniversary of the proclamation of the republic on March 23, 1956. 868, 875.

Anniversaries and Special Events Days

23 Birthday of John Bartram (March 23, 1699–September 22, 1777). American botanist who founded the first botanical garden in the United States. Known as the "father of American botany." 864.

23 Birthday of Sidney Hillman (March 23, 1887–July 10, 1946). American labor leader and union official in whose name the Sidney Hillman Foundation presents an annual award for a book dealing with race relations, civil liberties, trade-union development, or world understanding. 864.

23 Liberty Day, anniversary of Patrick Henry's March 23, 1775, speech in Richmond, Virginia, which concluded with the words "Give me liberty or give me death"; considered by historians to be the masterpiece of American patriotic oratory. 268, 866.

23 Anniversary of the establishment of the World Meteorological Organization, a specialized agency of the United Nations, on March 23, 1950, to facilitate an international system of standardizing and coordinating weather observations and collaborating data.

Anniversaries and Special Events Days

24 Birthday of Galen Clark (March 24, 1814–March 24, 1910). American naturalist who discovered the Mariposa Grove of giant sequoia, or redwood, trees in 1857. Mount Clark in Yosemite is named in his honor. 864.

24 Birthday of Andrew William Mellon (March 24, 1855–August 26, 1937). American financier and public official who gave his art collection to the nation in 1937 for the establishment of the National Gallery of Art. 864.

24 Birthday of William Morris (March 24, 1834–October 3, 1896). English poet, craftsman who designed fine furniture, wallpapers, and tapestries, and translator of Icelandic sagas. The William Morris Society was established in 1955 to revive interest in his ideas and works. 864.

24 Birthday of John Wesley Powell (March 24, 1834–September 23, 1902). American geologist and anthropologist who made the daring exploration of the Colorado and Green rivers in 1869; published the first classification of American Indian languages, was the first director of the United States Bureau of Ethnology. 268.

Holidays and Feast Days

25 Annunciation of the Lord, formerly called Annunciation of the Blessed Virgin Mary, a feast of the Incarnation commemorating the announcement by the Archangel Gabriel that Mary was to become the Mother of Christ. 5.

25 Feast of Saint Dismas, "the good thief," patron saint of prisoners, persons condemned to death, and funeral directors. 9.

Holidays and Civic Days

25 Greek Independence Day, a holiday celebrated with parades and dances in Greece and Cyprus and with a parade in New York to honor the day in 1821 when the Greek flag was first raised in revolt against Ottoman domination. 868, 875.

25 Annunciation Day, a religious and national holiday in Liechtenstein honoring the Annunciation of the Lord. 875.

25 Maryland Day, a legal holiday in Maryland celebrating the landing of the colonists sent to the New World in 1634 by Lord Baltimore under the leadership of his brother, Leonard Calvert. 856.

Anniversaries and Special Events Days

25 Birthday of Béla Bartók (March 25, 1881–September 26, 1945). Hungarian composer noted for the use of folk tunes in his concert works; famous for *Hungarian Folk Music*, a standard reference work in the field of music. 864.

25 Birthday of Gutzon Borglum (March 25, 1867–March 6, 1941). American sculptor and painter. Best known for his colossal head of Lincoln in the Capitol and for the Mount Rushmore Memorial figures of Washington, Jefferson, Lincoln, and Theodore Roosevelt. 339, 347.

25 Quarter Day, or Lady Day, a traditional day for paying rent in Ireland and England.

25 Birthday of Arturo Toscanini (March 25, 1867–January 16, 1957). Italian musician considered by critics to be the greatest virtuoso conductor of the first half of the twentieth century. 864.

25 Birthday of William Bell Wait (March 25, 1839–October 25, 1916). American educator and pioneer in the education of the blind, who devised an embossing machine for printing books for the blind and a typewriter for the blind. 864.

25 Birthday of John Winebrenner (March 25, 1797–September 12, 1860). American clergyman who founded the denomination known as the Church of God. 864.

Holy Days and Feast Days

26 Feast Day of Saint Braulio, patron saint of Aragon, one of the most popular saints in Spain. 9.

Holidays and Civic Days

26 Bangladesh Independence Day, a public holiday commemorating the proclamation of the establishment of Bangladesh on March 26, 1971. 868, 875.

26 Prince Jonah Kuhio Kalanianaole Day, a holiday in Hawaii celebrating the birthday and the contributions of Hawaii's first delegate to Congress. The day was formerly called Prince Kuhio, or Kuhio, Day. It is a day of festivals, parades, and balls depicting Hawaii's history and culture. 268.

Anniversaries and Special Events Days

26 Anniversary of the death of Sarah Bernhardt on March 26, 1923. French actress who has gone down in theatrical history as the "Divine Sarah." 738.

26 Camp David Accord Day, the anniversary of the March 26, 1979, signing by Israel and Egypt of the Camp David Treaty as a framework for establishing lasting peace in the Middle East. 874.

26 Birthday of Robert Frost (March 26, 1874–January 29, 1963). American Pulitzer Prize-winning poet especially known for his lyric poem "A Boy's Will" and the narrative poem "North of Boston"; poetry consultant at the Library of Congress. 268, 732.

26 Birthday of Louise Otto (March 26, 1819–March 13, 1895). German author and founder of the feminist movement in Germany. 738.

26 The Tichborne Dole, an annual event observed since the year 1150 in Alresford, Hampshire, in England. The head of the Tichborne family gives a gift of one gallon of flour for each adult and half a gallon for each child to every resident of the village to fulfill a deathbed promise and to avoid a curse on the house of Tichborne; special permission for allocation was given during World War II. 256.

26 Arbor Day in Spain, called Fiesta del Arbol, "fete of the tree." It began on March 26, 1895, when King Alfonso planted a pine sapling at a ceremony near Madrid.

Holidays and Civic Days

27 Resistance Day, a public holiday in Burma, honoring the movement of guerrilla forces to oppose invaders during World War II. 875.

Anniversaries and Special Events Days

27 Alaska Earthquake Day, the anniversary of the March 27, 1964, earthquake of ruinous consequences. 268, 695.

27 Birthday of Nathaniel Currier (March 27, 1813–November 20, 1888). American publisher and founder of the firm of Currier & Ives, printmakers who recorded American history from 1835 to the end of the century in famous prints which are now collector's items. 864.

27 Birthday of Wilhelm Konrad Röntgen (March 27, 1845–February 10, 1923). German scientist whose discovery of the x-ray made him the first recipient of the Nobel Prize in physics in 1901. 864.

27 Anniversary of the death of Constance Lindsay Skinner on March 27, 1939. American author and editor of the valuable Rivers of America series. The Constance Lindsay Skinner Award is presented annually in her honor by the Woman's National Book Association to an outstanding woman in the book world.

27 Birthday of Edward Steichen (March 27, 1879–March 25, 1973). World-known photographer and artist; associated for many years with the Museum of Modern Art; creator of such celebrated books of photographs as *The Family of Man*. 461, 864.

27 Birthday of the United States Navy; anniversary of the signing by President Washington on March 27, 1794, of the act to officially establish the navy.

Holidays and Civic Days

28 British Bases Evacuation Day, a holiday in Libya celebrating the closing of British military installations at Tobruk and El Adem on March 28, 1970. 868, 875.

Anniversaries and Special Events Days

28 Teachers' Day in Czechoslovakia, commemorating the life and work of John Comenius, seventeenth-century Moravian educational reformer. 34.

28 Birthday of Wade Hampton (March 28, 1818–April 11, 1902). American Confederate general, congressman, and governor of South Carolina. He represents South Carolina in Statuary Hall in a sculpture by Frederic Wellington Ruckstull. 870.

Holidays and Civic Days

29 Boganda Day, the anniversary of the March 29, 1959, death of Barthelemy Boganda; observed as a public holiday in the Central African Republic in tribute to the nation's first president. 875.

29 Memorial Day, or Commemoration Day, a holiday in Madagascar honoring the citizens who lost their lives in the 1947 revolt against French colonialism. 868, 875.

29 Taiwan Youth Day, a holiday of honor of young adults in the Republic of China. 875.

Anniversaries and Special Events Days

29 Delaware Swedish Colonial Day, the anniversary of the settlement on March 29, 1638, of the colony of New Sweden in Delaware; the day is commemorated by the Delaware Swedish Colonial Society and by churches, schools and community organizations. 268.

29 Birthday of Aleš Hrdlička (March 29, 1869–September 5, 1943). American anthropologist and author famous for his studies of American Indians; curator of the United States National Museum. 864.

29 Birthday of John Tyler (March 29, 1790–January 18, 1862). English ancestry; Virginia lawyer; elected to vice-presidency; succeeded to presidency on death of President Harrison one month after inauguration. Tenth president of the United States, 1841–45; an Episcopalian; buried at Hollywood Cemetery, Richmond, Virginia. 359–66, 370–72, 374, 378, 379.

29 Vietnam Veterans' Day, the anniversary of the March 29, 1973, withdrawal of American forces from the Vietnamese conflict. 413.

29 Birthday of Isaac Mayer Wise (March 29, 1819–March 26, 1900). American rabbi and educator, a principal founder of the Union of American Hebrew Congregations, and president of the Hebrew Union College. 20.

Holidays and Civic Days

c30 Seward's Day, a holiday in Alaska commemorating the March 30, 1867, purchase of Alaska from Russia; observed on the last Monday in March. 268.

Anniversaries and Special Events Days

30 Birthday of Clifford Whittingham Beers (March 30, 1876–July 9, 1943). American founder of the mental-hygiene movement; awarded the gold medal "for distinguished services for the benefit of mankind" by the National Institute of Social Sciences. 864.

30 Birthday of Jo Davidson (March 30, 1883–January 2, 1952). American sculptor whose work includes sculptures of many prominent people, including Woodrow Wilson, Anatole France, Walt Whitman, and Robert La Follette. 864.

30 Doctors' Day, a day of tribute to the medical profession and to the first use of ether as an anesthetic agent on March 30, 1842, by Dr. C. W. Long. 857, 866.

30 Birthday of Vincent van Gogh (Mrach 30, 1853–July 29, 1890). Dutch painter, lithographer, etcher, and a leader of the post-impressionist school. His letters to his brother, published under the title *Dear Theo*, are of continuing interest. 864.

30 Birthday of Francisco José de Goya (March 30, 1746–April 16, 1828). Spanish painter and etcher whose realism influenced nineteenth- and twentieth-century painters. 864.

30 Regina Medal Day, the anniversary of the first presentation of the Regina Medal for outstanding contributions to children's literature; awarded to Eleanor Farjeon on March 30, 1959. 5.

Holidays and Civic Days

31 Malta National Day, a public holiday commemorating the closing of the British military base on Malta on March 31, 1979. 875.

c31 Transfer Day, a holiday in the Virgin Islands on the last Monday of March commemorating the purchase of the islands by the United States from Denmark on March 31, 1917. 875.

Anniversaries and Special Events Days

31 Bunsen Burner Day, a day of tribute to Robert Wilhelm Eberhard von Bunsen born on March 31, 1811; inventor of the Bunsen burner. 866.

31 Birthday of René Descartes (March 31, 1596–February 1, 1650). French mathematician and philosopher who made contributions to theories of algebra and geometry and to the field of philosophy of pure reason. Called "the father of modern philosophy." 864.

31 Birthday of Edward FitzGerald (March 31, 1809–June 14, 1883). English poet celebrated for his translation of the *Rubáiyát of Omar Khayyám*. 864.

31 Birthday of Franz Joseph Haydn (March 31, 1732–May 31, 1809). Austrian composer, sometimes called "Papa" Haydn in recognition of his influence on instrumental music and on the development of the modern symphony. 783.

31 Birthday of Andrew Lang (March 31, 1844–July 20, 1912). Scottish author famous for Homeric translations and studies, fairy tales, children's books, folklore, history, biography, and fiction. 867.

31 Birthday of Robert Ross McBurney (March 31, 1837–December 27, 1898). American YMCA leader; first paid secretary of the YMCA in New York in 1862; responsible for the centralized system of leadership in effect in the YMCA.

c31 Oranges and Lemons Day, celebrated since 1920 on or near March 31 at Saint Clement Danes in London. It is a religious festival for children which ends with each child receiving an orange and a lemon as the bells ring out the old nursery rhyme: "Oranges and lemons, say the bells of Saint Clemens." 256.

31 Pearse Power Flight Day, anniversary of the powered flight made by New Zealand's Richard Pearse on March 31, 1903. 857.

April

The name for April, the fourth month of the year, comes either from *Aprilis*, the Roman derivation of Aphrodite, the Greek name for Venus, or from the Latin verb *aperire*, meaning "to open." The month begins with a day and ends with a night that are linked in many lands with age-old customs.

The first day is April Fools' Day, or All Fools' Day, which is a day at one time popular for pranks and harmless practical jokes. The origin of this day is not positively known. Records show that it has been going on at least since 1564, when January 1 was re-established in France as the first day of the year. The change confused many people, but in time it led to the fun of exchanging false greetings for the first of the year on the old day. April 1 coincides with the Zodiac sign of the fish, so the French call it Fooling the April Fish Day. A one-time April Fools' prank of the Scots was "hunting the gowk," which sent the victim on false errands; anyone who fell for this prank was called "a gowk," or cuckoo.

The last hours of the month of April are observed as Walpurgis Night in some parts of Europe. It is the custom in Scandinavian countries and in the mountains of Germany to light huge bonfires and hold gay events on the night of April 30 in remembrance of an old folkway that defended man and beast from witches and demons. In Sweden and Finland, university students start wearing their white velvet caps on that night and join together to sing spring songs. In some parts of Switzerland, a bachelor, if he observes old traditions, may plant a pine tree on the last day of April at the home of a girl he admires.

The sweet pea and the daisy are the flowers for April. The gem is the diamond.

Holidays and Civic Days

1 EOKA Day, a holiday in Cyprus, honoring the Greek National Union of Cypriot Fighters (EOKA) who campaigned against the British rule in 1955. 868, 875.

1 Islamic Republic Day, a holiday in Iran, celebrating the April 1, 1979, referendum which established the republic to replace the regime of the shah who left Iran on January 17, 1979. 868, 875.

1 San Marino National Day, the traditional date for the installation of the *Capitani Regginti*, or government officials; a holiday in San Marino. 868, 875.

Anniversaries and Special Events Days

1 Birthday of Edwin Austin Abbey (April 1, 1852–August 1, 1911). American painter and illustrator of editions of Shakespeare and Goldsmith. He painted the *Quest of the Holy Grail* murals in the Boston Public Library. 864.

1 April Fools' Day, or All Fools' Day, a day of practical jokes and high humor. It has various names. In Scotland it is Huntigowok Day, in the north of England it is April Noddy. In France it is called Fooling the April Fish Day. 20, 254, 269, 567, 572, 575, 614, 628, 642, 866.

1 Birthday of William Harvey (April 1, 1578–June 3, 1657). English physician, anatomist, and physiologist known for his discovery of the circulation of blood. 864.

c1 Hebrew University Day in Israel; observes the inauguration of the university of Jerusalem in 1925. 20.

1 Intolerance Day, established to confine intolerance to the most appropriate day of the year, April Fools' Day. 857.

1 Birthday of Sergei Rachmaninoff (April 1, 1873–March 28, 1943). Russian pianist and composer; last of the leading proponents of the musical tradition of Russian romanticism. 864.

1 Birthday of Edmond Rostand (April 1, 1868–December 2, 1918). French poet and playwright whose most frequently revived drama is *Cyrano de Bergerac*. 864.

1 Tiros I Launch Day, the anniversary of the American launching on April 1, 1960, of *Tiros I*, the first true weather satellite. 874.

Holy Days and Feast Days

2 Feast Day of Saint Francis of Paola, patron saint of sailors. 9.

Anniversaries and Special Events Days

2 Birthday of Hans Christian Andersen (April 2, 1805–August 4, 1875). Danish poet and novelist best known for fairy and folk tales. A literary award, the Hans Christian Andersen Prize, is presented biennially at each Congress of the International Board on Books for Young People, in honor of Hans Christian Andersen. International Children's Book Day is celebrated on Andersen's birthday. 858, 864.

2 Birthday of Frédéric Auguste Bartholdi (April 2, 1834–October 4, 1904). French sculptor whose work includes the Statue of Liberty in New York harbor, presented to the United States by the people of France in 1885 and dedicated in 1886. 296.

2 Mildred L. Batchelder Award Announcement Day; established by the Children's Services Division (now Association for Library Services to Children) of the American Library Association in 1966 to honor its former executive secretary with an annual award to an American publisher of an outstanding children's book originally published in a foreign language in a foreign country. 858.

2 International Children's Book Day observed on Hans Christian Andersen's birthday to stimulate interest, through the use of books, in the life styles, customs, and contributions of the peoples in nations throughout the world.

c2 Pascua Florida Day, a holiday in Florida, the Flower State, commemorating Florida State Day under the name given to it by Ponce de Leon in 1513; celebrated on April 2 unless that date falls on a Saturday or Sunday; in that event the governor of the state may proclaim either the preceding Friday or the following Monday as Pascua Florida Day. 268.

2 Birthday of Emile Zola (April 2, 1840–September 28, 1902). French novelist who became the leader of the school of naturalism in French literature. 772.

Anniversaries and Special Events Days

3 American Creed Day, anniversary of the acceptance by the United States House of Representatives, on April 3, 1918, of "The American Creed," written by William Tyler Page in 1917. 281.

3 Birthday of John Burroughs (April 3, 1837–March 29, 1921). American essayist and literary naturalist. A Burroughs Medal is presented annually in his memory by the John Burroughs Association for the year's best book in the field of natural history; the first recipient of this award was William Beebe. 864.

3 Birthday of Edward Everett Hale (April 3, 1822–June 10, 1909). American clergyman and author of *The Man without a Country*. 867.

3 Birthday of Washington Irving (April 3, 1783–November 28, 1859). American historian, essayist, and storyteller famous for the legends of Rip Van Winkle and Ichabod Crane. He was elected to the Hall of Fame for Great Americans in 1900. 864.

3 Anniversary of the beginning of the Pony Express on April 3, 1860. 866.

Holy Days and Feast Days

4 Feast Day of Saint Benedict the Moor; patron saint of North American Negroes; patron of the city of Palermo. 9.

4 Feast of Saint Isidore of Seville, a bishop, an educator and an encyclopedist called "the last of the ancient Christian philosophers"; declared a doctor of the church in 1722. 9.

Holidays and Civic Days

4 Liberation Day, a holiday in Hungary, the Magyar People's Republic, commemorating April 4, 1945, when the last German soldier was driven from Hungarian soil. 875.

4 Senegalese National Day, a public holiday in Senegal commemorating April 4, 1960, when agreements were completed to give sovereignty to Senegal, the oldest French colony in black Africa. 868, 875.

Anniversaries and Special Events Days

4 Birthday of Dorothea Lynde Dix (April 4, 1802–July 17, 1887). American philanthropist, author, and pioneer in the establishment or improvement of asylums for the mentally ill. 738, 749.

4 Anniversary of the establishment of the North Atlantic Treaty Organization (NATO) on April 4, 1949. 857.

c4 Student Government Day; observed in Massachusetts on the first Friday of April, to provide students with an insight into practical government. 857.

Holidays and Civic Days

5 Tomb-Sweeping Day, a national holiday in Taiwan, the Republic of China; a day of preparing tombs for traditional rites honoring the dead. 875.

Anniversaries and Special Events Days

5 Birthday of Joseph Lister (April 5, 1827–February 10, 1912). English physician, founder of aseptic surgery. 757.

5 Birthday of Algernon Charles Swinburne (April 5, 1837–April 10, 1909). English poet famous for his elegies and monographs on Shakespeare. 864.

5 Birthday of Booker Taliaferro Washington (April 5, 1856–November 14, 1915). American educator, author, and lecturer. The first black to be depicted on a United States postage stamp. He was elected to the Hall of Fame for Great Americans in 1945. 268, 759.

5 Birthday of Elihu Yale (April 5, 1649–July 8, 1721). English philanthropist for whom Yale University is named. 268.

Holidays and Civic Days

6 South Africa's Founder's Day, a holiday in the Republic of South Africa, honoring the founders of the nation. Also known as Van Riebeek Day in tribute to Jan Van Riebeek, the seventeenth-century explorer and founder of Cape Town. 868, 875.

6 Syrian Martyrs Day, a holiday in the Arab Republic of Syria memorializing the heroes of the nation. 875.

6 Chakri Day, a public holiday in Thailand, commemorating the foundation of the ruling dynasty by King Rama I. 868, 875.

Anniversaries and Special Events Days

6 Anniversary of the launching of the first communication satellite, the *Early Bird*, on April 6, 1965. 874.

6 North Pole Day, the anniversary of the April 6, 1909, discovery of the North Pole by Robert E. Peary and his party; the Peary expedition was declared the authentic first discovery by the National Geographic Society in 1911. 874.

6 Birthday of Raphael (April 6, 1483–April 6, 1520). Italian painter noted for his idealized madonnas and great frescoes; one of the masters of the Italian High Renaissance style. 864.

6 Anniversary of the death of William Strickland on April 6, 1854. American architect, the outstanding exponent of the Greek revival in the United States. He designed the first United States customhouse and the marble sarcophagus of Washington at Mount Vernon. 864.

Holidays and Civic Days

7 Mozambican Women's Day, a holiday in the People's Republic of Mozambique, honoring the women of the nation. 875.

Anniversaries and Special Events Days

7 Birthday of Walter Camp (April 7, 1859–March 14, 1925). American coach who did more than anyone else to develop the game of football; originator of the annual All-American selections. 867.

7 Birthday of William Ellery Channing (April 7, 1780–October 2, 1842). American Unitarian clergyman and author who played an influential role in the intellectual life of New England. Elected to the Hall of Fame for Great Americans in 1900. 864.

7 Birthday of David Grandison Fairchild (April 7, 1869–August 6, 1954). American botanist and explorer who traveled the globe in search of useful plants for introduction into the United States. The Fairchild Tropical Garden at Coral Gables, Florida, is named for him. 864.

7 Birthday of Gabriela Mistral (April 7, 1899–January 19, 1957). Chilean poet and educator who rose to important posts in the Chilean educational system and helped to reorganize the rural schools in Mexico. Her real name was Lucila Godoy de Alcayaga, but she is known by the pseudonym that combines the names of the poets D'Annunzio of Italy and Mistral of France. Winner of the 1945 Nobel Prize in literature. 738.

7 Birthday of William Wordsworth (April 7, 1770–April 23, 1850). English poet laureate famous for "I Wandered Lonely as a Cloud" and "Ode: Intimations of Immortality"; greatest poet of the English romantic movement. 747.

Holy Days and Feast Days

8 Feast Day of Saint Walter, patron saint of prisoners of war. 9.

Anniversaries and Special Events Days

8 Birthday of Harvey Cushing (April 8, 1869–October 7, 1939). American neurosurgeon, the leading brain specialist of his time; introduced blood-pressure determinations in the United States; author of the Pulitzer Prize-winning biography of Sir William Osler. 864.

8 Anniversary of the death of El Greco on April 8, 1614. The most influential master of Spanish painting, who reflected the zeal of Spain and set new patterns for artistic expression. 864.

Holy Days and Feast Days

9 Fast and Prayer Day, a religious and national holiday in the Republic of Liberia; a day dedicated to prayer, self-examination, and self-discipline. 875.

Holidays and Civic Days

c9 The Glarus Festival is a special Swiss celebration honoring the defeat of the Austrians by the men of Glarus on April 9, 1388. It is observed on the first Thursday in April with a pilgrimage to Nafels, during which the procession visits the eleven memorial stones that mark the Austrians' eleven unsuccessful attacks.

9 Tunisia Martyr's Day, a public holiday in Tunisia. 875.

Anniversaries and Special Events Days

9 Marian Anderson Day, the anniversary of Marian Anderson's concert on the steps of the Lincoln Memorial in Washington on April 9, 1939, after being denied the use of Constitution Hall by the Daughters of the American Revolution. 738.

9 Appomattox Day, the anniversary of the April 9, 1865, surrender of General Robert E. Lee, commander of the Army of Norther Virginia, to Ulysses S. Grant, commander-in-chief of the Union Army; the end of four years of conflict between the North and the South known as the American Civil War. 268.

9 Bataan Day, commemorating the surrender of the American and Philippine defenders of the Bataan peninsula on April 9, 1942. 874.

9 Birthday of Charles Pierre Baudelaire (April 9, 1821–August 31, 1867). French poet and critic whose *Les Fleurs du Mal* was an important influence on French symbolists and modern poets. 864.

9 Budget Day, a tradition in Britain, carrying out a custom of displaying to the public the dispatch box of the official papers by the chancellor of the exchequer on a route from No. 10 Downing Street to the House of Commons.

9 Churchill Day; anniversary of the April 9, 1963, proclamation granting honorary United States citizenship to Sir Winston Churchill. 857.

9 Anniversary of the establishment of the Golf Hall of Fame by the Professional Golfers' Association on April 9, 1941. 874.

Anniversaries and Special Events Days

10 Anniversary of the founding of the American Boccaccio Association, April 10, 1974, for the encouragement of Boccaccio studies among scholars of all disciplines.

10 Buchenwald Liberation Day, the anniversary of the April 10, 1945, liberation by Allied troops of Buchenwald, the first, and one of the worst, of the Nazi concentration camps.

10 Birthday of Matthew Calbraith Perry (April 10, 1794–March 4, 1858). American naval officer who reached Tokyo Bay on July 8, 1853, and later opened up diplomatic and trade relations between Japan and the United States. 864.

10 Birthday of Hugo Grotius (April 10, 1583–August 28, 1645). Dutch jurist and statesman; founder of the science of international law. 864.

10 Humane Day, anniversary of the incorporation of the American Society for the Prevention of Cruelty to Animals on April 10, 1866. 656, 664, 724, 769.

10 Frances Perkins Day, the anniversary of the birth on April 10, 1880, of the first woman member of a U.S. presidential cabinet. An appointee of Franklin Roosevelt, Frances Perkins served as secretary of labor from 1933 to 1945. 323, 738.

10 Birthday of Joseph Pulitzer (April 10, 1847–October 29, 1911). American journalist and publisher who, through his will, founded the Columbia University Graduate School of Journalism and the Pulitzer prizes in journalism, letters, and music. 685, 864.

10 Salvation Army Founder's Day, commemorating the birth of General William Booth on April 10, 1829. 20.

Holy Days and Feast Days

11 Feast of Saint Stanislaus, patron of Cracow, Poland, martyred on April 11, 1079. A symbol of Polish nationhood; canonized by Pope Innocent IV in 1253; one of the patron saints of Poland. 5, 9.

Holidays and Civic Days

11 Heroes Day, a holiday in Costa Rica, commemorating the Battle of Rivas of April 11, 1856, when Costa Ricans triumphed over foreign invaders. 875.

11 Liberation Day in Uganda, a holiday marking the end of the rule of the unpredictable, self-appointed president for life, Idi Aman. Kampala was taken by the Tanzanian relief forces on April 11, 1979. 868, 875.

Anniversaries and Special Events Days

11 Birthday of Charles Evans Hughes (April 11, 1862–August 27, 1948). American jurist, statesman, and eleventh chief justice of the United States Supreme Court. 864.

11 Anniversary of the authorization by Congress of the Distinguished Service Medal for the Merchant Marine on April 11, 1942. The first recipient was Edwin Fox Cheney, Jr.

Holidays and Civic Days

12 Halifax Resolves Day, or Halifax Independence Day, a holiday in North Carolina. It commemorates the Halifax Resolves of Independence adopted in North Carolina on April 12, 1776, which were influential in bringing about the adoption of the Declaration of Independence. 268, 856.

Anniversaries and Special Events Days

12 Birthday of Henry Clay (April 12, 1777–June 29, 1852). American statesman known as "the great compromiser" in the effort to preserve the Union. Elected to the Hall of Fame for Great Americans in 1900. He represents the state of Kentucky in a Statuary Hall sculpture done by Charles Henry Niehaus. 870.

12 Fort Sumter Day, anniversary of the bombardment of Fort Sumter on April 12, 1861, the beginning of the American Civil War. 268.

12 Birthday of Frederick G. Melcher (April 12, 1870–March 9, 1963). American publisher, editor, and a founder of Children's Book Week in 1919. Donor of the Newbery and Caldecott medals awarded annually for outstanding children's books.

12 Space Probe Day, anniversary of the first manned orbit around the earth achieved by Russian astronaut Yuri Gagarin on April 12, 1961. 874.

12 Space Shuttle Columbia Day, the anniversary of the successful American launching on April 12, 1981, of the world's first cargo shuttle capable of return into space to project scientific instruments and satellites into orbit for the benefit of mankind. 874.

Holidays and Civic Days

13 Chad National Day, a public holiday. President Tombalbaye was assassinated on April 13, 1975, following an army coup d'état. 868, 875.

13 Birthday of Thomas Jefferson (April 13, 1743–July 4, 1826). Welsh ancestry; Virginia lawyer; third president of the United States, 1801–09. No formal religious affiliation. Buried at Monticello, Albemarle County, Virginia. Elected to Hall of Fame for Great Americans in 1900. Thomas Jefferson's birthday is a holiday in Alabama. The University of Virginia Founders Day celebration at Charlottesville is held annually on Jefferson's birthday. 269, 302, 359–66, 369–74, 734, 768, 791, 818.

Anniversaries and Special Events Days

13 Birthday of John Hanson (April 13, 1721–November 22, 1783). American Revolutionary political leader. First president of the Congress of the Confederation. He represents the state of Maryland in Statuary Hall in a sculpture by Richard Edwin Brooks. 870.

13 John Hanson Day, observed in Maryland to honor the state's outstanding leader of the period of the American Revolution.

13 Huguenot Day, the anniversary of the signing of the Edict of Nantes, on April 13, 1598, is observed by the Huguenot Society of America. 20.

13 The Jefferson Memorial at Washington, D.C., was dedicated on the two-hundredth anniversary of Jefferson's birth, April 13, 1943. 843.

Holidays and Civic Days

14 Pan American Day, a holiday in Honduras. Pan American Day, established in 1931, honors the first International Conference of American States held on April 14, 1890, in Washington; observed in schools in the United States with special programs which interpret the folk songs, dance, and customs of the countries of the American hemisphere. 268.

Anniversaries and Special Events Days

14 Birthday of Junius Spencer Morgan (April 14, 1813–April 8, 1890). American merchant and philanthropist who was a benefactor of the Hartford Public Library, Trinity College, the Metropolitan Museum of Art, and other institutions. 864.

14 Birthday of Anne Mansfield Sullivan (April 14, 1866–October 20, 1936). American educator famous as the teacher and companion of Helen Keller. 738.

14 Anniversary of the dedication of the Taft Memorial Bell Tower in Washington, D.C., on April 14, 1959; a memorial to Robert Alphonso Taft, senator from Ohio.

Anniversaries and Special Events Days

15 Good Roads Day, first observed in Illinois on April 15, 1914, to call attention to the need for hard roads; re-observed in 1964 and in the 1970s with cavalcades of antique cars.

15 Malta Award Day, the anniversary of the awarding of the British George Cross on April 15, 1942, to the people of Malta in honor of their courage and valor in World War II.

15 Birthday of John Lothrop Motley (April 15, 1814–May 29, 1877). American historian and diplomat. Author of *The Rise of the Dutch Republic*. He was elected to the Hall of Fame for Great Americans in 1910. 864.

15 Birthday of Charles Willson Peale (April 15, 1741–February 22, 1827). American painter famous for his many portraits of George Washington. 864.

15 Birthday of Leonardo da Vinci (April 15, 1452–May 2, 1519). Italian painter, sculptor, scientist, and inventor; one of the greatest minds of all time. 778.

Holy Days and Feast Days

16 Feast of Saint Marie Bernarde Soubirous, popularly known as Saint Bernadette, whose visions led to the establishment of the Shrine of Lourdes, one of the great pilgrimage centers of modern times. 4, 34.

Holidays and Civic Days

16 De Diego Day, a public holiday in Puerto Rico commemorating the April 16, 1867, birth of the patriot José de Diego. 875.

Anniversaries and Special Events Days

16 Birthday of Herbert Baxter Adams (April 16, 1850–July 30, 1901). American historian; a founder and first secretary of the American Historical Association, in whose name the association offers an annual award for a book on history. 864.

16 Birthday of Anatole France (April 16, 1844–October 13, 1924). French novelist, poet, playwright, and critic who received the Nobel Prize in literature in 1921. 864.

16 Queen Margrethe's birthday, observed in Denmark with special events for children at Amalienberg Palace. The queen was born on April 16, 1940. 857.

16 Birthday of Wilbur Wright (April 16, 1867–May 30, 1912). American pioneer aviator who, with his brother Orville, invented the airplane. He was elected to the Hall of Fame for Great Americans in 1955. 465, 476.

Holidays and Civic Days

17 Flag Day in American Samoa, commemorating April 17, 1900, when the seven high chiefs voluntarily signed the Instrument of Cession at the invitation of President Theodore Roosevelt. It also commemorates the establishment of Samoan constitutional government on April 17, 1960. 875.

17 Evacuation Day, a holiday in the Arab Republic of Syria commemorating the withdrawal of French troops on April 17, 1946. 875.

17 American Academy of Arts and Letters Charter Day, the anniversary of the incorporation of the Academy by an Act of Congress signed by President Woodrow Wilson on April 17, 1916; awards and honors are conferred at an annual ceremonial held in May. 268.

17 Birthday of Isabel Barrows (April 17, 1845–October 25, 1913). American editor and pioneer penologist. 864.

17 Bay of Pigs Day, the anniversary of the April 17, 1961, unsuccessful attempt by Cuban exiles, with the help of the United States, to overthrow the regime of Fidel Castro. 874.

17 Children's Protection Day, observed annually in Japan as a day commemorating the passage of laws protecting juvenile delinquents.

17 Verrazano Day, observed in New York State to commemorate the discovery of New York harbor by Giovanni da Verrazano on April 17, 1524. 866.

Holidays and Civic Days

18 Zimbabwe Republic Day, a public holiday commemorating the anniversary of April 18, 1980, when Southern Rhodesia became the Republic of Zimbabwe. 868, 875.

Anniversaries and Special Events Days

18 Birthday of Clarence Seward Darrow (April 18, 1857–March 13, 1938). American lawyer associated with the Scopes trial and other dramatic court cases of the early twentieth century. His career is the subject of *The Story of My Life*. 864.

18 Birthday of Richard Harding Davis (April 18, 1864–April 11, 1916). American journalist and author, one of the first of the roving foreign correspondents. 864.

18 Panama Canal Day, the anniversary of the April 18, 1978, Senate approval of the full transfer of the Panama Canal to Panama by December 31, 1999. 874.

18 Paul Revere Night: the anniversary of the famous midnight ride made on April 18, 1775, to warn the American colonists that "the British are coming." 673, 866.

18 Anniversary of the San Francisco earthquake and fire of April 18, 1906; periodically commemorated with special events in California. 268, 695.

Holy Days and Feast Days

19 Feast Day of Blessed James Duckett, patron saint of booksellers and publishers. 9.

Holidays and Civic Days

c19 Patriots' Day, or Battles of Lexington and Concord Day, commemorating the first battle of the Revolutionary War, which occurred on April 19, 1775; observed in Maine and Massachusetts on the third Monday of April. 268.

19 Sierra Leone Republic Day, a national holiday, celebrating the establishment of the republic on April 19, 1971. The country was planned in the eighteenth century to be a home for natives of Africa who were waifs in London and for black refugees from the newly independent United States. 383, 853, 875.

c19 Sechselauten, Six Ringing Festival, a holiday in Zurich, Switzerland, on the third Sunday and Monday of April; originally a medieval guild holiday commemorating the ringing of the cathedral bells at six instead of seven o'clock for the end of the working day. The holiday begins on Sunday with processions of costumed children; Monday is a day of parades of guildsmen and the burning of effigies of Old Man Winter. 857, 875.

19 Landing of the 33 Patriots Day, a public holiday in Uruguay commemorating the landing of thirty-three patriotic exiles on April 19, 1825, to begin the campaign that ultimately resulted in the independence of Uruguay. 875.

19 Declaration of Independence and Day of the Indian, observed as a joint holiday in Venezuela. 875.

Anniversaries and Special Events Days

19 Boston Marathon Day, a popular competition for runners sponsored by the Boston Athletic Association; an annual event since 1896 held on Patriots' Day, the third Monday in April. 874.

19 Anniversary of the death of Simon Fraser on April 19, 1962. Canadian explorer and fur trader who explored the upper course of the Fraser River. 864

19 Parker Day, or John Parker Day, a remembrance day in tribute to John Parker, a captain of the minutemen, who gave the order on April 19, 1775, at Lexington, not to fire unless fired upon; remembered for the words "if they mean to have a war, let it begin here." 268.

19 Birthday of Roger Sherman (April 19, 1721–July 23, 1793). American patriot and stateman. The only man to sign all four of the major documents of American independence—the Articles of Association, the Declaration of Independence, the Articles of Confederation, and the Constitution. He represents the state of Connecticut in Statuary Hall in a sculpture done by Chauncey B. Ives. 292, 294, 870.

Anniversaries and Special Events Days

20 Easter Rising Day, the anniversary of the April 20, 1916, insurrection by Irish patriots rebelling against English rule; a tragic failure for the Irish but a day forever linked with 1916 as "the year one in Irish history and Irish life." 701.

20 Birthday of Daniel Chester French (April 20, 1950–October 7, 1931). American sculptor who was commissioned to create many statues of prominent Americans. His best-known work includes the seated figure of Abraham Lincoln in the Lincoln Memorial in Washington and the *Minute Man* at Concord. 339, 347.

Holy Days and Feast Days

21 Feast of Saint Anselm, archbishop of Canterbury from 1093 to 1109; defender of church rights in opposition to English kings; pre-eminent theologian known as "the father of scholasticism"; proclaimed doctor of the church in 1720. 14

21 Feast of Ridvan, a holy day in the Baha'i faith, commemorating the Declaration of Baha'u'llah, articulating a plan whereby all of the divergent peoples of the world may live in peace and harmony. 1, 854.

Holidays and Civic Days

21 Tiradentes Day in Brazil, commemorates the execution of the dentist José de Silva Xavier, a conspirator in the 1789 revolt against the Portuguese. 875.

21 Falkland Islands Day, a major holiday in the Falkland Islands celebrating the birth of Queen Elizabeth II on April 21, 1926; one of the few observances of the queen's birthday scheduled on her actual birth date.

21 Kartini Day in Indonesia, a tribute to Raden Adjeng Kartini, leader in the emancipation of Indonesian women. 875.

21 Natale di Roma, traditional day for observing the founding of Rome in 753 B.C., celebrated with parades and public speeches. 1.

21 San Jacinto Day, a legal holiday in Texas commemorating the 1836 Battle of San Jacinto through which the Texans won independence from Mexico. 268.

Anniversaries and Special Event Days

21 Birthday of Alexander Anderson (April 21, 1775–January 17, 1870). American engraver and illustrator who made the first wood engravings completed in the United States. His best-known work includes engravings for an edition of the plays of Shakespeare.

21 Birthday of Fredrik Bajer (April 21, 1837–January 22, 1922). Danish statesman and author; founder of the Danish Peace Society and the International Peace Bureau; recipient of the 1908 Nobel Peace Prize. 867.

21 Brasilia Day, a Brazilian day of observance; the anniversary of the proclamation naming Brasilia as the national capital of Brazil on April 21, 1960.

21 Birthday of Charlotte Brontë (April 21, 1816–March 31, 1855). English novelist famous for *Jane Eyre* and other novels interpreting women in conflict with their individual needs and social conditions. 738.

21 Birthday of Friedrich Froebel (April 21, 1782–June 21, 1852). German educator; founder of kindergarten system. 864.

21 Birthday of John Muir (April 21, 1838–December 24, 1914). American naturalist; advocate of forest conservation who discovered the glaciers in the High Sierras. The only stand of redwoods in the United States Park System is named the Muir Woods National Monument in his honor. 741.

Holidays and Civic Days

22 Arbor Day, a legal holiday in Nebraska commemorating the birthday of J. Sterling Morton, April 22, 1832, founder of Arbor Day and former governor of the state. Arbor Day was first celebrated in Nebraska on April 10, 1872, but was later changed to Morton's birth date. 268, 269, 430–40, 578.

Anniversaries and Special Events Days

22 Birthday of Alphonse Bertillon (April 22, 1853–February 13, 1914). French anthropologist; chief of the department of identification in the prefecture of police in Paris who devised the Bertillon system for identifying criminals. 864.

22 Earth Day, first observed internationally on April 22, 1970, to emphasize the necessity for the conservation of the natural resources of the world. 857.

22 Birthday of Henry Fielding (April 22, 1707–October 8, 1754). English novelist remembered for such novels as *The History of Tom Jones, a Foundling*. 864.

22 Queen Isabella Day, honoring the April 22, 1451, birth of the Spanish queen who financed Christopher Columbus; the day is observed in Spain and frequently proclaimed by the governors of a number of states in the United States. 276.

22 Birthday of Immanuel Kant (April 22, 1724–February 12, 1804). German philosopher who influenced such schools of philosophy as Kantianism and idealism; author of *The Critique of Pure Reason*. 864.

22 Birthday of Nikolai Lenin (Vladimir Ilich Ulyanov); April 22, 1870–January 21, 1924. Russian revolutionary leader and writer whose ideas and career laid the foundations for Soviet totalitarianism; first head of the Russian state. His birthday is observed in the Union of Soviet Socialist Republics. 864.

22 Birthday of Julius Sterling Morton (April 22, 1832–April 27, 1902). American politician who started Arbor Day in Nebraska in 1872. He represents Nebraska in Statuary Hall in a sculpture made by Rudulph Evans; his birthday is recognized annually by arboretum societies and observed as Arbor Day in Nebraska. 268, 870.

22 Birthday of J. Robert Oppenheimer (April 22, 1904–February 18, 1967). Theoretical physicist, director of the Los Alamos laboratory during the development of the atomic bomb. Received the Enrico Fermi Award of the Atomic Energy Commission in 1963. 871.

c22 Secretaries' Day, honoring the skills and contributions of secretaries; observed on varying days during Secretaries' Week. 857.

Holy Days and Feast Days

23 Feast of Saint George, a third-century martyr associated with the legend of George as the Christian knight who slew the dragon; a patron of knighthood in the Middle Ages; patron of England, Portugal, Germany, Genoa, Venice, and the Order of the Garter. 14.

Holidays and Civic Days

23 Saint George's Day, a holiday in Barcelona, Spain. It is also a holiday in Newfoundland on or near April 23.

Anniversaries and Special Events Days

23 Anniversary of the founding of the American Academy of Arts and Letters on April 23, 1904.

23 Birthday of James Buchanan (April 23, 1791–June 1, 1868). Scotch-Irish ancestry; Pennsylvania lawyer; fifteenth president of the United States, 1857–61. A Presbyterian and the only bachelor president. Buried at Woodward Hill Cemetery, Lancaster, Pennsylvania. 359–66, 370–72, 374, 378, 379.

23 Anniversary of the death of Miguel de Cervantes Saavedra on April 23, 1616. Leading Spanish novelist, playwright, and poet famed for the writing of *Don Quixote*. 864.

23 The Georgitt, or Saint George's Parade, an annual event in various Bavarian villages honoring the soldier saint of the Middle Ages and the protector of riders and their horses.

23 Birthday of Edwin Markham (April 23, 1852–March 7, 1940). American poet who wrote "The Man with the Hoe" and "Lincoln, the Man of the People." Markham has been called "the dean of American poets." 864.

23 Anniversary of the establishment of the Order of the Garter, the oldest and most illustrious of British orders of knighthood, on April 23, 1348. 285.

23 Birthday of Lester Bowles Pearson (April 23, 1897–December 27, 1972). Prime minister of Canada and ambassador to the United States; awarded the Nobel Peace Prize for his success in averting war at the time of the 1957 Suez crisis. 864.

c23 Peppercorn Day, an observance in Bermuda carrying out the Peppercorn ceremony, in which officials collect the annual rent of one peppercorn for the use of the Old State House in St. George; held on the most suitable day nearest April 23, Saint George's Day. 857.

23 Birthday of William Shakespeare (April 23, 1564–April 23, 1616). Traditional date for the commemoration of the birth of William Shakespeare, who was baptized on April 26, 1564; universally acknowledged to be the greatest dramatist and poet the world has known. His birthday is a festival day at Stratford-upon-Avon, his birthplace, and is observed by Shakespeare societies in many nations. 268, 654, 703.

23 Children's Day, a special program and activities day in Turkey honoring children as the symbol of modern Turkey; the day also commemorates the inauguration of the Grand National Assembly on April 23, 1923. 875.

23 Birthday of Joseph Mallord Turner (April 23, 1775–December 19, 1851). English landscape painter, admired for unusual use of light and color. 864.

Anniversaries and Special Events Days

24 Armenian Martyrs' Day, memorializing the Armenian victims of the Turkish massacres of 1915–16; observed by groups with Armenian backgrounds throughout the world.

24 Anniversary of the death of Daniel Defoe on April 24, 1731. English novelist renowned for _Robinson Crusoe_. 864.

24 Hostage Heroes Day, the anniversary of the death of eight Americans in the Iranian desert on April 24, 1980, in the ill-fated attempt to rescue the 52 Americans held hostage by Iranian militants in Teheran. 874.

24 Children's Day in Iceland, observed by children listening to an official address in the morning and being entertained with music and other events in the afternoon.

24 Anniversary of the establishment of the Library of Congress by authority of an Act of Congress on April 24, 1800. 268, 678, 866.

24 Birth of John Russell Pope (April 24, 1874–August 27, 1937). American architect whose work includes the National Gallery of Art and the Jefferson Memorial. 864.

Holy Days and Feast Days

25 Feast of Saint Mark, one of the four Evangelists, observed by the Roman Catholic, Greek Orthodox, Anglican, Episcopal and Lutheran churches; the remains of Saint Mark lie under the altar in the Basilica of Saint Mark in Venice. 4, 9.

Holidays and Civic Days

25 Anzac Day, an Australian and New Zealand holiday of veterans parades and church services, commemorating the courageous but sacrificial landing of the Australian and New Zealand Army Corps troops at Gallipoli in World War I. The word _Anzac_ is made up of the initials of the Australian and New Zealand Army Corps. 875.

25 Liberation Day, observed in Italy as a holiday to honor the freedom that came with the Allied victory in World War II. 875.

25 Portugal's Liberty Day, a national holiday and the anniversary of the April 25, 1974, coup which led to the downfall of the authoritarian corporate state that existed for 42 years under the Salazar-Caetano dictatorship. 868, 875.

25 Swaziland National Flag Day, a public holiday in Swaziland, honoring the nation's flag and the responsibilities of citizenship. 280.

Anniversaries and Special Events Days

25 Birthday of Charles Ferdinand Dowd (April 25, 1825–November 12, 1904). American educator and proponent of uniform time zones to replace the individual system whereby each city and railroad had its own time system. Dowd's ideas on standard time were adopted by most cities of the United States and by the railroads on November 18, 1883.

25 Birthday of Guglielmo Marconi (April 25, 1874–July 20, 1937). Italian electrician who perfected wireless telegraphy and experiments with short-waves and ultrashort waves. He was co-winner of the 1909 Nobel Prize in physics. 864.

Holidays and Civic Days

c26 Confederate Memorial Day, a holiday in Alabama, Georgia, and Mississippi on the last Monday in April; observed with tributes to the dead of the Civil War. 875.

c26 Fast Day, a holiday in New Hampshire observed on the fourth Monday in April commemorating the observance of a day of prayer and fasting that began in 1679. 268.

26 Union Day, a public holiday in Tanzania, celebrating the union of Tanganyika, Zanzibar, and Pemba into the United Republic of Tanzania on April 26, 1964. 868, 875.

Anniversaries and Special Events Days

c26 National Arbor Day in the United States, designated by presidental proclamation for observation on the last Friday of April; scheduled on varying dates throughout the country. 268, 430–40, 578.

26 Birthday of John James Audubon (April 26, 1785–January 27, 1851). American ornithologist and artist. His book *Birds of America* is recognized as the finest example of ornithological illustration; elected to the Hall of Fame for Great Americans in 1900. 268, 751.

26 Cape Henry Day, designated annually by proclamation of the governor of Virginia as a commemoration of the first landing on American soil of the expedition that founded Jamestown. 268.

26 Birthday of Michel Fokine (April 26, 1889–August 22, 1942). Russian-American dancer and choreographer; created *The Dying Swan* for Anna Pavlova; a major influence on twentieth-century classical ballet repertoire. 864.

26 Birthday of Esek Hopkins (April 26, 1718–February 26, 1802). American commodore; first commander-in-chief of the United States navy. 867.

26 Birthday of Frederick Law Olmsted (April 26, 1822–August 28, 1903). American landscape architect, noted for his design of Central Park in New York City and for the planning for Yosemite National Park and the Niagara Falls Park project. 864.

Holy Days and Feast Days

27 Feast of Saint Zita, a thirteenth-century servant noted for her diligence and austerities and for the help she gave to the poor and the imprisoned; patron saint of maids. 9.

Holidays and Civic Days

27 Saur Revolution day, a holiday in Afghanistan commemorating the Great Saur Revolution of April 27 and 28, 1978, a protest against the government's inability to carry out needed economic reforms. 868, 875.

27 Austrian Second Republic day, a civic day commemorating the foundation of the Second Republic of Austria on April 27, 1945. 868. 875.

27 Togo Independence day, a holiday in the Republic of Togo commemorating the establishment of Togo as a sovereign nation on April 27, 1960. 868, 875.

Anniversaries and Special Events Days

27 Birthday of Samuel Finley Breece Morse (April 27, 1791–April 2, 1872). American artist and inventor of the electric telegraph and the Morse code. He was elected to the Hall of Fame for Great Americans in 1900. 864.

27 Birthday of Ulysses Simpson Grant (April 27, 1822–July 23, 1885). Scottish ancestry; Illinois tanner; general-in-chief of the Union forces in the Civil War; eighteenth president of the United States. Methodist. Buried on Riverside Drive, New York City. Elected to the Hall of Fame for Great Americans in 1900. 359–36, 370–72, 374, 378, 379.

27 Anniversary of the death of Ferdinand Magellan on April 27, 1521. Portuguese navigator; often called "the first circumnavigator of the earth"; honored on Discoverers' Day. 864.

c27 National Christian College Day, established in 1941 to emphasize the importance of religion to higher education. The last Sunday in April was designated for its observance. 20.

Holidays and Civic Days

28 Maryland Admission Day. Maryland entered the Union on April 28, 1788, as the seventh state of the original thirteen to be admitted. 268, 856, 862.

Anniversaries and Special Events Days

28 Birthday of James Monroe (April 28, 1758–July 4, 1831). Scottish ancestry; Virginia lawyer; fifth president of the United States, 1817–25. Episcopalian. Buried in Hollywood Cemetery, Richmond, Virginia. Elected to the Hall of Fame for Great Americans in 1930. 359–66, 370–72, 374, 378, 379.

Holy Days and Feast Days

29 Feast of Saint Catherine of Siena, one of the greatest of Christian mystics; made patron saint in Italy in 1939 and declared a doctor of the church by Pope Paul VI in 1970. 5, 9.

Holidays and Civic Days

29 The Emperor's birthday, a holiday in Japan, honoring the birth on April 29, 1901, of His Majesty the Emperor Hirohito. 875.

Anniversaries and Special Events Days

29 Birthday of Sir Thomas Beecham (April 29, 1879–March 8, 1961). English conductor; founder of the London Philharmonic Orchestra in 1932; champion of the music of Frederick Delius. 864.

29 Birthday of Oliver Ellsworth (April 29, 1745–November 26, 1807). American jurist; third chief justice of the United States Supreme Court; major author of the Judiciary Act of 1789 establishing the federal court system. 864.

29 Birthday of Lorado Taft (April 29, 1860–October 30, 1936). American sculptor whose notable works include *Black Hawk* at Oregon, Illinois, and *Solitude of the Soul*, at the Chicago Art Institute. 864.

Holidays and Civic Days

30 Louisiana Admission Day. Louisiana entered the Union on April 30, 1812, as the eighteenth state. 268, 856, 862.

30 Queen Juliana's birthday, an official holiday in the Netherlands honoring the Queen Mother who was born on April 30, 1909, and abdicated on April 30, 1980, in favor of her daughter Beatrix. 857.

Anniversaries and Special Events days

30 May Day Eve. Maitag Vorabend, celebrated in various cantons of Switzerland carrying on the ancient traditions of lovers.

30 Anniversary of George Washington's first oath of office as president of the United States, administered on April 30, 1789, by Robert Livingston, chancellor of New York State. 371.

30 Anniversary of the first national holiday in the United States; authorized by an Act of Congress to honor the April 30, 1889, centennial of the inauguration of George Washington. The day was "hereby declared to be a national holiday throughout the United States."

30 Vappu Day, celebrated in Finland on the eve of May day to rejoice in the coming of spring. It is a day of parades of white-capped students and workers followed by a night of revelry. 849.

30 Walpurgis Night, an ancient festival to ward off witches, warlocks, and demons, is observed in the towns of the Harz Mountains of Germany, and in Finland and the Scandinavian countries, with bonfires and gala events. 20, 261, 268.

May

May, the fifth month of the year, may have been named for Maria, the Roman goddess of spring and growth, or for the *Majores*, a branch of the Roman senate. It is a month that is associated with flowers and mild weather in the northern hemisphere, but it is a winter month in the southern hemisphere.

The first day, called May Day, was once a popular festival honoring Flora, the goddess of flowers. It was a day of maypole dancing and other charming customs, many of which disappeared with the fast pace of progress in the Western world. In the last half of the twentieth century, May 1 has been celebrated as a favorite international holiday for workers of all kinds. At least 119 nations in the world celebrate Labor Day on May 1 with parades, speeches, and civic gatherings. In a few European countries such as Finland, the day is also a special spring festival for students.

May is "the month of Mary" for Roman Catholics throughout the world. The Virgin Mary is honored during the entire month with pilgrimages and observances at great cathedrals and at special shrines. In the United States it is the month when the Protestant, Roman Catholic, and Jewish faiths, each in its own way, observe National Family Week, which leads up to the most popular of May observances, Mother's Day.

The special flowers for the month of May are the hawthorn and the lily of the valley. The birthstone is the emerald.

Holidays and Civic Days

1 International Labor Day, a holiday in 119 nations of the world at the beginning of the 1980s; a day marking the solidarity of workers, the importance of high standards of productivity, and appreciation of the contributions of workers. 875.

1 Saint Joseph Worker Day, observed as a holiday in the Vatican City State. 5, 875.

Anniversaries and Special Events Days

1 Birthday of Joseph Addison (May 1, 1672–June 17, 1719). English essayist. 864.

1 Amtrak Day, the anniversary of the beginning (on May 1, 1971) of the unified rail passenger system in the United States. 874.

1 Bealtaine, an old May day Irish festival celebrated in some parts of the Irish countryside and a folk-memory in others; a day of welcoming the beginning of the summer season with the decorating of bushes and the lighting of bonfires.

1 Dewey Day, honors Admiral George Dewey and the anniversary of the Battle of Manila Bay of May 1, 1898. It is observed primarily by veterans organizations. 268.

c1 Old Dover Days, a festival observed in Dover, the capital of Delaware, during the first weekend in May to re-create the history and customs of Old Dover, a town formed by William Penn in 1683. 268.

1 Birthday of Benjamin Henry Latrobe (May 1, 1764–September 3, 1820). American architect who designed the Roman Catholic cathedral in Baltimore, the first cathedral to be constructed in the United States, and rebuilt the Capitol after it was burned by the British in 1814. 864.

1 Law Day, sponsored by the American Bar Association, is recognized by presidential proclamation; its aim is to further public knowledge, appreciation, and respect for law and its benefits to the citizen; observed by legal societies, schools, and the media. 268.

1 Lei Day, a Hawaiian flower festival, the only fete of its kind; dedicated to the lei as a symbol of Hawaiian beauty and friendship. 268.

1 Loyalty Day, observed in the United States by presidential proclamation. Special ceremonies are presented by the Veterans of Foreign Wars, on or near May 1, at Cooch's Bridge, Delaware, where the Stars and Stripes were first displayed in battle. 268.

1 May Day, the traditional day of flower festivals, is a spring festival in Turkey. The age-old rituals of hanging May baskets and dancing around the maypole are carried on by students and neighborhood groups in England and in some parts of the United States. 256.

1 Beatrix crowned Queen of the Netherlands on May 1, 1980, succeeding her mother, Queen Juliana who abdicated on April 30, 1980.

c1 Senior Citizens Day, the beginning of Senior Citizens Month, which is observed in Massachusetts and other states; senior citizens have been honored this month with annual presidential proclamations since 1963. 857.

1 Tamany's Day, or Saint Tamenend's Day, a modern re-creation of a May day celebration of colonial America; originated with the selection by Revolutionary soldiers of an Indian sage, Chief Tamenend, as a saint to compete with the British Saint George. 20.

Holy Days and Feast Days

2 Feast Day of Saint Athanasius, champion of the faith, who held out against Arian heresy; one of the four great Greek doctors of the church. 4, 9.

Anniversaries and Special Events Days

2 Birthday of Elias Boudinot (May 2, 1740–October 24, 1821). American lawyer, patriot-philanthropist; leader in the organization of the American Bible Society and its first president. 864.

2 Birthday of Theodor Herzl (May 2, 1860–July 3, 1904). Founder of modern Zionism; honored in Israel and in Jewish communities throughout the world. 1.

c2 Kentucky Derby Day, a day of horse racing held at Churchill Downs in Louisville, Kentucky, on the first Saturday of May; one of the most colorful and popular sporting events in the United States, with a history that goes back to the first Derby held on May 17, 1875. 268, 661.

Holy Days and Feast Days

3 Feast of Our Lady of Czestochowa, Queen of the Crown of Poland, is celebrated at the Polish National Shrine of Czestochowa in honor of the Virgin of Czestochowa. The shrine holds the venerated ikon of the mother of Christ. 34.

3 Feast of Saint James the Less, apostle whose name refers to the fact that he was shorter in stature and younger in age than James the Greater; martyred by being stoned to death. 9.

Holidays and Civic Days

c3 May Day, or Labour Day, celebrated as a holiday in England, Wales, Scotland, and Northern Ireland on the first Monday of May. 256.

3 Japanese Constitution Day, a national holiday in Japan which celebrates the establishment, on May 3, 1947, of a democratic form of government under parliamentary rule. 868, 875.

3 Moshoeshoe Day, a holiday in Lesotho honoring the birthday of Moshoeshoe II, king of Lesotho. 875.

3 Labour Day, a holiday in Queensland in Australia, celebrating the eight-hour working day with rallies for workers, picnics for families, and sporting events. 875.

3 Polish Constitution Day, Swieto Trzeciego Majo, commemorates the nation's first constitution, adopted in 1794. 868.

c3 Zambia Labour Day, a holiday paying tribute to workers and emphasizing in programs and events the importance of productivity to the nation; observed on the first Monday of May. 875.

Anniversaries and Special Events Days

3 Holy Cross Day, a festive day for Mexican construction workers; a day to place a flower-decorated cross on all structures under construction and to enjoy owners-sponsored parties.

3 Birthday of Niccoló Machiavelli (May 3, 1469–June 21, 1527). Italian political statesman and author whose fame is based on the books *The Prince* and *The Discourses*. 864.

3 Sun Day, proclaimed by the Carter administration on May 3, 1977, to focus public attention on the potentials of solar energy. 874.

3 Thatcher Day, the anniversary of the election on May 3, 1979, of Margaret Thatcher as Britain's first woman prime minister. 874.

Holy Days and Feast Days

4 Feast of Saint Florian, a fourth-century Roman Christian martyred during Diocletian's persecution; patron of Poland and Upper Austria. 4, 9.

Holidays and Civic Days

4 Rhode Island Declaration of Independence Day, a civic day commemorating through public meetings and school programs the Declaration of Independence proclaimed by the colony on May 4, 1776, two months before the Continental Congress made its declaration. 268.

4 Crown Prince Tupuoto Day, a holiday in Tonga honoring the birthday of the crown prince. 875.

Anniversaries and Special Events Days

c4 Humane Sunday, a day dedicated to the prevention of child abuse and cruelty to animals; sponsored by the American Humane Society, usually on the first Sunday of May. 664, 724.

4 Birthday of Thomas Henry Huxley (May 4, 1825–June 29, 1895). English biologist, educator, and writer; champion of the Darwinian theory of evolution. 864.

4 Kent Students' Memorial Day, commemorating the memory of four students killed during anti-war demonstrations at Kent State University on May 4, 1970; ceremonies include tributes to students martyred elsewhere. 649.

c4 McDonogh Day, a day of commemoration by New Orleans schoolchildren honoring John McDonogh, who died on October 26, 1850, leaving half of his fortune to found public schools in New Orleans; a request that children occasionally place flowers on his grave is honored on the first Friday in May by a march to his statue and appropriate ceremonies.

4 Birthday of Horace Mann (May 4, 1796–August 2, 1859). American educator and crusading champion of educational reforms; known as the "father of the public school system." He was elected to the Hall of Fame for Great Americans in 1900. 268, 864.

Holidays and Civic Days

5 Liberation Day in Denmark, marking the end on May 5, 1945, of five years of Nazi occupation during World War II.

5 Japanese Children's Day, a holiday in Japan honoring children with festivities and customs symbolizing strength of character and ideals. 875.

5 Cinco de Mayo, a holiday in Mexico, celebrating the defeat of the French at the Battle of Puebla in 1867. The day is also celebrated on Olvera Street in Los Angeles and in other cities of the United States with large Mexican-American populations. 868, 875.

5 Dutch Liberation Day, a holiday in the Netherlands, commemorating May 5, 1945, when the Nazi forces were driven out of Holland by the Allies. 875.

5 Children's Day in South Korea, a national holiday, honoring children with special events, excursions and visits with parents to parks and entertainment centers. 875.

5 Coronation day, a national holiday in Thailand, celebrating the crowning of King Bhumibol on May 5, 1950. The day is also known as Chulakongkron's Day, honoring the king who carried out a modernization program for the Thai government in the last quarter of the nineteenth century. 875.

Anniversaries and Special Events Days

c5 Anniversary of the organization of the American Bible Society in New York in May of 1816. 874.

5 Birthday of Sören Aabye Kierkegaard (May 5, 1813–November 11, 1855). Danish philosopher whose writings influenced such modern schools of thought as existentialism. 864.

5 Birthday of Karl Marx (May 5, 1818–March 14, 1883). German socialist whose best-known work is *Das Kapital*. 864.

5 Memorial day, the anniversary of the documented "first" among Memorial days in the United States; observed on May 5, 1866, at Waterloo, New York. 857.

5 Napoleon's Day, the anniversary of the May 5, 1821, death of Napoleon Bonaparte, eighteenth-century emperor of France; commemorated with an annual mass before his tomb in the Invalides in Paris attended by descendants of the Bonapartes and by admirers of Napoleon.

5 Birthday of Henryk Sienkiewicz (May 5, 1846–November 15, 1916). Polish novelist who wrote a patriotic trilogy dealing with Poland's struggle for freedom in the seventeenth century. He received the 1905 Nobel Prize in literature. 864.

Anniversaries and Special Events Days

6 Birthday of Phoebe Ann Coffin (May 6, 1829–June 2, 1921). American Universalist minister; first woman ordained as a minister in New England.

6 Birthday of Sigmund Freud (May 6, 1856–September 23, 1939). Austrian physician and psychoanalyst, who is called the "father of psychoanalysis." 864.

6 Birthday of John McCutcheon (May 6, 1870–June 10, 1949). American cartoonist who was awarded a Pulitizer Prize in 1931 for his cartoons on political events and everyday life; creator of the cartoon "Injun Summer," reprinted each fall in the *Chicago Tribune*. 864.

6 Birthday of Rear Admiral Robert Edwin Peary (May 6, 1856–February 20, 1920). American Arctic explorer; first to reach the North Pole, on April 6, 1909. 268.

6 Shepherd's and Herdsman's Day, an old folk-festival day in Bulgaria.

Holy Days and Feast Days

7 Feast Day of San Nicola; the people of Bari, in the Italian province of Apulia, celebrate the feast of San Nicola (Saint Nicholas) in May rather than on his regular feast day on December 6. May 7 and 8 is the anniversary of the transfer of the saint's relics from Myra, Asia Minor, to Bari.

Anniversaries and Special Events Days

7 Anniversary of the organization of the American Medical Association on May 7, 1847, at Philadelphia, with Dr. Jonathan Knight as the first president.

7 Birthday of Johannes Brahms (May 7, 1833–April 3, 1897). German composer, considered one of the foremost musicians of all times; honored by annual music festivals throughout the world. 864.

7 Birthday of Robert Browning (May 7, 1812–December 12, 1889). English poet who climaxed his career with the writing of *The Ring and the Book*. 864.

7 Lusitania Day; the anniversary of the attack on, and sinking of, the British passenger liner, the *Lusitania* on May 17, 1915; the act of a German submarine. 258.

7 Birthday of Sir Rabindranath Tagore (May 7, 1861–August 7, 1941). Hindu poet, philosopher, and artist. Author of *Gitanjali, The Religion of Man*, and other books. Awarded the Nobel Prize in literature in 1913. 864.

7 Birthday of Peter Ilich Tchaikovsky (May 7, 1840–November 6, 1893). Russian composer famous for his symphonies, orchestral works, and the familiar song "None but the Lonely Heart." 864.

Holy Days and Feast Days

c8 The Holy Blood Procession takes place on the streets of Bruges, Belgium, on the first Monday following May 2 to celebrate the spring day of 1150 when Count Thierry d'Alsace returned from the Crusades with the relic of the Holy Blood. The Passion play, *Sanguis Christi*, based on the story of the Holy Blood, is presented every five years. 34.

Holidays and Civic Days

8 Truman's Birthday, a holiday in Missouri commemorating the May 8, 1884, birth of Harry S. Truman, the thirty-third president of the United States and Missouri's most famous son; special ceremonies are held annually at Truman's gravesite in the courtyard of the Truman Library at Independence, Missouri. 875.

Anniversaries and Special Events Days

8 Anniversary of the death of Helena Petrovna Blavatsky on May 8, 1891. Russian theosophist who founded the Theosophical Society in New York and whose book *Isis Unveiled* became a classic in theosophical literature; the day is commemorated by theosophical societies throughout the world. 41, 738.

8 Birthday of Jean Henri Dunant (May 8, 1828–October 30, 1910). Swiss philanthropist and founder of the Red Cross Society who shared the Nobel Peace Prize in 1901; World Red Cross Day is celebrated on his birthday. 679.

8 Furry Day, a Helston, England, celebration originally honoring Saint Michael's victory over Satan, now a spring festival with the entire town in movement; men in top hats and women in fancy dresses dance in the streets to the Furry Dance that is as old as the custom itself. 256.

8 Birthday of Oscar Hammerstein (May 8, 1846–August 1, 1919). German-American opera impresario, playwright, and inventor who established the Manhattan Opera House for the presentation of popular musical events. 864.

8 Birthday of Miguel Hidalgo (May 8, 1753–July 31, 1811). Roman Catholic priest; organizer of a movement that became a social and economic revolution; known as "the father of Mexican independence." 864.

c8 Native American Day, observed in the United States on the second Saturday of May or the fourth Friday in September; celebrated in various regions of the United States through Indian festivals and cultural exhibitions. 268.

8 Stork Day, the traditional day for the arrival of the storks at Ribe, Denmark, to repair their nests on the tops of old houses; the stork population was reported to be diminishing in the 1970s.

8 Birthday of Harry S. Truman (May 8, 1884–December 26, 1972). English-Scotch-Irish ancestry; Missouri senator; vice-president who succeeded to the presidency on the death of Franklin D. Roosevelt; thirty-third president of the United States, 1945–53. Baptist. Devoted his retirement to building up the archives in the Truman Library at Independence, Missouri. Author of *Years of Decisions* and *Years of Trial and Hope*. Buried in the rear courtyard of the Truman Library in Independence, Missouri. 359–66, 369, 371–72, 374, 379, 380.

8 V-E (Victory in Europe) Day, commemorating the end of World War II in Europe with the signing of the unconditional surrender by the Germans in May of 1945. It is called Armistice Day in France. 268.

c8 Windmill Day, observed in the Netherlands on the second Saturday of May to display some three hundred windmills working throughout the country at the same time. 857.

8 World Red Cross Day, honoring Henri Dunant, the originator of the Red Cross movement. 677.

Holidays and Civic Days

9 Channel Islands Liberation Day, a holiday in the Channel Islands, a part of the United Kingdom situated off the northwest coast of France; a celebration of the anniversary of the removal of German occupation forces at the end of World War II. 875.

9 Czechoslovakia Liberation Day, a national holiday, commemorating the liberation of the nation on May 9, 1945, by the Soviet army and U.S. forces and the surrender of Germany, which terminated World War II on the European continent. 875.

9 USSR Victory Day, a national holiday, celebrating the German surrender of May 7, 1945, and honoring the millions of Russian citizens who died during World War II. 875.

Anniversaries and Special Events Days

9 Birthday of Sir James Matthew Barrie (May 9, 1860–June 9, 1937). Scottish playwright and novelist with a gift for whimsy. His most famous work is *Peter Pan*, which has provided a celebrated role for generations of famous actresses. 864.

9 Birthday of Belle Boyd (May 9, 1843–June 11, 1900). American actress who was, before her theatrical career, one of the most successful Confederate spies during the Civil War. 864.

9 John Brown Day, the anniversary of the birth on May 9, 1800, of John Brown, abolitionist with ambitious plans to liberate American slaves; convicted of treason and hanged on December 2, 1859; called a "martyr in the cause of human freedom;" his memory is commemorated by civil rights groups. 268.

9 North Pole Flight Day, anniversary of the first flight over the North Pole, achieved by Commander Richard E. Byrd of the United States Navy and Floyd Bennett on May 9, 1926. 268.

9 Birthday of José Ortega y Gasset (May 9, 1883–October 18, 1955). Spanish philosopher and humanist; known for *The Revolt of the Masses*, which advocates rule by the creative minority. 864.

Anniversaries and Special Events Days

10 Adler Planetarium Day, the anniversary of the opening of the Adler Planetarium in Chicago on May 10, 1930, the first public planetarium in the United States.

10 Burning of the Books Day, the anniversary of the massive burning of books in public squares in Germany on May 10, 1933, to demonstrate Hitler's intent to curb freedom of the press and freedom of expression of individual thought.

10 Confederate Memorial Day, a statewide holiday in both North and South Carolina honoring the memory of the Confederate soldiers and civilians lost during the Civil War. 875.

10 Fort Ticonderoga Day, the anniversary of the battle of May 10, 1775, when Ethan Allen and his Green Mountain Boys overwhelmed the British at Fort Ticonderoga, the first American victory in the War of Independence. 268.

10 Golden Spike Day, commemorating the completion of the railroads and the driving of a golden spike on May 10, 1869, to symbolize the unification of the East and the West by railroad; observed at the Golden Spike Historical Monument at Corrine, Utah. 688.

c10 Mother's Day. The first Mother's Day was held in Philadelphia on May 10, 1908, following suggestions made by Julia Ward Howe in 1872 and Anne Jarvis in 1907. The day received national recognition on May 9, 1914, when President Woodrow Wilson issued a proclamation asking American citizens to give a public expression of reverence to mothers. The selection of carnations as a symbol of the day, pink for a living mother and white for remembrance, was made in memory of President William McKinley, who always wore a white carnation, his own mother's favorite flower. In the United States, Mother's Day is now observed on the second Sunday in May. 268, 269, 270, 519–24, 582, 588.

Holidays and Civic Days

11 Minnesota Admission Day. Minnesota entered the Union on May 11, 1858, as the thirty-second state. 268, 856, 862.

Anniversaries and Special Events Days

11 International Mother's Day, observed on May 11, unites mothers of the world in an action program for peace.

11 Birthday of Mari Sandoz (May 11, 1901–March 10, 1966). Author of *Old Jules* and other books on the American pioneer period; Maria Sandoz Day was proclaimed by the Nebraska State Legislature to honor her birthday and work. 864.

Anniversaries and Special Events Days

12 Birthday of Robert Baldwin (May 12, 1804–December 9, 1858). Canadian statesman, exponent of representative government. 864.

12 Birthday of Lincoln Ellsworth (May 12, 1880–May 26, 1951). American engineer and polar explorer who led the first transarctic flights in 1926 and the first transantarctic flights in 1935. 867.

12 Garland Day in Abbotsbury, Dorsetshire, England; a ceremony left over from the old May Day festivities; observed by children who carry garlands from door to door and receive gifts for the welcoming of May; the garlands are later laid in front of the War Memorial. 256.

12 National Hospital Day has been observed annually on May 12 since 1921; observed by many hospitals and hospital associations with special programs honoring Florence Nightingale. 268.

12 Birthday of Florence Nightingale (May 12, 1820–August 13, 1910). English nurse and the founder of modern nursing; called the "lady with the lamp" during the Crimean War. She was the first woman to receive the Order of Merit. 268, 785, 788, 866.

12 Nurses' Day, International, a day honoring the dedication and the services of the nurses of the world; observed on May 12, the birthday of Florence Nightingale. 857.

12 Birthday of Gabriel Dante Rossetti (May 12, 1828–April 9, 1882). English poet and painter who was the most important member of the Pre-Raphaelites. 864.

12 Snellman Day, observed in Finland to honor the birth on May 12, 1806, of J. V. Snellman, journalist, statesman, and leader of the Nationalist movement; ceremonies are held at his statue in Helsinki. 849

c12 Tulip Time, a flower festival observed in Holland, Michigan, beginning on the Wednesday nearest May 15; celebrated since 1929 with beautiful plantings of tulips in Tulip Lanes and parks, and with parades, pageants, musicals, and exhibits at the Netherlands Museum. 268.

Anniversaries and Special Events Days

13 Jamestown Day, the anniversary of the establishment of the first permanent English settlement in America on May 13, 1607; commemorative services are held annually on the Sunday nearest May 13. 268.

13 The anniversary of the attempted assassination of Pope John Paul II in Saint Peter's Square at the Vatican on May 13, 1981. 874.

13 Birthday of Sir Arthur Sullivan (May 13, 1842–November 22, 1900). British composer who with William Gilbert created the unique and perennially popular Gilbert and Sullivan operettas. 728.

Holidays and Civic Days

14 Guinean Democratic Party Day, a holiday in the Republic of Guinea observing the anniversary of the foundation of the Guinean Democratic Party in 1947. 868, 875.

14 Liberian Unification and Integration Day, honors the beginning of the National Unification Party, which is dedicated to a unified Liberia. 875.

14 Kamuzu Day, a holiday in the Republic of Malawi, formerly Nyasaland, is a day of tribute to the republic's first president, Kamuzu Banda. 868, 875.

14 Flag Day, a holiday in Paraguay honoring the only flag in the world with different obverse and reverse; the horizontal stripes on the flag are red, white, and blue with the white stripes on the obverse charged with arms of the republic, and, on the reverse with a lion and an inscription, "Paz y Justicia." 280, 287.

14 Philippine Islands Constitution Day, a civic day honoring the ratification of the basic constitution on May 14, 1935. 868.

Anniversaries and Special Events Days

14 Anniversary of the baptism of Thomas Gainsborough (May 14, 1727–August 2, 1788). English portrait and landscape painter known for such paintings as *The Blue Boy*. 864.

14 Birthday of Robert Owen (May 14, 1771–November 17, 1858). Welsh manufacturer and educator; founder of British socialism and of the utopian colony at New Harmony, Indiana. 864.

14 Anniversary of the orbiting of *Skylab I*, the first United States manned space station on May 14, 1973; remained in space twenty-eight days. 874.

Holy Days and Feast Days

15 Feast Day of Saint Dympna, patron saint of the insane, particularly observed in Geel in Belgium, where the townspeople take care of the mentally or emotionally disturbed through a "boarding out" system. Pilgrimages are made to Saint Dympna's tomb in Geel. 4, 9.

15 Feast of Saint Isidore of the Husbandman (or Farmer), patron saint of Madrid and of farmers, celebrated annually in Spain with religious services in chapels in the fields followed by local fairs; it is an integral part of the Week of Bull Fights. The feast is also celebrated in all Mexican towns that have Saint Isidore as a patron saint. 4, 9.

Holidays and Civic Days

15 Israeli National Day, a holiday honoring the proclamation of the independence of Israel adopted on May 15, 1948; observed on or near the day of proclamation; the observance dates vary in accordance with the lunar calendar. 396.

15 Independence Observance Day, a holiday in Paraguay following the May 14 Flag Day celebration; Paraguay achieved independence on May 14, 1811, with the departure of the last of the Spanish royal governors. 868, 875.

Anniversaries and Special Events Days

15 Birthday of Lyman Frank Baum (May 15, 1856–May 6, 1919). American writer and playwright remembered chiefly for a series of books about the imaginary land of Oz; observed by the International Wizard of Oz Clubs. 864.

15 Police Memorial Day, a day set aside by the Congress of the United States to honor law enforcement officers killed in the line of duty. Police Week, established by presidential proclamation, is scheduled to include May 15. 866.

Holy Days and Feast Days

16 Feast of Saint Brendan, one of the most popular of Irish saints; founder of Irish monasteries, including Clonfert, and author of *Navigatio*, a saga of his voyage to the "land promised to the saints." The instructions in the sixth-century Brendan saga proved to be accurate and reliable for a twentieth-century adventurer. 4, 9.

16 Feast of Saint John Nepomucen, fourteenth-century Bohemian defender of the faith; patron saint of Czechoslovakia. 4, 9.

Anniversaries and Special Events Days

16 Birthday of Edmund Kirby-Smith (May 16, 1824–March 28, 1893). American soldier and educator. West Point graduate who served with the Confederate Army in the Civil War. He represents the state of Florida in Statuary Hall in a sculpture by C. Adrian Pillars. 870.

16 Birthday of Elizabeth Palmer Peabody (May 16, 1804–January 3, 1894). American educator and author; one of the famous Peabody sisters, a pioneer in championing the study of history in public schools and the founder of the first kindergarten in the United States in 1860. 864.

16 Birthday of William Henry Seward (May 16, 1801–October 10, 1872). American statesman; secretary of state under Abraham Lincoln; negotiator of the purchase of Alaska from Russia. 268.

Holidays and Civic Days

17 Discovery Day, a holiday in the Cayman Islands in the Caribbean celebrating the discovery of the islands by Columbus in 1503. 975.

17 Nauru Constitution Day, a national holiday in Nauru, honors the May 17, 1968, amendments to the basic constitution establishing a republic with a parliamentary system of government. 868, 875.

17 Norwegian Constitution Day, a holiday in Norway commemorating the adoption of the constitution in 1814; one highlight of the day is a spectacular parade in which all school children participate, each wearing a national costume and waving a Norwegian flag. Syttende Mai is also observed by Norwegian-American communities in all parts of the United States, particularly in the Midwest. 268, 868, 875.

17 Battle of Las Piedras Day, the anniversary of the end of the 1828 conflict between Uruguayan patriots and Brazil; a holiday in Uruguay. 868, 875.

Holy Days and Feast Days

18 Feast Day of Saint Eric of Sweden; martyr and lawgiver; patron saint of Sweden. 9.

Holidays and Civic Days

18 Haitian Flag Day, a holiday in Haiti honoring the flag which is vertically black and red with a small white panel in the center bearing the national arms. 280, 285.

c18 Armed Forces Day, the third Saturday in May, combines Army Day, once celebrated in April, Air Forces Day, formerly observed in September, and Navy Day, originally observed on Theodore Roosevelt's birthday; authorized for observance by a presidential proclamation of May 7, 1965, covering all succeeding years. 268, 269, 441–63.

c18 Feis Ceoil, an Irish music festival, first held in Dublin on May 18, 1897; now held regularly during the week of the second Monday in May to promote Irish music.

18 Mount St. Helen's Day, the anniversary of the May 18, 1980, eruption of one of the most beautiful mountains in the state of Washington, blowing off almost a cubic mile of its summit and creating major disasters for nature and people. 652, 704.

18 Harry R. Truman Day, the anniversary of the death of Harry R. Truman during the eruption of Mount St. Helen on May 18, 1980; a man of independent spirit who may become the most interesting legend of the 1980 disaster; articles and songs have been written to celebrate his long years of residency near the mountain and his refusal to leave despite ominous warnings.

Holy Days and Feast Days

19 Feast Day of Saint Dunstan, patron saint of goldsmiths. 4.

19 Feast Day of Saint Peter Celestine, patron saint of book-industry workers. 4.

19 Pardon of Saint Ivo, a French religious pilgrimage notable for pious devotion and displays of regional costumes and music; dedicated to Saint Ivo, patron saint of lawyers; attracts lawyers from many nations.

Holidays and Civic Days

19 Flag Day of the Army, a civic day in Finland honoring those who died to preserve their country's freedom. It is comparable to Memorial Day in the United States, with memorial services and the placing of wreaths on the graves of the war dead.

19 Youth and Sports Day, a holiday in Turkey which begins with young athletes carrying burning torches to locations where games and contests are held. The holiday commemorates in particular the day in 1919 when Kemal Ataturk landed in Samsum and began the national movement toward independence. 875.

Anniversaries and Special Events Days

19 Birthday of Carl Ethan Akeley (May 19, 1864–November 17, 1926). American naturalist who developed the museum technique of mounting animals in habitat groups. 864.

19 Anniversary of the organization of the Federated Boys' Clubs on May 19, 1906, now known as the Boys' Clubs of America, Inc.

19 Birthday of Ho Chi Minh (May 19, 1890–September 3, 1969). President of the Democratic Republic of Vietnam (North Vietnam) from 1945 to 1969; one of the most powerful Communist leaders of the twentieth century. 864.

Holy Days and Feast Days

20 Feast Day of Saint Bernardino of Siena, patron saint of publicity agents. 9.

Holidays and Civic Days

20 Cameroon Constitution Day, a public holiday in Cameroon, on the west coast of Africa, commemorating the ratification of the constitution on May 20, 1972. 868, 875.

20 Mecklenburg Day, the anniversary of the signing of the Mecklenburg Declaration of Independence on May 20, 1775, by citizens of Mecklenburg County, North Carolina; a holiday in North Carolina. 268, 875.

20 MPR Day in Zaire, a holiday, commemorating the foundation of the Mouvement Populaire de la Revolution, the sole political party in the Republic of Zaire. 868, 875.

Anniversaries and Special Events Days

20 Birthday of Honoré de Balzac (May 20, 1799–August 18, 1850). French novelist famous for the series *La Comédie Humaine*, which presents a panorama of French society covering the first half of the twentieth century. 864.

20 Botev Day, anniversary of the May 20, 1876, death of Khristo Botev, Bulgarian poet and hero in the revolutionary movement against the Turks; observed in Bulgaria with poetry festivals and concerts.

20 Eliza Doolittle Day, established in honor of the heroine of Bernard Shaw's *Pygmalion* to encourage the proper use of language. 866.

20 Lafayette Day, commemorating the May 20, 1834, death of the Marquis de Lafayette, French general who aided the armies of the American Revolution. 268.

20 Birthday of Rose Hawthorne Lathrop (May 20, 1851–July 9, 1926). American nun; daughter of Nathaniel Hawthorne, who dedicated her life to the care of people incurably ill with cancer. 864.

20 Birthday of John Stuart Mill (May 20, 1806–May 8, 1873). English economist, logician, and philosophical writer noted for his *Essay on Liberty*. 864.

20 Birthday of Sara Louisa Oberholtzer (May 20, 1841–February 2, 1930). American author and social reformer; organized the Anti-Tobacco Society and was a leader in establishing the school-savings movement in the United States. 864.

20 Birthday of Frédéric Passy (May 20, 1822–June 12, 1912). French economist and pacifist; founder of the International and Permanent League of Peace. Shared the first Nobel Peace Prize with Jean Henri Dunant in 1901. 679.

20 Birthday of Sigrid Undset (May 20, 1882–June 10, 1949). Norwegian novelist famous for *Kristin Lavransdatter*. She was awarded the 1928 Nobel Prize for literature. 864.

20 Weights and Measures Day, anniversary of the May 20, 1875, signing of a treaty establishing the International Bureau of Weights and Measures. 857.

Holidays and Civic Days

21 Battle of Iquique Day, or Navy Day, a holiday in Chile celebrating victory in the naval battle of May 21, 1879; the day honors the Chilean navy. 875.

Anniversaries and Special Events Days

21 Anniversary of the organization of the American Red Cross, on May 21, 1881, by Clara Barton, who became its first president. 268.

21 Birthday of Glenn Hammond Curtiss (May 21, 1878–July 23, 1930). American aviator and aeronautical inventor who set many pioneer flying records, established the first flying school, and invented the flying boat and the first heavier-than-air craft intended for transatlantic flight. 864.

21 Birthday of Albrecht Dürer (May 21, 1471–April 6, 1528). German painter and printmaker; the major artist of German Renaissance altarpieces, religious works, and engravings. 864.

21 Birthday of Elizabeth Gurney Fry (May 21, 1780–October 12, 1845). English prison reformer who founded an association to improve conditions for women prisoners at Newgate. 738.

21 The Anasternarides Feast, celebrated at Macedonia in Greece in accordance with classic and Byzantine traditions, including the old barefoot dance on beds of coals.

21 Lilies and Roses Day, observed annually at the Tower of London in commemoration of the May 21, 1471, death of Henry VI, founder of both Eton College and King's College; services are attended by representatives of the two colleges carrying lilies and roses for the traditional ceremonial. 256.

21 Lindbergh Flight Day, commemorating the landing of Charles A. Lindbergh in Paris on May 21, 1927, which concluded the first successful nonstop transatlantic flight. 268, 473, 866.

21 Birthday of Alexander Pope (May 21, 1688–May 30, 1744). English poet and essayist known for his *Essay on Man*; outstanding satirist of the English Augustan period. 864.

Holy Days and Feast Days

22 Feast of Saint Julia of Corsica, a slave who was tortured and crucified for her faith; a patron saint of Corsica. 4, 9.

22 Feast Day of Saint Rita of Cascia, called La Abogada de Impossibles, "the saint of desperate cases," in Spanish-speaking countries. 4, 9.

Holidays and Civic Days

22 Sovereignty and Thanksgiving Day, a holiday in Haiti honoring the head of state, the Haitian culture, and the traditions of thanksgiving. 875.

22 Heroes Day, a holiday in the Democratic Socialist Republic of Sri Lanka, a day honoring the citizens who sacrificed their lives for their country in the insurrection of 1971. Sri Lanka ratified its basic constitution on May 22, 1972. 875.

Anniversaries and Special Events Days

22 Birthday of Mary Cassatt (May 22, 1844–June 14, 1926). American artist noted for her pictures of mothers and children at home. 738.

22 Birthday of Sir Arthur Conan Doyle (May 22, 1859–July 7, 1930). British novelist known as the creator of the fictional detective Sherlock Holmes of Baker Street; observed by the Baker Street Irregulars and other Sherlock Holmes societies. 864.

c22 Jumping Frog Jubilee Day, an event featuring a frog-jumping contest inspired by a Mark Twain short story; observed around May 22 at Angel's Camp, California. 268.

22 National Maritime Day, a presidential proclamation day honoring the SS *Savannah* which made the first transatlantic voyage under steam propulsion in 1819. 268, 269, 866.

22 Birthday of Richard Wagner (May 22, 1813–February 13, 1883). German composer famous for *Tannhäuser, Lohengrin, Parsifal,* and *The Ring of the Nibelungs.* 817.

Holy Days and Feast Days

23 Declaration of Bab, a holy day in the Baha'i faith, commemorating Bab's prophecy of the coming of a spiritual leader who would inaugurate a new era in religious history. 1, 854.

23 Feast Day of Saint Ivo of Chartres, patron saint of lawyers. 9.

Holidays and Civic Days

23 Jamaican Labour Day, a public holiday in Jamaica in tribute to the Jamaican worker. 875.

23 South Carolina Admission Day. South Carolina entered the Union on May 23, 1788, as the eighth state. 268, 856, 862.

Anniversaries and Special Events Days

23 Birthday of James Buchanan Eads (May 23, 1820–March 8, 1887). American engineer and inventor. One of his major achievements was the construction of the Eads Bridge at St. Louis, Missouri. He was elected to the Hall of Fame for Great Americans in 1920. 864.

23 Birthday of Margaret Fuller (May 23, 1810–July 19, 1850). American writer and critic who is credited as being the first professional book-review editor, with columns running in the *New York Tribune* beginning in 1844. 738.

23 Birthday of Carolus Linnaeus (May 23, 1707–January 10, 1778). Swedish naturalist who developed new methods of classifying plants; his *Species Plantarum* is the official bible of botanical nomenclature. His home and gardens in Uppsala are maintained as a monument and memorial. 864.

c23 Mayoring Day in Rye, Sussex, England, a ceremonial day in late May that carries on the old custom of the hot-penny scramble in which the new mayor tosses hot pennies to children; a ritual that may go back to the time when Rye minted its own coins and they were distributed hot from the molds. 262.

Holidays and Civic Days

24 Independence Battle Day, a holiday in Ecuador, commemorating the Battle of Pinchincha which liberated Ecuador from Spanish rule on May 24, 1822. 868, 875.

c24 Victoria Day, or Empire Day, is celebrated in England to commemorate the birth of Queen Victoria on May 24, 1819; ceremonies and customs reflect life in far-flung posts of the British Commonwealth. It is a public holiday in the countries of the British Commonwealth on varying days in May. It is observed in Canada on the first Monday preceding May 25 to honor Victoria and to pay tribute to the reigning monarch's "official" birthday. 875.

Anniversaries and Special Events Days

24 Bulgarian Day of Slavonic Letters, observed on May 24 in tribute to Bulgarian culture, education, and communications; also called Education Day.

c24 La Fête des Saintes Maries (Festival of the Holy Maries) on May 24–25 attracts thousands of gypsies for a holiday at Les Saintes-Maries-de-la-Mer in France, honoring their patron Sara and Saints Marie Jacobe and Marie Salome. 20, 34.

24 Birthday of Lillian M. Gilbreth (May 24, 1878–January 2, 1972). Engineer and pioneer in time-motion studies. Mother of twelve children, who became part of the American literary scene with the publication of *Cheaper by the Dozen* by Frank B. Gilbreth, Jr., and Ernestine Gilbreth Carey. 864.

24 Birthday of Jan Christian Smuts (May 24, 1870–September 11, 1950). South African soldier and statesman, originator of the concept of the British Commonwealth of Nations, leader in the establishment of the League of Nations and the United Nations. 864.

Holy Days and Feast Days

25 Feast of Saint Bede the Venerable; author of the *Ecclesiastical History of the English Nation*, a primary source of early English history; declared a doctor of the church in 1899. 4, 9, 14.

Holidays and Civic Days

25 Argentine National Day, a holiday in Argentina commemorating the revolts against Spain that began on May 25, 1810, securing a measure of autonomy and leading to an outright declaration of independence on July 9, 1816. 868, 875.

25 Africa Day, or African Freedom Day, or Africa Liberation Day, a holiday in the nations of Chad, Liberia, Mali, Mauritania, Zambia, and Zimbabwe. It is a day celebrating freedom from colonial rule and a day of appreciation of African cooperation. 868, 875.

25 OAU Day, a holiday in the Republic of Equatorial Guinea, honoring the Organization of African Unity which was created by thirty African leaders on May 25, 1963, to achieve, among other goals, a better life for the people of Africa. 868, 875.

25 Jordan Independence Day, a holiday in the Hashemite Kingdom of Jordan commemorating the establishment of a constitutional monarchy. 868, 875.

25 Sudanese Revolution Day, a holiday in Sudan honoring the May 25, 1969, assumption of governmental power by a 10-man Revolutionary Council. 868, 875.

Anniversaries and Special Events Days

25 Birthday of Ralph Waldo Emerson (May 25, 1803–April 27, 1882). American essayist, poet, and lecturer. Elected to the Hall of Fame for Great Americans in 1900. 293, 725, 782, 819.

25 Birthday of John Raleigh Mott (May 25, 1865–January 31, 1955). American religious and social worker; general secretary of the International Committee of the Young Men's Christian Association; organizer of the World's Student Christian Federation. Received the Nobel Peace Prize in 1946 with Emily Greene Balch. 1, 679.

25 Yugoslavian Day of Youth, a children's and young people's holiday celebrated in Yugoslavia on Marshall Tito's birthday; a day combining exhibits of children's work with other festivities. 875.

Holy Days and Feast Days

26 Feast of Saint Augustine of Canterbury, a sixth-century Benedictine monk who became the first archbishop of Canterbury; the feast is celebrated by the Anglican and Episcopal churches on May 26, and by the Roman Catholic church on May 27 as an optional memorial. 4, 9, 14

26 Feast of Saint Philip Neri, sixteenth-century founder of the Oratorians; restorer of the faith in secular Rome; the apostle of Rome who became the patron saint of Rome. 4, 9.

Holidays and Civil Days

26 Guyana Independence Day, an historic day in Guyana commemorating the agreement which gave independence on May 26, 1966, to the former British colony of British Guiana; the new name means "land of waters." 868, 875.

Anniversaries and Special Events Days

26 Anniversary of the transfer of the American Flag House, the Betsy Ross home, to the city of Philadelphia on May 26, 1941; a gift from the Betsy Ross Memorial Association.

26 Dunkirk Day, the anniversary of the May 26 to June 3, 1940, evacuation of the bulk of the British Expeditionary Force from Dunkerque on the coast of France to avoid total annihilation; the successful cooperation of civilian and naval craft in effecting the evacuation and the return of the force to England was called "a moral triumph in the face of a military catastrophe." 698, 719.

Holidays and Civic Days

c27 Confederate Memorial Day, observed in Virginia on the last Monday of May; observed in other southern states on varying dates during April and May. 875.

Anniversaries and Special Events Days

27 Birthday of Arnold Bennett (May 27, 1867–March 27, 1931). English novelist best known for *The Old Wives' Tale* and his Five Towns novels, set in the towns which make up the county borough of Stoke-on-Trent, England. 864.

27 Birthday of Amelia Jenks Bloomer (May 27, 1818–December 30, 1894). American social reformer who fought for temperance and women's rights but is remembered chiefly for her advocacy of "sensible" dress, which she demonstrated by the wearing of full trousers that came to be known as "bloomers." 864.

27 Birthday of Rachel Louise Carson (May 27, 1907–April 14, 1964). American biologist whose book *Silent Spring* published in 1962 aroused worldwide concern for the dangers of environmental polution. 735, 738.

27 Birthday of Isadora Duncan (May 27, 1878–September 14, 1927). American dancer who developed interpretive dancing through adaptations of the classical dances of Greece. 738.

27 Birthday of Julia Ward Howe (May 27, 1819–October 17, 1910). American author, social reformer, author of "The Battle Hymn of the Republic," and first woman member of the American Academy of Arts and Letters. 742.

27 Children's Day in Nigeria, honoring boys and girls of the more than one hundred distinct tribal communities that are a part of the Federation of Nigeria.

Anniversaries and Special Events Days

28 Birthday of Louis Agassiz (May 28, 1807–December 14, 1873). Swiss-born American teacher, naturalist, biologist, geologist, and ichthyologist. His bibliography consists of more than 425 published books and papers. Established the Museum of Comparative Zoology at Harvard, the model of all American natural-history museums, and founded the Anderson School of Natural History on Penikese Island, Buzzards Bay, Massachusetts, the forerunner of all marine and lacustral stations. Elected to the Hall of Fame for Great Americans in 1915. 268, 864.

Holy Days and Feast Days

29 Ascension of Baha'u'llah, the anniversary of the death on May 29, 1892, of the great spiritual leader of Baha'i; a holy day beginning at 3 A.M. on May 29 observed by Baha'is throughout the world. 1, 854.

Holidays and Civic Days

29 Rhode Island Admission Day. Rhode Island entered the Union on May 29, 1790, as the thirteenth state, the last of the thirteen original colonies to ratify the United States Constitution. 268, 856, 862.

29 Wisconsin Day, the anniversary of Wisconsin's becoming the thirtieth state of the Union, on May 29, 1848. 268, 856, 862.

Anniversaries and Special Events Days

29 Birthday of Gilbert Keith Chesterton (May 29, 1874–June 14, 1936). English journalist, novelist, poet, and critic; creator of the fictional priest-detective, Father Brown. 864.

29 Birthday of Patrick Henry (May 29, 1736–June 6, 1799). American Revolutionary statesman who said, "Give me Liberty or give me Death." He was elected to the Hall of Fame for Great Americans in 1920. 268, 867.

29 Birthday of John Fitzgerald Kennedy (May 29, 1917–November 22, 1963). Irish ancestry; World War II hero; Roman Catholic; Massachusetts senator; thirty-fifth president of the United States, 1961–63; author of *Profiles in Courage* and *A Nation of Immigrants*; assassinated in Dallas, Texas; buried in Arlington National Cemetery. 359–366, 369–372, 374, 379.

29 Oak Apple Day, or Royal Oak Day, or Nettle Day, observed in parts of England in honor of the May 29, 1660, restoration of King Charles II, saved from his pursuers in the Battle of Worcester by an oak apple tree. 256.

29 Anniversary of the adoption on May 29, 1916, of the official flag of the president of the United States. 280.

29 Royal Hospital Founder's Day, observed annually since 1692 by the Chelsea Pensioners at the Royal Hospital, Chelsea, London, in honor of the birthday of Charles II, founder of the hospital.

Holy Days and Feast Days

30 Feast Day of Saint Ferdinand III, patron saint of engineers. 4, 9.

30 Feast Day of Joan of Arc, commemorating the fifteenth-century Maid of Orleans, white-armored leader of the French forces fighting the British; a martyr of the Hundred Years' War; the second patron saint of France. 4, 9.

Anniversaries and Special Events Days

30 Birthday of Countee Cullen (May 30, 1903–January 9, 1946). American poet; a leader of the Harlem Renaissance; author of *The Black Christ and Other Poems* and *The Ballad of the Brown Girl*. 864.

c30 De Soto Landing Day, the anniversary of the landing in Florida, on May 30, 1539, of Hernando de Soto, Spanish explorer; celebrated with a week-long series of parades, historical pageants and balls at Bradenton, Florida. 268.

30 Birthday of Alice Sophia Stopford Green (May 30, 1847–May 28, 1929). Irish historian, champion of Irish independence who served in the first Irish senate from 1922 until her death; author of *The Making of Ireland and Its Undoing*.

30 Anniversary of the dedication of the Hall of Fame for Great Americans on the campus of New York University on May 30, 1901.

30 Anniversary of the dedication on May 30, 1922, of the Lincoln Memorial, designed by Henry Bacon and housing the seated Lincoln statue done by Daniel Chester French, in Washington, D.C. 339.

Holy Days and Feast Days

31 Feast of the Visitation, commemorates the visit of Mary to her cousin Elizabeth after the Annunciation and before the birth of John, the precursor of Christ; a feast that celebrates with the Magnificat, one of the few New Testament canticles. 5.

Holidays and Civic Days

31 Royal Brunei Malay Regiment Day, a holiday in Brunei celebrating the anniversary of the formation of the famous military regiment. 868, 875.

31 South African Republic Day, or Union Day, celebrated in the Union of South Africa as a public statutory holiday honoring the unification of the South African colonies in 1910 and the establishment of the republic in 1961. 868, 875.

c31 Spring Bank Holiday, celebrated in the United Kingdom on the last Monday of May; a day of sports, picnics, or engagement in old customs such as cheese rolling at Cooper's Hill, Gloucestershire, or Morris dancing at Bampton, Oxfordshire. 265.

c31 Memorial day, a holiday proclaimed annually by the president of the United States; observed by all states in the Union except South Carolina which observes Confederate Memorial day on May 10, and Virginia which observes Confederate Memorial day on May 31; the national Memorial day is observed by forty-eight states on the last Monday in May. 268, 269, 355–58, 609.

Anniversaries and Special Events Days

31 Johnstown Flood Day, the anniversary of the collapse of the Conemaugh Dam and the consequent flooding of Johnstown, Pennsylvania, on May 31, 1889, with a tragically high loss of life. 874.

31 Anniversary of the death of Tintoretto on May 31, 1594. Italian painter of the late Renaissance famous for *The Last Supper*. 864.

31 Birthday of Walt Whitman (May 21, 1819–March 26, 1892). American poet, author of the great elegy. "When Lilacs Last in the Dooryard Bloom'd" and the famous *Leaves of Grass*. Known as the "good gray poet," Whitman was elected to the Hall of Fame for Great Americans in 1930. 268.

June

June, the sixth month in the Gregorian calendar, was named according to legend for Juno, the goddess of women and of marriage. If this is true, it is an appropriate name since June is a favored month for weddings, although modern brides no longer necessarily cling to tradition. Some authorities, however, claim that the month was named for *Juniores*, the lower branch of the Roman senate, or that it was associated with the consulate of Junius Brutus.

Many traditional events are associated with the month of June. Among the most famous are the great flower festivals of the world. June has long been commencement time, when young people are graduated from schools and colleges. It is also the month when the British celebrate the official, not the real, birthday of Queen Elizabeth in order to assure favorable weather for the public ceremonies. The most ancient of June festivals are those associated with Midsummer Eve in northern countries where bonfires have added to the merrymaking and festivities from time immemorial.

The special flower for the month of June is the rose, and the gems are the moonstone, the pearl, and the alexandrite.

Holy Days and Feast Days

1 Feast of Saint Justin Martyr, the first Christian apologist; a layman martyred in Rome; patron saint of philosophers. 4.

Holidays and Civic Days

1 Cape Verde Children's Day, a holiday in the Republic of Cape Verde honoring the children living on the ten islands of the republic situated in the Atlantic Ocean. 875.

1 Kentucky Statehood Day is observed in many ways, from mountain laurel festivals to patriotic programs, in commemoration of the entrance of Kentucky into the Union as the fifteenth state on June 1, 1792. 268, 856, 862.

1 Madaraka Day, a public holiday in Kenya; also called Responsibility Day, or Self-Government Day, designed as a day for rejoicing in freedom. 875.

1 Samoan Independence Days, celebrated as holidays during the first three days in June to honor Western Samoan independence gained on January 1, 1962. The June days were chosen for the festivals to avoid the rainy season typical of January in Samoa. 875.

1 Tennessee Statehood Day, a commemoration of the admission on June 1, 1796, of Tennessee as the sixteenth state in the Union. 268, 856, 862.

1 Tunisian National Holiday, a two-day holiday commemorating the promulgation of the constitution of Tunisia on June 1, 1959. 868.

Anniversaries and Special Events Days

1 Birthday of Philip Kearny (June 1, 1814–September 1, 1862). American general; leader of the New Jersey Volunteers in the Civil War. He represents New Jersey in Statuary Hall in a sculpture by Henry Kirke Brown. 870.

1 Birthday of Jacques Marquette (June 1, 1937–May 18, 1675). French Jesuit missionary and explorer of the territory of the Wisconsin, Mississippi, and Illinois rivers. He represents the state of Wisconsin in a Statuary Hall sculpture by Gaetano Trentanove. 268, 870.

1 Birthday of John Masefield (June 1, 1878–May 12, 1967). Fifteenth British poet laureate; best known for poems of the sea such as *Salt Water Ballads*; awarded the Order of Merit in 1935. 864.

1 Mint Julep Day, the anniversary of the June 1, 1845, introduction of mint juleps to New College, Oxford, by William Trapier of South Carolina; a festival day that has continued through the years with the use of Trapier's own recipe.

1 Elfreth's Alley Day, observed in Philadelphia with an open house on the oldest residential street in the United States.

1 Birthday of Brigham Young (June 1, 1801–August 29, 1877). American Mormon leader; president of the Morman church; founder of Salt Lake City. 268, 864.

Holy Days and Feast Days

2 Feast Day of Saint Erasmus, patron saint of sailors. It is frequently called Saint Elmo's Day. 4, 9.

Holidays and Civic Days

2 Italian Republic Day, an historic day in Italy commemorating the proclamation of the republic established by the referendum of June 2, 1946. The majority vote was cast for the republic as opposed to the retention of the monarchy. 868.

2 Supreme Head of State's Birthday, a holiday in Malaysia honoring the birthday of the Yang di-Pertuan. 875.

2 Youth Day, a holiday in Tunisia, honoring the young people of the nation. 875.

Anniversaries and Special Events Days

2 Birthday of Thomas Hardy (June 2, 1840–January 11, 1928). English novelist and poet, author of *The Return of the Native* and other novels. 790.

2 Seaman's Day, celebrated in Iceland to honor the nation's sailors and fishermen who represent the lifeline of the country's economy.

Holidays and Civic Days

3 Confederate Memorial Day, a holiday in Louisiana, honoring the soldiers who died in the Civil War. 875.

Anniversaries and Special Events Days

c3 Jefferson Davis Day. Birthday of Jefferson Davis (June 3, 1808–December 6, 1889). American soldier, legislator, and president of the Confederate States of America. His birthday is celebrated in Alabama, Florida, Georgia, Louisiana, Mississippi, and South Carolina. Alabama and Mississippi observe the day on the first Monday in June. In Arkansas, Jefferson Davis's birthday is a memorial day. Jefferson Davis represents the state of Mississippi in Statuary Hall in a sculpture done by Augustus Lukeman. 268, 269, 870.

c3 Jack Jouett Day, observed in Virginia to honor the anniversary of the June 3, 1781, ride of Jack Jouett from Cuckoo Tavern to Charlottesville to warn Thomas Jefferson of the approach of the British and to allow for his escape. 268.

3 Memorial to Broken Dolls Day, a Buddhist ceremony in Japan attended by little girls and their mothers, at which time all broken dolls are enshrined by a priest. 251.

3 The anniversary of the June 3–6, 1942, Battle of Midway, the brilliant American campaign which shattered the Japanese fleet and turned the tide in the war in the Pacific. 417.

Holidays and Civic Days

4 Labour Day, a holiday in the Bahamas, celebrated with pageantry, parades, picnics, and colorful displays. 875.

4 Flag Day of the Finnish Armed Forces, commemorating the June 4, 1867, birth of Marshall Carl Gustaf Mannerheim, Finland's great military leader.

4 Emancipation Day in the Kingdom of Tonga, a holiday celebrating June 4, 1970, when Tonga became fully independent. 868, 875.

Holy Days and Feast Days

5 Feast Day of Saint Boniface, patron saint of Germany, celebrated in the Roman Catholic and the Anglican churches in honor of the missionary who is known as "the apostle of Germany." 4, 9.

Holidays and Civic Days

5   Denmark Consitution Day, a holiday honoring the constitution signed on June 5, 1849, and the new constitution adopted on June 5, 1953. 868, 875.

5   President's Birthday, a holiday in the Republic of Equatorial Guinea celebrating the birth of President Teodoro Oblang Nguema Mbasogo. 875.

5   Seychelles Liberation Day, a national holiday in the Seychelles Islands celebrating a coup on June 5, 1977, which changed the government leadership. 868, 875.

Anniversaries and Special Events Days

5   Birthday of John Couch Adams, (June 5, 1819–January 21, 1892). English astronomer who first observed the planet Neptune. The Adams Prize, awarded biannually at Cambridge University, commemorates his discovery. 864.

5   Birthday of George Thorndike Angell (June 5, 1823–March 16, 1909). American lawyer; pioneer reformer in crime prevention; one of the founders of the American Humane Education Society.

5   Birthday of Ruth Fulton Benedict (June 5, 1887–September 17, 1948). American anthropologist and humanist whose book *Chrysanthemum and the Sword* aided in the determination of American policy toward the Japanese following World War II. 738.

5   Birthday of Jabez Lamar Monroe Curry (June 5, 1825–February 12, 1903). American educator and statesman; president of the Southern Educational Board; the founder of grade schools and normal schools throughout the South. He represents the state of Alabama in Statuary Hall in a sculpture by Dante Sodini. 870.

5   Anniversary of the beginning of the Six-Day War, June 5–10, 1967, between Israel and the forces of Egypt, Syria, and Jordan. 874.

5   Anniversary of the baptism of Adam Smith (June 5, 1723–July 17, 1790). Scottish economist and philosopher celebrated for his *Inquiry into the Nature and Causes of the Wealth of Nations*. 864.

5   World Environment Day, observed by the members of the United Nations in accordance with a resolution of the June 1972 Stockholm Conference on the Human Environment supporting a day on which all people may undertake activities reaffirming the worldwide need for the preservation of the environment. 866.

Holidays and Civic Days

6   Korean Memorial Day, a holiday in the Republic of Korea honoring the victims of war with memorial services at the National Cemetery in Seoul. 875.

6   Constitution and Flag Day in Sweden, recognizing the adoption of the Swedish constitution of June 6, 1809, and honoring June 6, 1523, when Gustavus I ascended the throne. 868, 875.

Anniversaries and Special Events Days

6   Allied Landing Observances Day at Normandy, France, honoring D Day, June 6, 1944, when the Allies invaded Europe under the command of Dwight Eisenhower.

6   Birthday of Pierre Corneille (June 6, 1606-October 1, 1684). French dramatist whose masterful plays are frequently revived on the modern stage. 864.

6   Birthday of Nathan Hale (June 6, 1755–September 22, 1776). American soldier, known as the "martyr spy" of the American Revolution, who spoke the words "I only regret that I have but one life to lose for my country." 268.

6   Birthday of Thomas Mann (June 6, 1875–August 12, 1955). German novelist famous for *Buddenbrooks*, for four novels about the biblical Joseph, and for *The Magic Mountain*; awarded the Nobel Prize in literature in 1929. 864.

6   Birthday of Aleksandr Sergeyevich Pushkin (June 6, 1799–February 10, 1837). Russian poet frequently called "the founder of modern Russian literature." 864.

c6   The annual Sibelius festival is held in Helsinki, Finland, around June 6 in tribute to the nation's greatest composer. 849.

6 Birthday of John Trumbull (June 6, 1756–November 10, 1843). American painter known for the historical paintings in the rotunda of the Capitol in Washington and for portraits of Washington, Adams, and Jefferson. 864.

6 Anniversary of the baptism of Diego Velásquez on about June 6, 1599. Spanish painter famous for portraits of Philip IV, and of princes, admirals, jesters, and dwarfs. 864.

6 YMCA Founding Day, the anniversary of the founding on June 6, 1844, of the Young Men's Christian Association; founded by George Williams of London, the organization spread over the globe in the twentieth century, with the YMCA established in eighty-six countries by the end of the 1970s. 268.

Holidays and Civic Days

7 Foundation Day, a public holiday in Western Australia commemorating the 1838 creation of the colony that became a part of the Commonwealth of Australia in 1900. 875.

Anniversaries and Special Events Days

7 Birthday of Susan Elizabeth Blow (June 7, 1843–March 26, 1916). American educator who pioneered in the establishment of public kindergartens and training schools for kindergarten teachers; called the "mother of the kindergarten in the public schools of the United States." 867.

7 Boone Day, the anniversary of the day, June 7, 1769, when Daniel Boone, the great frontiersman first saw the forests and woodlands of present-day Kentucky; observed annually by Kentucky Historical Society. 268.

7 Birthday of Paul Gauguin (June 7, 1848–May 8, 1903). French painter and author who described his life in Tahiti in *Noa Noa* and *Intimate Journals*. 864.

Anniversaries and Special Events Days

8 Birthday of Frank Lloyd Wright (June 8, 1867–April 9, 1959). American architect famous for the Imperial Hotel in Japan, the Solomon R. Guggenheim Museum in New York, and other buildings. Wright established the Taliesin Fellowship for experimentation in the arts. 268, 771.

Holy Days and Feast Days

9 Feast Day of Saint Columba, Abbot of Iona, secondary patron of Ireland, who is associated with the story of how the robin got its red breast by pulling out the thorns piercing the Lord's forehead on the day of the Crucifixion. 4, 9.

9 Feast of Saint Ephraem, fourth-century Syrian known for his writings and for the introduction of hymns in public worship; creator of Nisibeian hymns and canticles and called "the harp of the Holy Spirit"; declared a doctor of the church in 1920. 4, 9.

Anniversaries and Special Events Days

9 Birthday of John Howard Payne (June 9, 1791–April 9, 1852). American songwriter, playwright, and actor, remembered for writing "Home, Sweet Home." 864.

9 Senior Citizens Day, observed in Oklahoma, to honor older Americans and their contributions to society. 857.

9 Birthday of George Stephenson (June 9, 1781–August 12, 1848). English inventor who perfected the locomotive. 864.

Holidays and Civic Days

10 Portugal National Day, or Camões Memorial Day, a national fete day in Portugal and its territories commemorating the death on June 10, 1580, of Luiz Vaz de Camões, Portugal's immortal poet. 875.

Anniversaries and Special Events Days

10 Anniversary of the establishment of Alcoholics Anonymous, founded by William G. Wilson and Dr. Robert Smith on June 10, 1935. 866.

10 Lidice Day, anniversary of the razing of the village of Lidice in Czechoslovakia and the massacre of its people by the Nazis on June 10, 1942.

c10 Rose Day at Manheim, Pennsylvania, observed on the second Sunday of June; an annual ritual fulfilling the terms of the deed for the Lutheran church from Baron William Stiegel, which requires that the church pay "Therefor unto the said Henry William Steigel, his heirs or assigns . . . the rent of one red rose if demanded."

Holy Days and Feast Days

11 Feast of Saint Barnabas, originally named Joseph and renamed Barnabas by the apostles; served with Paul as a missionary in the Middle East and Asia Minor. 4, 9.

Holidays and Civic Days

11 King Kamehameha Day, a holiday in Hawaii celebrating with many festivities the victories and achievements of King Kamehameha I who unified the Hawaiian Islands in the eighteenth century. 268, 811.

11 American Bases Evacuation Day, a holiday in Libya celebrating the closing of U.S. facilities at Wheelus Air Force Base near Tripoli on June 11, 1970. 875.

c11 Queen Elizabeth's Birthday, a holiday in the Solomon Islands honoring the official birthday of Britain's queen, held in England in June by proclamation. 875.

Anniversaries and Special Events Days

11 Birthday of Ben Jonson (June 11, 1572–August 6, 1637). English playwright and poet famous for *Volpone*, or *The Fox*, and other important plays of the Elizabethan period. 864.

11 Birthday of Jeannette Rankin (June 11, 1880–May 18, 1973). American pacifist, crusader for social and election reform, first woman member of the Congress of the United States. 738, 864.

Holy Days and Feast Days

12 Feast of Saint Leo III, the ninth-century pope who crowned Charlemagne in Rome, an act that founded the Holy Roman Empire; a patron of the arts who helped rebuild and decorate churches in Rome and Ravenna. 4, 9

Holidays and Civic Days

12 Helsinki Day, celebrated in Finland since 1959 to commemorate the founding of the city of Helsinki in 1550. 849.

12 Peace with Bolivia Day, a holiday in Paraguay honoring the peace settlement of 1938 that officially ended the 1932–35 war with Bolivia over disputed ownership of the Chaco Boreal. 868, 875.

12 Philippine Independence Day, a public holiday since 1962, commemorating June 12, 1898, when independence from Spain was declared. 868, 875.

c12 Official, or public, birthday of Elizabeth II; scheduled for late May or early June by proclamation in the hope of assurance of favorable weather for the ceremonies held at the Parade Ground behind St. James Park. The ceremony includes Trooping the Color, the most brilliant and imposing of all British military parades. The queen's actual birth date is April 21, 1926. 875.

Anniversaries and Special Events Days

12 Birthday of Anne Frank (June 12, 1929–March [?], 1945). German-Dutch adolescent of sensitivity and talent whose diary of two years of hiding from the Germans was published under the title *The Diary of a Young Girl*; the exact day of her death is unknown. 864.

12 Birthday of Charles Kingsley (June 12, 1819–January 23, 1875). English clergyman, novelist, and poet remembered for the novels *Westward Ho!* and *Hereward the Wake*. 864.

Holy Days and Feast Days

13 Feast of Saint Anthony of Padua, a Franciscan friar and the order's first lector in theology, a famous preacher known by his contemporaries as "the hammer of the heretics"; declared a doctor of the church in 1946; the patron saint of the poor and the oppressed. Alms gathered on his feast day are called "Saint Anthony's bread." 4, 9.

Holidays and Civic Days

13 Saint Anthony's Day, a religious holiday in Lisbon, Portugal, where Anthony of Padua was born; commemorates the memory of a great advocate of the poor and the helpless. Saint Anthony's Day is also the occasion for religious and festival celebrations in many localities in the United States where churches are named for Saint Anthony. 875.

13 Reform Movement Day, a holiday in the Yemen Arab Republic commemorating the anniversary of the 1974 reforms leading to the establishment of a central government. 868, 875.

Anniversaries and Special Events Days

c13 Children's Day, traditionally observed in the United States on the second Sunday in June or on the last day of the Sunday-school year; a day of dedication to children and of participation of children and young people in the church services of many denominations. 857.

c13 Race Unity Day, dedicated to the basic principle that the achievement of understanding and unity among the races of the world will be the foundation of permanent peace; sponsored by the Baha'is and observed on the second Sunday in June. 857.

13 Birthday of William Butler Yeats (June 13, 1865–January 29, 1939). Irish poet, dramatist and leader of the Irish literary revival; received the Nobel Prize in literature in 1923. 864.

Holidays and Civic Days

c14 Queen Elizabeth's Day, a holiday in Australia and in Fiji celebrating the birthday of Britain's queen; held on a Monday near the day the celebration is officially observed in England. 875.

14 Flag Day, a holiday in Pennsylvania honoring the flag of the United States with special events and flag displays. 875.

Anniversaries and Special Events Days

14 Anniversary of the first presentation of the Caldecott Medal; awarded annually to the artist of the most distinguished American picture book for children published in the United States during the preceding year; first presented on June 14, 1938, to Dorothy P. Lathrop for *Animals of the Bible*. 858, 863.

14 Anniversary of the establishment of the Canadian Library Association (Association Canadienne des Bibliothèques) on June 14, 1946.

14 Flag Day is observed in the United States to commemorate the adoption of the Stars and Stripes by the Continental Congress on June 14, 1777. Flag Day has been a legal holiday in Pennsylvania since 1937; observed by all other states through the display of the flag on public buildings and homes or special programs. 269, 280–88.

14 Birthday of Robert Marion La Follette (June 14, 1855–June 18, 1925). American statesman, reform leader, presidential candidate for the Progressive party; exponent of the "Wisconsin idea." He represents the state of Wisconsin in Statuary Hall in a sculpture done by Jo Davidson. 870.

14 Anniversary of the day, June 14, 1954, when the pledge of allegiance to the flag of the United States was amended by Congress and approved by President Eisenhower to add the words "under God," so that the last line of the pledge now reads "One Nation under God indivisible, with liberty and justice for all." 281.

14 Birthday of Harriet Elizabeth Beecher Stowe (June 14, 1811–July 1, 1896). American novelist and humanitarian; author of *Uncle Tom's Cabin*. Elected to the Hall of Fame for Great Americans in 1910. 738, 864.

Holy Days and Feast Days

15 Feast Day of Saint Vitus, patron saint of dancers, actors, comedians, and epilepsy sufferers. 4, 9.

Holidays and Civic Days

15 Arkansas Admission Day. Arkansas was admitted to the Union as the twenty-fifth state on June 15, 1836. 268, 856, 862.

Anniversaries and Special Events Days

15 Birthday of Edvard Grieg (June 15, 1843–September 4, 1907). Norwegian composer who established a new musical image for his country; famous for the *Peer Gynt* suites and arrangements of songs and Norwegian dances; commemorated annually by the Grieg music festivals in Norway. 864.

15 Idaho Pioneer Day has been a legal holiday since 1910 and commemorates with picnics, pioneer reunions, and other festivities the founding of the first permanent white settlement at Franklin on June 15, 1860. 268.

15 Indian Citizenship Day, anniversary of the passage of a law by Congress on June 15, 1924, granting citizenship to American Indians. 874.

15 Farmer's Day, observed in Korea, and official day for the transplanting of rice seedlings.

15 Magna Charta Day, anniversary of the day, June 15, 1215, when King John signed the Magna Charta, the first important document in the history of human freedom. 20, 857.

15 Oregon Treaty Day, anniversary of the signing of the Oregon Treaty on June 15, 1846, by the United States and Great Britain, to fix the northwest boundary at the 49th parallel extending to the Pacific. 268.

15 Valdemar's Day, commemorating the victory of King Valdemar's troops on June 15, 1219, observed throughout Denmark. It is also the Danish Flag Day, honoring the oldest flag in the world, one which, according to legend, came down from heaven to bring victory to King Valdemar. 280, 868, 875.

Holy Days and Feast Days

16 Feast Day of the Madonna of Carmine, a Neapolitan saint said to heal ailments in various parts of the body; observed in Italy and by Italian Americans.

Anniversaries and Special Events Days

16 Bloomsday, a day of appreciation of James Joyce which attracts scholars and admirers to gatherings in Dublin; a commemorative day recalling the June 16, 1904, events associated with Leopold Bloom, a major character in Joyce's *Ulysses*. 833.

16 Soweto Day, proclaimed by the United Nations General Assembly as a day of solidarity with the struggling people of South Africa and as a memorial of the 1976 protest of the oppressed peoples of Soweto, South Africa. 868.

16 Tereshkova Day, the anniversary of the piloting of a Russian space craft by Valentina Tereshkove, the first woman in space. The flight lasted from June 16 to June 19, 1963. 874.

Holidays and Civic Days

17 Bunker Hill Day, a holiday in Boston and Suffolk County, Massachusetts, commemorating the June 17, 1775, Battle of Bunker Hill; celebrated with commemorative services, parades, exhibitions, and dinners. 268.

17 National Day, a holiday in the Federal Republic of Germany; a day of prayer in West Germany dedicated to the goals of German unity. 875.

17 Iceland Independence Day, a holiday commemorating the establishment of Iceland as a republic on June 17, 1944, and honoring the birth on June 17, 1811, of Jon Sigurdsson, the nation's outstanding nineteenth-century leader. 868, 875.

Anniversaries and Special Events Days

17 Birthday of Charles Gounod (June 17, 1818–October 18, 1893). French composer whose Marguerite in the opera *Faust* was the first operatic role for a lyric soprano. 864.

17 Children's Day, observed as National Children's Day in Indonesia with carefully planned recreational and cultural programs for children presented at the end of the school day. 875.

17 Birthday of James Weldon Johnson (June 17, 1871–June 26, 1938). American poet and anthologist; first black to be admitted to the Florida bar; founder and secretary of the National Association for the Advancement of Colored People; awarded the Spingarn Medal in 1925.

17 Okinawa Day, the anniversary of the signing on June 17, 1971, of a treaty between the United States and Japan returning Okinawa, seized during World War II, to Japan. 874.

17 Anniversary of the establishment of the Union of Kalmar, created by Queen Margaret of Denmark on June 17, 1397, for the purpose of unifying Denmark, Norway, and Sweden in the interest of lasting and unbroken peace.

17 Watergate Day, anniversary of the June 17, 1972, break-in at the Democratic Headquarters in Washington; occasioned the congressional investigations of 1972–74. 268

17 Birthday of John Wesley (June 17, 1703–March 2, 1791). English evangelical preacher; founder of Methodism; influential leader in the eighteenth-century revival movement in North America. 20, 34.

Holidays and Civic Days

18 Evacuation Day, a holiday in the Arab Republic of Egypt commemorating the 1956 departure of the last of the British occupation troops from their Suez Canal bases. 875.

Anniversaries and Special Events Days

18 Birthday of Henry Clay Folger (June 18, 1857–June 11, 1930). American industrialist; collector of Shakespeareana, now bequeathed to the American people in the Folger Shakespeare Library in Washington, D.C. 864.

18 Anniversary of the adoption of the Library Bill of Rights by the Council of the American Library Association, June 18, 1948.

18 War of 1812 Declaration Day, the anniversary of the June 18, 1812, declaration by Congress of war with Great Britain; a war resulting from Britain's violation of American rights on the high seas. 268.

18 Waterloo Day, anniversary of the Battle of Waterloo, lost by Napoleon in 1815. 660.

Holidays and Civic Days

19 Algeria Righting Day, a holiday in Algeria, commemorating the overthrow on June 19, 1965, of the Ben Bella government and the establishment of a governing Revolutionary Council. 868, 875.

19 Independence Day in the State of Kuwait, a civic day noting the establishment of sovereignty on June 19, 1961, and the termination of an 1899 treaty with Britain. 868, 875.

19 Laos Independence Day, a holiday commemorating the treaty of July 19, 1949, through which Laos became a sovereign state within the French union, with full sovereignty achieved on December 24, 1954. 868.

19 Emancipation Day, or Juneteenth Day, a holiday in Texas commemorating June 19, 1865, when Texas slaves were told of the Emancipation Proclamation, more than two years after the act was signed. 268.

19 Labour Day, a holiday in the Republic of Trinidad and Tobago celebrated with festivals and sports which are outstanding elements in the culture of the two islands. 875.

19 Artigas Day, the anniversary of the June 19, 1764, birth of General José Gervasio Artigas, father of Uruguayan independence; a public holiday in Uruguay. 868, 875.

Anniversaries and Special Events Days

19 Birthday of Sir John Barrow (June 19, 1764–November 23, 1848). English geographer; chief founder of the Royal Geographical Society in 1830. 864.

c19 Father's Day. The first Father's Day was held on June 19, 1910. The idea originated with Mrs. John Bruce Dodd and was promoted by the Ministerial Association and the YMCA of Spokane, Washington. Father's Day was officially approved by President Calvin Coolidge in 1924. The rose is the official Father's Day flower—a white rose for remembrance, a red rose for the living. Father's Day is now observed on the third Sunday in June. 268, 269, 582, 588, 714, 866.

19 Birthday of Blaise Pascal (June 19, 1623–August 19, 1662). French philosopher, mathematician, and scientist whose work on the pressure of liquids resulted in Pascal's law. 864.

Holidays and Civic Days

c20 Flag Day, a holiday in Argentina honoring the national flag with a history that goes back to 1812; observed annually on or near June 20. 280.

20 West Virginia Admission Day. West Virginia entered the Union on June 20, 1863, as the thirty-fifth state; a legal holiday. 268, 856, 862.

Anniversaries and Special Events Days

20 Bald Eagle Day, proclaimed by President Reagan in 1982 as National Bald Eagle Day, a special day in a year-long observance of the Bicentennial Year of the American Bald Eagle. The Bald Eagle was approved on June 20, 1782, by Congress as the emblem for the Great Seal of the United States. 834.

20 Anniversary of the establishment of the Lifesaving Medal of the United States, awarded by the Treasury Department, authorized by Act of Congress on June 20, 1874. The first award was presented to Lucian M. Clemons, keeper of the United States Lifesaving Service Station, on June 19, 1876, for saving the men of the schooner *Conseulo* on May 1, 1875. 458.

c20 Anniversary of the first of the famous Portland rose festivals on June 20, 1907, in Portland, Oregon, with exhibitions of roses and a "human rosebud" parade. It has been held ever since during the rose season in June. 268.

20 Birthday of Helen Miller Shepard (June 20, 1868–December 21, 1938). American philanthropist whose many gifts included the establishment of a Hall of Fame for Great Americans at New York University in 1900.

Holy Days and Feast Days

21 Feast of Saint Aloysius Gonzaga, sixteenth-century Jesuit teacher of catechism to the poor and provider of aid to plague victims; declared "protector of young students" by Pope Benedict XIII and patron of Catholic youth by Pope Pius XI. 4, 9.

Holidays and Civic Days

21 New Hampshire Admission Day. New Hampshire entered the Union on June 21, 1788, the ninth of the thirteen original United States. 268, 856, 862.

Anniversaries and Special Events Days

21 Birthday of Daniel Carter Beard (June 21, 1850–June 11, 1941). American naturalist, writer, and illustrator who organized the first Boy Scout troop in the United States. 864.

21 Birthday of Rockwell Kent (June 21, 1882–March 13, 1971). American painter and illustrator of the American scene; one of the most popular artists of the first half of the twentieth century. 864.

Holy Days and Feast Days

c22 Feast Day of Saint Alban, early Christian martyr of Britain, celebrated with an annual rose festival at Saint Alban's Cathedral, Hertfordshire, England. 14.

22 Feast of Saint Paulinus of Nola, fifth-century bishop of Nola in Italy; known for his charities and for his poetry. Honored as one of the foremost Latin poets of the patristic period. His feast day is celebrated in conjunction with an annual Lilies of Nola spectacle in Nola, Italy. 4, 9.

22 Feast Day of Saint Thomas More, English humanist and martyr. A medal is presented annually in his name by the Thomas More Association for the most distinguished contribution to Catholic publishing during the year. 14.

Holidays and Civic Days

22 Schoolteachers Day in El Salvador, a public holiday. 875.

c22 Organic Act Day, a holiday in the Virgin Islands in honor of the Organic Act, or constitution granted the islands by the United States on June 22, 1936; celebrated on or near June 22. 868, 875.

22 Corrective Move Day, a holiday in the People's Democratic Republic of Yemen honoring the reforms of June 1974 which strengthened a central government. 868, 875.

Holy Days and Feast Days

23 Feast Day of Saint Joseph Cafasso, patron saint of prisons. 9.

Holidays and Civic Days

23 Midsummer Eve, a time of rejoicing and merriment over the return of summer; a holiday in Finland and in Sweden. 849.

23 Luxembourg National Day, a public holiday with major celebrations in Luxembourg City celebrating the official birthday of the grand duke. 875.

Anniversaries and Special Events Days

23 Birthday of Irvin Shrewsbury Cobb (June 23, 1876–March 10, 1944). American author, actor, and humorist; the first winner of the O. Henry Award for the best short story of the year in 1922. 864.

23 Midsummer Eve, a time of festivity, revivals of ancient rituals and the burning of bonfires in parts of Great Britain; observed by such groups as the Companions of the Most Ancient Order of Druids. 256.

23 Birthday of Carl Milles (June 23, 1875–September 19, 1955). Swedish-American sculptor whose monumental sculpture is to be found in Europe and the United States. The *Meeting of the Waters* at St. Louis is a good example of his work. 864.

Holy Days and Feast Days

24 Solemnity of Saint John the Baptist, commemorating the birth of the precursor of the Messiah; the only saint except the Blessed Virgin Mary whose birthday is honored with a religious feast; his death is commemorated on August 29. 4, 9

Holidays and Civic Days

c24 Newfoundland Discovery Day, a holiday in Newfoundland celebrating its discovery on June 24, 1497, by John Cabot; observed on or near the discovery date. 875.

24 Saint Jean Baptise Day, a major holiday in Quebec, Canada; a day of religious observance and of spectacular gaiety involving parades, street dancing, carnival events, bonfires, and fireworks. 875.

24 San Juan Day, a civic festival in Puerto Rico honoring Saint John the Baptist with concerts, street dances, and night-long beach parties concluding with a church service at dawn. San Juan Day is also celebrated with comparable customs in New York City, in California, and in other sections of North America that have large Hispanic-American populations. 875.

24 Midsummer Day, a festive time of rejoicing over the return of summer; a holiday in Sweden continuing the merriment of Midsummer Eve.

24 Battle of Carabobo Day, a holiday in Venezuela commemorating a battle of the Venezuelan war of independence fought at Carabobo, west of Caracas, on June 24, 1821, which assured the freedom of Venezuela. 868.

24 Fisherman's Day, a holiday in Zaire celebrating not only the Day of Fishers but also the promulgation of the constitution and the establishment of currency. 868, 875.

Anniversaries and Special Events Days

24 Birthday of Henry Ward Beecher (June 24, 1813–March 8, 1887). American Congregational clergyman, reformer, lecturer, and author. Elected to Hall of Fame for Great Americans in 1900. 268, 813.

24 Berlin Airlift Day, the anniversary of the June 24, 1948, start of the U.S. airlift of supplies to Berlin blockaded by the communists. The blockade ended on May 12, 1949. 874.

24 Birthday of Horatio Herbert Kitchener (June 24, 1850–June 5, 1916). British military leader who avenged the death of General Gordon and became a national hero in 1898; one of the twelve original members of the Order of Merit. 864.

24 Day of the Indian, or Dia del Indio, celebrated in Peru and other Latin American countries to preserve and enjoy native customs, musical contests, folklore, and poetry, horsemanship exhibits, sports, and general feasting.

24 Inti Raymi pageant, the Feast of the Sun, celebrated annually in Cuzco, Peru; a re-creation of an ancient Inca ceremony with ovations and homage to the sun.

24 Bannockburn Day in Scotland, commemorates June 24, 1314, when Robert Bruce won independence for Scotland by expelling the English. 844.

Holidays and Civic Days

25 Independence Day, a public holiday in the People's Republic of Mozambique, which achieved independence on June 25, 1975, thus ending 477 years of Portuguese control of a country that was first colonized in 1505. 868, 875.

25 Virginia Ratification Day. Virginia entered the Union on June 25, 1788, the tenth of the thirteen original United States to do so. 268, 856, 862.

Anniversaries and Special Events Days

25 Custer Day, anniversary of "Custer's last stand" at the Battle of the Little Big Horn, Montana, on June 25, 1876. 268.

Holidays and Civic Days

26 Madagascar Independence Day, a holiday in the Democratic Republic of Madagascar located in the Indian Ocean off the southeast coast of Africa. The nation achieved independence on June 26, 1960. 868, 875.

26 Somalia Independence Day, a public holiday in the African east-coast republic, commemorating the June 26, 1960, agreement on Somali self-government. 868, 875.

Anniversaries and Special Events Days

26 Birthday of Bernard Berenson (June 26, 1865–October 6, 1959). American art critic whose *Italian Painters of the Renaissance* was the most influential book in its field in the twentieth century. 801.

26 Birthday of Pearl Buck (June 26, 1892–March 6, 1973). American author noted for *The Good Earth* and other novels of life in China; recipient of the Nobel Prize in literature in 1938. 864.

26 Anniversary of the dedication of the Mackinac Straits Bridge connecting Lower and Upper Michigan on June 26, 1958.

26 Anniversary of the creation of the Order of Merit, a British order designed as a special distinction for eminent men and women, on June 26, 1902. Florence Nightingale is the only woman to have received this honor. 285.

26 United Nations Charter Day, commemorates the signing of the charter in five official languages, Chinese, English, French, Russian, and Spanish, on June 26, 1945. 268.

Holy Days and Feast Days

27 Feast of Saint Cyril of Alexandria, fifth-century bishop of Alexandria; a defender of the faith against Nestorianism; proclaimed doctor of the church in 1882. 4, 9.

Holidays and Civic Days

27 Djbouti National Day, a holiday honoring independence achieved on June 27, 1977, by the Republic of Djbouti, formerly French Somaliland. 868, 875.

Anniversaries and Special Events Days

27 Birthday of Helen Adams Keller (June 27, 1880–June 1, 1968). The most accomplished blind woman of the twentieth century; author of *The Story of My Life, Helen Keller's Journal*, and other books and articles; her birthday is honored annually by many associations for the blind. 268, 738.

27 Korean War Day, the anniversary of the June 27, 1950, entry of the United States into the Korean conflict in response to the appeal of the UN Security Council to its member nations to aid the Republic of Korea in repelling aggression from North Korea. An armistice signed on July 27, 1953, ended the hostilities. 268.

27 Anniversary of the first presentation on June 27, 1922, of the Newbery Medal, awarded annually to the author of the most distinguished contribution to American literature for children published during the preceding year; the first recipient was Hendrik van Loon for *The Story of Mankind*. 858, 863.

27 Birthday of Charles Stewart Parnell (June 27, 1846–October 6, 1891). Irish political leader active in the Home Rule party, which opposed British control. 864.

27 Anniversary of the death of Joseph Smith, founder and leader of Mormonism, at the hands of a mob at Carthage, Illinois, on June 27, 1844. 864.

27 Anniversary of the death of James Smithson, June 27, 1829. English scientist whose will established the Smithsonian Institution in Washington, D.C. 864.

Anniversaries and Special Events Days

28 Mnarja Folk Festival Day, celebrated in Malta with the re-creating of customs dating from the Middle Ages.

28 Birthday of Luigi Pirandello (June 28, 1867–December 10, 1936). Italian dramatist and novelist whose plays have been translated into thirty-three languages; awarded the Nobel Prize in literature in 1934. 864.

28 Birthday of Jean-Jacques Rousseau (June 28, 1712–July 2, 1778). French philosopher and author of great influence; author of the celebrated *Confessions* and other works. 864.

28 Birthday of Peter Paul Rubens (June 28, 1577–May 30, 1640). Flemish painter famous for historical and religious scenes and portraits of kings, clergymen, and scholars. 864.

28 Sarajevo Day, the anniversary of the assassination in Sarajevo on June 28, 1914, of the heir to the Austro-Hungarian throne, Archduke Francis Ferdinand and his wife; an act that flamed the tensions that started World War I. 268, 874.

28 Versailles Treaty Day, the anniversary of the signing of the Treaty of Versailles on June 28, 1919, officially ending World War I. 268.

Holy Days and Feast Days

29 Feast of Saint Peter and Saint Paul, a commemoration of the martyrdom of the two greatest of apostles; Peter by crucifixion and Paul by beheading. 4, 9.

Holidays and Civic Days

29 Saints Peter and Paul Day, a religious and national holiday in Colombia, Costa Rica, Peru, San Marino, the Vatican City State, and Venezuela, honoring one of the oldest of saints' days in the Christian calendar.

29 Seychelles Republic Day, the anniversary of June 29, 1976, when Seychelles, located in the Indian Ocean, became a republic. The people of Seychelles celebrated their independence for three months and are reported to regard themselves as "the happy heirs of Paradise Lost." 868, 875.

Anniversaries and Special Events Days

29 Birthday of William E. Borah (June 29, 1865–January 19, 1940). American statesman and lawyer, opponent of America's affiliation with the League of Nations. He represents the state of Idaho in Statuary Hall in a sculpture done by Bryant Baker. 870.

29 Birthday of William James Mayo (June 29, 1861–July 28, 1939). American surgeon, specialist in cancer and gallstones, a member of the medical family who developed the world-famous Mayo Clinic. 864.

Holidays and Civic Days

30 Guatemala Army Day, a holiday in Guatemala honoring the soldiers of the nation; once celebrated as Revolution Day in tribute to the June 30, 1871, revolt for agrarian reform. 875.

30 Zaire Independence Day, commemorating the establishment of the nation, formerly the Democratic Republic of the Congo, on June 30, 1960. 868.

Anniversaries and Special Events Days

c30 Independence Sunday, observed in Iowa on the Sunday preceding July 4 as a tribute to the Declaration of Independence and its meaning for all Americans. 857.

July

The month of July, the seventh month in the Georgian calendar, was named for Julius Caesar, the Roman who reformed the calendar in 44 B.C..

July is an important month in the United States because of July 4, the birthday of the nation. It was on July 4, 1776, that the Continental Congress, meeting in Philadelphia, adopted the Declaration of Independence. July 4 is now a legal holiday for all Americans. The United States Independence Day is also observed with ceremonies in England, Norway, Sweden, Denmark, Guatemala, the Philippines, Canal Zone, and Guam, and at all American embassies in foreign lands.

July is one of the most important months for bullfights and the continuance of old customs. An example is the Fiesta de San Fermen at Pamplona in Spain, which is dangerously exciting because the bulls are still allowed to run wild on the streets just before the bullfights, as they did in olden times.

Japan also observes an ancient July festival associated with four-footed animals. This is a Japanese horse festival that has been held for over six hundred years. It lasts for three days, during which a thousand horsemen clad in ancient armor and helmets joust and compete in archery and horsemanship.

The July flowers are the water lily and the larkspur, and the birthstone is the ruby.

Holy Days and Feast Days

1 Pilgrimage to the shrine of the saint Oliver Plunkett, the martyred Catholic primate of Ireland, an annual event in Drogheda, County Louth, Ireland. 9, 34.

Holidays and Civic Days

1 Burundi Independence Day, a public holiday commemorating the proclamation of sovereignty for the African nation on July 1, 1962. 868.

1 Dominion Day, or Canada Day, a national holiday commemorating the confederation of the provinces of Canada into the Dominion of Canada under the terms of the British North America Act of July 1, 1867. 578, 866.

1 Ghana Republic Day, commemorating the change from dominion status to that of a republic in the British Commonwealth on July 1, 1960. 868.

1 Half-Year Day, a public holiday in Hong Kong providing a midyear day of relaxation for all citizens. 875.

1 Rwanda Independence Day, a public holiday in the Central African republic, commemorating the granting of sovereignty on July 1, 1962, to the former Belgian trust territory. 868, 875.

1 Union Day, a holiday in the Somali Democratic Republic, celebrating the merger of the British Somaliland Protectorate and the Italian Trusteeship Territory of Somalia on July 1, 1960, and the creation of the Somali Republic on that day. 868, 875.

1 Day of Freedom, a holiday in the Republic of Surinam commemorating the abolition of slavery in 1863; celebrated with festivals and fairs. 875.

Anniversaries and Special Events Days

1 Explorer I Day, the anniversary of the launching of the American space satellite, *Explorer I*, on July 1, 1958; a flight which confirmed the existence of the Van Allen radiation belts that girdle the earth. 874.

1 Gettysburg Day, anniversary of the beginning of the Battle of Gettysburg on July 1, 1863, one of the most decisive conflicts of the American Civil War; observed with annual commemorative services at Gettysburg. 268, 659.

1 Birthday of James Sloan Gibbons (July 1, 1810–October 17, 1892). American banker; abolitionist; remembered for the refrain of the patriotic song "We Are Coming, Father Abra'am, Three Hundred Thousand More." 864.

1 American Stamp Day, anniversary of the issuance of the first United States postage stamps on July 1, 1847; observed by philatelic societies.

c1 The Strážnice folk festival, celebrated in Czechoslovakia during the first two weeks in July, with hundreds of folk singers and dancers participating.

1 Birthday of Walter White (July 1, 1893–March 21, 1955). American author; longtime secretary of the National Association for the Advancement of Colored People; awarded the Spingarn Medal in 1937 for his fight against lynching. 864.

Anniversaries and Special Events Days

2 Corso del Palio (Race for the Palio) Day, a festival horse-racing day in Siena, Italy, in honor of the armless Madonna di Provenzano.

2 Birthday of Thomas Cranmer (July 2, 1489–March 21, 1556). Archbishop of Canterbury and chief author of *The English Book of Common Prayer*. 20.

2 Anniversary of the authorization on July 2, 1926, of the Distinguished Flying Cross of the United States "for heroism or extraordinary achievement while participating in an aerial flight." The first recipient was Charles Augustus Lindbergh, who received the medal on June 11, 1927, for his solo Atlantic flight. 458.

c2 Anniversary of the official establishment of the national Statuary Hall in the United States Capitol on July 2, 1864, when Congress approved an act authorizing the president "to invite each and all the states to provide and furnish statues, in marble or bronze, not exceeding two in number for each state, of deceased persons who have been citizens thereof, and illustrious for their historic renown or for distinguished civic or military services." 870.

Holy Days and Feast Days

3 Feast of Saint Thomas the Apostle celebrated in the Roman Catholic church on July 3, the date of the transfer of his relics. 4, 9.

Holidays and Civic Days

3 Algerian Independence Day, commemorating the passage of a self-determination referendum on July 3, 1962, ending 130 years of French rule and establishing permanent independence for the African nation. 868, 875.

3 Idaho Admission Day. Idaho became the forty-third state on July 3, 1890. 268, 856, 862.

Anniversaries and Special Events Days

3 Anniversary of the assumption of command of the Continental Army by George Washington at Cambridge, Massachusetts, on July 3, 1775. 268.

3 Birthday of Franz Kafka (July 3, 1883–June 3, 1924). Austrian novelist and essayist whose work expresses the frustrations and anxieties of modern man. 864.

3 Birthday of Alfred Korzybski (July 3, 1879–March 1, 1950). Polish-born American scientist, author, pioneer in semantics, founder of general semantics. His best-known book is *Science and Sanity*.

Holidays and Civic Days

4 Alaska's F-Day, or Flag Day, is the anniversary of July 4, 1959, when the forty-ninth star was officially added to the field of blue of the United States. 280–81.

c4 Caricom Day, a holiday in Barbados, in Guyana, and in St. Vincent celebrating the establishment of the Caribbean Community on July 4, 1973, with goals of supporting a common market, cooperating in noneconomic areas, and coordinating foreign policies for the ten member states located in the Caribbean; a holiday observed on or near July 4. 868, 875.

4 Hawaii's F-Day, or Flag Day, is the anniversary of July 4, 1960, when the fiftieth star was officially added to the American flag as a symbol of Hawaii's statehood. 280–81.

4 Philippine-American Friendship Day, a public holiday in the Philippine Islands, with floral ceremonies at the American battle monuments and other observances honoring American freedom. 875.

4 The Fourth of July, or Independence Day, the birthday of the United States. It celebrates the signing of the Declaration of Independence on July 4, 1776; a holiday in each of the fifty states, the District of Columbia, the Canal Zone, Guam, Puerto Rico, and the Virgin Islands. It is also observed in friendship by Denmark, Norway, Sweden, and England. 268, 269, 289–309, 567, 866.

4 Anniversary of the authorization of the fifty-star flag as the official flag of the United States on July 4, 1960. 281.

c4 Zambia Heroes' Day, a holiday in the south-central African nation of Zambia, formerly Northern Rhodesia; a memorial day observed on the first Monday in July to honor the nation's citizens who perished in the fight for independence. 875.

Anniversaries and Special Events Days

4 Anniversary of the death of Chaim Nachman Bialik on July 4, 1934. Hebrew poet famous for his elegiac poem *In the City of Slaughter* and for his support of the Zionist movement. 767.

4 Birthday of Calvin Coolidge (July 4, 1872–January 5, 1933). English ancestry; Massachusetts lawyer; vice-president who succeeded to the office of the presidency upon the death of President Harding; thirtieth president of the United States, 1923–29. Congregationist. Buried at Plymouth, Vermont. 359-66, 370–72, 374, 379.

4 Entebbe Day, the anniversary of the July 4, 1976, Israeli commando raid on the Entebbe airport in Uganda to free 103 hostages held prisoners by Palestinian guerrillas in a hijacked French airliner. 874.

4 Birthday of Stephen Collins Foster (July 4, 1826–January 13, 1864). American composer and writer of songs that reflect the sentiment of pre–Civil War America. Elected to the Hall of Fame for Great Americans in 1940. Memorial and commemorative observances are held in Foster's honor on or near January 13, the anniversary of his death. 268.

4 Garibaldi Day in Italy, commemorates the July 4, 1807, birthday of Giuseppi Garibaldi, the most forceful figure in the unification of Italy in the nineteenth century. 864.

4 Birthday of Nathaniel Hawthorne (July 4, 1804–May 19, 1864). American novelist whose home was the Old Manse in Concord, Massachusetts. His most famous book is *The Scarlet Letter*. He was elected to the Hall of Fame for Great Americans in 1900. 787.

4 Tom Sawyer Fence-painting Day, a contest based on the famous episode in *Tom Sawyer* by Mark Twain; observed in Hannibal, Missouri, on the Fourth of July. 268.

Holidays and Civic Days

5 Cape Verde Independence Day, a holiday in the Republic of Cape Verde honoring the receipt of the instruments of independence from Portugal on July 5, 1975. 875.

c5 Family Day, a public holiday in Lesotho, a former British High Commission Territory in Africa; celebrated on the first Monday of July. 875.

5 Peace and National Unity Day, a holiday in Rwanda, celebrating the goals of an official movement to promote peace and unity, national development, and the eradication of feudalism. 875.

5 Tonga's King's Day, a holiday in the kingdom of Tonga, celebrating both the anniversary of the coronation of His Majesty King Taufa'ahau Tupou IV on July 4, 1967, and his birthday. 875.

5 Venezuela Independence Day, a holiday in Venezuela honoring the declaration of independence by the Congress of Cabildos on July 5, 1811. Venezuela was the first South American country to declare its independence from Spain. 868, 875.

5 Fighter's Day, a holiday in Yugoslavia honoring the nation's war veterans; the day is also known as Warrior's Day. 875.

Anniversaries and Special Events Days

5 Birthday of Phineas Taylor Barnum (July 5, 1810–April 7, 1891). American showman; pioneer advertiser; manager of Jenny Lind's concert tour; and author. 268.

5 Birthday of Dwight Filley Davis (July 5, 1879–November 28, 1945). American public official; donor in 1900 of the Davis Cup, the most prized team trophy in international tennis. 874.

5 Birthday of Davis Glasgow Farragut (July 5, 1801–August 14, 1870). American naval officer, Civil War hero of the Battles of New Orleans and Mobile Bay. Elected to the Hall of Fame for Great Americans in 1900. 268.

5 Birthday of Wanda Landowska (July 5, 1879–August 16, 1959). Polish pianist and harpsichordist responsible for a revival of interest in early musical instruments. 738.

5 Birthday of Cecil John Rhodes (July 5, 1853–March 26, 1902). English colonial statesman; developer of Rhodesia; founder of the coveted Rhodes Scholarships at Oxford University. 864.

5 Anniversary of the founding of the Salvation Army in London by William Booth on July 5, 1865. 20.

Holidays and Civic Days

6 Malawi Republic Day, a national holiday commemorating the proclamation of July 6, 1965, changing the former British Protectorate of Nyasaland into the Republic of Malawi. 868, 875.

c6 Unity Day, a public holiday in Zambia, formerly Northern Rhodesia, observed on the first Tuesday of July to honor the goals of all African people. 868, 875.

Anniversaries and Special Events Days

6 Anniversary of the death of Jan Huss on July 6, 1415. Czech religious reformer who was burned at the stake; his death is commemorated in Czechoslovakia. 1, 34.

6 Birthday of John Paul Jones (July 6, 1747–July 18, 1792). American naval officer of the Revolutionary period and founder of the American navy. A national monument was erected in his honor in Potomac Park in Washington. He was elected to the Hall of Fame for Great Americans in 1925. 268, 452, 463.

6 Birthday of Eino Leino (July 6, 1878–January 10, 1926). Finnish poet, playwright, and novelist who expressed the aspirations of the Finnish people. 849.

6 Luxembourg Remembrance Day, a memorial day with special tributes to U.S. General George Patton, Jr., and his men of the Third Army who liberated the grandduchy in 1945.

6 Anniversary of the establishment of the United States Medal of Freedom on July 6, 1945, awarded to civilians for meritorious acts or service against the enemy on or after December 7, 1941. 458.

Holidays and Civic Days

7 Independence Day, a holiday in the Solomon Islands, celebrating the granting of independence to the islands on July 7, 1978. 868.

7 Saba Saba Peasants' Day, or Farmer's Day, a holiday in the United Republic of Tanzania; officially celebrated in a different region of the country each year with traditional dances, sports, activities, processions, rallies, and fairs. 875.

Anniversaries and Special Events Days

7 Anniversary of the death of Thomas Hooker on July 7, 1647. American colonial clergyman whose interpretation of the theory that the people have the right to choose their public officials gave him the name "the father of American democracy." 20.

7 The Star Festival, or Tanabata, a Japanese festival based on a legend about two stars who meet only on the seventh night of the seventh month.

7 The Fiesta de San Fermin, celebrated at Pamplona, Spain, during the week that includes July 7. It is the festival at which the bulls are allowed to run in the streets before the bullfights.

Holy Days and Feast Days

8 Feast of Saint Kilian, a seventh-century Irish monk who evangelized Baden and Bavaria; the patron saint of Bavaria. 4, 9.

Anniversaries and Special Events Days

8 Olive Branch Petition Day, the anniversary of the July 8, 1775, signing, by colonial moderates, of a petition addressed to King George III as an effort to avoid the American Revolutionary War.

8 Anniversary of Commodore Matthew Perry's historic visit to Japan beginning July 8, 1853, which opened up the East to world trade.

8 Birthday of John Davison Rockefeller (July 8, 1839–May 23, 1937). American industrialist and philanthropist, head of the Standard Oil Company, and benefactor of the University of Chicago, the Rockefeller Foundation, and other important institutions. 864.

Holy Days and Feast Days

9 Martyrdom of the Bab, a Baha'i holy day, commemorating the martyrdom suffered on July 9, 1850, by the Bab, a prophet of the Baha'i faith. 1, 854.

Holidays and Civic Days

9 Independence Day, a holiday in Argentina commemorating the formal proclamation of independence from Spain on July 9, 1816, which was forecast by the May revolution of 1810. 868, 875.

Anniversaries and Special Events Days

9 Birthday of Elias Howe (July 9, 1819–October 3, 1867). American inventor and manufacturer who invented the sewing machine. He was elected to the Hall of Fame for Great Americans in 1915. 864.

9 Anniversary of the July 9, 1918, authorization of the Distinguished Service Cross of the United States Army to honor extraordinary heroism on the part of persons serving the army in any capacity. 458.

Holy Days and Feast Days

10 Feast of Our Lady of Mount Carmel, a principal feast of the Carmelite order of friars, a commemorative or optional memorial day in the Roman Catholic calendar.

10 Feast of the Virgin of Begoña at Bilbao, Spain, a river festival featuring the carrying of the Virgin along the coast at the head of a procession of gaily decked ships.

Holidays and Civic Days

10 Independence Day, a public holiday in the Bahama Islands commemorating the proclamation of sovereignty on July 10, 1973. 868, 875.

10 Wyoming Statehood Day, commemorating its admission to the Union on July 10, 1890, as the forty-fourth state; the first state to grant the vote to women through its original constitution. 268, 856, 862.

Anniversaries and Special Events Days

10 Birthday of Mary McLeod Bethune (July 10, 1875–May 18, 1955). American educator, founder of Bethune-Cookman College, and founder and president of the National Council of Negro Women. 322, 759.

10 Birthday of Sir William Blackstone (July 10, 1723–February 14, 1780). English jurist whose fame rests on his influential *Commentaries on the Laws of England*. 864.

10 Birthday of John Calvin (July 10, 1509–May 27, 1564). Protestant theologian and reformer, author of *Institutes of the Christian Religion*. 1.

10 Birthday of Toyohiko Kagawa (July 10, 1888–April 23, 1960). Japanese social reformer and evangelist, a leader in the Japanese labor movement and in the establishment of cooperatives. 1.

10 Birthday of Nikola Tesla (July 10, 1856–January 7, 1943). Croatian scientist; discoverer of the rotating magnetic field. 864.

Holy Days and Feast Days

11 Feast of Saint Benedict II, elected pope in 683; named patron of Europe in 1964 by Pope Paul VI. 4, 9.

Holidays and Civic Days

11 Mongolian Revolution Day; the national holiday in the Mongolian People's Republic commemorating the July 1921 revolution against Chinese occupation. Mongolia was proclaimed a republic on November 26, 1924, when complete autonomy was realized for a country once known as Outer Mongolia. 868, 875.

Anniversaries and Special Events Days

11 Birthday of John Quincy Adams (July 11, 1767–February 23, 1848). English ancestry; Massachusetts lawyer; secretary of state to Monroe; sixth president of the United States, 1825–29; a Unitarian; died in the Hall of Congress; buried at Unitarian Church, Quincy, Massachusetts. Elected to the Hall of Fame for Great Americans in 1905. 359–66, 370–72, 374, 378, 379.

11 Bawming the Thorn Day, a generations-old tradition in Appleton, Cheshire, England, based on the ancient worship of trees; primarily a festival in which children garland and dance around a hawthorn tree. 256.

11 Birthday of Colin Purdie Kelly (July 11, 1915–December 10, 1941). American army captain and aviator, first United States air hero of World War II, posthumously awarded the Distinguished Service Cross. 864.

11 Birthday of George William Norris (July 11, 1861–September 2, 1944). American statesman and congressman from Nebraska who was instrumental in the establishment of the Tennessee Valley Authority. The first TVA dam was named in his honor. Author of the Twentieth Amendment, known as the "lame duck" amendment, which provided for inauguration of a newly elected president on January 20 instead of March 4. 864.

11 Anniversary of the dedication of the United States Air Force Academy at Lowry Air Base, Colorado, on July 11, 1955.

Holidays and Civic Days

12 Orangeman's Day, or Orange Day, dedicated to the anniversary of the Battle of the Boyne of 1690; a statutory public holiday in Northern Ireland. 20, 866.

12 Kiribati Independence Day, the anniversary of July 12, 1979, when Kiribati, formerly the Gilbert Islands located in the mid-Pacific around the point where the international dateline cuts the equator, achieved independence. 868.

12 São Tomé and Principe National day, a public holiday, honoring the July 12, 1975, agreement with Portugal which gave full independence to the Democratic Republic of São Tomé and Principe. 868, 875.

Anniversaries and Special Events Days

12 Anniversary of the authorization of the Medal of Honor by Congress on July 12, 1862, to honor noncommissioned officers and privates who distinguish themselves in actual conflict by gallantry and intrepidity at the risk of life beyond the call of duty. The first award was made to six members of a Union army raiding party. 458.

12 Birthday of Sir William Osler (July 12, 1849–December 29, 1919). Canadian physician and teacher noted for his research on the circulatory system. 864.

12 Birthday of Henry David Thoreau (July 12, 1817–May 6, 1862). American author most famous for the book *Walden, or Life in the Woods*. Elected to the Hall of Fame for Great Americans in 1960. 777, 814.

Holy Days and Feast Days

13 Festival of Our Lady of Fátima, commemorating the vision of the Virgin Mary to the Dos Santos children in the village of Fátima in Portugal in 1917. 5.

Holidays and Civic Days

c13 President's Day, a holiday in Botswana observed on or near July 13. The first president of Botswana, Sir Seretse Khama, reelected three times, died on July 13, 1980. 868, 875.

13 Night Watch, or La Retraite aux Flambeaux, a French half-day holiday celebrating the eve of the fall of the Bastille and followed by Bastille Day, a full holiday. 875.

Anniversaries and Special Events Days

13 Birthday of Nathan Bedford Forrest (July 13, 1821–October 29, 1877). American cavalry commander in the Confederate army whose famous motto was "Get thar fastest with the mostest." 864.

c13 Reed Dance Day, a festival day in Swaziland, celebrated on the second Monday in July as a tribute from the Swazi girls to the queen mother, known as Ndlovukazi, or "she-elephant."

Holy Days and Feast Days

14 Feast of Saint Camillus de Lellis, founder of the Camellians, an order dedicated to the sick; declared patron of the sick by Pope Leo XIII, and patron of nurses and nursing groups by Pope Pius XI. 4, 9.

Holidays and Civic Days

14 Bastille Day, or Fête Nationale, the national festival of France, commemorating the storming of the Bastille in 1789 by citizens and the release of political prisoners. Also called "holiday of all free men," Bastille Day is observed in all French territories and provinces and by French societies throughout the world. 268, 388, 866, 868, 875.

14 Iraq 1958 Revolution Day, a holiday celebrating the army-led revolution of July 14, 1958, which ended the rule of Hashemite dynasty. 868, 875.

Anniversaries and Special Events Days

14 Birthday of Florence Bascom (July 14, 1862–June 18, 1945). American geologist. First woman to receive a degree from Johns Hopkins University and the first woman to receive a Ph.D. from any American university.

14 Birthday of Gerald Rudolph Ford (July 15, 1913–). English ancestry. Episcopalian. Thirty-eighth president of the United States, August 9, 1974–Jaunary 20, 1977. 361, 365, 371, 372, 374.

14 Birthday of Jules Mazarin (July 14, 1602–March 9, 1661). French statesman, Roman Catholic cardinal, and founder of the Mazarin Library. 864.

14 Birthday of Emmeline Pankhurst (July 14, 1858–June 14, 1928). English woman-suffrage leader who used militant methods of campaigning and was sentenced to prison. She lived to see the passage of the Representation of the People Act on June 9, 1928, which gave full and equal suffrage to women. A memorial statue to her was erected near the Houses of Parliament in London. 793.

14 Birthday of James Abbott McNeill Whistler (July 14, 1834–July 17, 1903). American artist and wit. Elected to the Hall of Fame for Great Americans in 1930. 268, 808.

Holy Days and Feast Days

15 Feast of Saint Bonaventure, thirteenth-century philosopher and theologian known as "the seraphic doctor"; author of the official Franciscan biography of Saint Francis; declared a doctor of the church in 1588. 4, 9.

15 Feast of Saint Swithin, a popular English saint buried at Winchester Cathedral; traditionally associated with the prophecy that if it rains on Swithin's Day it will rain for forty days. 4, 14.

15 Feast Day of Saint Vladimir of Kiev, honored by Russian and Ukrainian Christians. 4, 9.

Holidays and Civic Days

15 The Sultan's Birthday, a holiday in the sultanate of Brunei, honoring the birth of His Highness the Sultan, who was crowned on August 1, 1968. 875.

Anniversaries and Special Events Days

c15 Black Ship Day, a festival observed in Yokosuka, Shimoda, and other ports of Japan around July 15 to commemorate the arrival of Commodore Perry in 1853; observed in other ports on varying days.

15 Anniversary of the baptism of Inigo Jones (July 15, 1573–June 21, 1652). English architect whose restoration of Saint Paul's Cathedral in London, and other buildings, revived classic architecture. 864.

15 Birthday of Clement Clarke Moore (July 15, 1779–July 10, 1863). American scholar and poet. Best known for the poem called *A Visit from Saint Nicholas*. 122.

15 Birthday of Rembrandt van Rijn (July 15, 1606–October 4, 1669). Dutch painter and etcher, foremost member of the Dutch school of painting. 798.

Holidays and Civic Days

16 La Paz day, a municipal holiday celebrating the foundation of the city in 1548; La Paz, the seat of government in Bolivia is one of the highest capitals in the world. 875.

Anniversaries and Special Events Days

16 District of Columbia Day, the anniversary of the establishment on July 16, 1790, of the District of Columbia and the authorization of Washington as the permanent capital of the United States.

16 Czar Nicholas Day, the anniversary of the July 16, 1918, murder of Czar Nicholas II and his family by the Bolsheviks.

16 Birthday of Mary Baker Eddy (July 16, 1821–December 3, 1910). Founder of the Church of Christ, Scientist and author of *Science and Health with Key to the Scriptures* and other books. 20, 738.

Holidays and Civic Days

17 July Revolution Day, a holiday in Iraq, sometimes called Peaceful Revolution Day, commemorating the coup which overthrew the Arif regime in 1968. 868, 875.

17 Constitution Day, a holiday in the Republic of Korea (South Korea) commemorating the constitution adopted in 1963. 868, 875.

17 Muñoz Rivera Day, celebrated in Puerto Rico to honor the July 17, 1859, birth of Luis Muñoz Rivera, patriot and journalist. 875.

Anniversaries and Special Events Days

17 Apollo-Soyuz Day, the anniversary of the docking of Russian and American space vehicles on July 17, 1975; the first Soviet-American union in space. 874.

17 P.O.W.-M.I.A. Recognition Day, a day of remembrance of and tribute to American prisoners of war and those missing in action; a day established by a presidential proclamation. 874.

Holidays and Civic Days

18 Uruguay Constitution Day, a public holiday commemorating the adoption of the 1951 constitution providing for a collegiate form of government. 868, 875.

Anniversaries and Special Events Days

18 Birthday of Laurence Housman (July 18, 1865–February 20, 1959). English illustrator, author, and playwright remembered particularly for the play *Victoria Regina*. 864.

18 Railroad Day, marking the completion of the Grand Trunk line, the first international railroad on the North American continent, on July 18, 1853. 688.

18 Birthday of William Makepeace Thackeray (July 18, 1811–December 24, 1863). English novelist and satirical humorist famous for *Vanity Fair* and *The History of Henry Esmond*. 864.

Holidays and Civic Days

19 Burma Martyrs Day, a holiday in Burma commemorating the assassination of General Aung San and his colleagues on July 19, 1947. 868, 875.

19 Sandinista Revolution Day, a holiday in Nicaragua celebrating the July 19, 1979, victory of the Sandinista National Liberation Front and the end of the Somoza regime that had lasted more than four decades. 868, 875.

Anniversaries and Special Events Days

19 Birthday of Mary Ann Ball Bickerdyke (July 19, 1817–November 8, 1901). American nurse known as Mother Bickerdyke for her services to the Union armies in the West during the Civil War. 867.

19 Birthday of Charles Horace Mayo (July 19, 1865–May 26, 1939). American surgeon, specialist in goiters and preventive medicine; cofounder of the Mayo Clinic. 864.

Holidays and Civic Days

20 Independence Day in Colombia, celebrating the declaration of independence issued on July 20, 1810. 868, 875.

Anniversaries and Special Events Days

20 Anniversary of the establishment of the Legion of Merit Medal by Act of Congress on July 20, 1942, for meritorious service performed by individuals in the armed services of the United States or by citizens of other nations. 458.

20 Moon Day, the anniversary of the historic landing on the moon on July 20, 1969, of the United States *Apollo II*, manned by astronauts Neil A. Armstrong and Edwin Aldrin, Jr., who became the first men to engage in explorations of the moon's surface. 268, 284, 286, 672, 866.

20 Birthday of Francesco Petrarch (July 20, 1304–July 18, 1374). Italian lyric poet and scholar. Major figure in the Renaissance. 864.

Holy Days and Feast Days

21 Feast of Saint Lawrence of Brindisi, a sixteenth-century Capuchin famed for his preaching in the post-Reformation period; proclaimed a doctor of the church in 1959. 4, 9.

21 Feast Day of Saint Victor, patron saint of cabinetmakers. 4, 9.

Holidays and Civic Days

21 Belgium Independence Day, a holiday commemorating the accession of the first Belgian king, Leopold I, following separation from the Netherlands on July 21, 1831. 868, 875.

21 Liberation Day, a holiday in Guam in honor of July 21, 1944, when forces of the United States Army and Marines freed the island from the Japanese, who had seized it in December 1941. 875.

Anniversaries and Special Events Days

21 Birthday of Ernest Hemingway (July 21, 1899–July 2, 1961). American novelist, short-story writer, and world traveler. His book *The Old Man and the Sea* won the Pulitzer Prize in 1953. He was awarded the Nobel Prize in literature in 1954. 787.

21 Birthday of Paul Julius Reuter (July 21, 1816–February 25, 1899). German journalist and founder of Reuter's News Agency, which pioneered in gathering news from all over the world. 864.

21 Women's Hall of Fame, dedicated on July 21, 1979; located at Seneca Falls, New York, recognized as the birthplace of the Women's Rights movement.

Holy Days and Feast Days

22 Feast of Mary Magdalen, the repentant sinner, one who cared for the needs of Christ and the apostles in their travels; the first to whom Christ appeared after the Resurrection. 4, 9.

c22 Hurricane Supplication Day, observed on the fourth Monday of July in the Virgin Islands; a day of prayer for safety in the hurricane season. 875.

Holidays and Civic Days

22 Polish National Liberation Day, a holiday in Poland honoring the end of the war in 1944 and a constitution enacted on July 22, 1952. 875.

22 The King's Birthday, a holiday in the kingdom of Swaziland, honoring His Majesty Sobhuza II, who became the Ngwenyama (the Lion), or head of state, in 1921. 875.

Anniversaries and Special Events Days

22 Birthday of Stephen Vincent Benét (July 22, 1898–March 13, 1943). American poet and novelist who received the Pulitzer Prize in poetry in 1929 for *John Brown's Body* and in 1944 for the posthumously published *Western Star*. 864.

22 Birthday of Emma Lazarus (July 22, 1849–November 19, 1887). American poet and essayist who wrote *The New Colossus*, the closing lines of which are engraved on the pedestal of the Statue of Liberty. 296.

22 Robert E. Lee Citizenship Day, the anniversary of the July 22, 1975, restoration of the citizenship of Robert E. Lee, commander of the Army of Northern Virginia in the American Civil War. 874.

22 Spooner's Day, a day of remembrance of the English clergyman William Spooner, born on July 22, 1844; Spooner achieved lasting fame for his continuous but unintentional transposition of words into amusing slips of the tongue. 866.

Holy Days and Feast Days

23 Feast of Saint Bridget, or Birgitta, fourteenth-century founder of the Order of the Most Holy Trinity, the Brigettines; patron saint of Sweden. 4, 9.

Holidays and Civic Days

23 Revolution Anniversary Day, a holiday in the Arab Republic of Egypt and in Libya, commemorating July 23, 1952, when the Revolutionary Command terminated the Egyptian royal regime and declared Egypt to be a republic. 868, 875.

Anniversaries and Special Events Days

23 Birthday of Charlotte Saunders Cushman (July 23, 1816–February 17, 1876). American actress known for her portrayal of Lady Macbeth. She was elected to the Hall of Fame for Great Americans in 1915. 864.

Holidays and Civic Days

c24 Juhannus Day, the midsummer festival in Finland, celebrating the longest day in the year and the feast of St. John; usually observed on the Saturday closest to June 24 with feasting, dances, and bonfires. 849.

c24 Pioneer Day in Utah, a legal holiday celebrating the entry of Brigham Young and the Mormon pioneers into the valley of the Salt Lake in 1847 and the establishment of the first settlement in the area. It has been observed every year since 1849 on varying dates near July 24. 268.

24 Bolivar Day, a holiday in Venezuela honoring the July 24, 1783, birth of Simon Bolivar, the South American soldier-statesman known as "the liberator." 868, 875.

Anniversaries and Special Events Days

24 Birthday of John Middleton Clayton (July 24, 1796–November 9, 1856). American statesman, senator from Delaware, and secretary of state under Zachary Taylor. He represents the state of Delaware in Statuary Hall in a sculpture done by Bryant Baker. 870.

24 Birthday of Amelia Earhart (Putnam) (July 24, 1898–July 2, 1937). American aviatrix. The first woman to fly an airplane across the Atlantic and winner of many aviation "firsts." The first woman to receive the Distinguished Flying Cross. 470, 474, 752.

24 Valencia Fair Days, begin on July 24 in Valencia, Spain. As a celebration of the Battle of Flowers, carnations are thrown in mock battles and festivities.

Holy Days and Feast Days

25 Feast of Saint Christopher, the Christbearer who, according to legend, found the weight of a child growing heavier as he carried him across the river. The child was Christ and with him Christopher carried the weight of the sins of the world. Christopher is the patron saint of travelers and of motorists. 4, 9.

25 Feast of Saint James the Greater; apostle, the first to be martyred, when he was beheaded in Jerusalem by Herod Agrippa I in A.D. 42. Traditions connect James with preaching in Spain; he is the patron saint of Spain. 4, 9.

c25 Reek Sunday, observed in Ireland on the last Sunday in July; a traditional day for the pilgrimage up Croagh Patrick, the steep holy mountain in Mayo named for Saint Patrick; one of the most popular pilgrimages of Ireland. 34.

Holidays and Civic Days

25 Guanacaste Day, anniversary of the annexation of Guanacaste province; a public holiday in Costa Rica.

25 Commonwealth Day, celebrated in Puerto Rico in honor of July 25, 1952, when the constitution of the Commonwealth of Puerto Rico was proclaimed. 875.

25 Netherlands Independence day, a civic day recognizing the events of the nineteenth century which assured autonomy under a constitutional monarchy for the kingdom of the Netherlands. 868, 875.

25 Tunisian Republic Day, anniversary of the proclamation of July 25, 1957, which abolished the monarchy and established the republic; a national holiday in Tunisia. 868, 875.

Anniversaries and Special Events Days

25 Birthday of Davidson Black (July 25, 1884–March 15, 1934). Canadian doctor and professor of anatomy whose contributions to anthropology in studying protohuman remains and in identifying the "Peking man" brought him international fame. 864.

25 Birthday of Flora Adams Darling (July 25, 1840–January 6, 1910). American author and founder of patriotic societies of which the most important is the Daughters of the American Revolution, which she founded with Mary S. Lockwood on October 11, 1890.

Holy Days and Feast Days

26 Feast Day of Saint Anne, patron saint of Canada, patroness of housewives and of miners, mother of the Virgin Mary, wife of Joachim; celebrated throughout the world. The pilgrimage to the Basilica of Sainte Anne de Beaupré in the province of Quebec is one of the major pilgrimages on the North American continent. The shrine at Beaupré has been called the Lourdes of the New World. 4, 9.

26 Feast of Joachim and Anne, commemorates the parents of Mary; a memorial in the Roman Catholic church calendar. 4, 9.

Holidays and Civic Days

26 Cuban Revolution Day, a holiday in Cuba commemorating Fidel Castro's "26th of July Movement" of 1953 against the Batista military dictatorship. 389, 875.

26 Liberian Independence Day, a holiday commemorating the establishment of the Free and Independent Republic of Liberia on July 26, 1847, following its founding by the American Colonization Society, as a place to send free Negroes from the United States, by authority of a charter granted by the Congress of the United States in 1816. 868, 875.

26 Maldives Independence Day, commemorating July 26, 1965, when the British recognized the full independence of the Sultanate of the Maldives, the group of islands in the Indian Ocean that became the Republic of the Maldives. 868, 875.

26 New York Ratification Day. New York entered the Union on July 26, 1788, the eleventh of the thirteen original United States to do so. 268, 856, 862.

Anniversaries and Special Events Days

26 Bellman Day, a commemorative day in Stockholm honoring Carl Michael Bellman, eighteenth-century troubadour, whose songs and poems are enjoyed in twentieth-century Sweden.

26 Birthday of Constantino Brumidi (July 26, 1805–February 19, 1880). Italian-American painter whose lifework was the painting of portraits and frescoes for the Capitol in Washington, D.C. 864.

26 Birthday of George Catlin (July 26, 1796–December 23, 1872). American artist who made special studies and portraits of American Indians. His work is displayed in the Catlin Gallery of the United States National Museum and at the American Museum of Natural History in New York. 867.

26 Birthday of George Clinton (July 26, 1739–April 20, 1812). American Revolutionary War soldier; first governor of the state of New York; twice vice-president of the United States; lawyer. He represents the state of New York in Statuary Hall in a sculpture done by Henry Kirke Brown. 864, 870.

26 Birthday of Serge Koussevitzky (July 26, 1874–June 4, 1951). Russian-American bass player, conductor of the Boston Symphony Orchestra, and founder of the Berkshire Music Center. 864.

26 Birthday of George Bernard Shaw (July 26, 1856–November 2, 1950). Irish-English dramatist, critic, novelist, and pamphleteer. Recipient of the Nobel Prize in literature in 1925, using the money to establish an institution for the study of Scandinavian literature in Great Britain, since, in his case, the money was "a life belt thrown to a man who had already reached shore." A Bernard Shaw Day is observed on his birthday by Shaw societies throughout the United States. 780, 782.

Holy Days and Feast Days

27 Feast Day of Saint Pantaleon, patron saint of physicians. 4.

Holidays and Civic Days

27 Barbosa Day, observed in Puerto Rico in honor of the July 27, 1857, birth of José Celso Barbosa, black physician and political hero of the nineteenth century. 875.

Anniversaries and Special Events Days

27 Korean War Armistice Day, anniversary of the end of the Korean conflict that began on June 25, 1950, and ended on July 27, 1953. 268.

Holidays and Civic Days

c28 Independence Day in Peru, a holiday commemorating the declaration of independence from Spain on July 28, 1821, which led to war and complete freedom in 1824. This holiday is celebrated for two days. 868, 875.

Anniversaries and Special Events Days

28 Joseph Lee Day, sponsored by the National Recreation Association to commemorate the July 28, 1937, death of the "father of the playground movement." 864.

28 Birthday of Beatrix Potter (July 28, 1866–December 22, 1943). English author and illustrator, famous for *The Tale of Peter Rabbit*, which has been translated into many languages. 864.

28 Founder's Day for the Volunteers of America, honors the birth of Ballington Booth on July 28, 1859.

28 Anniversary of the death of John Peter Zenger on July 28, 1746. American printer and journalist tried for seditious libels. His acquittal is considered the first important victory for the freedom of the press in the colonies. 268.

Holy Days and Feast Days

29 Feast of Saint Martha, sister of Lazarus, who attended to household duties, with some resentment, while her sister sat and listened at the feet of Christ; the patron saint of innkeepers, housekeepers, cooks, and laundresses. 4, 9.

29 Feast Day of Saint Olaf, patron saint of Norway since 1164; ceremonies commemorate the death of King Olaf in battle and honor his support of the Christian faith. 4, 9.

Anniversaries and Special Events Days

29 Anniversary of the ratification of the International Atomic Agency on July 29, 1957. Its purpose is to ensure peaceful benefits of atomic research to peoples throughout the world.

29 Birthday of Dag Hammarskjöld (July 29, 1905–September 18, 1961). Swedish economist; second secretary-general of the United Nations; posthumously awarded the Nobel Peace Prize in 1961. 679, 864.

29 Birthday of Don Marquis (July 29, 1878–December 30, 1937). American journalist, poet, and playwright; creator of Archy, the cockroach, and Mehitabel, the cat, the newspaper philosophers of the 1920s. 864.

29 Olsok Eve festival; celebrated in Norway with bonfires and folk dancing in honor of Saint Olaf, the martyr king Olav Haraldsson, who brought Christianity to Norway and was killed in the first Battle of Stiklestad, July 29, 1030; frequently called Norway Day in the United States and observed in Norwegian-American communities.

29 Royal Wedding Day, anniversary of the marriage of Charles, Prince of Wales and Lady Diana Spencer on July 29, 1981; "the wedding of the century," observed by the world through television. 874.

29 Somers Day, observed in Bermuda to recall the 1609 day when Sir George Somers and his party were wrecked on the coast and formed the Plantation of the Somers' Islands, later named Bermuda.

29 Birthday of Booth Tarkington (July 29, 1869–May 19, 1946). American author who won the Pulitzer Prize in 1919 for *The Magnificent Ambersons* and in 1922 for *Alice Adams*. Perhaps best known for *Penrod*. 864.

29 Birthday of Alexis de Tocqueville (July 29, 1805–April 16, 1859). French statesman and author of a famous four-volume work called *Democracy in America*, which won the Montyon Prize of the French Academy in 1836. 864.

29 Umutomboko Ceremony Day, a festival in north-central Zambia carrying out the traditions of honor to the chief of the Luunda people in Luapula Province.

Holidays and Civic Days

30 Vanuatu Independence Day, a holiday in the Republic of Vanuatu, formerly New Hebrides, commemorating the achievement of independence on July 30, 1980, and the establishment of the republic. 868, 875.

Anniversaries and Special Events Days

30 Birthday of Emily Brontë (July 30, 1818–December 19, 1848). English author, famous for the novel *Wuthering Heights*. 785.

30 Crater Day in Virginia, commemorates July 30, 1864, the occasion of an unsuccessful attempt of the Union forces to take Petersburg by blowing up the forts, causing craters in the earth; observed by veterans and civic organizations. 268.

30 Birthday of Henry Ford (July 30, 1863–April 7, 1947). American inventor, automobile manufacturer, and philanthropist whose fortune and family established the Ford Foundation. 864.

30 Birthday of James Edward Kelly (July 30, 1855–May 25, 1933). American sculptor who chose subjects from American history for his work and became known as the "sculptor of American history."

30 Marseillaise Day. The "Marseillaise," the national anthem of France, was sung in Paris for the first time on July 30, 1792, by five hundred men from the port city of Marseilles, which gave its name to the French national anthem.

30 Anniversary of the organization of the WAVES, women's reserve unit of the United States Naval Reserves, on July 30, 1942.

Holy Days and Feast Days

31 Feast Day of Saint Ignatius of Loyola; founder and patron of the Society of Jesus; patron saint of retreats and retreatants. Ignatius was the author of the classic book *Spiritual Exercises*. 4, 9.

Holidays and Civic Days

31 Saint Ignatius of Loyola Day, a holiday in Bilbao, Spain, honoring the founder of the Society of Jesus, the Jesuits. 4, 9.

31 Parents' Day in Zaire, a two-day holiday honoring the parents of the nation. 875.

Anniversaries and Special Events Days

31 Birthday of John Ericsson (July 31, 1803–March 8, 1889). American inventor of the screw propeller, pioneer in modern naval construction, builder of the famous *Monitor*; memorials to him have been built in New York; Worcester, Massachusetts; and Sweden. 268.

31 Birthday of James Kent (July 31, 1763–December 12, 1847). American lawyer, jurist, and famous legal commentator. He was elected to the Hall of Fame for Great Americans in 1900.

August

August, the eighth month of the year, was named for the Roman emperor Augustus. In many countries it is a traditional time for music festivals, fairs, expositions, and family holidays.

The one religious day in August that is observed around the world is August 15, the Feast of the Assumption of Mary, a holy day and a holiday in many Roman Catholic countries. On this day the Italian, Spanish, and Latin American peoples cherish age-old religious processions often followed by fiesta activities.

The flowers for August are the gladiolus and the poppy. The birthstones are the sardonyx and the peridot.

Holy Days and Feast Days

1 Feast of Saint Alphonsus Liguori, eighteenth-century founder of the Redemptorists; proclaimed a doctor of the church in 1871; patron of confessors and moralists. 4, 9.

Holidays and Civic Days

c1 Bahamas Emancipation Day, a holiday in the West Indian Bahamas group, commemorating the emancipation of British slaves in 1838; now celebrated on the first Monday of August. 868, 875.

1 Benin Independence Day, the anniversary of August 1, 1960, when Benin, called Dahomey until 1975, achieved full independence as the People's Republic of Benin. 868.

c1 Colorado Day, a legal holiday in Colorado in honor of the admission of Colorado to the Union in 1876 as the thirty-eighth state. 268, 856, 862.

1 Peking Army Day, observed in Peking, China, with military parades; revived in 1981 after cancellations lasting two decades. 875.

1 Swiss Confederation Day, anniversary of the foundation of the Swiss Confederation on August 1, 1291; a nationally celebrated holiday in Switzerland and one that has a significance comparable to the Fourth of July in the United States. 868, 875.

Anniversaries and Special Events Days

1 Birthday of William Clark (August 1, 1770–September 1, 1838). American soldier and explorer; a leader of the Lewis and Clark expedition, which set up a route to the Pacific and stimulated the westward expansion of the American nation. 739.

1 Birthday of Richard Henry Dana (August 1, 1815–January 6, 1882). American author, lawyer, and sailor, best known for his book *Two Years before the Mast*. 864.

1 Birthday of Francis Scott Key (August 1, 1779–January 11, 1843). American lawyer and author of the national anthem "The Star-Spangled Banner"; honored on Defenders' Day. 268.

1 Lammas Day, once an important British festival day, historically important as the forerunner of America's Thanksgiving and Canada's Harvest Festival. 20, 256, 831.

1 Birthday of Herman Melville (August 1, 1819–September 28, 1891). American author; his major book, *Moby Dick*, won Melville a permanent place in world literature. 268.

1 Birthday of Maria Mitchell (August 1, 1818–June 28, 1889). American astronomer and first woman to be elected to the American Academy of Arts and Sciences. She was elected to the Hall of Fame for Great Americans in 1905. 738.

Holy Days and Feast Days

2 Feast of Our Lady of Angels, a religious and national holiday in Costa Rica; a day of pilgrimage to the basilica in Cartago, the site of the black stone statue of the Virgin called La Negrita.

c2 Feast Day of Saint Wilfred, a day of processions and ceremonials in Ripon, Yorkshire, England, recalling the return from exile of the seventh-century bishop, later saint, Wilfred of York; observed on the first Saturday of August. 4.

Holidays and Civic Days

2 Picnic Day, a holiday in the Northern Territory of Australia, whose capital is Darwin. 875.

2 Freedom Day, a holiday in Guyana celebrating the enactment of the Emancipation Act of 1837, which freed the slaves when Guyana was the colony of British Guiana. 875.

c2 Jamaican Independence Day, a holiday commemorating the achievement of independence for Jamaica on August 6, 1962; observed on the first Monday in August, celebrated with agricultural, arts, and crafts exhibits, awards competitions, dancing, and singing. 868, 875.

2 Saint Elias Day, or National Day, a holiday in Macedonia, now a part of the Republic of Yugoslavia. The day commemorates the August 2, 1903, uprising of the Macedonians against Turkey. 857, 875.

2 Discovery Day, a holiday in the Republic of Trinidad and Tobago celebrating the discovery of the two islands by Columbus on his third voyage to the Western Hemisphere in 1498. 868, 875.

2 Farmers' Day, a holiday in the Republic of Zambia honoring the farmers of the nation and reflecting the government's policy of agricultural diversification. 875.

Anniversaries and Special Events Days

2 Birthday of Pierre Charles L'Enfant (August 2, 1754–June 14, 1825). French army engineer and an officer in the American Revolutionary army; honored as the designer of the plans for the city of Washington, D.C. 268.

2 Birthday of Henry Steel Olcott (August 2, 1832–February 17, 1907). American spiritualist and first president of the Theosophical Society.

2 Harriet Quimby Day, the anniversary of the August 2, 1911, licensing of Harriet Quimby as America's first woman pilot.

Holidays and Civic Days

3 Guinea-Bissau Martyrs Day, a holiday in Guinea-Bissau honoring the martyrs of colonization. 875.

3 Niger Independence Day, a national holiday in the Republic of Niger celebrating independence on August 3, 1960 after having been a territory of French West Africa from 1904. 868, 875.

3 President Bourguiba's Birthday, a holiday in Tunisia honoring the president of the republic who has served as head of state since July 20, 1957, and was elected president for life in November 1974. 875.

Anniversaries and Special Events Days

3 Birthday of Ernest (Ernie) Taylor Pyle (August 3, 1900–April 18, 1945). American journalist and spokesman of the American soldier; the most famous American correspondent in World War II. 864.

3 Birthday of Lady Isabella Caroline Somerset (August 3, 1851–March 12, 1921). English philanthropist; temperance worker; successor to Frances Willard as president of the world WCTU; founder of a pioneer farm colony for alcoholic women in 1895, the first institution of its kind in England.

Anniversaries and Special Events Days

4 Coast Guard Day, anniversary of the establishment on August 4, 1790, of the Revenue Cutter Service, which merged with the Life Saving Service in 1915 to become the United States Coast Guard. 446, 866.

4 Birthday of Oliver Perry Morton (August 4, 1823–November 1, 1877). Indiana's Civil War governor who represents his state in Statuary Hall in a sculpture made by Charles Henry Niehaus. 870.

4 Nautilus Day, the anniversary of the August 4, 1958, passage of the atomic-powered submarine, *Nautilus*, under the North Pole. Commander William R. Anderson was awarded the Legion of Merit and the submarine's officers and men were presented with the Presidential Unit Citation for their pioneering achievement. 268.

4 Birthday of Gasper Núñez de Arce (August 4, 1832–June 9, 1903). Spanish poet known as the "Spanish Tennyson."

c4 Peer Gynt Festival Days, observed in Norway beginning about August 4 to re-create the folklore and pageantry of the historical Peer Gynt, known to the world through the dramatic play of Ibsen.

4 Birthday of Percy Bysshe Shelley (August 4, 1792–July 8, 1822). English poet in whose honor the Poetry Society of America presents the annual Shelley Memorial Award to a living American poet. 864.

Holy Days and Feast Days

5 The Feast of the Dedication of Our Lady of the Snows of the Church of Saint Mary Major in Rome. A feast of thanksgiving that includes a shower of white blossoms commemorating the August 5 snowfall of the third century that outlined the shape of a basilica. 5.

Holidays and Civic Days

5 Upper Volta Independence Day, a civic day in Upper Volta, which became an independent nation on the African continent on August 5, 1960. 868, 875.

Anniversaries and Special Events Days

5 Birthday of Mary Ritter Beard (August 5, 1876–August 14, 1958). American historian who in numerous books concentrated on women's roles in society; collaborated with her husband Charles in the writing of American history.

5 Clipping the Church Day, observed on Saint Oswald's Day at Guiseley, Yorkshire, England; a day of carrying out an old custom of embracing the church by joining hands and moving around the church in a wide ring; observed in other parts of England on days appropriate to their parish church calendars. 256.

5 Birthday of John Eliot (August 5, 1604–May 21, 1690). American clergyman, "the apostle to the Indians"; author of a catechism which was the first book printed in an American Indian language; his translation of the Bible into the Pequot language, completed in 1663, was the first Bible printed on the American continent. 20.

5 Birthday of Guy de Maupassant (August 5, 1850–July 6, 1893). French novelist and one of the greatest short-story writers of the nineteenth century. 864.

c5 Rush-Bearing Day, observed at Grasmere, England, on the Saturday nearest Saint Oswald's Day, August 5; a ceremony in which children carry garlands and rushes to the churchyard where Wordsworth is buried. 256.

Holy Days and Feast Days

6 Feast of the Transfiguration of the Lord, a commemoration of the revelation to Peter, James, and John of Christ's role as the fulfillment of the law and the prophets. 5.

Holidays and Civic Days

6 Bolivian Independence Day, a public holiday in Bolivia commemorating the proclamation of independence from Peru declared at the Congress of Chuquisaca on August 6, 1825; the day is a part of two-day national festival. 868, 875.

6 Accession Day, a holiday in the United Arab Emirates commemorating the accession of the ruler of Abu Dhabi and president of the federation of the Supreme Council of the United Arab Emirates. 875.

Anniversaries and Special Events Days

6 Birthday of Sir Alexander Fleming (August 6, 1881–March 11, 1955). Scottish bacteriologist who discovered penicillin; corecipient of the Nobel Prize in medicine in 1945. 864.

6 Hiroshima Day, anniversary of the dropping of the first atomic bomb on Hiroshima, from a B-29 Superfortress on August 5 (U.S. time), August 6 (Japan time), 1945. Hiroshima is now a city dedicated to world peace and the site of the Atomic Bomb Casualty Commission, which is dedicated to medical and biological research. 684, 700.

Holiday and Civic Days

7 Battle of Boyacá Day, a public holiday in Colombia commemorating the victory of the South American insurgents over the Spanish forces on August 7, 1819. 868, 875.

Anniversaries and Special Events Days

7 Birthday of Ralph Johnson Bunche (August 7, 1904–December 9, 1971). A founder and leader of the United Nations. Winner of the 1950 Nobel Peace Prize for the negotiation of an Arab-Israel truce. The first black to receive the Nobel Prize. 679, 796.

7 Birthday of Nathanael Greene (August 7, 1742–June 19, 1786). American Revolutionary War general who represents Rhode Island in Statuary Hall in a sculpture done by Henry Kirke Brown. 870.

7 Anniversary of the dedication on August 7, 1927, of the International Peace Bridge honoring the peace that exists between Canada and the United States.

7 The anniversary of the establishment of the Order of the Purple Heart, a United States decoration for military merit created by George Washington on August 7, 1782, for enlisted men and noncommissioned officers. The first recipients were Sergeants Daniel Bissel, Daniel Brown, and Elijah Churchill of the Connecticut regiment, who were honored on May 9, 1783. 458.

Holy Days and Feast Days

8 Feast Day of Saint Dominic, founder of the Dominican Order; patron saint of astronomers and of the Dominican Republic. 4, 9.

Holidays and Civic Days

8 Bhutan, a Himalayan kingdom known as the "land of dragons," became an independent monarchy on August 8, 1949. 868.

Anniversaries and Special Events Days

8 Birthday of Charles Bulfinch (August 8, 1763–April 4, 1844). American architect who introduced the styles of Christopher Wren and Robert Adam into American architecture; the first professional architect in the United States. 864.

8 Matthew Henson Day, the anniversary of the birth on August 8, 1866, of Matthew A. Henson, the black explorer who with Peary discovered the North Pole in 1909; the recipient of a Congressional Medal in 1945 for his contributions to science. 864.

8 Birthday of Ernest Orlando Lawrence (August 8, 1901–August 27, 1958). American physicist, inventor of the cyclotron, recipient of the 1939 Nobel Prize in physics; recipient of the first Sylvanus Thayer Award from West Point. 864.

8 Birthday of Henry Fairfield Osborn (August 8, 1857–November 6, 1935). American paleontologist and author who broadened public understanding of paleontology through instructive museum displays. 864.

Holidays and Civic Days

9 Singapore National Day, a public holiday, honoring August 9, 1965, when Singapore was separated from the Federation of Malaysia and became an independent sovereign state. 875.

Anniversaries and Special Events Days

9 Birthday of William Thomas Green Morton (August 9, 1819–July 15, 1868). American dentist who received an award from the French Academy of Science in 1852 for the application of the discovery of etherization to surgical operation. He was elected to the Hall of Fame for Great Americans in 1920. 864.

9 Nagasaki Memorial Day, a memorial observance in Nagasaki, Japan, for the victims of the second atomic bombing on August 9, 1945; also called "the moment of silence." 684.

9 Resignation Day, anniversary of the resignation of Richard M. Nixon on August 9, 1974; the first president of the United States to resign from executive office. 268, 371.

9 Birthday of Izaak Walton (August 9, 1593–December 15, 1683). English biographer and author famous for *The Compleat Angler*. 864.

Holy Days and Feast Days

10 Feast Day of Saint Lawrence of Rome for whom the St. Lawrence River is named; patron saint of cooks, invoked against rheumatism and fire and for the protection of vineyards; a notable festival in his honor is held at the Escorial in Madrid. 4, 9.

Holidays and Civic Days

10 Ecuador Independence Day, a holiday commemorating the August 10, 1809, proclamation of independence; celebrated throughout Ecuador with patriotic events. 868, 875.

10 Herbert Hoover Day, a commemorative day at President Hoover's birthplace in West Branch, Iowa; observed with programs by civic organizations at West Branch and throughout the country by the Boys' Club of America. 857.

10 Missouri Admission Day. Missouri entered the Union as the twenty-fourth state on August 10, 1821. 268, 856, 862.

Anniversaries and Special Events Days

10 Birthday of Camillo Benso di Cavour (August 10, 1810–June 6, 1861). Italian statesman, premier of Italy, major leader in Italian unification. 864.

10 Birthday of Herbert Clark Hoover (August 10, 1874–October 20, 1964). German-Swiss ancestry; Iowa-born mining engineer; administrator and humanitarian; thirty-first president of the United States, 1929–33. Chairman, Commission on Organization of the Executive Branch. Society of Friends. Founded the Hoover Library on War, Revolution, and Peace at Stanford University. Buried at West Branch, Iowa. 359–66, 370–72, 374, 378, 378.

10 The anniversary of the signing by President James K. Polk of the act establishing the Smithsonian Institution on August 10, 1846.

Holy Days and Feast Days

11 Feast of Saint Clare, founder of the Franciscan order of nuns known as the Poor Clares; recognized with Saint Francis for leadership and influence in the growth and spread of the Franciscans; patron saint of television. 4, 9, 748.

Holidays and Civic Days

11 Chad Independence Day, a holiday celebrating independence gained by Chad on August 11, 1960, the official celebration is frequently scheduled for a January date to avoid the torrential August rains. 868, 875.

11 The King's Accession day, a holiday in the Hashemite Kingdom of Jordan celebrating King Hussein's accession to the throne on August 11, 1952. 875.

11 Zimbabwe Heroes Days, a two-day holiday in Zimbabwe honoring the heroes of the nation. 875.

Holidays and Civic Days

12 The Queen's Birthday, a holiday in Thailand, celebrating the birthday of Her Majesty Queen Sirikit. 875.

Anniversaries and Special Events Days

12 Birthday of Katharine Lee Bates (August 12, 1859–March 28, 1929). American educator and writer, author of the text for the national hymn "America the Beautiful." 864.

12 Birthday of Robert Mills (August 12, 1781–March 3, 1855). American architect, the first to study exclusively in the United States; his most memorable work is the Washington Monument. 268, 425.

12 Ponce de Leon Day, a festival day in Puerto Rico honoring the arrival of Ponce de Leon in 1508. 268.

12 The Glorious Twelfth, the day the grouse season begins in Scotland; a day honored by Scots around the world even by those who have never participated in the great national sport. 844.

Holidays and Civic Days

13 Proclamation of Independence Day in the Central African Republic, a holiday honoring the establishment of complete independence on August 13, 1960. 868, 875.

13 The Three Glorious Days, a three-day holiday in the People's Republic of Congo; the days of festivity include Independence day honoring August 15, 1960, when the country achieved its sovereignty. 875.

13 Women's Day, a holiday in Tunisia, celebrating the independence of women and honoring their contributions to the nation. 875.

Anniversaries and Special Events Days

13 Birthday of John Logie Baird (August 13, 1888–June 14, 1946). Scottish inventor known as "the father of television." 864.

13 Berlin Wall Day, the anniversary of the erection on August 13, 1961, of the concrete wall sealing the border between East and West Berlin to halt the exodus of people to the West. The placement of wreaths and quiet memorial services for the victims of escape attempts have been a symbol of West Berlin resentment of the curtailment of human rights. 658.

13 William Caxton Day, anniversary of the birth on August 13, c1422, of William Caxton, who, in 1477, printed the first book in English; a day of recognition observed by collectors and literary organizations. 864.

13 Lefthanders Day, celebrated in 1982 on Friday, August 13, by Lefthanders International to promote the rights of left-handed people and to encourage manufacturers to consider their special needs.

13 Birthday of Annie Oakley (August 13, 1860–November 3, 1926). American markswoman whose personality and exploits are re-created in pageants of the American West. 802.

13 Lucy Stone Day, the anniversary of the birth of Lucy Stone on August 13, 1818; a leading suffragist and abolitionist; known for her insistence on keeping her maiden name after marriage, thus inspiring generations of Lucy Stoners; honored by many organizations including the Lucy Stone League in New York City, a center for studies on the status of women. 268, 738.

Holidays and Civic Days

14 Bahrain proclaimed its status as an independent emirate on August 14, 1971, ending 110 years of formal British protection. 868.

14 Assumption Eve, a holiday in France in anticipation of the Feast of the Assumption. 875.

14 Liberty Tree Day, observed in Massachusetts to memorialize the American colonists' challenge to the British governor in placing, on August 14, 1765, two effigies in a Boston elm tree, soon to be known as "the liberty tree."

14 Pakistan Independence Day, a holiday commemorating the establishment of Pakistan as a free nation on August 14, 1947. 868, 875.

Anniversaries and Special Events Days

14 Atlantic Charter Day, observed in the United States by presidential proclamation; honors the Atlantic Charter, signed by President Franklin Roosevelt and Winston Churchill on August 14, 1941, on which the signatories based their "hopes for a better future for the world" and outlined the eight points that were later incorporated in the United Nations declaration. 268.

c14 Bud Billiken Day, a children's day observed in Chicago on or near August 14 in honor of Bud Billiken, the mythical godfather of Chicago's black children, created in 1923 by Robert S. Abbott, founder of the *Chicago Defender* newspaper.

14 Birthday of John Galsworthy (August 14, 1867–January 31, 1933). English author famous for *The Forsyte Saga*. He received the Order of Merit in 1929 and was the recipient of the Nobel Prize in literature in 1932. 864.

14 Social Security Day, the anniversary of the August 14, 1935, signing by President Franklin Roosevelt of the law creating the American social security system. 874.

14 V-J Day, the anniversary of the August 14, 1945, announcement that Japan had surrendered to the Allies, thus ending the war in the Pacific. The official ratification occurred on September 2, 1945. 268.

Holy Days and Feast Days

15 Feast of the Assumption of the Blessed Virgin Mary, commemorates the taking of Mary, body and soul, into heaven at the end of her earthly life; a Solemnity in the Roman Catholic church. 5.

Holidays and Civic Days

15 Assumption Day, a religious and national holiday in thirty-eight nations of the world honoring one of the oldest and most solemn feasts of Mary, her assumption into heaven.

15 Congo Independence Day, one of the Three Glorious Days celebrated as holidays in August. Congo became an independent republic on August 15, 1960. 868, 875.

15 Mother's Day, a holiday in Costa Rica honoring the mothers of the nation on Assumption Day. 875.

15 Napoleon's Day, a holiday in Corsica, a department of France, celebrating the birth of Napoleon I on August 15, 1769.

15 Independence Day in India, a holiday commemorating August 15, 1947, when the Indian Independence Act went into effect. 868, 875.

15 Korean Republic Day, a holiday in the Republic of Korea celebrating the 1945 liberation from Japan and the August 15, 1948 proclamation of the republic for south Korea. 868, 875.

15 Liechtenstein National Day, a holiday of festivities honoring both the Day of the Assumption and associations with the royal family. 875.

15 Military Regime Day, a holiday in the Republic of Niger honoring the Supreme Military Council as the highest organ of government since 1974. 868.

15 Foundation of Panama, a holiday in Panama City commemorating its settlement on the Pacific coast in 1518. 875.

Anniversaries and Special Events Days

15 Chauvin Day, a name-day associated with a French soldier, Nicholas Chauvin, who idolized Napoleon to an extreme, his arrogant boastfulness led to the long-lasting use of the term *chauvinism*. 866.

15 Birthday of Thomas Edward Lawrence (August 15, 1888–May 19, 1935). British soldier and author known as Lawrence of Arabia. 864.

15 Birthday of Sir Walter Scott (August 15, 1771–September 21, 1832). Scottish novelist and poet famous for such books as *Ivanhoe, Rob Roy,* and *Quentin Durward.* 864.

Holidays and Civic Days

16 Cyprus Independence Day, the anniversary of the August 16, 1960, agreement between the British and the Greek and Turkish Cypriots to provide independence for Cyprus. 789.

16 Political Restitution Day, or Dominican Restoration Day, commemorating the restoration of independence in 1963; a public holiday in the Dominican Republic. 868, 875.

16 Bennington Battle Day, August 16, a legal holiday in Vermont honoring the Green Mountain Boys' victory over the British in 1777. 268.

Anniversaries and Special Events Days

16 Elvis Presley Day, the anniversary of the death of the popular rock-singer on August 16, 1977. The day is commemorated by Elvis Presley clubs and individual fans. 874.

16 Anniversary of the death of Duncan Phyfe on August 16, 1854. American cabinetmaker famous for fine furniture; honored in museum collections. 864.

16 Madonna del Voto Day, celebrated in Sienna, Italy, with the second of the two great annual horseraces held in honor of the Virgin; the first, the Race for the Palio, is held on July 2.

Holidays and Civic Days

17 San Martín Day, a holiday in Argentina, commemorates the death of José Francisco de San Martín on August 17, 1850, with special events honoring the most famous Argentine of all time. 868, 875.

17 Gabon Independence Day, a public holiday in the equatorial nation on the west coast of Africa, commemorating independence secured on August 17, 1960. 868, 875.

17 Indonesia Independence Day, a holiday honoring the proclamation of independence made by the Indonesian Revolutionaries on August 17, 1945, the decisive day for full independence achieved on December 27, 1949. 868.

Holy Days and Feast Days

18 Feast Day of Saint Helena, discoverer of the True Cross, mother of the Emperor Constantine. 4, 9.

Anniversaries and Special Events Days

18 Birthday of Meriwether Lewis (August 18, 1774–October 11, 1809). American explorer and coleader of the Lewis and Clark expedition into the American Northwest. 268, 739.

c18 Klondike Gold Discovery Day, a holiday in the Yukon commemorating the discovery of gold on August 17, 1896; observed on the Friday immediately preceding August 18. 781, 866.

Anniversaries and Special Events Days

19 National Aviation Day, honoring the Wright brothers and other pioneer aviators. 268, 269, 464–76, 866.

19 Birthday of Edith Nesbit (August 19, 1858–May 4, 1924). English author, cofounder of the Fabian Society, who is remembered for her lively stories of the adventures of the Bastable children. 864.

19 Birthday of Manuel Luis Quezon (August 19, 1878–August 1, 1944). Philippine statesman; first president of the Philippine Commonwealth. 268.

19 Birthday of Orville Wright (August 19, 1871–January 30, 1948). American aviator and inventor who made the first self-powered airplane flight in history on December 17, 1903. 465, 476.

Holy Days and Feast Days

20 Feast of Saint Bernard, twelfth-century abbot and monastic reformer; called the second founder of the Cistercian order; known as the "mellifluous doctor" because of his eloquence; proclaimed a doctor of the church in 1830. 4, 9.

Holidays and Civic Days

20 Constitution Day, a holiday in Hungary, the Magyar People's Republic, commemorating the institution of a constitution in 1949. 868, 875.

Anniversaries and Special Events Days

20 Czechoslovakia Invasion day, the anniversary of the August 20, 1968, invasion of Czechoslovakia to stop a movement to restore civil rights; a day commemorated by Americans of Czech and Slovak descent. 874.

20 Birthday of Benjamin Harrison (August 20, 1833–March 13, 1901). English ancestry; Indiana lawyer and soldier; twenty-third president of the United States, 1889–93. Presbyterian. Buried at Indianapolis, Indiana. 359–66, 370–72, 374, 378, 379.

20 Birthday of Bernardo O'Higgins (August 20, 1778–October 24, 1842). Chilean general and statesman called "the liberator of Chile." 864.

20 Birthday of Oliver Hazard Perry (August 20, 1785–August 23, 1819). American naval officer famous for the statement "We have met the enemy and they are ours." 268.

Holidays and Civic Days

c21 Hawaii Statehood Day, a holiday honoring Hawaii's admission to the Union as the fiftieth state on August 21, 1959; observed on the third Friday of August. 268, 856, 862, 866.

Anniversaries and Special Events Days

21 The anniversary of the organization of the American Bar Association, one of the chief sponsors of Law Day, on August 21, 1878, at Saratoga, New York.

21 Birthday of Roark Bradford (August 21, 1896–November 13, 1948). American writer and humorist whose short-story collection *Ol' Man Adam an' His Chillun* was adapted by Marc Connelly for the play *Green Pastures*.

21 Anniversary of the Lincoln-Douglas debates of 1858, a major political event of the nineteenth century. 346, 352.

Holy Days and Feast Days

22 Feast of the Queenship of Mary, a memorial commemorating Mary as the queen of heaven, angels, and men. 5.

Anniversaries and Special Events Days

22 King Richard III Day, anniversary of the death of the last of the Plantagenets, slain in battle on August 22, 1485; observed by Richard III societies in the United States and England.

Holy Days and Feast Days

23 Feast of Saint Rose of Lima, a sixteenth-century mystic and woman of great piety; canonized in 1671 as the first saint in the New World; patron saint of South America. 4, 9.

Holidays and Civic Days

23 Romanian Liberation Day, a public holiday commemorating the coup that deposed the Fascist Iron Guard dictatorship in Romania on August 23, 1944. 868, 875.

Anniversaries and Special Events Days

23 Sacco and Vanzetti Memorial Day; the anniversary of the execution of Nicola Sacco and Bartolomeo Vanzetti on August 23, 1927; a case that aroused worldwide protests against the convictions and a proclamation of vindication from the governor of Massachusetts on July 19, 1977.

23 The anniversary of the August 23, 1948, organization of the World Council of Churches in Amsterdam. The member churches, as of 1980, represent over one hundred countries throughout the world.

Holy Days and Feast Days

24 Feast of Saint Bartholomew, one of the twelve apostles who spent his life preaching until he was martyred; his feast is celebrated on August 25 in the Eastern Orthodox and the Eastern Catholic churches. 4, 9.

Holidays and Civic Days

24 Liberian Flag Day, observed in Liberia to honor the flag and the 1847 convention that approved the flag design with eleven stripes representing the eleven men who signed the declaration of independence and the first constitution. 280.

Anniversaries and Special Events Days

24 Birthday of Sir Max Beerbohm (August 24, 1872–May 20, 1956). English caricaturist and critic, best known for his caricature portraits of literary and political figures. 864.

24 Vesuvius Day, the anniversary of the eruption of Mount Vesuvius on August 24, A.D. 79 burying the cities of Pompeii and Herculaneum under ash that preserved the artifacts of the period for study and observation by later generations. 695.

24 Birthday of William Wilberforce (August 24, 1759–July 29, 1833). Crusader against oppression and slavery in the British Empire. His name was given to Wilberforce College in Ohio. 20.

Holy Days and Feast Days

25 Feast Day of Saint Genesius, patron saint of secretaries, actors, and lawyers. 4, 9.

25 Feast of Saint Louis, thirteenth-century French king, founder of the Sorbonne, a Crusader, a man of great charity and piety, responsible for the building of some of the most beautiful cathedrals in France. 4, 9.

Holidays and Civic Days

25 French Liberation Day, celebrating the end of the Nazi occupation of Paris with the arrival of the Allied forces on August 25, 1944; observed with special ceremonials in Paris despite the general population exodus that takes place in August, the favorite month for holidays in France.

25 Paraguay Constitution Day, a public holiday commemorating the revision of the constitution adopted on August 25, 1967. 868, 875.

25 Uruguayan Independence Day, a holiday in Uruguay commemorating the declaration of independence from Brazil proclaimed on August 25, 1825. 868, 875.

Anniversaries and Special Events Days

25 Birthday of Bret Harte (August 25, 1836–May 5, 1902). American poet and novelist, best known for his short stories "The Luck of Roaring Camp" and "The Outcasts of Poker Flat." 864.

Anniversaries and Special Events Days

26 Birthday of Sir John Buchan (August 26, 1875–February 11, 1940). Scottish statesman and author; governor-general of Canada. 864.

26 Birthday of Lee De Forest (August 26, 1873–June 30, 1961). American inventor, known as "the father of radio" for his 1906 invention of the three-electrode vacuum tube. 864.

26 Birthday of James Harlan (August 26, 1820–October 5, 1899). American congressman and secretary of the interior. Represents the state of Iowa in Statuary Hall in a sculpture by Nellie V. Walker. 870.

26 Krakatoa Day, the anniversary of the August 26, 1883, volcanic eruptions in the Netherland Indies that made history not only for the Indonesian area but also for the entire world since the eruption affected oceanic and atmospheric currents for years. 695.

26 Woman's Equality Day, or Susan B. Anthony Day, the anniversary of the proclamation of final approval of the Nineteenth Amendment, on August 26, 1920, which gave voting privileges to women; observed by presidential proclamation in the United States. 268, 866.

Holy Days and Feast Days

27 Feast of Saint Monica, a fourth-century Christian whose conduct made her a model for Christian mothers; the patron saint of married women. 4, 9.

Holidays and Civil Days

27 Lyndon B. Johnson's Birthday, a holiday in Texas, honoring the August 27, 1908 birth of Lyndon Baines Johnson, the thirty-sixth president of the United States. 875.

Anniversaries and Special Events Days

27 Birthday of Theodore Herman Dreiser (August 27, 1871–December 28, 1945). American author who made his reputation with such naturalistic novels as *Sister Carrie* and *An American Tragedy*; awarded the Merit Medal of the American Academy of Arts and Letters in 1944. 864.

27 Birthday of Lyndon Baines Johnson (August 27, 1908–January 22, 1973). Thirty-sixth president of the United States; promulgator of legislation for the "great society" program; member of the Church of the Disciples of Christ; author of *The Vantage Point*, an interpretation of the Johnson administration. Buried at the Johnson ranch near Johnson City, Texas. 359–61, 365, 369, 371, 372, 374, 379.

27 Birthday of Hannibal Hamlin (August 27, 1809–July 4, 1891). American statesman; vice-president in Lincoln's first administration; United States minister to Spain. He represents the state of Maine in Statuary Hall in a sculpture by Charles E. Tefft. 870.

27 Mountbatten Assassination Day, the anniversary of the August 27, 1979, assassination in Donegal Bay of Lord Mountbatten, British World War II hero and the last viceroy of India. 776.

27 Anniversary of the birth on August 27, 1910, of Mother Teresa, Roman Catholic missionary and founder of the Missionaries of Charity; known around the world for her selfless dedication to the sick, the homeless, and the dying destitute. Mother Teresa was awarded the Nobel Peace Prize in 1979. 804.

27 Anniversary of the death of Titian on August 27, 1576. Italian painter famous for the altarpiece *The Assumption of the Virgin* and other great religious paintings. 864.

Holy Days and Feast Days

28 Feast Day of Saint Augustine of Hippo; doctor of grace; patron saint of students for the priesthood. Saint Augustine is remembered as the man whose worldly background caused him to pray "Make me pure—but not yet"; he became one of the greatest figures in the Christian church; author of *Confessions* and *The City of God*. 4, 9.

Anniversaries and Special Events Days

28 Birthday of Johann Wolfgang von Goethe (August 28, 1749–March 22, 1832). German poet, dramatist, novelist, philosopher, statesman, and scientist. *Faust*, one of Goethe's major works, has been translated into all of the major languages of the world.

28 Anniversary of the Spanish landing in 1565 at the site of present-day St. Augustine, Florida. 268.

Holy Days and Feast Days

29 The Martyrdom of Saint John, beheaded by King Herod at the insistence of Salome, commemorated on August 29 in honor of one of the greatest and most popular of saints; called "the feast of the beheading" in the Greek Orthodox church. 4, 9.

Anniversaries and Special Events Days

29 Birthday of Henry Bergh (August 29, 1811–March 12, 1888). American philanthropist; founder and first president of the Society for the Prevention of Cruelty to Animals; commemorated through the observance of Humane Days. 769.

29 Birthday of Oliver Wendell Holmes (August 29, 1809–October 7, 1894). American poet, essayist, and novelist. His best-known poems include "The Chambered Nautilus" and "The Wonderful One-Hoss Shay." He was elected to the Hall of Fame for Great Americans in 1910. 268.

29 Birthday of John Locke (August 29, 1632–October 28, 1704). English philosopher who wrote *An Essay Concerning Human Understanding*. 864.

29 Birthday of Maurice Maeterlinck (August 29, 1862–May 6, 1949). Belgian dramatist, poet, and essayist, author of such dramas as *Pelléas et Mélisande*, the basis of an opera by Claude Debussy, and *L'Oiseau Bleu*. Awarded the 1911 Nobel Prize in literature for his contributions to drama. 864.

Holidays and Civic Days

c30 Liberation Day, a holiday in Hong Kong commemorating the end of Japanese occupation on August 30, 1945; observed on the last Monday in August. 875.

c30 Lammas Fair Day, a day of fair and festival events celebrated for over 350 years in Ballycastle, Ireland, on the last Tuesday of August; a tradition of the day is the feasting on dulse and yellowman, an age-old custom.

30 Huey P. Long Day, a holiday in Louisiana, celebrating the August 30, 1893, birth of the state's most articulate U.S. senator; popularly known as the Kingfish. 268, 875.

30 Rose of Lima Day, a public holiday in Peru honoring the patroness of South America whose feast day is celebrated by the church on August 23. 875.

30 Victory Day, a holiday in Turkey in tribute to the memory of warriors who died in the 1922 Battle of Dumlupinar, the final battle for Turkish independence. 875.

c30 Summer Holiday, celebrated in all of the United Kingdom, except Scotland, on the last Monday of August; a free day for sports and family outings. 875.

Anniversaries and Special Events Days

30 Birthday of Huey Pierce Long (August 30, 1893–September 10, 1935). Louisiana politician and lawyer; governor of the state and exponent of a "share-the-wealth" plan. He represents the state of Louisiana in Statuary Hall in a sculpture by Charles Keck. His birthday is a holiday in Louisiana. 268, 870.

Holidays and Civic Days

31 Merdeka Day, a holiday in Malaysia, celebrating the achievement of the status of independence within the British Commonwealth on August 31, 1957; celebrated with parades, fireworks, and festivities. 868, 875.

31 Trinidad and Tobago Independence Day, a public holiday commemorating the independence achieved on August 31, 1962, within the British Commonwealth of Nations. 868, 875.

Anniversaries and Special Events Days

31 Anniversary of the chartering on August 31, 1960, of the Agricultural Hall of Fame to honor farm men and women who have contributed to America's greatness.

31 Anniversary of the death of John Bunyan on August 31, 1688. English preacher renowned for *Pilgrim's Progress*. 1, 864.

31 Festal Day, observed by the Order of the Eastern Star on August 31, the birthday of Robert Morris, who was one of the founders of the Order of the Eastern Star in the United States.

31 Birthday of DuBose Heyward (August 31, 1885–June 16, 1940). American novelist whose novel *Porgy* was used as the basis for George Gershwin's opera *Porgy and Bess*. 864.

31 Anniversary of the August 31, 1981, death of Joseph H. Hirshhorn, financier, uranium mining tycoon, art collector, and founder and donor to the nation of the Hirshhorn Museum and Sculpture Garden in Washington, D.C. 690.

31 Birthday of Ramón Magsaysay (August 31, 1907–March 17, 1957). Philippine statesman; recipient of the United States Legion of Merit in 1952; president of the Philippines. 864.

31 Birthday of Maria Montessori (August 31, 1870–May 6, 1952). Italian educator, founder of the Montessori method of teaching. 738.

31 Solidarity Day, the anniversary of the August 31, 1980, signing of the Gdansk Agreement by the Polish government and Lech Walesa, Polish labor leader; an agreement which gave birth to the Polish Solidarity movement aiming at the right to form independent trade unions and the right to strike. 667.

September

September, the ninth month in our calendar, received its name from the Latin numeral *septem*, meaning "seven," because it was the seventh month in the old Roman calendar. It became the ninth month when Julius Caesar changed the calendar to make January the first month. The middle of September brings autumn to the northern hemisphere and the beginning of spring to the southern hemisphere.

September is an important month in military history since it marks the official end of World War II, the signing of the unconditional surrender papers by Japan on September 2, 1945. Battle of Britain Week, which honors the British airmen who drove back the German planes on September 15, 1940, the most decisive air battle of World War II, is observed in September in Britain. September is also a special month for veterans who belong to the American Legion because their organization was chartered on September 16, 1919. September also honors the mothers who lost their sons and daughters in military service with a day called Gold Star Mother's Day, which is observed in late September.

The flowers for September are the morning glory and the aster, and the birthstone is the sapphire.

Holy Days and Feast Days

1 Feast of Saint Fiacre, seventh-century hermit, founder of a hospice for travelers; the patron saint of the cabdrivers of Paris, whose vehicles are called *fiacres*, because the first coach was located near the Hotel Saint-Fiacre. 9.

Holidays and Civic Days

1 Libyan National Day, a holiday, commemorating the deposition of the king on September 1, 1969, and the formation of the Socialist People's Libyan Arab Jamahiriyah. 868, 875.

1 United Arab Republics Day, a holiday in the Arab Republic of Syria commemorating the referendum of September 1, 1971, approving a Confederation of Arab Republics. 868, 875.

1 Presidential Message Day, the opening of the Mexican Congress on September 1; a public holiday in Mexico. 875.

Anniversaries and Special Events Days

1 Birthday of Sir Roger David Casement (September 1, 1864–August 3, 1916). Irish martyr patriot. 864.

1 Birthday of Elizabeth Harrison (September 1, 1849–October 31, 1927). American educator, leader in the kindergarten movement, and one of the founders of the organization that became the National Congress of Parents and Teachers. 864.

Holidays and Civic Days

2 Independence Day in Vietnam honoring September 2, 1945, when Ho Chi Minh proclaimed the establishment of a Democratic Republic of Vietnam. The official date of Vietnamese independence is recorded as March 8, 1949. 868, 875.

Anniversaries and Special Events Days

2 Birthday of Eugene Field (September 2, 1850–November 4, 1895). American journalist; author of children's verses, of which the most familiar are "Little Boy Blue" and "Wynken, Blynken, and Nod." 268.

c2 Birthday of Henry George (September 2, 1839–October 29, 1897). American economist best known for his book *Progress and Poverty*. 864.

2 Anniversary of the signing of the unconditional surrender by Japan on September 2, 1945, which officially ended World War II in the Pacific.

2 Birthday of Lydia Kamekeha Liliuoka-
lani (September 2, 1838–November 11,
1917). Queen of the Hawaiian Islands, over-
thrown in 1893 but remembered as the author
of several songs including "Aloha Oe"
(Farewell to Thee). 864.

2 London Fire Days, anniversary of the
Great Fire of London which began on
September 2, 1666, and raged for three days;
re-created in a diorama at the Museum of
London.

Holy Days and Feast Days

3 Feast of Saint Gregory I, the Great,
consecrated pope on September 3, 590;
a molder of the Roman liturgy and known for
the Gregorian chant; the last of the traditional
doctors of the church; canonized by acclama-
tion upon his death. 4, 9.

Holidays and Civic Days

3 Independence Day in Qatar, a national
holiday celebrating September 3, 1971,
when the State of Qatar, on a peninsula in the
Persian gulf, won full independence from Britain. 868, 875.

3 Saint Marinus Day, a holiday in the
Republic of San Marino, a land-locked
nation surrounded by Italian territory. The
holiday commemorates the nation's official
foundation day and Saint Marinus, the country's patron saint. 868, 875.

3 Commemoration of September 3, 1934,
Day, a public holiday in Tunisia honoring the beginning of the independence movement. 868.

Anniversaries and Special Events Days

c3 Labor Day, a public holiday, celebrated in the United States and Canada
on the first Monday in September. Labor Day
in the United States was founded by Peter J.
Maguire in tribute to American industry. The
day became a holiday for federal employees in
1894, and was quickly approved as a holiday in
the individual states. 268, 269, 323–338, 605.

3 Birthday of John Humphrey Noyes
(September 3, 1811–April 13, 1886).
American social reformer and author; founder
of the Oneida Community. 864.

3 Birthday of Louis Henri Sullivan
(September 3, 1856–April 4, 1924).
American architect who established the princi-
ple that form should follow function. 864.

3 Treaty of Paris Day, the anniversary of
the signing on September 3, 1783, of the
treaty between the United States and England
ending the Revolutionary War. 268.

Holidays and Civic Days

4 Birthday of the city of Los Angeles,
celebrated with a variety of observances, especially on Olvera Street, the oldest
street in the city, to honor the September 4,
1781, founding of the city. 268.

Anniversaries and Special Events Days

c4 Birthday of Daniel Hudson Burnham
(September 4, 1846–June 1, 1912).
American architect; pioneer in fireproof sky-
scraper construction; developer of the Burnham Plan, the "think big" plan, used for many
years as the basis for city planning in Chicago.
864.

4 Birthday of Dadabhai Naoroji
(September 4, 1825–June 30, 1917). In-
dian statesman; first Indian member of the
British Parliament.

4 Birthday of Robert Raikes (September
4, 1736–April 5, 1811). English Sunday-
school pioneer who was a major force in the
development of the religious-education movement. 20.

4 Birthday of Marcus Whitman (September 4, 1802–November 29, 1847).
American pioneer and missionary physician
whose faith in the future of the state of Oregon
and representations to the federal governemnt
led to the securing of Oregon for the United
States. 268.

Anniversaries and Special Events Days

5 Anniversary of the first meeting of the
Continental Congress in Philadelphia
on September 5, 1774. 268.

5 Labor Parade Day; the anniversary of the first Labor Day holiday parade in the United States; held on September 5, 1882, in New York City. Labor Day in the United States was initiated by Peter J. Maguire in tribute to American industry. 336.

c5 Regatta Day, observed in Malta on or near September 5; commemorates the siege in 1565 when the Maltese turned back the Turkish invaders and the siege of 1943 inflicted by the German forces. 857.

Holidays and Civic Days

6 Pakistan Defense Day, a public holiday in Pakistan. 875.

6 Somhlolo Day, in Swaziland, a public holiday, celebrating the achievement of independence on September 6, 1968, for the Kingdom of Swaziland in southern Africa. Named for Somhlolo or Subhuza, the nation's nineteenth-century chief. 868, 875.

Anniversaries and Special Events Days

6 Birthday of Jane Addams (September 6, 1860–May 21, 1935). American social worker, advocate of international peace, founder of Hull House in Chicago. She shared the Nobel Peace Prize with Nicholas Murray Butler in 1931. A Jane Addams Children's Book Award, given annually to the children's book that "best combines literary worth with a strong statement of faith in people," is presented by the Women's International League for Peace and Freedom and the Jane Addams Peace Association. Observance of her birthday occurs at Hull House in Chicago and in programs of social agencies and peace organizations. 268, 738, 749, 806, 858.

c6 Grandparents' Day, established by a presidential proclamation signed on September 6, 1979; observed throughout the United States on the first Sunday after Labor Day. 697.

6 Lafayette's Birthday, a day of recognition honoring the September 6, 1757, birth of the Marquis de Lafayette, who served in Washington's army during the American Revolution. 268, 419.

6 Birthday of Heinrich Melchior Mühlenberg (September 6, 1711–October 7, 1787). American Lutheran clergyman, chief founder of the Lutheran church in the United States, known as the "patriarch of the Lutheran church in America." 20.

Holy Days and Feast Days

7 Feast of Our Lady of the Rosary, commemorates Mary through the mysteries of the rosary focused on events in the lives of both Mary and Christ. The feast was instituted to commemorate the Christian victory over invading Mohammedans at Lepanto on October 7, 1571.

Holidays and Civic Days

7 Brazil Independence Day, a holiday honoring Dom Pedro's proclamation of independence from Portugal, declared on September 7, 1822. 868, 875.

Anniversaries and Special Events Days

7 Birthday of Ferdinand Vandiveer Hayden (September 7, 1829–December 22, 1887). American geologist who participated in the 1859–86 geological and geographical surveys of the United States; a leader in the movement to preserve Yellowstone as a federal park.

Holy Days and Feast Days

8 Feast of the Nativity of the Blessed Virgin Mary, honoring Mary's birthday as a Jewish child and as a lineal descendant of the royal family of David; observed by the Roman Catholic countries of the world. 5.

Holidays and Civic Days

8 Andorra National Day, a holiday in the Andorran coprincipality of the eastern Pyrenees honoring the Notre Dame of Meritxell; a folklore event and pilgrimage based on the finding of an unusual figure under an almond tree blooming out of season. 875.

8 Guinea-Bissau Independence Day, the anniversary of the establishment, on September 8, 1974, of Guinea-Bissau as a sovereign nation; terminating five centuries of colonial rule for the former territory of Portuguese Guinea. 868, 875.

Anniversaries and Special Events Days

8 Birthday of Lodovico Ariosto (September 8, 1474–July 6, 1533). Italian poet; author of *Orlando Furioso*, an epic of Roland recognized as a classic example of Renaissance literature.

8 Birthday of Anton Dvořák (September 8, 1841–May 1, 1904). Czech composer famous for the *New World Symphony*, which was composed in Iowa. 864.

8 International Literacy Day, established by the United Nations to foster universal literacy with assistance and materials. 784, 866.

8 Birthday of Frédéric Mistral (September 8, 1830–March 25, 1914). French poet who used Provençal, the dialect of southern France, as his medium; a corecipient of the 1904 Nobel Prize in literature. 864.

8 Pardon Day, the anniversary of the pardon issued by President Gerald Ford on September 8, 1974, to his predecessor, Richard Nixon, who resigned the presidency on August 9, 1974; the pardon was granted in an effort to heal the divisive wounds suffered by the nation as a result of the Watergate break-in and subsequent congressional inquiries. 371.

8 The Sheriff's Ride Ceremony, an annual event at Lichfield, England, observed on the day of the Feast of the Nativity of the Blessed Virgin Mary to fulfill the terms of Queen Mary's Charter of 1553, which created the city. 256.

8 Birthday of Robert Taft (September 8, 1889–July 31, 1953). American congressman; drafter of the Taft-Hartley Act of 1947; known as "Mr. Republican."

8 Roy Wilkins Day, the anniversary of the death on September 8, 1981, of the long-time executive director of the National Association of Colored People; a quiet, effective force in the movement to advance justice and opportunities for minorities. 821.

Holy Days and Feast Days

9 Feast of Saint Peter Claver, seventeenth-century missionary; defender of and minister to slaves; named patron of missionary work with blacks in 1896; a patron saint of Colombia. 4, 9.

Holidays and Civic Days

9 Bulgarian National day, or Freedom Day, a holiday in Bulgaria commemorating September 9, 1944, when Bulgarian partisans and Soviet troops joined to drive out the Nazis. 875.

9 California Admission Day, a legal holiday in California commemorating the day in 1850 when California was admitted to the Union. 268, 856, 862.

9 Independence Day in North Korea; the anniversary of the founding of the Democratic People's Republic of Korea on September 9, 1948. 868, 875.

9 Jeune Genevois, a holiday in Geneva, Switzerland, a day of enjoyment of Geneva's celebrated garden show. 875.

Anniversaries and Special Events Days

9 Birthday of Armand Jean du Plessis de Richelieu (September 9, 1585–December 4, 1642). Cardinal of the Roman Catholic church and French statesman of tremendous political power; founder of the French Academy and the Jardin des Plantes. 864.

9 Salerno Day, anniversary of the Allied landing at Salerno, Italy, on September 9, 1943; observed by veterans associations.

9 Birthday of Count Leo Tolstoy (September 9, 1828–November 20, 1910). Russian novelist, moral philosopher, and social reformer, famous for *War and Peace* and *Anna Karenina*. 864.

9 United States Day, the anniversary of September 9, 1776, when the Second Continental Congress ruled that the words *United States* should replace the term *United Colonies* as the official name of the new nation; a day commemorated in the programs of many civic organizations. 866.

Holidays and Civic Days

10 Belize National Day, a holiday in Belize, formerly British Honduras, commemorating the 1798 Battle of St. George's Cay, won by a few local baymen over a superior Spanish force. 868, 875.

Anniversaries and Special Events Days

10 Birthday of Sir John Soane (September 10, 1753–January 20, 1837). English architect whose art collection and fortune formed the basis of the Soane Museum in London. 864.

10 Birthday of Franz Werfel (September 10, 1890–August 26, 1945). Austrian novelist, dramatist, and poet whose most popular novel was *The Song of Bernadette*.

Holidays and Civic Days

11 Ethiopian New Year, a holiday in Ethiopia celebrating the first day of Maskaram, the first month in the Coptic church calendar; a day of rejoicing in age-old customs which also celebrates the 1978 reunion of parts of Eritrea with Ethiopia. 875.

11 Jinnah Day, anniversary of the September 11, 1948, death of Quaid-i-Azam Mohammed Ali Jinnah, the founder of a free and independent Pakistan; a public holiday in Pakistan. 392.

Anniversaries and Special Events Days

11 Birthday of Erastus Flaval Beadle (September 11, 1821–December 18, 1894). American publisher of dime novels of interest to collectors as authentic Americana. 867.

11 Birthday of David Herbert Lawrence (September 11, 1885–March 2, 1930). English writer whose most famous novel is *Lady Chatterley's Lover*. 864.

11 Birthday of William Sidney Porter, "O. Henry" (September 11, 1862–June 5, 1910). American short-story writer and journalist; author of the most deftly plotted stories in American literature. 864.

Holidays and Civic Days

12 Ethiopia National Day, a public holiday. On September 12, 1974, the Ethiopian Empire was officially terminated and Emperor Haile Selassie was deposed. 868, 875.

12 Defenders' Day, a holiday in Maryland, commemorating the September 12, 1814, battle of North Point near Baltimore; a day in the War of 1812 followed by the September 14 bombardment of Fort McHenry, an unsuccessful attack that inspired Francis Scott Key to write down the words of "The Star-Spangled Banner"; Defenders' Day is celebrated with many splendid patriotic events. 268.

12 Saudi Arabia National Day, the single nationwide secular holiday celebrated in the Saudi Arabian Kingdom; an outstanding event commemorating the progress of the nation. 875.

Holy Days and Feast Days

13 Feast of Saint John Chrysostom, fourth-century patriarch of Constantinople, a brilliant preacher called "the golden-mouthed" because of his eloquence; proclaimed a doctor of the church in 451; named patron of preachers in 1909. 9.

Holidays and Civic Days

13 Knabenschiessen, a holiday in Zurich, Switzerland. The major attraction of the day is a boys' shooting contest. 875.

Anniversaries and Special Events Days

13 John Barry Day, the anniversary of the death on September 13, 1803, of John Barry, naval hero of the American Revolution, the nation's first commodore; John Barry Day is commemorated by the Knights of Columbus, by the city of Philadelphia, and through proclamations by the governors of Pennsylvania, New Jersey, Rhode Island, and Massachusetts. 268, 452.

13 Birthday of Adolf Meyer (September 13, 1866–March 17, 1950). American psychiatrist and neurologist who, with Clifford Beers, began the mental-hygiene movement. 864.

13 Birthday of John Joseph Pershing (September 13, 1860–July 15, 1948). American general; commander-in-chief of the Allied Expeditionary Force in World War I; United States Army Chief of Staff; winner of the 1932 Pulitzer Prize in history for *My Experiences in the World War*. 864.

13 Battle of Quebec, anniversary of the decisive battle of the French and Indian War won on the Plains of Abraham near the city of Quebec on September 13, 1759. The victory of Wolfe's forces assured the dominance of English influence on the North American continent.

13 Birthday of Walter Reed (September 13, 1851–November 22, 1902). American physician and surgeon who made important studies in the causes of typhoid and yellow fever. Walter Reed Hospital in Washington, D.C., is named in his honor. Dr. Reed was elected to the Hall of Fame for Great Americans in 1945. 864.

13 Birthday of Arnold Schönberg (September 13, 1874–July 13, 1951). Austrian-American composer who had a revolutionary influence on modern music through his use of the twelve-tone scale. 864.

Holy Days and Feast Days

14 Pilgrimage of the Black Madonna, one of the major pilgrimage days to the basilica in Einsiedeln, Switzerland; the anniversary of the September 14, 948, consecration of the church which shelters the Black Madonna, a statue of the Virgin darkened by centuries of lighted candles. 34.

14 Feast of the Triumph of the Cross, or the Exaltation of the Holy Cross, commemorates the finding in 326, by Saint Helena, mother of Constantine, of the cross on which Christ was crucified. 5.

Holidays and Civic Days

14 Battle of San Jacinto Day, a national holiday in Nicaragua commemorating the defeat of foreign invaders on September 14, 1856. 875.

Anniversaries and Special Events Days

14 National Anthem Day, observed in the United States, and particularly in Maryland, to honor Francis Scott Key and the writing of the verses of "The Star-Spangled Banner" on the morning of September 14, 1814, following the bombardment of Fort McHenry. 268, 694.

14 Birthday of Karl Taylor Compton (September 14, 1887–June 22, 1954). American physicist, atomic-bomb scientist; recipient of many awards, including the French Legion of Honor. 867.

14 Anniversary of the death of Dante Alighieri on September 14, 1321. The greatest of all Italian poets, known throughout the world for his *Divine Comedy*. 1.

14 Birthday of Jan Garrigue Masaryk (September 14, 1886–March 10, 1948). Czechoslovak statesman.

14 Birthday of Margaret Sanger (September 14, 1883–September 6, 1966). Founder and international leader of the birth-control movement; first president of both the American Birth Control League and the International Planned Parenthood Federation; her birthday is commemorated by Planned Parenthood associations and groups. 727.

Holy Days and Feast Days

15 Feast of Our Lady of Sorrows, a memorial to the griefs and sorrows of Mary in her association with Christ. 5.

Holidays and Civic Days

15 Independence Day in Costa Rica, commemorating the overthrow of Spanish rule in 1821. Traditionally, on the eve of this day the president lights a liberty torch in the old capital of Cartago, and on September 15 addresses school children. 868, 875.

15 Independence Day, a holiday in El Salvador, commemorating the September 15, 1821, revolt against Spain and the achievement of independence. 868, 875.

15 Independence Day, a holiday in Guatemala, commemorating the anniversary of September 15, 1821, when the government of the captaincy-general won independence from Spain. 868, 875.

15 Independence Day, a holiday in Honduras commemorating September 15, 1821, when Honduras joined other provinces in Central America in declaring independence from Spain. 868, 875.

15 Nicaragua Independence Day, commemorating the September 15, 1821, proclamation of independence for the five provinces of Central America, of which Nicaragua was one. 868, 875.

15 Respect for the Aged Day, a holiday in Japan; a day of honor and ceremonials for the older generations. 875.

Anniversaries and Special Events Days

15 Battle of Britain Day, celebrated annually in England in honor of September 15, 1940, when British airmen drove back the invading German planes in the most decisive air battle of World War II. 666.

15 Birthday of James Fenimore Cooper (September 15, 1789–September 14, 1851). American novelist famous for the Leather Stocking Tales, which include *The Last of the Mohicans* and *The Deerslayer*. He was elected to the Hall of Fame for Great Americans in 1910. 787.

15 Birthday of François de La Rochefoucauld (September 15, 1613–March 17, 1680). French moralist, famous for his *Maxims*.

15 Birthday of William Howard Taft (September 15, 1857–March 8, 1930). English ancestry; Ohio lawyer; governor of the Philippines, 1901–4; secretary of war under Theodore Roosevelt; twenty-seventh president of the United States, 1909–13. Chief justice of the Supreme Court, 1921–30. Unitarian. Buried in Arlington National Cemetery. 359–366, 370–372, 374, 378, 379.

Holidays and Civic Days

c16 Mexican Declaration of Independence Day, a legal holiday in Mexico comparable in significance to July 4 in the United States, with celebrations beginning on September 15; the president of Mexico gives the famed *grito*, the cry of independence, during the major ceremonies. 868.

16 Papua New Guinea, a national holiday celebrating the achievement of full sovereignty on September 16, 1975, for the people who live on the eastern half of the island of New Guinea. 868.

16 Singapore Independence Day, a civic day in the Republic of Singapore honoring the sovereignty that was reached on September 16, 1963. 868.

Anniversaries and Special Events Days

16 Anniversary of the death of Anne Bradstreet on September 16, 1672. American poet, first woman of letters in America. 738.

16 Cherokee Strip Day, a festival day in Oklahoma commemorating September 16, 1893, when land runs were organized by the government for prospective homesteaders to race to claim land; celebrations in the Cherokee Strip communities last several days as the pioneer spirit of '93 is re-enacted with parades, picnics, dances, and pageantry. 268.

16 American Legion Charter Day, anniversary of the chartering by Congress on September 16, 1919, of the American Legion, composed of honorably discharged veterans. It was founded during a caucus of members of the First Expeditionary Force held from March 15–17, 1919.

16 Mayflower Day, the anniversary of the September 16, 1620, departure of the Pilgrims from Plymouth, England, bound for the New World in a small vessel called "the Mayflower." 655.

16 Birthday of Alfred Noyes (September 16, 1880–June 28, 1958). English poet whose work has been set to music by Edward Elgar and others. Noyes's best-known single poem is "The Highwayman." 864.

16 Birthday of Francis Parkman (September 16, 1823–November 8, 1893). Distinguished American historian and author. Elected to the Hall of Fame for Great Americans in 1915. 864.

Holy Days and Feast Days

17 Feast of Saint Robert Bellarmine; friend of Galileo; authority on ecclesiology and church-state relations; declared a doctor of the church in 1930. 9.

Holidays and Civic Days

17 Day of the National Hero, a holiday in Angola honoring the victims in the anti-Portuguese revolts of 1961–62 and the civil wars in 1975. 868, 875.

17 Citizenship Day, honoring new Americans, replaced "I Am an American Day" and Constitution Day in the United States in 1952; proclaimed annually by the president of the United States; it is the beginning of Constitution Week. 268.

Anniversaries and Special Events Days

17 Bloodiest Day, the anniversary of the Civil War battle at Antietam fought on September 17, 1862; noted by historians as America's bloodiest day on its own soil. 675.

17 Constitution Day, the anniversary of the signing of the Constitution of the United States on September 17, 1787. The historic event is commemorated during Constitution Week which is scheduled to include the official day, and is honored on Citizenship Day. 268.

17 Steuben Day, commemorating the birth, on September 17, 1730, of Friedrich von Steuben, a German officer charged with training the Continental forces in the American Revolution; observed in the major cities of the United States. 268.

Holy Days and Feast Days

18 Feast of Saint Joseph of Cupertino, a seventeenth-century priest who is reputed to have had the gift of levitation; patron saint of air travelers and pilots. 4

Holidays and Civic Days

18 Victory of Uprona Day, a holiday in Burundi, celebrating the September 18, 1961, victory at the polls of the Unite et Progres National Party (UPRONA) which led to internal self-government in 1962. 868, 875.

18 Independence Day in Chile, a holiday honoring the first declaration of independence issued on September 18, 1810. Chile achieved complete independence from Spain on February 12, 1818, after seven years of bitter warfare. 868.

Anniversaries and Special Events Days

18 Birthday of Samuel Johnson (September 18, 1709–December 13, 1784). English poet, essayist, critic, and dictionary maker, author of the *Rambler* and *Lives of the Poets*; his birthday is celebrated annually in his hometown of Lichfield, England. 850.

18 Birthday of Joseph Story (September 18, 1779–September 10, 1845). American jurist, associate justice of the United States Supreme Court whose writings helped to form American legal thought. Elected to the Hall of Fame for Great Americans in 1900. 864.

18 Birthday of Clark Wissler (September 18, 1870–August 25, 1947). American anthropologist, the first to develop a systematic concept of culture areas, which he used in studying and writing many fine books about the American Indian.

Holy Days and Feast Days

19 Feast of Saint Januarius, whose relics in the cathedral in Naples include a vial of blood which seems to liquefy in response to the prayers of the countless faithful; patron saint of blood banks and of Naples. 4, 9.

Holidays and Civic Days

19 Chilean Armed Forces Day, a holiday in the Republic of Chile, celebrated as a part of the Independence Day honors and festivities of September 18. 875.

Anniversaries and Special Events Days

19 Birthday of Charles Carroll (September 19, 1737–November 14, 1832). American Revolutionary leader; signer of the Declaration of Independence. He represents the state of Maryland in Statuary Hall in a sculpture done by Richard Edwin Brooks. 870.

19 Birthday of Arthur Rackham (September 19, 1867–September 6, 1939). English artist whose illustrations of literary classics, such as *Grimm's Fairy Tales*, have attracted worldwide appreciation. 864.

19 Washington's Farewell Day, the anniversary of Washington's farewell address of September 19, 1796; remembered for its warnings against public debt, large military developments, and permanent alliances with foreign powers. 874.

19 World Peace Day, sponsored by the Spiritual Assembly of the Baha'is of the United States to encourage American leadership in world peace. 857.

Anniversaries and Special Events Days

20 Airborne Operations Day, a commemorative day in the Netherlands honoring the airborne landing in 1944 in the Battle of Arnhem.

c20 Harvest-Moon Days, the period of the full moon closest to the autumn equinox; a time for traditional harvest festivals. 22.

Holy Days and Feast Days

21 Feast of Saint Matthew, one of the twelve apostles; author of the first gospel; martyr; patron saint of tax collectors. 4, 9.

Holidays and Civic Days

21 Belize Independence Day, commemorating the achievement of independence on September 21, 1981, of a one-time British colony, 8,500 square miles in size with a 200-mile coral barrier reef. The first independence ceremonies held on September 21, 1981. 868.

21 Malta Independence Day, a civic day in the Republic of Malta honoring the achievement of independence on September 21, 1964. 868.

Anniversaries and Special Events Days

21 Birthday of Kwame Nkrumah (September 21, 1909–April 27, 1972). President of Ghana; first to lead an African country to independence; author of *Toward Colonial Freedom* and *Africa Must Unite*. 864.

21 Press Sunday, a day of tribute to the freedom of the press and to the first newspapers published in the United States.

21 Birthday of Girolamo Savonarola (September 21, 1452–May 23, 1498). Italian religious reformer. 1.

21 Birthday of Herbert George Wells (September 21, 1866–August 13, 1946). English novelist, sociological writer, and historian whose most important work of nonfiction is the *Outline of History*. 864.

Holidays and Civic Days

22 Mali Independence Day, a national holiday, honoring the establishment of independence for the Republic of Mali on September 22, 1960. 868.

Anniversaries and Special Events Days

22 Birthday of Michael Faraday (September 22, 1791–August 25, 1867). English scientist who made the greatest electrical discovery of all time, the generation of electricity by means of magnetism. 864.

Holidays and Civic Days

c23 Autumnal Equinox Day, a holiday in Japan that is observed either on September 23 or 24 to celebrate the first day of autumn and to memorialize family ancestors. 875.

Anniversaries and Special Events Days

23 Frontier Day, anniversary of the first frontier celebration, held in Cheyenne, Wyoming, on September 23, 1897, later extended to a week-long event. Frontier Days are now observed in many communities and counties in the United States on varying dates or weeks. 268.

23 Lewis and Clark Expedition Day, the anniversary of the end on September 23, 1806, of the two-year exploration of the West by Meriwether Lewis and William Clark, an expedition that made possible the opening up of the northwest territory. 268, 739.

23 Birthday of John Lomax (September 23, 1870–January 26, 1948). American folklorist; collector of folk songs; founder of the American Folklore Society and its first president. 864.

23 Birthday of William Holmes McGuffey (September 23, 1800–May 4, 1873). American educator; author of the Eclectic Readers, which are collector's items. 864.

23 Birthday of John Sevier (September 23, 1745–September 24, 1815). American pioneer and soldier who was famous as an Indian fighter. He represents the state of Tennessee in Statuary Hall in a sculpture done by Belle Kinney Scholz and Lee F. Scholz. 870.

Holy Days and Feast Days

24 Feast of Our Lady of Mercy, a religious and general holiday in the Dominican Republic; observed with a pilgrimage and processions.

c24 Feast of the Ingathering, or Harvest Festival, celebrated in England around September 24 with the decorating of churches with flowers, fruits and vegetables for special services of harvest thanksgiving.

24 Feast Day of Nuestra Señora de las Mercedes, a holiday in the Dominican Republic; known as Mercedes Day. 875.

Holidays and Civic Days

24 Third Republic Day, a holiday in Ghana commemorating the nation's return to a parliamentary democracy on September 24, 1979, ending a military regime. 868, 875.

24 Guinea-Bissau Independence holiday, commemorating the proclamation of independence for Guinea-Bissau on September 24, 1973. On September 10, 1974, Portugal officially recognized the independence of the Republic of Guinea-Bissau, formerly Portuguese Guinea. 868.

Anniversaries and Special Events Days

24 Birthday of Francis Scott Key Fitzgerald (September 24, 1896–December 21, 1940). American novelist, identified with the "lost-generation school," whose novel *This Side of Paradise* was one of the most famous books in the 1920s. 864.

24 Birthday of John Marshall (September 24, 1755–July 6, 1835). American lawyer, jurist, fourth chief justice of the Supreme Court, founder of the American system of constitutional law. He was elected to the Hall of Fame for Great Americans in 1900. 805.

c24 Native American Day, a day of recognition of the heritage and contributions of American Indians; observed on the fourth Friday of September or on the second Saturday of May; formerly American Indian Day. 525–43.

24 Schwenkenfelder Thanksgiving Day, observed by the members of the Schwenkenfelder Society in the Pennsylvania Dutch country in commemoration of the safe arrival of its first members in 1733 and 1734.

Holidays and Civic Days

25 Mozambican Popular Liberation Forces Day, or Army Day, honoring the defenders of the nation, a holiday in the People's Republic of Mozambique. 875.

25 Kamarampaka Day, a holiday in the Republic of Rwanda; a day marking the opening of sessions of the National Assembly and the anniversary of the September 25, 1961, referendum which abolished the monarchy. 868, 875.

Anniversaries and Special Events Days

25 Birthday of William Faulkner (September 25, 1897–July 6, 1962). American novelist; author of the series known as the "Yoknapatawpha cycle"; awarded the Nobel Prize in literature in 1955. 864.

c25 Hunting and Fishing Day, a presidential proclamation day in the United States; observed on the fourth Saturday of September to underscore the importance of sports-persons in conservation of natural resources. 857.

25 Sandra O'Connor Day, the anniversary of the September 25, 1981, oath-of-office ceremonies for Sandra O'Connor, first woman justice on the U.S. Supreme Court. 874.

25 Pacific Ocean Day, the anniversary of the discovery of the Pacific Ocean by Vasco Nuñez de Balboa on September 25, 1513. 857.

Holy Days and Feast Days

26 Feast of Saint Cosmas, widely known for his medical skill; martyred with his brothers for their faith; a patron of physicians. 9.

26 Feast of Martyrs of North America, honors eight priests who lost their lives trying to bring the Christian faith to the American Indians. 20.

Holidays and Civic Days

26 Yemen Arab Republic National Day, a holiday celebrating the September 26, 1962, seizure of the government by officers of the army and their proclamation of the establishment of a republic. 868.

26 Y.A.R. National Day, a holiday in the People's Democratic Republic of Yemen, celebrating the September 26, 1962, revolt against the harsh rule of the royalists; a revolution that led to the establishment of the republic. 868.

Anniversaries and Special Events Days

26 Birthday of Edith Abbott (September 26, 1876–July 28, 1957). American social worker, dean of the University of Chicago School of Social Service Administration, authority on public assistance and immigration problems.

26 Birthday of Thomas Stearns Eliot (September 26, 1888–January 4, 1965). Poet and playwright renowned for *The Waste Land*; awarded the Nobel Prize in literature in 1948. 864.

26 Birthday of George Gershwin (September 26, 1898–July 11, 1937). American composer famed for such compositions as *Rhapsody in Blue* and *Porgy and Bess*. 268, 820.

Holy Days and Feast Days

27 Feast of the Finding of the True Cross, commemorating the fourth-century finding of the cross on which Christ was crucified, celebrated in Ethiopia on September 27 in accordance with the Julian calendar. 875.

27 Feast of Saint Vincent de Paul, seventeenth-century founder of the Vincentians and cofounder of the Sisters of Charity, dedicated to the alleviation of human misery; declared patron of all charitable organizations and groups by Pope Leo XIII. 9.

Anniversaries and Special Events Days

27 Birthday of Samuel Adams (September 27, 1722–October 2, 1803). American patriot, signer of the Declaration of Independence, governor of Massachusetts. Represents Massachusetts in Statuary Hall in a sculpture done by Anne Whitney. 727, 870.

27 Birthday of Sándor Kisfaludy (September 27, 1772–October 28, 1844). Hungarian poet who is considered the founder of the Hungarian school of lyric poetry.

27 Birthday of Alfred Thayer Mahan (September 27, 1840–December 1, 1914). American naval officer and historian whose major work is *The Influence of Sea Power upon History*. 864.

27 Birthday of Thomas Nast (September 27, 1840–December 7, 1902). American illustrator and cartoonist whose work so influenced politics and public opinion that Abraham Lincoln called him "our best recruiting sergeant"; creator of the donkey and elephant emblems of the Democratic and Republican parties. 864.

Holy Days and Feast Days

28 Feast of Saint Wenceslaus, duke of Bohemia martyred in his attempt to convert the Czechs in the tenth century; a symbol of Czech christianity and patron saint of Czechoslovakia. 9.

Holidays and Civic Days

c28 Meskel, or True Cross Day, a holiday in Ethiopia commemorating the finding of the True Cross by Saint Helena; observed on or near September 28 with communal and family festivities at the end of the Ethiopian rainy season. 875.

28 Referendum Day, a public holiday in Guinea, on the west coast of Africa, commemorating the public vote, on September 28, 1958, for complete independence. 868.

28 Confucius' Birthday, or Teachers' Day, a public holiday in Taiwan (Republic of China). 875.

Anniversaries and Special Events Days

c28 Cabrillo Day, observed in California as part of a six-day festival honoring Juan Rodriguez Cabrillo, Portuguese navigator, who discovered California on September 28, 1542. 268.

28 Birthday of Georges Clemenceau (September 28, 1841–November 24, 1919). French editor and statesman who presided at the Versailles Peace Conference; called "le tigre" and "le pere de la victoire" by his fellow Frenchmen. 755.

c28 Good Neighbor Day, observed on the fourth Sunday of September in the United States to promote understanding and good relationships. 857.

28 Anniversary of the death of Pope John Paul I on September 28, 1978; a religious and general holiday in the Vatican City State. 5.

28 Birthday of Francis Turner Palgrave (September 28, 1824–October 24, 1897). English poet and critic best known for his classic anthology the *Golden Treasury of the Best Songs and Lyrical Poems in the English Language.*

28 The Fiesta of San Miguel, celebrated in San Miguel de Allende, Mexico, a four-day fete lasting from September 28 to October 1.

28 Birthday of Kate Douglas Wiggin (September 28, 1856–August 24, 1923). American educator and author; cofounder of the first free kindergarten in the Far West, who started to write books for children in her own school. She is remembered for *The Birds' Christmas Carol* and *Rebecca of Sunnybrook Farm*. 864.

28 Birthday of Frances Elizabeth Caroline Willard (September 28, 1839–February 18, 1898). American temperance reformer, editor, author, and president of the Woman's Christian Temperance Union. Elected to the Hall of Fame for Great Americans in 1910. 268, 738.

Holy Days and Feast Days

29 Feast of Saint Michael and All Angels, celebrated by Anglican, Episcopal, and Lutheran churches on September 29 and on November 8 by the Eastern Orthodox churches adhering to the Julian calendar. The Roman Catholic church commemorates Saint Michael on September 29 in the Solemnity of the Feast of Saints Michael, Gabriel, and Raphael, Archangels. Saint Michael is the patron saint of policemen, grocers, paratroopers, and radiologists. 4, 5.

Holidays and Civic Days

29 Constitution Day in Brunei, a public holiday honoring the promulgation of a constitution on September 29, 1959, for the Sultanate of Brunei. 868, 875.

29 Battle of Boquerón Day, a public holiday in Paraguay commemorating the end of a 1930 border conflict. 875.

Anniversaries and Special Events Days

29 Birthday of Enrico Fermi (September 29, 1901–November 28, 1954). Italian physicist, noted for his studies in nuclear physics, his work on the atomic-bomb project, and his teaching at the Institute of Nuclear Studies at the University of Chicago. He was awarded the 1938 Nobel Prize in physics for his research in radioactive substances. 864.

c29 Gold Star Mothers Day, observed on the last Sunday of September by presidential proclamation to honor the mothers "whose sons and daughters died in line of duty in the Armed Forces of the United States." 857.

29 Michaelmas Day, a festival honoring the Feast of Saint Michael, archangel and "warrior saint," with customs which range from feasting on goose dinners to returning the herds of cattle from high mountain slopes to valley farms in anticipation of traditional forms of Michaelmas merry-making.

29 Birthday of Horatio Nelson (September 29, 1758–October 21, 1805). English admiral who is remembered for his battle-signal "England expects that every man will do his duty"; the monument to Nelson in Trafalgar Square is one of the best-known monuments in the world. 864.

Holy Days and Feast Days

30 Feast of Gregory the Enlightener, or Illuminator, an evangelist to the Armenians; the patron saint of Armenia. 9.

30 Feast Day of Saint Jerome, patron saint of students of scripture and of librarians. Jerome, whose translation of the Bible into Latin is known as the Vulgate, is venerated as a doctor of the church. 4, 9.

Holidays and Civic Days

30 Botswana Day, a holiday commemorating September 30, 1966, when the Bechuanaland Protectorate became the thirtieth African nation to receive full independence as the Republic of Botswana. 868, 875.

October

October, the tenth month in the Gregorian calendar, received its name from the Latin numeral *octo*, meaning "eight," because in the days of the old Roman calendar it was the eighth month.

One of the notable days in October is Columbus Day, October 12, honoring the discovery of America by the Italian map-maker and explorer, Christopher Columbus. It is celebrated as Discovery Day in Central and South America and was set aside as a holiday in the United States in 1892 by President Harrison.

Hawaii has a special October event called the Aloha Festival, sometimes described as the "Mardi Gras of the Pacific." It is observed with pageantry, street dancing, hula festivals, luaus, parades, and fancy balls.

October gave its name to one of the best-known German fall festivals. Oktoberfest started on October 17, 1810, the wedding day of King Ludwig I. It still retains the name, even though the festivities may start in September, with October having only a partial share of the time schedule.

An important October day for the entire world is October 24, United Nations Day, which commemorates the founding of the United Nations on October 24, 1945. It is a holiday for many of the member nations and is generally observed by all nations as a way of publicizing the aims and achievements of the world organization.

The month ends with Halloween or All Hallow's Eve. It is a religious festival in some countries but a trick-or-treat night in the United States, when small children in costume roam through their neighborhoods to solicit candy or cookies.

The flowers for October are the calendula and the cosmos. The birthstones are the opal and the tourmaline.

Holy Days and Feast Days

1 Feast of Saint Therese of Lisieux, nineteenth-century nun known as "the little flower;" author of *The Story of a Soul*, one of the most widely read spiritual autobiographies; declared co-patron of the missions with Saint Francis Xavier in 1927, and co-patroness of France with Joan of Arc in 1944. 4, 9.

Holidays and Civic Days

1 Cameroon Unification Day, an historic day commemorating the joining of East and West Cameroon into the United Republic of Cameroon on October 1, 1961. 868.

1 National Days, a two-day holiday in the People's Republic of China, commemorating the action of the Communists, under the leadership of Chairman Mao Tse-tung, proclaiming the establishment of the People's Republic of China on October 1, 1949, at the country's new capital at Peking. 868, 875.

1 Korean Armed Forces Day, a public holiday in South Korea honoring the armed forces of the Republic of Korea. 875.

1 Nigeria National Day, a holiday in Nigeria celebrating the October 1, 1979, end of thirteen years of military rule. 868, 875.

Anniversaries and Special Events Days

1 Agricultural Fair Day, the anniversary of the first agricultural fair in the United States, the Berkshire Cattle Show, held at Pittsfield, Massachusetts, on October 1, 1810. Launched with a quotation from George Washington that "the multiplication of useful animals is a common blessing to mankind," it became the forerunner of the state fairs today.

1 Birthday of Annie Besant (October 1, 1847–September 20, 1933). English theosophist and philosophical writer who, through long residence in India, was instrumental in acquainting Europeans with Hindu thought. 785.

1 Birthday of Jimmy Carter (October 1, 1925–). English ancestry, Baptist. Thirty-ninth president of the United States, January 20, 1977–January 20, 1981. 361, 365, 371, 372, 374.

1 Day of the Caudillo, observed in Spain to mark the establishment of the Spanish state by General Francisco Franco on October 1, 1936.

1 Birthday of Rufus Choate (October 1, 1799–July 13, 1859). American lawyer, author, and statesman; preeminent among American advocates. Elected to the Hall of Fame for Great Americans in 1915.

1 Birthday of John Peter Gabriel Muhlenberg (October 1, 1746–October 1, 1807). American revolutionary general, Lutheran pastor, and congressman. He represents the state of Pennyslvania in Statuary Hall in a sculpture done by Blanche Nevin. 870.

Holy Days and Feast Days

2 Feast of the Guardian Angels, commemorates the angels protecting humanity from physical and spiritual dangers. 5.

Holidays and Civic Days

2 Guinea Republic Day, a public holiday, anniversary of the proclamation of the Republic of Guinea on October 2, 1958. 875.

2 Gandhi Day, a holiday in India, commemorating with ceremonials the birth on October 2, 1869, of Mahatma Gandhi, Hindu statesman and spiritual leader honored throughout the world for his philosophy and example of nonviolence. 1, 392.

c2 Missouri Day, observed throughout the state of Missouri on the first Monday in October to commemorate the state's history with special programs and exercises. 268, 856, 862.

Anniversaries and Special Events Days

2 Birthday of Mohandas Karamchand Gandhi (October 2, 1869–January 30, 1948). Hindu statesman and spiritual leader whose anniversaries are commemorated by his countrymen and honored throughout the world. 1, 392.

2 Birthday of Cordell Hull (October 2, 1871–July 23, 1955). American statesman, United States secretary of state, contributor to "good-neighbor" policies, planner of a postwar world organization, known as the "father of the United Nations"; recipient of the Nobel Peace Prize in 1945. 679, 864.

2 Birthday of Ruth Bryan Rohde (October 2, 1885–July 26, 1954). American public official, congresswoman, and first woman ever appointed to head a United States diplomatic post, serving as minister to Denmark for three years.

Holidays and Civic Days

3 Morazán Day, a holiday in Honduras in honor of Francisco Morazán, early nineteenth-century Honduran statesman whose dream was a unified Central America. 875.

3 Korean Foundation Day, a holiday in the Republic of Korea, commemorating with special events the mythical founding of Korea by Gangun in 2333 B.C. 875.

Anniversaries and Special Events Days

3 Birthday of George Bancroft (October 3, 1800–January 17, 1891). American diplomat, historian, and public official. Author of *History of the United States*, which he treated as an illustration of a divine plan for democracy, freedom, and equality. Served as United States minister to Great Britain, to Prussia, and to the German empire. Elected to the Hall of Fame for Great Americans in 1910. 268.

3 Birthday of William Crawford Gorgas (October 3, 1854–July 4, 1920). American sanitarian, surgeon-general of the United States Army, famous for his success in controlling yellow fever, an achievement that permitted the completion of the Panama Canal. He was elected to the Hall of Fame for Great Americans in 1950. 864.

3 Birthday of John Gorrie (October 3, 1803–June 16, 1855). American physician and inventor; an innovator in artificial cooling for hospitals and mechanical refrigeration. He represents the state of Florida in Statuary Hall in a sculpture done by C. Adrian Pillars. 870

3 Leyden Day, observed in the Netherlands and by the Holland Society of New York to commemorate the lifting of the Siege of Leyden in 1573–74, through a tempest that carried the Spanish fleet out into the ocean. 857.

3 Birthday of Sir Patrick Manson (October 3, 1844–April 9, 1922). British physician and parasitologist who is known as "the father of tropical medicine."

3 Anniversary of the death of Myles Standish on October 3, 1656. English colonist in America whose memory has been perpetuated by Longfellow's *The Courtship of Miles Standish*. 268.

Holy Days and Feast Days

4 Feast Day of Saint Francis of Assisi, patron saint of Italy, of Catholic action, and of merchants. Saint Francis, brother to men, animals, and birds, and founder of the Franciscan order, is universally honored. 4, 748, 763.

Holidays and Civic Days

4 Labour Day, a holiday in the Australian Capital Territory and in New South Wales celebrating the eight-hour working day achieved in 1871; a day of sports, picnics, and rallies. 875.

4 Lesotho Independence Day, a public holiday honoring October 4, 1966, when Basutoland became a sovereign member of the British Commonwealth under the name of the Kingdom of Lesotho. 868, 875.

Anniversaries and Special Events Days

4 Gregorian Calendar Day, the anniversary of the October 4, 1582, adoption of the Gregorian calendar by Roman Catholic countries, a calendar which corrected a ten-day error in the Julian calendar. 865.

4 Birthday of Rutherford Birchard Hayes (October 4, 1822–January 17, 1893). Scottish ancestry; Ohio lawyer; Civil War solider; governor of Ohio; nineteenth president of the United States, 1877–81. Methodist. Buried at Fremont, Ohio. 359–66, 370–74, 378, 379.

4 Birthday of Frederic Remington (October 4, 1861–December 26, 1909). American artist and author famous for his on-site drawings and paintings of frontier life, Indians, and horses. 864.

4 Sputnik Day, the anniversary of the October 4, 1957, launching by the Soviets of the world's first unmanned, earth-orbiting satellite. 857, 866.

4 Ten-Four Day, observed by truckdrivers and other users of citizen band radios in the tenth month and on its fourth day in recognition of 10-4 as a code terminating a conversation or message. 857.

Holidays and Civic Days

5 National Sports Day, a public holiday in Lesotho, formerly Basutoland. 875.

5 Portuguese Republic Day, a public holiday in Portugal, honoring the proclamation of the republic on October 5, 1910. 875.

Anniversaries and Special Events Days

5 Birthday of Chester Alan Arthur (October 5, 1831–November 18, 1886). Scotch-Irish ancestry; New York teacher and lawyer; vice-president succeeding the assassinated President Garfield; twenty-first president of the United States, 1881–85. Episcopalian. Buried at Albany, New York. 359–66, 370–72, 374, 378, 379.

5 Birthday of Jonathan Edwards (October 5, 1703–March 22, 1758). American theologian, philosopher, and college president who has been called "the greatest American mind of the colonial period." He was elected to the Hall of Fame for Great Americans in 1900. 1, 864.

Holidays and Civic Days

6 Armed Forces Day, a holiday in Egypt, commemorating October 6, 1973, when Egyptian forces crossed the Suez Canal into the Sinai in the war against Israel. Sadat, the hero of the crossing, was assassinated while viewing the Armed Forces Day parade on October 6, 1981. 875.

Anniversaries and Special Events Days

6 Anniversary of the organization of the American Library Association on October 6, 1876, in Philadelphia.

6 Birthday of Albert Jeremiah Beveridge (October 6, 1862–April 27, 1927). American politician and author, best known for *The Life of John Marshall*. An Albert J. Beveridge Award is given by the American Historical Association for an outstanding book in history. 867.

6 Sadat Assassination Day, the anniversary of the assassination of Egypt's President Anwar el-Sadat during a military parade in Nasser City, near Cairo, on October 6, 1981. Sadat shared the Nobel Peace Prize with Israel's Menachem Begin in 1978.

c6 Universal Children's Day, observed on the first Monday of October; established by the United Nations to honor children with special programs to call the attention of governments to the needs of children. 626.

6 Birthday of George Westinghouse (October 6, 1846–March 12, 1914). American inventor who invented the air brake. Elected to the Hall of Fame for Great Americans in 1955. 864.

Holidays and Civic Days

c7 Deed of Cession Day, a holiday in Fiji marking the ceding of Fiji to the British crown in 1874; celebrated around October 7. 868.

7 Foundation Day, a holiday in the German Democratic Republic commemorating the enactment of a constitution on October 7, 1949. 868, 875.

7 Expulsion of the Fascist Settlers Day, a holiday in Libya celebrating the 1970 expulsion of several thousand Italians in residence in the country. 875.

7 Constitution Day, a holiday in the Union of Soviet Socialist Republics, honoring the 1977 constitution of the socialist state. 875.

Anniversaries and Special Events Days

c7 Child Health Day, observed on the first Monday of October by presidential proclamations; proclaimed for the first time in the United States on May 1, 1928. 857.

7 Lepanto Day, the anniversary of the Greek victory over the Turks at Lepanto on October 7, 1571; a day of commemoration.

7 Birthday of Martha McChesney Berry (October 7, 1866–February 27, 1942). American educator and founder of the Berry schools for children in the mountain districts around Georgia. The recipient of many awards; voted in 1931 one of the twelve greatest American women. 864.

7 Birthday of James Whitcomb Riley (October 7, 1849–July 22, 1916). Known as "the Hoosier poet"; considered by some critics as "the Burns of America." Among his many popular poems is "When the Frost Is on the Punkin." His birthday is an occasion for annual tributes in schools and communities in Indiana. 268.

7 Birthday of Caesar Rodney (October 7, 1784). American patriot, signer of the Declaration of Independence who represents Delaware in Statuary Hall in a sculpture done by Bryant Baker. 870.

Anniversaries and Special Events Days

8 Chicago Fire Day, anniversary of the catastrophic fire which began on October 8, 1871, and destroyed most of the city. The Chicago fire was one of the sparks in the establishment of Fire Prevention Day, observed on October 9. 268, 696, 702.

8 Peshtigo Fire Day, anniversary of the beginning on October 8, 1871, of the forest fire at Peshtigo, Wisconsin; considered to be one of the most disastrous fires in history. 695.

8 Birthday of Eddie Rickenbacker (October 8, 1890–July 23, 1973). American aviator known as the "ace of aces" of World War I. Author of *Fighting the Flying Circus, Seven Came Through*, and an autobiography. 470.

Holy Days and Feast Days

9 Feast Day of Saint Denis, patron saint of Paris and of France. 4.

9 Feast of Saint Louis Bertran, sixteenth-century missionary to Colombia; patron saint of Colombia. 4.

Holidays and Civic Days

9 Guayaquil's Independence Day, a national holiday in Ecuador, honoring October 9, 1820, when the city declared itself free from Spain. 875.

9 Hangul Day, anniversary of the proclamation of the Korean alphabet devised by King Sejong in 1446; a public holiday in South Korea. 875.

9 Uganda Independence Day, a national holiday commemorating the achievement of autonomy for the African nation of Uganda on October 9, 1962, after nearly seventy years of British rule. 868, 875.

Anniversaries and Special Events Days

9 Birthday of Lewis Cass (October 9, 1782–June 17, 1866). American statesman, soldier, and author. Governor of the Michigan territory who improved relations with the Indians. He represents the state of Michigan in Statuary Hall in a sculpture done by Daniel Chester French. 870.

c9 Fire Prevention Day, anniversary of the Chicago Fire of October 8–9, 1871; observed in the United States as a part of a week including October 9 dedicated to public information and fire-prevention education; by presidential proclamation. 268.

c9 Husain Day, commemorated by the Shiites, a branch of Islam, as a memorial to the martyrdom of Husain, grandson and third successor of Mohammed, on October 9, 680. The story of the martyrdom is recited in Moslem halls and in reenacted in religious dramas on succeeding days.

9 Leif Ericson Day, established in the United States by presidential proclamation in 1964 and proclaimed annually. A day of tribute to the landing of the Norsemen in Vinland on the North American continent in about A.D. 1000. The day is observed with special events and programming in Norwegian-American communities in the United States, and is a commemorative day in Iceland and in Norway. 268, 705, 866.

9 Birthday of Martin Elmer Johnson (October 9, 1884–January 13, 1937). American explorer and photographer of savage tribes and wild-animal life for the American Museum of Natural History. 864.

9 Day of National Dignity, a commemorative day in Peru recalling October 9, 1968, governmental seizure of the oil fields on behalf of the Peruvian nation.

Holy Days and Feast Days

10 Feast of Saint Francis Borgia, sixteenth-century Jesuit, a leader in the Counter-Reformation; a patron saint of Portugal. 9.

10 Anniversary of the cannonization on October 10, 1982, of Father Maximilian Kolbe, Polish Conventual Franciscan who was martyred in the Auschwitz prison camp in 1941 when he heroically and unselfishly offered his life to save a fellow prisoner. 810.

c10 White Sunday, observed on the island of American Samoa on the second Sunday in October. It is a children's day and everyone is dressed in white.

Holidays and Civic Days

c10 Fiji Day, a holiday in the Fiji Islands honoring October 10, 1970, when Fiji became a sovereign nation within the British Commonwealth. The holiday is observed on or near October 10. 868.

10 Physical Education Day, or Sports Day, a public holiday in Japan, commemorating the Tokyo Olympics of 1964. 875.

10 Kruger Day, a holiday in South Africa, honoring the October 10, 1825, birth of Paulus Kruger, South African statesman known as Oom Paul. 875.

10 Double Tenth Day, a public holiday in Taiwan (Republic of China); commemorates the anniversary of the Proclamation of the Republic of Sun Yat-sen on October 10, 1911, and the anniversary of the revolts that overthrew the Manchu dynasty in 1911. 251.

Anniversaries and Special Events Days

10 Samuel Fraunces Memorial Day, established in memory of the first White House steward and the proprietor of the eighteenth-century inn that is one of New York's historic preservations.

10 Aleksis Kivi Day, a school holiday in Finland commemorating the October 10, 1834, birth of the author of the greatest play (*Kullervo*) and the greatest novel (*Seitsemän veljestä*) in the Finnish language. 849.

10 Birthday of Fridtjof Nansen (October 10, 1861–May 13, 1930). Norwegian Arctic explorer; awarded the 1922 Nobel Peace Prize. 679, 864.

10 Anniversary of the founding of the United States Naval Academy on October 10, 1845, at Annapolis, Maryland. 450.

10 Oklahoma Historical Day, a commemoration of the anniversary of the birth on October 10, 1758, of Major Jean Pierre Chouteau; a pioneer called "the father of Oklahoma" through his establishment of the first permanent non-Indian settlement in the state; major observances are held at Salina, which is the settlement he founded, and special programs are presented in educational institutions throughout the state in Chouteau's honor. 268.

10 Birthday of Giuseppe Verdi (Octoer 10, 1813–January 27, 1901). Italian operatic composer famous for *Aïda, Rigoletto, Il Trovatore,* and *La Traviata.* 864.

10 Birthday of Benjamin West (October 10, 1783–March 11, 1820). Anglo-American painter famous for historical paintings; one of the first to paint his subjects in contemporary dress rather than in Greek or Roman togas. 864.

Holidays and Civic Days

c11 Canadian Thanksgiving Day, a holiday observed on the second Monday of October throughout Canada to celebrate bountiful harvests and the blessings of life on Canadian soil. 875.

11 Beginning of Independence Wars Day, a holiday in Cuba honoring the guerrilla wars of the 1950s led by Fidel Castro to overthrow the Batista regime. 875.

c11 Farmers Day is celebrated with Columbus Day in Florida; observed on the second Monday of October. 875.

11 Panama Revolution Anniversary Day, a holiday in Panama celebrating the overtaking on October 11, 1968, of an elitist government by the National Guard; this holiday is also Panama's Columbus Day. 875.

11 Eight-Hour Day, a holiday in South Australia, a labour-day celebration for the people of the region honoring the establishment of an eight-hour working day in 1871. 875.

11 Monday after Children's White Sunday, a holiday in Western Samoa following White Sunday which is a festival day for children.

Anniversaries and Special Events Days

11 Pulaski Memorial Day, a presidential proclamation day observed in communities in Georgia, Illinois, Indiana, Nebraska, and Wisconsin to commemorate the October 11, 1779, death of General Casimir Pulaski, native of Poland and hero of the American Revolution. 268, 723.

11 Birthday of Eleanor Roosevelt (October 11, 1884–November 7, 1962). American humanitarian; official United States delegate to the United Nations; wife of the thirty-second president of the United States; author of *This Is My Story* and other books. 738, 749, 866.

11 Anniversary of the opening of the Second Vatican Council by Pope John XXIII on October 11, 1962. 5.

11 Birthday of Sir George Williams (October 11, 1821–November 6, 1905). English founder of the Young Men's Christian Association. 268.

Holidays and Civic Days

c12 Columbus Day, a holiday in forty-two of the fifty states in the United States, the District of Columbia, Guam, Puerto Rico, and the Virgin Islands; observed on October 12 in Maryland and Oklahoma, and on the second Monday in October in forty states. Columbus Day has been observed in the United States since 1892, when it was set aside by President Harrison as a holiday called Discovery Day. 269, 271–79, 624, 631, 866.

12 Day of the Race, a holiday in Chile, Colombia, Costa Rica, and Paraguay celebrating the fifteenth-century discovery of the Americas. October 12 is observed as a holiday called Dia de la Hispanidad in Panama; as America's Discovery Day in Honduras; and as Columbus Day in Belize, Ecuador, El Salvador, Mexico, and Venezuela; and as Discovery Day in the Bahamas. 875.

12 Equatorial Guinea Independence Day, a public holiday in Equatorial Guinea in honor of the achievement of sovereignty on October 12, 1968, which ended its status as a Spanish colony. 868, 875.

c12 Discoverers' Day, a holiday in Hawaii honoring Pacific and Polynesian navigators and all other discoverers; observed on the second Monday of October. 875.

12 Hispanity Day, or the national Day of Spanish Consciousness, a national holiday in Spain which honors the landfall in the New World by Christopher Columbus in 1492. 875.

c12 Columbus Day and Puerto Rico Friendship Day, a holiday in the Virgin Islands celebrated on the second Monday of October to honor both Discovery Day and a good neighbor. 875.

Anniversaries and Special Events Days

12 Birthday of Helena Modjeska (October 12, 1840–April 9, 1909). Polish-American actress noted for Shakespearean roles who was barred from Poland because of her anti-Russian speeches. 867.

12 Harvest Festival, a festive day in Nigeria celebrating the harvesting of yams; celebrated with drumming and dancing, feasts, and the traditional wearing of animal masks and native costumes.

Holy Days and Feast Days

13 Feast of Edward the Confessor, last of the Saxon kings of England; builder of Saint Peter's Abbey at Westminster, site of the present cathedral; a man whose piety earned him the epithet "the confessor." 4, 14.

Holidays and Civic Days

13 Assassination of the Hero of the Nation Day, a day of remembrance in Burundi commemorating the death of a popular twentieth-century leader and prime minister-elect, Prince Louis Rwagasore. 868.

Holidays and Civic Days

14 Yemen National Day, a public holiday for the People's Democratic Republic of Yemen in honor of the revolts of 1962. 875.

14 Founders Day and Youth Day, a holiday in the Republic of Zaire honoring both the founders of the nation and youth, the future of the nation. 875.

Anniversaries and Special Events Days

14 Birthday of Joseph Duveen (October 14, 1869–May 25, 1939). English art connoisseur who gave the British Museum the gallery in which the Elgin marbles are housed. 864.

14 Birthday of Dwight David Eisenhower (October 14, 1890–March 28, 1969). Pennsylvania German ancestry; World War II general; statesman; Columbia University president; man of letters; thirty-fourth president of the United States, 1953–61; Presbyterian. Author of *The White House Years*. Buried at Abilene, Kansas. President Eisenhower's birthday has been designated as National Friendship Day in the United States. 359–66, 368–69, 371–72, 374, 378–79.

14 Battle of Hastings Day, the anniversary of the October 14, 1066, victory of the Normans under William the Conqueror over the Saxons under Harold; the first and most decisive battle in the Norman Conquest and one of the most famous days in English history.

14 Peggy Stewart Day, observed in Maryland to honor the sinking of the tealaden brig *Peggy Stewart* in Annapolis harbor on October 14, 1774, a protest against the stamp taxes. 268.

14 Birthday of William Penn (October 14, 1644–July 30, 1718). Founder of Pennsylvania and famed leader of the Society of Friends. Elected to the Hall of Fame for Great Americans in 1935. His birthday is observed in Pennsylvania on or near October 14, with events honoring him and the state that is named for him. 20, 268.

Holy Days and Feast Days

15 Feast of Saint Teresa of Avila, sixteenth-century nun famed for her spiritual writings; proclaimed the first woman doctor of the church in 1970; a patron saint of Spain. 4, 9.

Holidays and Civic Days

15 Evacuation Day in Tunisia, a holiday in Tunisia celebrating the French withdrawal from the naval base at Bizerte in 1962. 868, 875.

Anniversaries and Special Events Days

c15 Ether Day, commemorates the first public use of ether to deaden pain in a surgical operation, administered by Dr. William Thomas Green Morton in 1846. The day is observed periodically by the Massachusetts General Hospital in Boston. 866.

15 Birthday of Friedrich Nietzsche (October 15, 1844–August 25, 1900). German philosopher whose most influential work is *Thus Spoke Zarathustra*. 864.

15 Birthday of Virgil (October 15, 70 B.C.–September 21, 19 B.C.). Roman poet, author of *The Aeneid*, the national epic of Rome. 864.

15 White Cane Safety Day, dedicated to the visually handicapped by presidential proclamation. 857.

15 World Poetry Day, a day of tribute established "to unite the nations of the world by the invisible ties of poetry."

Holy Days and Feast Days

16 Feast of Saint Gall, an Irish-born priest-missionary known as "the apostle of Switzerland." He is the patron saint of Switzerland. 9.

16 Feast Day of Saint Gerard Majella, patron saint of mothers; saint of "happy delivery." 4, 9.

Anniversaries and Special Events Days

16 Birthday of David Ben-Gurion (October 16, 1886–December 6, 1973). Israel's first prime minister and leading statesman in the struggle to make Palestine a refuge for the Jewish people and an independent nation. 729.

16 National Boss Day, a day of tribute to employers; observed by women employees. 857.

16 Birthday of Eugene Gladstone O'Neill (October 16, 1888–November 27, 1953). American playwright, the first to win the Nobel Prize in literature; a three-time recipient of the Pulitzer Prize for drama. 864.

16 Birthday of Noah Webster (October 16, 1758–May 28, 1843). American lexicographer whose name is synonymous with *dictionary*. 268.

16 World Food Day, observed on the anniversary of the founding of the Food and Agriculture Organization on October 16, 1945; a day sponsored by the United Nations to broaden citizen understanding of the problems of hunger, malnutrition, and poverty that exist in all parts of the world. 731, 866.

Holidays and Civic Days

17 Dessalines Day, a holiday in Haiti commemorating the death on October 17, 1806, of Jean Jacques Dessalines, revolutionist who was proclaimed emperor of Haiti in 1805. 868.

17 Mothers' Day, a two-day holiday in Malawi honoring all of the mothers of the nation. 875.

Anniversaries and Special Events Days

17 Black Poetry Day, the anniversary of the birth on October 17, 1711, of Jupiter Hammon, the first black in the United States to publish his own poetry. 815.

17 Burgoyne's Surrender Day, anniversary of the October 17, 1777, surrender at Saratoga, the turning point in the American Revolutionary War; observed in New York State. 866.

Holy Days and Feast Days

18 Feast day of Saint Luke, evangelist, "the beloved physician," and author of the third gospel and the Acts of the Apostles; patron saint of doctors, painters, and artists in general, supposedly because he painted a portrait of the Virgin Mary from life, and/or because of his style of writing. 4.

Holidays and Civic Days

c18 Alaska Day, celebrated as a holiday in the forty-ninth state, to commemorate the formal transfer of Alaska to the United States on October 18, 1867; observed on the third Monday of October. 268, 866.

18 Heroes Day, a holiday in Jamaica honoring citizens of heroic stature in the nation. 875.

c18 Hurricane Thanksgiving Day, a holiday in the Virgin Islands, a day of thanksgiving for the ending of the hurricane season. 875.

Anniversaries and Special Events Days

c18 Sweetest Day, observed on the third Saturday in October; originating as a day for spreading cheer among the unfortunate, it is now an occasion to remember anyone with a kind act or remembrance. 269, 857.

18 Birthday of Florence Dahl Walrath (October 18, 1877–November 7, 1958). American humanitarian, founder of the Cradle Society, organized in 1923 to prepare children for adoption.

Holy Days and Feast Days

19 Feast of Saint Isaac Jogues, Jesuit missionary who served in Quebec and what is now New York State in the seventeenth century; one of the martyrs of North America. 9.

19 Feast of Saint Paul of the Cross, eighteenth-century cofounder of the Passionists; gifted and popular preacher; canonized in 1867. 9.

19 Feast of Saint Peter of Alcantara, the sixteenth-century founder of the Alcantarines; declared patron of Brazil in 1862. 4.

19 Feast of Saint René Goupil, the first of the North American martyrs; a surgeon active in seventeenth-century Jesuit missions in Canada and the United States; patron saint of anesthetists. 4.

Anniversaries and Special Events Days

19 Birthday of John McLoughlin (October 19, 1784–September 3, 1857). American pioneer in the Oregon Territory. He represents the state of Oregon in Statuary Hall in a sculpture by Gifford MacGregor Proctor. 870.

19 Yorktown Day, observed in commemoration of the surrender on October 19, 1781, of Cornwallis and his troops to General George Washington; the day has been celebrated by the people of Yorktown, Virginia, every year since 1881; special patriotic services are also conducted by the National Park Service at the Yorktown Monument. 268.

Holy Days and Feast Days

20 Birth of Bab, a Baha'i holy day rejoicing in the birth of the spiritual leader the Bab, "the gate of God"; a commemorative day on which all work is suspended. 1, 854.

Holidays and Civic Days

20 Revolution Day in Guatemala, a holiday celebrating the overthrow of the regime of Jorge Ubico y Castaneda in 1944. 875.

20 Kenyatta Day, a public holiday in Kenya, honoring Jomo Kenyatta, the nation's first prime minister, affectionately called the "grand old man." 381.

Anniversaries and Special Events Days

20 Birthday of John Dewey (October 20, 1859–June 1, 1952). American educator and philosopher whose watchword was "learning by doing." 864.

20 Birthday of Sir Christopher Wren (October 20, 1632–February 25, 1723). English architect whose great public buildings include Saint Paul's Cathedral. 864.

Holy Days and Feast Days

21 Feast Day of Saint Ursula, patron saint of teachers and young people in general. 4.

Holidays and Civic Days

21 Saint Ursula's Day, a holiday in the British Virgin Islands honoring Saint Ursula, the patron saint of teachers and young people. 875.

21 Honduras Army Day, observed in Honduras, sometimes called Ousting of Lozano Diaz Day, commemorating an October 1956 revolt. 875.

21 Somalia Revolution Days, celebrated in the Somali Democratic Republic on October 21–22, to honor the take-over of the government on October 21, 1969, by the police and the army. 868, 875.

Anniversaries and Special Events Days

21 Birthday of Samuel Taylor Coleridge (October 21, 1772–July 25, 1834). English poet, critic, and philosopher. 864.

21 Birthday of Alfred Bernhard Nobel (October 21, 1833–December 10, 1896). Swedish chemist and engineer who invented dynamite and other explosives and left his fortune for the Nobel Prizes. *See also* Nobel Prize Presentation Day, December 10. 679.

21 Trafalgar Day, a day of observance in commemoration of the Battle of Trafalgar, October 21, 1805, when Lord Nelson defeated French-Spanish fleets. Ceremonies include a naval parade from London's Mall to Trafalgar Square where after a short service wreaths are placed at the foot of Nelson's Column.

Holidays and Civic Days

22 Jidai Matsuri, or Festival of the Eras, observed in Kyoto, Japan, since 1895 as a ceremonial day reviewing the main periods of Kyoto's and Japan's histories from the eighth to the nineteenth centuries.

c22 Labour Day, a public holiday in New Zealand, observed on the last Monday in October. 875.

22 Anniversary of the beginning of the Pontificate of John Paul II; a religious and general holiday in the Vatican City State. 5.

Anniversaries and Special Events Days

22 Cuban Missile Crisis Day, the anniversary of President John Kennedy's October 22, 1962, declaration of intent to remove Soviet offensive weapons and installations from Cuba. 268.

22 Anniversary of the Revocation of the Edict of Nantes by Louis XIV on October 22, 1685, which deprived the French Protestants of religious freedom and resulted in the Huguenot emigration to Holland and England and eventually to the United States. 20.

22 Birthday of Franz Liszt (October 22, 1811–July 31, 1886). Hungarian composer and pianist, famous for the *Hungarian Rhapsodies*, symphonic poems for orchestra, and many piano compositions. 864.

22 Anniversary of the death of Jean Grolier de Servières on October 22, 1565. French bibliophile for whom the Grolier Society in New York is named and who is honored annually by the society on the anniversary of his death.

Holidays and Civic Days

23 Hungarian Revolution Day, the anniversary of the October 23, 1956 Hungarian revolt against the Communist government; the uprising was suppressed by the Soviet army but the day is commemorated by Americans of Hungarian descent.

Anniversaries and Special Events Days

23 Birthday of Robert Bridges (October 23, 1844–April 21, 1930). Poet laureate of England, remembered especially for his work *The Testament of Beauty*.

23 Swallows of Capistrano Day, the traditional day for swallows to leave the San Juan Capistrano Mission in California. *See also* Swallows Day, March 19. 866.

Holidays and Civic Days

24 Suez Day, a holiday in the Arab Republic of Egypt commemorating the Egyptian-Israeli cease-fire of October 24, 1973, which restored control of the Suez Canal to Egypt. 875.

24 United Nations Day, commemorating the founding of the United Nations on October 24, 1945; a holiday in Haiti, Mauritius, and Swaziland; a half-day holiday in Nepal. 268, 269, 583, 624, 754, 866.

24 Zambia Independence Day, a public holiday of two-days duration, celebrating October 24, 1964, when Northern Rhodesia became the independent Republic of Zambia. 868, 875.

Anniversaries and Special Events Days

24 Birthday of Sarah Josepha Hale (October 24, 1788–April 30, 1879). American author and pioneer woman editor of *Godey's Lady's Book*. The Friends of the Richards Free Library at Newport, New Hampshire, present an annual award in her name to an individual who has made a lifetime contribution to literature associated with New England. 268.

24 Birthday of Anton van Leeuwenhoek (October 24, 1632–August 26, 1723). Dutch microscopist and biologist; known as "the father of microscopy" and the first biological scientist. 864.

Holy Days and Feast Days

25 Feast Day of Saint Crispin, patron saint of shoemakers. 4.

Holidays and Civic Days

c25 Gospel Day, a holiday in the Cook Islands, commemorating the arrival of the Christian gospel at Aitutaki in 1823. 875.

25 Halloween holiday, a national free day in Ireland dedicated to merrymaking and parties. October 25 is called a Bank Holiday in some parts of Ireland. 613.

25 Taiwan Restoration Day, commemorates the return of Taiwan to the Chinese Nationalists in 1945 after fifty years of Japanese occupation. 868, 875.

25 King Chulalongkorn Memorial Day, a holiday in Thailand commemorating the birth of Rama V, responsible for the modernization of the Thai government during the last quarter of the nineteenth century. 868, 875.

Anniversaries and Special Events Days

25 Birthday of Georges Bizet (October 25, 1838–June 3, 1875). French composer whose most famous work is the opera *Carmen*.

25 Birthday of Richard Evelyn Byrd (October 25, 1888–March 11, 1957). American naval officer and polar explorer who made five important expeditions to the Antarctic. He received the Congressional Medal of Honor in 1926. 268.

25 Guernica Day, the anniversary of the October 25, 1981, release of Picasso's painting *Guernica* to the Prado Museum in Madrid after being on loan to the New York Museum of Modern Art for forty-four years. 874.

25 Birthday of Thomas Babington Macaulay (October 25, 1800–December 28, 1859). English essayist, poet, historian, and statesman, famous for *Horatius at the Bridge* and his *History of England*. 864.

25 Birthday of Pablo Ruiz Picasso (October 25, 1881–April 8, 1973). Spanish-born painter and sculptor; founder of the Cubist school and leader in the surrealistic movement in France. 864.

Holy Days and Feast Days

26 Feast Day of Saint Demetrios, patron saint of Salonika, Greece, honored by the Greeks with annual ceremonials that had their origin in the Middle Ages.

Holidays and Civic Days

26 Austria National Day, a holiday commemorating the withdrawal of the Soviet Union's occupying troops on October 26, 1955, and the regaining of national freedom. It is also Flag Day for Austria. 868, 875.

Anniversaries and Special Events Days

26 International Red Cross Day, anniversary of the establishment of the worldwide Red Cross organization at an October 26, 1863, meeting of nations in Geneva.

Holy Days and Feast Days

27 Feast of Saint Frumentius, fourth-century bishop of Ethiopia, called Abuna, or "our father," a title which remains in use in the twentieth century; the patron saint of Ethiopia. 4.

Holidays and Civic Days

27 Angam Day, a holiday in the Republic of Nauru in the western Pacific, celebrating the day on which the population of Nauru, the smallest independent republic in the world, reached the pre-World War II level. 868, 875.

27 Thanksgiving and Independence Day, a holiday in St. Vincent. Independence was granted to St. Vincent by the United Kingdom on October 27, 1979. 875.

27 Zaire's Naming Day, a holiday commemorating the adoption of the name *Zaire*, meaning "river," for the country known as the Congo. On October 27, 1971, Zaire celebrated its new name, a new flag, and a new anthem. The holiday is sometimes called the Three Zs Day. 868, 875.

Anniversaries and Special Events Days

27 Navy Day, anniversary of establishment of the American navy on October 27, 1775; observed as Navy Day since 1922. 268.

27 Birthday of Theodore Roosevelt (October 27, 1858–January 6, 1919). Dutch ancestry; New York assemblyman; naturalist; conservationist; explorer; man of letters; twenty-sixth president of the United States, 1901–9. Awarded Nobel Peace Prize in 1906. Member of the Reformed Dutch church. Buried at Oyster Bay, New York. Elected to the Hall of Fame for Great Americans in 1950. 350–66, 370–72, 374, 378, 379.

27 Birthday of Dylan Marlais Thomas (October 27, 1914–November 9, 1953). British poet whose verse has been compared to surrealist painting. 864.

c27 Frances E. Willard Day, observed by temperance associations and schools on the fourth Friday in October to honor the American temperance leader. 268.

Holy Days and Feast Days

28 Feast Day of Saint Jude, patron saint of deperate cases. 4.

Holidays and Civic Days

28 Ochi Day, a holiday in Greece, commemorating October 28, 1940, when Greece entered World War II on the side of the Allies after saying *ochi* (no) to the demands of the Italian invaders. 875.

Anniversaries and Special Events Days

28 Czechoslovak Independence Day, the anniversary of the proclamation of independence and the establishment of the Republic of Czechoslovakia on October 28, 1918; celebrated in the United States and other countries by persons of Czech and Slovak descent with religious services and cultural programs. 268.

c28 Punky Night, observed on the last Thursday of October in Hinton St. George, Somerset, England; a celebration for both children and adults who carry candlelit punkies carved out of mangel-wurzels, a variety of beet, and sing old punky songs, hoping to win a prize for the best carved punky. 256, 265.

28 Statue of Liberty Dedication Day, anniversary of the dedication of the Statue of Liberty on October 28, 1886. 296.

Holidays and Civic Days

29 Tanzania Naming Day; the United Republic of Tanganyika and Zanzibar changed its name on October 29, 1964, to the United Republic of Tanzania. 868.

29 Turkey's Republic Day, a holiday in Turkey commemorating October 29, 1923, when Turkey became a republic; the celebrations usually last two days. 868, 875.

Anniversaries and Special Events Days

29 Black Tuesday, the anniversary of the October 29, 1929, stock market crash that brought ruin to the financial world and precipitated the great depression of the 1930s. 268.

29 Birthday of James Boswell (October 29, 1740–May 19, 1795). English author, famous as a diarist and as the biographer of Dr. Samuel Johnson. 850.

29 Anniversary of the formation of the National Organization for Women (NOW), organized on October 29, 1966, "to press for true equality for all women in America."

29 Aniversary of the death of Sir Walter Raleigh on October 29, 1618. English military and naval commander of expeditions to North America. 864.

Anniversaries and Special Events Days

30 Birthday of John Adams (October 30, 1735–July 4, 1826). English ancestry; Massachusetts teacher, lawyer, diarist, and letter writer; second president of the United States, 1797–1801. Unitarian. Buried in First Unitarian Church at Quincy, Massachusetts. Elected to the Hall of Fame for Great Americans in 1900. 302, 359–66, 370–72, 374, 378, 379, 791.

Holidays and Civic Days

31 Antigua Independence Day, the anniversary of the achievement of independence on October 31, 1981, by a West Indies nation. 868.

31 Nevada Admission Day, a legal holiday, celebrating Nevada's admission to the Union on October 31, 1864, as the thirty-sixth state. 268, 856, 862.

Anniversaries and Special Events Days

31 Halloween, All Hallows' Eve, or Beggars' Night, a festival for children, known in the United States as Trick-or-Treat night, when costumed youngsters roam their neighborhoods with open bags for treats and with soap for the windows of their absent or ungiving neighbors. 269, 493–518, 572, 582, 588, 589, 607, 624, 628, 831, 866.

31 Houdini Day, the anniversary of the October 31, 1926, death of Harry Houdini, American magician, illusionist, and writer, famed for his escape techniques and for his exposure of fraudulent mediums. The day is commemorated by organizations of amateur and professional magicians. 496, 502, 503.

31 Birthday of John Keats (October 31, 1795–February 23, 1821). English poet trained as a surgeon. *The Eve of St. Agnes* and other poems assure him a permanent place in world literature. Keats, known as the "poet's poet," is buried in the Protestant cemetery in Rome. 774.

31 Birthday of Juliette Gordon Low (October 31, 1860–January 17, 1927). American youth leader and founder of the Girl Scouts in America. 268.

31 National Magic Day, honoring the skills of magicians and commemorating the death of the great magician Harry Houdini on October 31, 1926. 497, 510.

c31 Reformation Day, commemorating Luther's signing of the theses. The Sunday preceding October 31 is usually observed as Reformation Sunday in Lutheran churches. Called Luther's Theses Day in some parts of Germany in memory of October 31, 1517, when Martin Luther posted his ninety-five theses in Wittenberg. 1, 268.

31 UNICEF Day, a day set aside by presidential proclamation in the United States and observed in many nations for the purpose of aiding the United Nations International Children's Fund. 268.

31 Birthday of Sir George Hubert Wilkins (October 31, 1888–Nov. 30/Dec. 1, 1958). Australian polar explorer; the first to fly an airplane in the Antarctic and to fly over both polar regions. 864.

November

November, the eleventh month in the Gregorian calendar, received its name from the Latin numeral *novem* because it was the ninth month in the Julian calendar.

The month of November includes the oldest special day to have originated in the United States. In 1621, Governor William Bradford of Massachusetts proclaimed a day for feasting, prayer, and thanksgiving. It had its forerunner in the harvest-home celebrations of England, but it was a very special day for the Pilgrims. The idea spread throughout the states but was not universally celebrated until Sarah Josepha Hale, the editor of *Godey's Lady's Book*, persuaded President Lincoln to issue a general proclamation in 1863. Since then, Thanksgiving Day has been observed as a holiday by all states and territories of the United States.

November also has a traditional day for revelry. It is Guy Fawkes Day, the anniversary of the November 5, 1605, gunpowder plot to blow up the English Parliament and the king. It is observed throughout England and in many parts of the British Commonwealth. It is a popular festival for children and students. It is said that the undergraduates at Oxford University fill the streets on Guy Fawkes night lighting fireworks. The students who get into trouble on this night are eligible to join the Bowler Hat Club, whose members vow to promote the use of the Bowler hat. In other parts of England, the celebration centers around big bonfires. In Nassau and in the Caribbean, Guy Fawkes parades are accompanied by calypso bands.

The chrysanthemum is the November flower, and the gem is the topaz.

Holy Days and Feast Days

1 All Saints Day, a religious festival honoring Christian saints of all ages and stations, known and unknown; observed universally by all Western churches, a day of obligation in the Roman Catholic church. 1, 5.

Holidays and Civic Days

1 Algerian Revolution Day, a public holiday in Algeria, commemorating the revolution begun by the National Liberation Front on November 1, 1954, against the French administration and armed forces. 868, 875.

1 All Saints Day, a religious and national holiday in thirty-six nations of the world commemorating the saints in heaven. 269. 875.

1 Chiang Kai-shek Day, a holiday in Taiwan honoring the birth on November 1, 1887, of Chiang Kai-shek, president of the Republic of China from 1948 to his death in 1975. 875.

1 Recreation Day, a holiday in northern Tasmania, one of the federated states of the Commonwealth of Australia. 875.

Anniversaries and Special Events Days

1 Birthday of Sholem Asch (November 1, 1880–July 10, 1957). American novelist famous for novels and plays in English and in Yiddish.

1 Author's Day, observed since November 1, 1928, by study clubs to honor the work of writers who have developed American literature and to encourage authors "to lend their talents to making a better America."

1 Birthday of Charles Brantley Aycock (November 1, 1859–April 4, 1912). American politician and educational reformer. Governor of North Carolina, best known for the establishment of a rural high school system in that state. He represents North Carolina in Statuary Hall in a sculpture done by Charles Keck. 870.

1 Birthday of Stephen Crane (November 1, 1871–June 5, 1900). American author who is famous for the novel *The Red Badge of Courage*. 864.

1 Birthday of Crawford Williamson Long (November 1, 1815–June 16, 1878). American surgeon who pioneered in the use of ether for anesthesia. He represents the state of Georgia in Statuary Hall in a sculpture by J. Massey Rhind. 870.

Holy Days and Feast Days

2 All Souls Day, a memorial commemorating the faithful departed; a day of prayers for the dead that began in the earliest days of Christianity. 1, 5.

Holidays and Civic Days

2 Memorial Day, a religious and national holiday in Brazil commemorated with services for All Souls' Day and with the observance of local customs at grave sites. 875.

2 All Souls' Day, a religious and national holiday in Ecuador, El Salvador, the French West Indies, Macao, Mexico, San Marino, Uruguay, and the Vatican City State; a day of commemoration for the faithful departed, which in most of the countries includes both church services and traditional ceremonials at cemeteries. 875.

c2 Melbourne Cup Day, a holiday in the Melbourne, Australia, metropolitan area; the only public holiday in the world dedicated to a horse race; the Melbourne Cup Day has been held since 1867 and is scheduled for the first Tuesday in November. 875.

2 North Dakota Admission Day. North Dakota entered the Union on November 2, 1889, as the thirty-ninth state. 268, 856, 862.

2 Portugal's Dia de Finados, "Day of the Dead"; observed with special masses and processions to cemeteries, followed by open-air feasts of wine and chestnuts.

2 South Dakota Admission Day. South Dakota entered the Union on November 2, 1889, as the fortieth state. 268, 856, 862.

Anniversaries and Special Events Day

2 Balfour Declaration Day, a semi-holiday in Israel in commemoration of the establishment of a Jewish national home on November 2, 1917. 1, 20.

2 Birthday of Daniel Boone (November 2, 1734–September 26, 1820). American pioneer explorer, settler, and surveyor, subject of many books, honored particularly in the state of Kentucky. Elected to the Hall of Fame for Great Americans in 1915. 268.

2 Birthday of Warren Gamaliel Harding (November 2, 1865–August 2, 1923). Scotch-Dutch descent; Ohio newspaper editor and publisher; twenty-ninth president of the United States, 1921–23. Baptist. Buried at Marion, Ohio. 359–66, 370–72, 374, 378, 379.

2 Birthday of James Knox Polk (November 2, 1795–June 15, 1849). Scotch-Irish ancestry; Tennessee lawyer; eleventh president of the United States, 1845–49. Methodist. Buried at Nashville, Tennessee. 359–66, 370–72, 374, 378, 379.

Holy Days and Feast Days

3 Feast Day of Saint Hubert of Liége, patron saint of hunters, of the hunt, of dogs, and of victims of hydrophobia; especially honored at the Church of Saint Hubert in Luxembourg; Saint Hubert's mass officially opens the hunting season in Belgium. 4.

3 Feast of Saint Martin de Porres, a Dominican lay brother at Rosary Convent in Lima, Peru; known for his work with the poor and with African slaves; patron of interracial justice. 9.

Holidays and Civic Days

3 Father of Texas Day, or Austin Day, observed in Austin, Texas, to honor Stephen Austin's birth in 1793.

3 Cuenca Independence Day, a holiday in Ecuador honoring the declaration of independence for the city declared on November 3, 1820. 875.

3 Dominica Independence Day, the anniversary of the achievement of independence on November 3, 1978, for a West Indies nation. It is a two-day celebration. 875.

3 Culture Day, a national holiday in Japan established to encourage public interest in freedom and in cultural activities; before World War II, November 3 was reserved for the Emperor Meiji's birthday, honoring the man who led his country out of feudalism. 875.

3 Independence from Colombia Day, a holiday in Panama commemorating the revolution-inspired separation of Panama from Colombia and the declaration of November 3, 1903, establishing independence. 395.

Anniversaries and Special Events Days

3 Birthday of Stephen Fuller Austin (November 3, 1793–December 27, 1836). American pioneer and Texas colonizer. Represents the state of Texas in Statuary Hall in a sculpture done by Elisabet Ney. 870.

3 Birthday of William Cullen Bryant (November 3, 1794–June 12, 1878). American poet; one of the most influential newspaper editors of the mid-nineteenth century. His best-known poem is "Thanatopsis," first published in 1817. Bryant was elected to the Hall of Fame for Great Americans in 1910. 864.

Holy Days and Feast Days

4 Feast of Saint Charles Borromeo, sixteenth-century scholar, archbishop of Milan, and cardinal, whose great achievements were ecclesiastical administration and the religious education of the laity, particularly children. 4.

Holidays and Civic Days

4 Panama Flag Day, a holiday in Panama celebrated in conjunction with the nation's Independence Day on November 3. 280.

4 John Paul II Namesday, a religious and general holiday in the Vatican City State. 875.

c4 Liberty Day, a holiday in the Virgin Islands, observed on the first Monday of November to honor the establishment in 1915 of the first press in the Virgin Islands. 875.

Anniversaries and Special Events Days

4 Birthday of James Fraser (November 4, 1876–October 11, 1953). American sculptor who designed the Indian head and buffalo on the pre-1938 United States five-cent coins and whose sculpture includes statues of Alexander Hamilton, General George Patton, Jr., and other famous Americans.

4 Hostage Day, the anniversary of the overtaking, on November 4, 1979, of the U.S. Embassy in Teheran, a crisis that lasted 444 days with 52 Americans held in captivity by militant Iranian students. 710.

4 Mischief Night, observed in many districts of northern and midland England on the eve of Guy Fawkes' Day; a young people's night dedicated to merriment, pranks, and high-spirited antics. 256.

4 Will Rogers Day, observed in Oklahoma by proclamation of the governor to commemorate the birth on November 4, 1879, of the great American humorist; Will Rogers represents the state of Oklahoma in Statuary Hall in the nation's Capitol. His birthday is celebrated with special events at the Will Rogers Memorial in Claremore. 745, 779, 797.

4 Victory of Vittorio Veneto, a day honoring the Italian Unknown Soldier, observed in Rome at the tomb in the monument to Victor Emmanuel II.

4 Anniversary of the establishment on November 4, 1946, of the United Nations Educational, Scientific and Cultural Organization (UNESCO), an autonomous organization affiliated with the United Nations to enlist educational, scientific, and cultural institutions in the service of peace and the ennoblement of man. 754, 874.

Holidays and Civic Days

5 First Call for Independence Day, a holiday in El Salvador, commemorating the first battle for freedom from Spain led by Padre José Matias Delgado on November 5, 1811. 875.

c5 Thanksgiving Day, a public holiday in Liberia, observed on the first Thursday of November. 875.

c5 Election day in the United States, the first Tuesday after the first Monday in November; a legal or optional holiday in twenty-three of the fifty states of the United States in years of general and presidential elections. 268.

5 Arbor Day, a holiday in Western Samoa. 875.

Anniversaries and Special Events Days

5   Birthday of Rui Barbosa (November 5, 1849–March 1, 1923). Brazilian statesman, jurist, essayist, and strong advocate of human and civil liberties whose private library has become a national shrine.

5   Guy Fawkes Day, the anniversary of the November 5, 1605, Gunpowder Plot to blow up Parliament and the king; observed in England and in other parts of the British Commonwealth with bonfires, fireworks, and revelries. 20, 254, 256, 261, 628, 866.

5   Birthday of Ida Minerva Tarbell (November 5, 1857–January 6, 1944). American biographer of Lincoln and author of the influential *History of the Standard Oil Company*. 864.

5   World Community Day, observed on the first Friday in November to encourage action in support of peace and justice; a day sponsored by Church Women United. 857.

Anniversaries and Special Events Days

6   Gustavus Adolphus Day, a commemorative day in Sweden, honoring the great Swedish king who died in battle on November 6, 1632.

6   Birthday of James Naismith (November 6, 1861–November 28, 1939). Canadian-American educator and physical-education leader who invented the game of basketball as a class assignment in 1891. 867.

6   Birthday of Ignace Jan Paderewski (November 6, 1860–June 29, 1941). Polish pianist, composer, and statesman. 825.

Holy Days and Feast Days

7   Feast Day of Saint Willibrord, patron saint of Holland. 4.

Holidays and Civic Days

7   Bangladesh Revolution Day, a holiday in Bangladesh celebrating the November 7, 1975, take-over of the government by a military group. 868, 875.

7   October Socialist Revolution Day, the anniversary of the Great October Revolution of 1917; a holiday celebrated on November 7 and 8 by the Union of Soviet Socialist Republics with major military parades and patriotic events held in Moscow. 868, 875.

Anniversaries and Special Events Days

7   Bolshevik Revolution Day, the anniversary of the overthrow of the Russian government on November 7 by a revolutionary group called the Bolshevik, or majority segment of the Russian Social Democratic Labor party.

7   Birthday of Marie Sklodowska Curie (November 7, 1867–July 4, 1934). Polish-French chemist and physicist, the only person whose name appears twice on the Nobel Prize list. 775, 788.

7   Birthday of Andrew Dickson White (November 7, 1832–November 4, 1918). American educator and diplomat; first president of Cornell University; cofounder and first president of the American Historical Association. 867.

Holy Days and Feast Days

8   Saints, Doctors, Missionaries, and Martyrs Day, observed by the Church of England in memory and commemoration of the "unnamed saints of the nation." 14.

Holidays and Civic Days

8   Prince Charles Day, a holiday in Fiji and in the Solomon Islands celebrating the November 14, 1948, birth of Britain's heir apparent. 875.

8   Montana Admission Day. Montana entered the Union on November 8, 1889, as the forty-first state. 268, 856, 862.

8   The Queen's Birthday, a holiday in Nepal celebrating the birthday of Her Majesty the Queen. 875.

Anniversaries and Special Events Days

8   Birthday of Edmund Halley (November 8, 1656–January 14, 1742). English astronomer who won lasting fame for his studies of comets. 864.

8   Birthday of Margaret Mitchell (November 8, 1900–August 16, 1949). American novelist famous for *Gone with the Wind*, which was awarded the 1937 Pulitzer Prize in fiction. 864.

8   Dunce Day, the anniversary of the November 8, 1308, death of Duns Scotus, medieval scholastic, responsible for the introduction of the word *dunce* into the language; a day of recognition of the folly of being a dunce. 857.

Holy Days and Feast Days

9   Feast of the Dedication of Saint John Lateran, commemorating the first public consecration of a church, the Basilica of the Most Holy Savior in Rome, on November 9, 324; the basilica has been called Saint John Lateran since the twelfth century in honor of John the Baptist. 5.

Anniversaries and Special Events Days

9   Crystal Night, the anniversary of the street riots of November 9 and 10, 1938, when Nazi storm troopers raided Jewish homes and synagogues; the name came from the shattering of glass in Jewish homes and stores. 1, 676.

9   Iqbal Day, the anniversary of the birth on November 9, 1877, of Allama Iqbal, Pakistan's great philosopher-poet; the day is observed in Pakistan and by Iqbal Societies in the United States and other countries; Iqbal was honored in Pakistan in 1977 with the issuance of a commemorative Iqbal Centenary Year stamp.

c9   The Lord Mayor's Day, held annually on the second Saturday of November; dates from 1215; a day of civic pageantry in which the lord mayor of London drives in state to the Guildhall for ceremonials and on to the law courts to take the oath of office. 256.

9   Birthday of Elijah Parish Lovejoy (November 9, 1802–November 7, 1837). American newspaperman killed in a mob attack on his presses; known as "the martyr abolitionist" of the Civil War period. 864.

9   Sadie Hawkins Day, a day created in the mind of Alfred Gerald Caplin, a cartoonist popularly known as Al Capp, for his comic strip *Li'l Abner*; introduced on November 9, 1928, as an occasion upon which the spinsters of Dogpatch might rightfully pursue the unattached males; observed on occasion by students and social groups. 857.

9   Tree Festival Day, an Arbor Day and national agricultural festival in Tunisia.

Holy Days and Feast Days

10   Feast of Saint Leo I, the Great; consecrated pope on September 29, 440; instrumental in dissuading Attila from sacking Rome in 452; a rebuilder of Rome after the plundering of the city by the Vandal Genseric; defender of the faith against the errors of Pelagianism; proclaimed a doctor of the church in 1574. 4.

Anniversaries and Special Events Days

10   Birthday of Sir Jacob Epstein (November 10, 1880–August 21, 1959). Anglo-American sculptor who gained fame with his controversial bronze figures and unidealized portraits. 864.

10   Anniversary of the death of Kemal Atatürk on November 10, 1938. Turkish patriot, founder and first president of the Turkish Republic; known as "the father of the Turks." 864.

10   Birthday of Nicholas Vachel Lindsay (November 10, 1879–December 5, 1931). American poet remembered as the vagabond poet who wrote *General William Booth Enters into Heaven* and *The Congo*. He was the first American poet invited to appear at Oxford University. 864.

10 Birthday of Martin Luther (November 10, 1483–February 18, 1546). German religious reformer and translator of the Bible whose stand led to the establishment of the Lutheran church. Also famous for the writing of hymns, of which "A Mighty Fortress Is Our God" is the most familiar. Luther Day is observed by the Protestants of Germany and commemorated by Lutheran churches on November 10. 1, 20.

10 Birthday of the United States Marine Corps, celebrated annually by the marines to commemorate the founding of the corps on November 10, 1775. 268.

10 Polish Solidarity Day, the anniversary of November 10, 1980, when Solidarity, formed in August of 1980, was declared to be a legal workers union. Outlawed by the government in 1982, the movement lives underground in Poland. The day is observed by Polish-Americans with dignified demonstrations and programs of support for the Polish workers.

Holy Days and Feast Days

11 Feast of Saint Martin of Tours, the bishop of Tours and the outstanding pioneer of Western monasticism before Saint Benedict; his shrine at Tours became an important pilgrimage center; a patron saint of France and of wine growers, tavern keepers and beggars. 4.

Holidays and Civic Days

11 Angola Independence Day, the anniversary of November 11, 1975, when independence became effective for the People's Republic of Angola located in southwest Africa on the Atlantic coast. 868, 875.

11 Remembrance Day, a holiday in Bermuda honoring the dead of two World Wars with military parades and ceremonials. 875.

11 The King's Birthday, a national holiday in the Kingdom of Bhutan, a Himalayan country located between the Tibetan Plateau and the Assam-Bengal Plains of northeastern India. 875.

11 Armistice Day, the anniversary of the November 11, 1918, signing of the armistice between the Allied and Central powers ending the first World War; a holiday called Armistice Day in Belgium, French Guinea, Saint Pierre and Miquelon, and Tahiti. 20, 875.

11 Remembrance Day, a public holiday in Canada commemorating the end of World Wars I and II. 875.

11 Cartagena Independence Day, a holiday in Colombia commemorating the declaration of independence for the port city in 1811 after years of Spanish rule. 868, 875.

11 Maldives Republic Day, a two-day holiday, commemorating November 11, 1968, when the Sultanate was abolished and the country took the official name of the Republic of Maldives. 868, 875.

11 Polish Independence Day, the anniversary of the birth of modern Poland, November 11, 1918, the day the country regained its liberty after 125 years of partition among Prussia, Russia, and Austria. Celebrated until World War II on November 11. Observed on November 7 in conjunction with the Soviet Revolution holiday until 1981 when the government permitted observance on November 11. 868.

11 Veterans' Day, a holiday in the United States honoring the members of the armed forces who served in World War I and II, Korea, and Vietnam. 269, 410–18, 866.

11 Washington Admission Day, the commemoration of Washington's admission to the Union as the forty-second state on November 11, 1889; observed as a holiday in conjunction with Veterans' Day; schools commemorate Admission Day on the preceding Friday with programs focused on the history of the state and its laws. 268, 865, 862.

Anniversaries and Special Events Days

11 Beggar's Day, an old tradition in the Netherlands carried out by children pretending to be beggars as they go from door to door on the day of Saint Martin, the patron saint of beggars.

11 Concordia Day, a day of commemoration in the island of St. Maarten in the Caribbean honoring the 1648 agreement to divide the island between the Dutch and the French.

11 Birthday of Fyodor Dostoyevsky (November 11, 1821–February 9, 1881). Russian novelist famed for such books as *The Brothers Karamazov* and *Crime and Punishment*. 864.

11 Birthday of Ephraim McDowell (November 11, 1771–June 25, 1830). American surgeon; pioneer in abdominal surgery who performed the first recorded ovariotomy in the United States. He represents the state of Kentucky in Statuary Hall in a sculpture by Charles Henry Niehaus. 870.

11 Martinmas, or Martin's Mass, or Martin's Goose Day, a festival day and night in many parts of Europe highlighted by revelry, the lighting of bonfires, and feasting on stuffed goose and other traditional foods. 20.

11 Anniversary of the entombment of the Unknown Soldier of World War I in the Tomb of the Unknowns at Arlington, Virginia, on November 11, 1921. An Unknown Soldier of World War II and one from the Korean conflict were interred in crypts on either side of the Tomb of the Unknown Soldier on Memorial Day, 1958. 414.

Holy Days and Feast Days

12 Birth of Baha'u'llah, a Baha'i holy day celebrating the birth of the divine messenger whose name means "the glory and splendor of God" and whose teachings are directed to the unity of mankind and the creation of harmony throughout the universe. 1, 854.

Holidays and Civic Days

12 Austrian Republic Day, observed in Austria in honor of November 12, 1918, when Austria declared itself a republic.

12 Sun Yat-sen Day, a holiday in Taiwan, the Republic of China, honoring Dr. Sun Yat-sen, the leader of the Chinese Nationalist party, born on November 12, 1866. 713, 875.

Anniversaries and Special Events Day

12 Birthday of Juana Inés de La Cruz (November 12, 1651–April 12, 1695). Mexican poet-nun considered to be the greatest woman of the colonial period of Spanish America, next to Rose of Lima; known as "the first feminist of Spanish America." 738.

12 Birthday of Elizabeth Cady Stanton (November 12, 1815–October 26, 1902). American woman-suffrage reformer. Her birthday is observed by women's organizations as Elizabeth Cady Stanton Day. 268, 738, 740.

12 Birthday of Sun Yat-sen (November 12, 1866–March 12, 1925). Leader of the Chinese Nationalist party; his birthday is a national holiday in Taiwan, the Republic of China. 713.

Holy Days and Feast Days

13 Feast of Saint Frances Xavier Cabrini, celebrated on November 13 to commemorate her beatification on November 13, 1938; founder of the Missionary Sisters of the Sacred Heart; first American citizen to be proclaimed a saint in the Roman Catholic church; patron saint of emigrants and hospital administrators. 9.

13 Feast of Saint Nicholas I, the ninth-century pope who effectively established the supreme authority of the papacy in church affairs over emperors, kings, and other rulers; a patron of learning and the arts. 9.

Anniversaries and Special Events Days

13 Birthday of Edwin Thomas Booth (November 13, 1833–June 7, 1893). American tragedian famous for his interpretation of *Hamlet*. Founded the Players in 1888, a famous club for actors. Elected to the Hall of Fame for Great Americans in 1925. 268.

13 Birthday of Louis Dembitz Brandeis (November 13, 1856–October 5, 1941). American associate justice of the United States Supreme Court, for whom Brandeis University, inaugurated in 1948, was named. 730.

13 Anniversary of the publication on November 13, 1830, of "Old Ironsides" by Oliver Wendell Holmes, which prevented the scrapping of the battleship *Constitution*, now a national memorial in the United States. 451, 829.

13 Pacific Balloon Day, the anniversary of the first successful crossing of the Pacific Ocean on November 13, 1981, a 6,000-mile voyage.

13 Birthday of Robert Louis Stevenson (November 13, 1850–December 3, 1894). Scottish novelist, poet, and essayist famous for *Treasure Island, A Child's Garden of Verses*, and many other books. Known as Tusitala, or "teller of tales," in Samoa, where he died at Vailema, the destination of a literary pilgrimage for travelers in the area. 736.

13 Anniversary of the November 13, 1982, dedication of the Vietnam Veterans Memorial in Washington, D.C. On the walls of the memorial are inscribed the names of the 57,939 Americans killed or missing in the Vietnam conflict. 413.

Holidays and Civic Days

14 Prince of Wales's Birthday, a holiday in the British Virgin Islands and on St. Kitts, a member of the West Indies Associated States; honoring the birth on November 14, 1948, of Prince Charles, heir apparent to the British throne. 875.

14 King Hussein Day, a national holiday in the Hashemite Kingdom of Jordan, honoring His Majesty King Hussein who was born November 14, 1935. 875.

Anniversaries and Special Events Days

14 Birthday of Robert Fulton (November 14, 1765–February 24, 1815). American artist, civil engineer, and inventor famous for the development of the steamboat. He was elected to the Hall of Fame for Great Americans in 1900. He represents the state of Pennsylvania in Statuary Hall in a sculpture done by Howard Roberts. 870.

14 Birthday of Claude Monet (November 14, 1840–December 5, 1926). French landscape and still-life painter who applied scientific principles of light to the art of painting; considered one of the greatest landscape painters in the world. 864.

14 Birthday of Jawaharlal Nehru (November 14, 1889–May 17, 1964). First prime minister of independent India. 765, 864.

14 Birthday of Frederick Jackson Turner (November 14, 1861–March 14, 1932). American historian best known for *The Frontier in American History*. His work *The Significance of Sections in American History* received the Pulitzer Prize in 1933. 864.

Holy Days and Feast Days

15 Feast Day of Saint Albertus Magnus, patron saint of scholars, students, medical technologists, and scientists; known in his day as Doctor Universalis because of his extensive knowledge. 4.

15 Feast Day of Saint Leopold, observed in particular in Vienna and at Klosterneuburg with a wine festival and a pilgrimage to Saint Leopold's shrine. The popular name for Saint Leopold's Day is *Fasslrutschen*. 4.

Holidays and Civic Days

15 Dynasty Day, or Fête de la Dynastie, a holiday in Belgium honoring the king's patron saint's day. 875.

15 Proclamation of the Republic Day in Brazil, a holiday with military parades and ceremonies honoring the proclamation of November 15, 1889, which dethroned Dom Pedro II. 868, 875.

Anniversaries and Special Events Days

15 Birthday of Sir William Herschel (November 15, 1738–August 25, 1822). Anglo-German astronomer who built his own telescope and discovered the planet Uranus. His work was carried on with distinction by his son, Sir John Frederick William Herschel. 864.

15 Anniversary of the death on November 15, 1978, of Margaret Mead, distinguished American anthropologist. Her studies of primitive societies existing in the South Pacific in the twentieth century were major contributions to anthropology and to investigations of cultural conditioning in modern society. 737, 795.

15 Birthday of Marianne Craig Moore (November 15, 1887–February 5, 1972). American poet; winner of the Pulitzer Prize in poetry in 1951, the 1952 National Book Award, and the 1953 gold medal of the National Institute of Arts and Letters; decorated by France for her translation of *The Fables of La Fontaine*. 794.

15 Birthday of William Pitt, the elder (November 15, 1708–May 11, 1778). British statesman, known as 'the great commoner"; advocate of a conciliatory policy toward the American colonies. 864.

15 Seven-Five-Three Festival Day, observed by parents in Japan as a day of thanksgiving for the safety of girls, aged seven and three, and boys, aged five and three; a tradition that is a legacy from old Japan. 251.

Holy Days and Feast Days

16 Feast of Saint Margaret of Scotland, known for personal piety, work with the poor and support of the clergy; declared patroness of Scotland in 1673. 9, 14.

Holidays and Civic Days

16 Oklahoma Statehood Day, honoring admission of Oklahoma to the Union as the forty-sixth state on November 16, 1907. 268, 856, 862.

Anniversaries and Special Events Days

16 Carib Settlement Days, observed for several days beginning on November 16 to re-enact the first Carib settlement in Belize in 1823. 875.

16 Birthday of William Christopher Handy (November 16, 1873–March 28, 1958). American composer best known for his *St. Louis Blues* and called "the father of the blues." 864.

Holy Days and Feast Days

17 Feast of Saint Elizabeth of Hungary, thirteenth-century Franciscan tertiary dedicated to caring for the sick, the aged and the poor; patron saint of nursing and nursing service. 4, 14.

17 Feast of Saint Hilda, patron saint of business and professional women. 4.

Holidays and Civic Days

17 Penance Day, a religious and national holiday in the Federal Republic of Germany; called Buss and Bettag Day, it is dedicated to repentance and prayer. 875.

17 Zaire Armed Forces Day, a holiday in the Republic of Zaire in Central Africa, honoring the army, the navy, and the air force. 875.

Holidays and Civic Days

18 Vertieres Day, a holiday in Haiti, commemorating the November 18, 1803, Haitian victory over the French in the Battle of Vertieres. 875.

18 Oman National Days, celebrated as a four-day holiday in the Sultanate of Oman to honor Sultan Qaboos bin Said's official birthday, the nation's heritage, and the Sultan's development program. 875.

Anniversaries and Special Events Days

18 Birthday of Louis Jacques Daguerre (November 18, 1789–July 10, 1851). French inventor famous for the development of a method of producing permanent pictures called the "daguerreotype process." 864.

18 Birthday of Clarence Shepard Day (November 18, 1874–December 28, 1935). American author of *Life with Father*. A Clarence Day Award for "outstanding work in encouraging the love of books and reading" was established in 1960 by the American Textbook Publishers Institute and is administered by the American Library Association; the first recipient was Lawrence Powell, librarian, bibliophile, and author. 864.

18 Birthday of Asa Gray (November 18, 1810–January 30, 1888). American botanist, one of the great creators of a systematic American flora. He was elected to the Hall of Fame for Great Americans in 1900. 864.

c18 World Fellowship Day, a sponsored by the Young Women's Christian Association as a part of World Fellowship Week, the climax of a year-round program of cooperation among the YWCAs of sixty-nine countries.

Anniversaries and Special Events Days

19 Birthday of George Rogers Clark (November 19, 1752–February 13, 1818). American soldier and surveyor; conqueror of the Old Northwest during the Revolutionary War. A memorial bridge over the Wabash River at Vincennes, Indiana, is named in his honor. 268, 739.

19 Equal Opportunity Day, anniversary of Lincoln's Gettysburg Address of November 19, 1863; ceremonies commemorating Lincoln's address are held at the National Cemetery under the sponsorship of the Sons of Union Veterans and the Lincoln Fellowship of Pennsylvania.

19 Birthday of James Abram Garfield (November 19, 1831–September 19, 1881). English ancestry; Ohio educator and congressman; general in the Civil War; twentieth president of the United States, November 1880 to September 1881. Shot after six and a half months in office. Disciple of Christ. Buried in Lake View Cemetery, Cleveland, Ohio. He represents the state of Ohio in Statuary Hall in a sculpture done by Charles Henry Niehaus. 359–66, 370–72, 374, 378–79.

19 Gettysburg Address Day, anniversary of the November 19, 1863, consecration of the Gettysburg National Cemetery during which President Lincoln delivered a 270-word message which lives in history as the Gettysburg Address, one of the greatest speeches of all time. 268, 350, 866.

19 Birthday of Ferdinand Marie de Lesseps (November 19, 1805–December 7, 1894). French engineer and diplomat remembered as the planner and engineer of the Suez Canal, which opened in 1869. 864.

Holidays and Civic Days

19 Garifuna Settlement Day, a holiday in Belize centered around a colorful re-enactment of the events of the first Carib settlement in Belize in 1823. 875.

19 Mali Army Coup Day, a holiday in Mali, the anniversary of a bloodless coup on November 19, 1968, which ended the regime of Modibo Keita. 875.

19 Prince Rainier Day, a holiday in Monaco honoring His Serene Highness Rainier III who has been the reigning monarch of Monaco since 1949. 875.

19 Discovery Day, Puerto Rico, a holiday in honor of the day Puerto Rico was discovered by Columbus on his second voyage in 1493. 875.

Holidays and Civic Days

20 Mexico Revolution Day, anniversary of the Mexican Revolution of 1910, a legal holiday throughout Mexico commemorating the revolt of the common people against poverty and the dictatorship of Porfirio Diaz. 875.

Anniversaries and Special Events Days

20 Birthday of Selma Lagerlöf (November 20, 1858–March 16, 1940). Swedish novelist; the first woman to receive the Nobel Prize in literature, which she was awarded in 1909. In 1914 she was elected to the Swedish Academy, the first woman to be admitted. 867.

20 Rights of the Child Day, anniversary of the adoption of the Declaration of the Rights of the Child by the General Assembly of the United Nations on November 20, 1959.

20 Birthday of Peregrine White (November 20, 1620–July 22, 1704). First child born in New England of English parents.

Holidays and Civic Days

21 North Carolina entered the Union as the twelfth state on November 21, 1789. 268, 856, 862.

Anniversaries and Special Events Days

21 Birthday of William Beaumont (November 21, 1785–April 25, 1853). American surgeon whose distinct contribution was a study of digestion and digestive processes through observation of a patient whose stomach was exposed because of a gunshot wound. 864.

21 Birthday of Jean François Marie Voltaire (November 21, 1693–May 30, 1778). French author and freethinker known for the romance *Candide* and for his social-philosophical articles. 864.

Holy Days and Feast Days

22 Feast Day of Saint Cecilia, patron saint of musicians, religious music, and of organ builders, for whom many choirs and musical societies have been named; special concerts are presented in Rome on this day. 4.

Holidays and Civic Days

22 Lebanese Independence Day, a holiday celebrating the achievement of independence declared on November 22, 1943. 875.

Anniversaries and Special Events Days

22 Anniversary of the death of Ann Bailey on November 22, 1825. American pioneer woman who became the heroine of Fort Lee, Virginia, when she rode one hundred miles in 1791 to secure gunpowder to save the fort from an Indian attack. 864.

22 Birthday of George Eliot (Mary Ann Evans) (November 22, 1819–December 22, 1880). English novelist famous for her books *Silas Marner, Mill on the Floss*, and others, for which she is considered one of the most distinguished English novelists of her time. 738, 785.

22 Birthday of Charles de Gaulle (November 22, 1890–November 9, 1970). French general, statesman, president and leader of the Fifth Republic; author of *The Edge of the Sword*. 864.

Holidays and Civic Days

23 Labor Thanksgiving Day, a holiday in Japan honoring the workers and the resources of the nation. 875.

23 Repudiation Day in Maryland, commemorates Frederick County's refusal to observe the Stamp Act in 1765; a partial holiday in the county. 268.

Anniversaries and Special Events Days

23 The anniversary of the founding of the Horatio Alger Society on November 23, 1961, to further the Algerian philosophy "strive and succeed."

23 Birthday of José Clemente Orozco (November 23, 1883–September 7, 1949). Mexican painter, modern master of fresco painting. 864.

23 Birthday of Franklin Pierce (November 23, 1804–October 8, 1869). English ancestry; New Hampshire lawyer; fourteenth president of the United States, 1853–57. Episcopalian. Buried at Minot Cemetery, Concord, New Hampshire. 359–66, 370–372, 374, 378, 379.

Holidays and Civic Days

24 Zaire New Regime Day, a holiday in the Republic of Zaire commemorating the end of rebellion and the start of a new government structure on November 24, 1964, based on the philosophy and teaching of President Mobutu. 868, 875.

Anniversaries and Special Events Days

c24 John F. Kennedy Day, observed in Massachusetts on the last Sunday in November as a memorial to the thirty-fifth president of the United States, a native son of Massachusetts.

24 Anniversary of the death of John Knox on November 24, 1572. Scottish preacher, leader of the Protestant Reformation in Scotland. 1.

c24 Onion Market Day, an autumn festival held on the fourth Monday of November in Bern, Switzerland, to commemorate the granting of market privileges to the men of Fribourg for their assistance in rebuilding Bern after the great fire of 1405.

24 Birthday of Friar Junípero Serra (November 24, 1713–August 28, 1784). Spanish priest-missionary, founder of the California missions. He represents the state of California in Statuary Hall in a sculpture done by Ettore Cadorin. Since 1948, a Serra pageant re-enacting Father Junípero Serra's arrival at San Diego has been presented annually at the old mission near Carmel, California. 870.

24 Birthday of Zachary Taylor (November 24, 1784–July 9, 1850). English ancestry; Louisiana-born soldier, known as Old Rough and Ready, twelfth president of the United States, 1849–50, died in the White House after one year and four months in office. Episcopalian. Buried near Louisville, Kentucky. 359–66, 370–72, 374, 378, 378, 379.

Holy Days and Feast Days

25 Feast Day of Saint Catherine of Alexandria, patroness of philosophers, jurists, maidens, and women students. 4.

Holidays and Civic Days

25 Surinam Independence Day, a public holiday in the Republic of Surinam located on the north-central coast of South America. Surinam gained full independence on November 25, 1975. 868, 875.

c25 Thanksgiving Day, a legal holiday in the United States, by presidential proclamation; a day of thanksgiving and praise observed by all states and territories on the fourth Thursday of November. 33, 269, 400–9, 567, 582, 607, 608, 624, 631.

Anniversaries and Special Events Days

25 Birthday of Andrew Carnegie (November 25, 1835–August 11, 1919). American iron and steel manufacturer; benefactor of libraries. 268, 858.

25 Birthday of Carrie Nation (November 25, 1846–June 9, 1911). American temperance leader who used a hatchet to implement her campaign against saloons. 738.

25 New York City Evacuation Day, the anniversary of the November 25, 1783, withdrawal of British troops from New York City and the official occupation of the city by General Washington and officials of the state. 268.

Holidays and Civic Days

c26 Thanksgiving Holiday, the day after Thanksgiving, a holiday, usually for state agencies in Florida, Illinois, Iowa, Kansas, Maine, Minnesota, Nebraska, North Carolina, Oklahoma, Texas, and Washington. 875.

Anniversaries and Special Events Days

26 Constitution Thanksgiving Day, November 26, 1787, proclaimed by George Washington as a day of Thanksgiving following the adoption of the constitution.

c26 John Harvard Day, commemorating the birth in 1607 of John Harvard, chief founder of Harvard, honoring his bequest of a library and funds for the new college. 268.

26 Sojourner Truth Day, the anniversary of the death on November 26, 1883, of a leading black abolitionist of the nineteenth century who adopted the name *Sojourner* as a symbol of her lecture tours, which espoused abolition and women's rights. 738.

Holy Days and Feast Days

27 Day of the Covenant, a Baha'i holy day commemorating the covenant in Baha'u'llah's last will and testament, which made clear that the establishment of the kingdom of God on earth depends upon the pure and selfless dedication and obedience of the believers. 1, 854.

Anniversaries and Special Events Days

27 Birthday of Robert R. Livingston (November 27, 1746–February 26, 1813). American statesman and jurist; member of the Continental Congress and chancellor of New York State, who administered Washington's first oath of office as president. Robert Livingston represents New York state in Statuary Hall in a sculpture by Erastus Dow Palmer. 870.

27 Birthday of José Asunción Silva (November 27, 1865–May 24, 1896). Colombian poet famous for *Nocturno III* and for his flexibility in verse forms, which had great influence on Spanish-American poetry.

27 Birthday of Chaim Weizmann (November 17, 1874–November 9, 1952). Israeli statesman and scientist who was instrumental in the British formulation of the Balfour Declaration that a national home for the Jews would be established in Palestine; Israel's first president. Weizmann Day is observed on his birthday at Tel Aviv. 767.

Holy Days and Feast Days

28 Ascension of 'Abdu'l-Baha, a Baha'i holy day commemorating the death on November 28, 1921, of the early twentieth-century guardian of the faith and the friend of all humanity. 1, 854.

28 Feast of the Miraculous Medal, a Roman Catholic observance that owes its origin to the apparitions made by Mary to Saint Catharine Laboure in 1830, during which the form and the elements of the miraculous medal were revealed. 5.

Holidays and Civic Days

28 Albanian Independence Day, a public holiday in Albania commemorating the proclamation of independence of November 28, 1912, issued at the end of the Balkan War that terminated Turkish rule. The observance is followed with Liberation Day activities on November 29. 868, 875.

28 Chad Republic Day, a holiday commemorating the proclamation of the republic of November 28, 1958, which gave Chad the status of a member state in the French community. 868, 875.

28 Independence Day in the Republic of Mauritania, a holiday honoring November 28, 1960, the day of achievement of sovereignty after more than a half century of being a French protectorate and colony. 868, 875.

28 Independence from Spain Observance Day, a holiday in Panama, commemorating the 1821 achievement of independence from Spain. 868, 875.

Anniversaries and Special Events Day

28 Birthday of Henry Bacon (November 28, 1866–February 16, 1924). American architect who specialized in the classic Greek style. One of his most important works is the Lincoln Memorial in Washington, D.C., completed in 1920. 347.

28 Teheran Conference Day, the anniversary of the beginning of the Teheran Conference, held from November 28 to December 1, 1943, attended by Roosevelt, Churchill, and Stalin, which resulted in the Allied decision to open a second front in Western Europe in World War II. 268.

Holidays and Civic Days

29 Albania Liberation Day, a public holiday celebrating the November 29, 1944, proclamation of liberation as invasions of German and Italian troops of World War II were terminated. 875.

29 President Tubman's Birthday, a public holiday in Liberia honoring the November 19, 1895, birth of William Tubman, who served as the nation's president for twenty-seven years. 853.

29 Yugoslavian Proclamation of the Republic Days are observed on November 29 and 30 as public holidays in commemoration of the proclamation of the Federal People's Republic of Yugoslavia in 1945. 868, 875.

Anniversaries and Special Events Days

29 Birthday of Louisa May Alcott (November 29, 1832–March 6, 1888). American novelist and author of *Little Women* and other books that appeal to many generations of readers. 864.

29 Eve of Saint Andrew's Day, a traditional festive time for girls playing *Andrzejki*, or Andrew's games, to discover who will find husbands during the year; observed in Poland.

29 Birthday of Andrés Bello (November 29, 1781–October 15, 1865). Chilean poet, journalist, and statesman. Author of some of the greatest poetry of South America, he also developed Bello's code, which put an end to juridical anarchy in Chile. 864.

Holy Days and Feast Days

30 Feast of Saint Andrew, apostle, celebrated by the Western Christian churches and by the Eastern churches using the Gregorian calendar. Saint Andrew is the patron saint of Scotland, Greece, and Russia and of fishermen and golfers. 4, 14.

Holidays and Civic Days

30 Barbados Independence Day, a holiday commemorating November 30, 1966, when the West Indian island became an independent member of the British Commonwealth of Nations. 868, 875.

30 Benin National Day, a public holiday. On November 30, 1975, this West African nation officially changed its name from Dahomey to the People's Republic of Benin. 868, 875.

30 Bonifacio Day, a National Heroes' Day, a public holiday in the Philippines, commemorating the November 30, 1863, birth of Andres Bonifacio, the Philippine patriot who led the 1896 revolt against the Spanish. 875.

30 Youth Day, a holiday in the Republic of Upper Volta, honoring youth with special events and festivities. 875.

30 Independence Day, a holiday in the People's Democratic Republic of Yemen honoring November 30, 1967, as the day of new sovereignty when independence was declared and South Arabia was renamed the People's Republic of Southern Yemen; a further name change occurred on December 1, 1970: the People's Democratic Republic of Yemen. 868.

Anniversaries and Special Events Days

c30 Saint Andrew Society of New York Day, an observance scheduled on or near Saint Andrew's Day; the society provides support for exchange of Scottish and American graduate students and for exhibits in the United States of books and manuscripts from Scotland.

30 Birthday of Sir Winston Churchill (November 30, 1874–January 24, 1965). British statesman; a prime minister; symbol of the British spirit during World War II; author of many books, including *The Second World War*; Churchill Day is observed on April 9 in the United States. 780.

30 Birthday of Samuel Langhorne Clemens, "Mark Twain" (November 30, 1835–April 21, 1910). American author, humorist, and lecturer whose most famous books are *The Adventures of Tom Sawyer* and *The Adventures of Huckleberry Finn*. He was elected to the Hall of Fame for Great Americans in 1920. An annual birthday party honoring Samuel Clemens is held on November 30 in the Mark Twain Memorial House in Hartford, Connecticut, sometimes called "the birthplace of Tom Sawyer." 268, 787, 858.

30 Anniversary of the death on November 30, 1952, of Sister Elizabeth Kenny, a nursing sister and developer of the Kenny Method of alleviating the suffering of polio victims. 864.

30 Birthday of Jonathan Swift (November 30, 1667–October 19, 1745). English clergyman, poet, political writer, and satirist remembered particularly for *Gulliver's Travels*. 864.

December

December is the twelfth and last month in the Gregorian calendar. It was the tenth month in the ancient Roman calendar, and its name comes from the Latin word *decem*, meaning "ten."

December is the most festive month of the year. It is the month when Christians all over the world celebrate the birth of Christ, and many activities are carried out in preparation for that great day. The season of preparation, which is called Advent in the Christian calendar, begins on the fourth Sunday before Christmas.

December is a month of happy traditions. Many people keep up customs that have been in their families for generations. They cook special dishes that originated with their forefathers, such as the English plum pudding or the Swedish lutefisk and other delicacies. December is the month for the singing of Christmas carols, the trimming of the tree, the writing of Christmas cards, and the selection of gifts for Christmas giving.

December is the month of Santa Claus in the United States and the month of Saint Nicholas in the countries of Europe. This saint has a feast day on December 6, and on that day he brings fruit and cakes to children if they have been good.

The last day of December closes the year. In Japan it is a time to take stock and pay debts. December 31 is called Hogmanay Day in Scotland, and it is a day when adults exchange presents and give cakes to children. It is also Saint Sylvester's Day, which is observed in Germany and Belgium with customs that anticipate the New Year. In Belgium, the last child out of bed on the morning of December 31 is a "Sylvester," a lazy one who has to pay a tribute to early risers. In the United States, the last hours of December constitute New Year's Eve, a time of merrymaking for adults and Watch Night parties for young people.

The poinsettia has come to be the flower that is symbolic of December. Holly and mistletoe are also special December floral decorations used at Christmas time.

December has two birthstones. They are the turquoise and the zircon.

Holy Days and Feast Days

1 Feast Day of Saint Edmund Campion in whose name the annual Campion Award is given by the Catholic Book Club to recognize eminence in the field of Catholic letters. 9.

1 Feast Day of Saint Eligius, patron saint of jewelers and metalworkers. 4.

Holidays and Civic Days

1 Central African Republic Independence Day, a national holiday with festivities celebrating the proclamation of the republic on December 1, 1958. 868.

1 Mocidade Day, a holiday in Portuguese Guinea, honoring the youth of the country.

Anniversaries and Special Events Days

1 Matilda Newport Day, a festival day in Liberia honoring a pioneer widow who ignited a cannon with her pipe during the 1822 siege by African tribesmen and thus saved her country. 853.

1 Rosa Parks Day, the anniversary of December 1, 1955, when Rosa Parks defied the rules of the Montgomery, Alabama, bus system and refused to relinquish her seat to a white man. Her courageous action led to a confirmation by the U.S. Supreme Court of the unconstitutionality of the bus-seating practice, and Rosa Parks came to be known among blacks as "the mother of the Civil Rights Movement." 857.

Holidays and Civic Days

2 Republic Day, a holiday in Laos honoring the establishment of the Lao People's Democratic Republic on December 2, 1975. During its long history Laos had been a kingdom, known as Lanxang, "the land of a million elephants." 868.

2 United Arab Emirates National Day, a public holiday celebrating the December 2, 1971, realization of independence and the union of seven of the former Trucial States located in an area once known as the Pirate Coast of the eastern Arabian peninsula. 868.

Anniversaries and Special Events Days

2 Atom Day, the anniversary of the successful conclusion on December 2, 1942, of scientific projects, carried on in the west stand of Stagg Field on the University of Chicago campus, that opened up the Atomic Age. 874.

2 Birthday of Henry Thacker Burleigh (December 2, 1866–September 12, 1949). Black American composer and choir director widely known for arrangements of Negro spirituals, notably "Deep River"; awarded the Spingarn Medal in 1916. 864.

2 Monroe Doctrine Day, the anniversary of the declaration by President James Monroe in his annual message to Congress on December 2, 1823, which established a policy of American opposition to European intervention in the Americas. 268.

2 Pan American Health Day, observed by presidential proclamation in the United States to focus on hemispheric cooperation in the field of public health. 857.

Holy Days and Feast Days

3 Feast Day of Saint Cassian, patron saint of stenographers. 4.

3 Feast Day of Saint Francis Xavier, patron saint of all Christian missions; patron saint of Borneo, Australia, and China; patron of the Propagation of the Faith. 4.

Holidays and Civic Days

3 Illinois Admission Day. Illinois entered the Union as the twenty-first state on December 3, 1818. 268, 856, 862.

Anniversaries and Special Events Days

3 Birthday of Cleveland Abbe (December 3, 1838–October 28, 1916). American meteorologist known as "the father of the weather bureau"; influential in establishing the use of standard time throughout the United States; initiated the publication of daily weather forecasts.

3 Heart Transplant Day, the anniversary of the first human heart transplant performed by Dr. Christian Barnard in Cape Town, South Africa, on December 3, 1967. 866.

3 Sir Rowland Hill Day, anniversary of the birth of Sir Rowland Hill, who introduced the first postage stamp in the world in England in 1840; observed by philatelic societies. 857.

3 Birthday of Ellen Henrietta Richards (December 3, 1842–March 30, 1911). American chemist; founder of the home-economics movement; first president of the American Home Economics Association. 864.

3 Birthday of Gilbert Charles Stuart (December 3, 1755–July 9, 1828). American portrait painter who painted Washington, Jefferson, Madison, and other great Americans of his day. Elected to the Hall of Fame for Great Americans in 1900. 268.

Holy Days and Feast Days

4 Feast Day of Saint Barbara, patron saint of firemen, artillery men, architects, stonemasons, and mathematicians; protectress against lightning, fire, sudden death, and impenitence; the day is considered the beginning of the Christmas season in parts of France, Germany, and Syria. 4, 74, 158.

4 Feast of Saint John Damascene, one of the last of the great Greek fathers; his poems are used in the Greek liturgy and his eloquent use of the Greek language caused him to be called Chrysorrhoas, or "gold-pouring"; proclaimed a doctor of the church in 1890. 4.

Anniversaries and Special Events Days

4 Day of the Artisans, observed in Mexico to honor the workers of the nation.

4 Birthday of Thomas Carlyle (December 4, 1795–February 5, 1881). Scottish essayist and historian called "the sage of Chelsea." His *French Revolution* established his reputation. 864.

4 Birthday of Edith Louisa Cavell (December 4, 1865–October 12, 1915). English nurse, heroine of World War I who was executed by the Germans. A monument to her memory stands in St. Martin's Place, Trafalgar Square, London. 738.

4 Birthday of John Cotton (December 4, 1584–December 23, 1652). American Puritan clergyman who had great influence in the Massachusetts Bay colony. 864.

Holidays and Civic Days

5 Discovery Day, a national holiday in Haiti, commemorating its discovery by Christopher Columbus in 1492. 875.

c5 Thailand National Day, a public holiday, honoring the reigning king, Bhumibol Adulyadej, who was born on December 5, 1927. 868, 875.

Anniversaries and Special Events Days

5 Birthday of Walt Disney (December 5, 1901–December 15, 1966). American motion-picture and television producer; pioneer in the creation of animated motion-picture cartoons; creator of such cartoon characters as Mickey Mouse and Donald Duck; organizer of the first Disneyland in 1955. 864.

5 Saint Nicholas Eve; a traditional night for the filling of stockings with candies and small gifts to delight children; observed in the Netherlands, Switzerland, Germany, and other sections of western Europe. 56, 85, 158.

5 Anniversary of the founding of Phi Beta Kappa on December 5, 1776, at the College of William and Mary.

5 Prohibition Repeal Day, the anniversary of the ratification on December 5, 1933, of the Twenty-first Amendment to the Constitution; a day when the sale of alcoholic beverages became legal after thirteen years of prohibition. 268.

5 Birthday of Martin Van Buren (December 5, 1782–July 24, 1862). Dutch ancestry; New York lawyer and eighth president of the United States, 1837–41. Reformed Dutch churchman. Buried at Kinderhook, New York. 359–66, 370–72, 374, 378–79.

Holy Days and Feast Days

6 Feast of Saint Nicholas, fourth-century bishop of Myra; celebrated on December 6 by the Western churches using the Gregorian calendar and on December 19 by Eastern Orthodox churches using the Julian calendar. Saint Nicholas is the patron saint of Russia and Greece. 20, 840.

Holiday and Civic Days

6 Bophuthatswana Independence Day granted on December 6, 1977, by South Africa, the second black homeland, consisting of a half-dozen unconnected areas, within the boundaries of South Africa. 868.

6 Finnish Independence Day, a holiday in Finland commemorating the December 6, 1917, declaration of freedom from Russia. 849, 868.

6 Irish Republic Constitution Day, the anniversary of the implementation, on December 6, 1922, of the first constitution of the Irish Republic with jurisdiction over 26 of the 32 counties of Ireland. 868.

Anniversaries and Special Events Days

6 Birthday of Joyce Kilmer (December 6, 1886–July 30, 1918). American poet and critic who is remembered especially for a single poem called "Trees." 5.

6 Birthday of John Singleton Mosby (December 6, 1833–May 30, 1916). American lawyer; Confederate soldier who organized Mosby's Partisan Rangers; credited with originating the phrase "the solid South." 864.

6 Sinterklaas, or Saint Nicholas Day, a festive occasion for celebrating Old World customs of gift-giving on Saint Nicholas Day and for retelling the legends of Saint Nicholas, the prototype of the American Santa Claus. Sinterklaas is observed by Dutch communities and by Saint Nicholas societies in the United States. 71, 85.

Holy Days and Feast Days

7 Feast of Saint Ambrose, fourth-century bishop, a major figure in the rise of Christianity in the West; the patron saint of beekeepers and domestic animals. 4.

Holidays and Civic Days

7 Delaware Day, a commemorative day, celebrates the anniversary of the adoption of the federal Constitution by Delaware on December 7, 1787, making Delaware the first state in rank in the thirteen original states of the United States. 268, 866.

7 Ivory Coast Independence Observance Day, a holiday commemorating the establishment on December 7, 1960, of the Ivory Coast Republic as an independent nation on the west coast of Africa. 868, 875.

Anniversaries and Special Events Days

7 Birthday of Giovanni Lorenzo Bernini (December 7, 1598–November 28, 1680). Italian architect, sculptor, and painter; one of the architects of Saint Peter's Church in Rome. 864.

7 Birthday of Matthew Heywood Campbell Broun (December 7, 1888–December 18, 1939). American journalist and first president of the American Newspaper Guild. 864.

7 Birthday of Willa Sibert Cather (December 7, 1873–April 24, 1947). American author considered to be one of the country's outstanding twentieth-century writers. She is particularly remembered for *A Lost Lady*, *O Pioneers*, and *Death Comes for the Archbishop*. *One of Ours* was awarded a Pulitzer Prize. 738.

7 Anniversary of the founding on December 7, 1875, of the Native Sons of the West, an organization of native-born Californians.

7 Pearl Harbor Day, anniversary of the Japanese attack on Pearl Harbor, the Philippines, and Guam on December 7, 1941. Civil Defense Day is observed on the anniversary of Pearl Harbor to emphasize the role of civil defense in the security of the United States. 461, 544–49.

Holy Days and Feast Days

8 Solemnity of the Immaculate Conception, a holy day of obligation in the Roman Catholic church, commemorating the preservation of the Virgin Mary from original sin from the moment of her conception. 1, 5.

Holidays and Civic Days

8 Mothers' Day, a holiday in Panama honoring all mothers on the day of the Immaculate Conception. 875.

Anniversaries and Special Events Days

8 Birthday of Björnstjerne Björnson (December 8, 1832–April 26, 1910). Norwegian novelist and dramatist and one of his nation's most ardent patriots. He received the 1903 Nobel prize in literature.

8 Birthday of Padraic Colum (December 8, 1881–January 11, 1972). Irish poet, folklorist, dramatist, and essayist. His *Collected Poems* reveal his deep involvement with the lore and the legends of Ireland. 864.

8 John Lennon Day, the anniversary of Lennon's death by assassination, December 8, 1980; commemorated by Beattle fans in New York City, Liverpool, and other parts of the world with quiet gatherings, listening or singing his songs, or vigils of prayers and meditations. 762.

8 Anniversary of the death on December 8, 1978, of Golda Meir, a dominant figure in the history of Israel, one of the original signers of Israel's Proclamation of Independence, the first woman member of the Israeli legislature, and Israel's fourth prime minister. 738, 767, 803.

8 Birthday of Jean Sibelius (December 8, 1865–September 20, 1957). Finnish composer, famous for *Valse Triste, Finlandia*, and his symphonic music. 849.

8 Mother's Day in Spain; has long been associated with the Feast of the Immaculate Conception; a day of joyful family celebrations throughout the country. 875.

8 School Reunion Day, the traditional day of school celebrations and alumni reunions in Spain.

8 Beach Day, or Blessing of the Waters Day, a festive day in Uruguay, marking the beginning of the beach season on the "Uruguayan Riviera"; sometimes called Family Day.

8 Birthday of Eli Whitney (December 8, 1765–January 8, 1825). American inventor and manufacturer who invented the cotton gin. He was elected to the Hall of Fame for Great Americans in 1900. 268.

Holidays and Civic Days

9 Tanzania Independence and Republic Day, a holiday in Tanzania to honor the achievement of independence on December 9, 1961; celebrated with parades of army units, schoolchildren, Boy Scouts and Girl Guides and with exhibitions by tribal dancers. 868, 875.

Anniversaries and Special Events Days

9 Birthday of John Milton (December 9, 1608–November 8, 1674). English poet best known for *Paradise Lost* and *Paradise Regained*. 1.

Holidays and Civic Days

10 MPLA Foundation Day, a holiday in Angola commemorating the December 10, 1977, transformation of the Popular Movement for the Liberation of Angola into the MPLA-Labor party which controls the government of Angola. 868, 875.

10 Burma National Day, a holiday in the Socialist Republic of the Union of Burma, commemorating the ratification of the treaty providing for Burmese autonomy outside the British dominions. 868.

10 Human Rights Day, a holiday in Equatorial Guinea honoring the adoption of the Universal Declaration of Human Rights by the United Nations on December 10, 1948. 875.

10 Mississippi entered the Union on December 10, 1817, as the twentieth state. 268, 856, 862.

10 Thailand Constitution Day, a public holiday commemorating the December 10, 1932, constitution, the first for the Thai people. 868, 875.

10 Wyoming Day, a historic day in the state of Wyoming commemorating the adoption of woman's suffrage in Wyoming Territory on December 10, 1869. 268.

Anniversaries and Special Events Days

10 Birthday of Zachariah Chandler (December 10, 1813–November 1, 1879). American merchant and politician who was among those who signed the call for the Jackson, Michigan, meeting that is said to have founded the Republican party. He represents the state of Michigan in Statuary Hall in a sculpture done by Charles Henry Niehaus. 870.

10 Gallaudet Day, the anniversary of the December 10, 1787, birth of Thomas H. Gallaudet, founder of the first free school for the deaf in the United States; observed by organizations and institutions working with the deaf. 286.

10 Human Rights Day, the anniversary of the adoption of the Universal Declaration of Human Rights on December 10, 1948; an official United Nations holiday. 268, 722, 866.

10 Nobel Prize Presentation Day, the anniversary of the 1896 death of Alfred Bernhard Nobel, founder of the annual Nobel Prizes. Awards are presented in Stockholm with the reigning monarch officiating. The Peace Prize is presented in Oslo, Norway. 679.

Holidays and Civic Days

11 Indiana Day, observed throughout the state with patriotic programs commemorating the admission of the state to the Union on December 11, 1816, as the nineteenth state. 268, 856, 862.

11 Upper Volta Republic Day, commemorates December 11, 1958, when Upper Volta's territorial assembly voted to become an autonomous state within the French community. 868, 875.

Anniversaries and Special Events Day

11 Abdication Day, the anniversary of the abdication of England's King Edward VIII on December 11, 1936, a situation necessitated by his intent to marry a divorced commoner, the American Wallis Warfield Simpson. 857.

11 Birthday of Hector Berlioz (December 11, 1803–March 8, 1869). French composer noted for his contributions to dramatic instrumental music. 864.

11 Birthday of Fiorello Henry La Guardia (December 11, 1882–September 20, 1947). American lawyer, mayor of the city of New York, congressman, first director of the Federal Office of Civilian Defense; called "the little flower." 770.

11 Scaling Day, or the Escalade, celebrated in Geneva, Switzerland; honors the night of December 11, 1602, when the citizens routed the Savoyards, who were scaling the walls of their city. Shops sell chocolate bonbons representing the soup pots the women used on that night to throw hot water on the invaders.

Holy Days and Feast Days

12 Fiesta of Our Lady of Guadalupe, Mexico's greatest religious festival, commemorates with religious ceremonies and pilgrimages the appearance of the Blessed Virgin to an Indian boy in 1531. Conchero dancers, processions, and fireworks honor Mexico's patroness, Our Lady of Guadalupe, who in 1945 was crowned "the queen of wisdom and of the Americas." This feast is also celebrated in the Southwest of the United States, where Spanish influence prevails, and on Olvera Street in Los Angeles. 5, 258.

Holidays and Civic Days

c12 Jamhuri Day, or Kenya Independence Day, a holiday in Kenya commemorating the proclamation of sovereignty for Kenya as declared on December 12, 1963. 868, 875.

12 Pennsylvania Admission Day. Pennsylvania entered the Union on December 12, 1787, as the second of the thirteen original states. 268, 856, 862.

12 Washington D.C., Birthday, anniversary of the decision on December 12, 1800, to establish Washington as the permanent capital of the United States government.

Anniversaries and Special Events Days

12 Crossword Puzzle Day, the anniversary of the publication of Arthur Wynne's first crossword puzzle in the *New York World* on December 12, 1913; the intent of Editor Wynne was "to brighten the paper's Fun Section."

12 Birthday of John Jay (December 12, 1745–May 17, 1829). American lawyer, jurist, statesman, and diplomat; first chief justice of the United States Supreme Court. 268, 791.

12 Birthday of Gustave Flaubert (December 12, 1821–May 8, 1880). French writer and novelist of the school of naturalism, famous for *Madame Bovary*.

Holy Days and Feast Days

13 Feast of Saint Andrew the First-Called, or Saint Andrew the Apostle, celebrated on December 13 by Eastern Orthodox churches governed by the Julian calendar. 4.

13 Feast Day of Saint Lucy, patroness of writers, of people with eye trouble, and of lights. 4.

Holidays and Civic Days

13 Saint Lucia Day, a holiday on the island of St. Lucia, honoring Saint Lucy; a popular but unproved belief among St. Lucians is that their island was discovered by Columbus on Saint Lucy's Day. 875.

13 Malta Republic Day, a national holiday, commemorating the attainment of the position of a republic within the British Commonwealth on December 13, 1974. 868, 875.

Anniversaries and Special Events Days

13 Birthday of Phillips Brooks (December 13, 1835–January 23, 1893). American Episcopal bishop, remembered in the twentieth century as the author of the Christmas hymn "O Little Town of Bethlehem." He was elected to the Hall of Fame for Great Americans in 1910. 813.

13 Birthday of Clark Mills (December 13, 1810–January 12, 1883). American sculptor and bronze founder who made equestrian statues of Andrew Jackson and George Washington, did the bronze casting of Thomas Crawford's *Freedom*, or *Armed Liberty*, for the dome of the Capitol, and took a life mask of Abraham Lincoln. 339.

13 Lucia Day, an important festival in Sweden, honoring Saint Lucia, "the queen of light," with the candlelight parade through Stockholm; the reigning queen wears a crown of lighted candles, receives the Lucia jewel, and is awarded a trip to the United States to visit Swedish-American communities that also celebrate the festival of lights. 268.

13 Operation Three Circles, the anniversary of the December 13, 1981, imposition of martial law in Poland, a measure designed to crush the Solidarity union movement through restrictions on union activity, the banning of assemblies, and the enforcement of curfews and identity checks on Polish citizens.

Holy Days and Feast Days

14 Feast of Saint John of the Cross, the sixteenth-century founder of the Discalced Carmelites; one of the greatest mysticists of all times whose writings are among the world's spiritual classics; called the "doctor of mystical theology"; proclaimed a doctor of the church in 1926. 4.

14 Feast Day of Saint Spyridon, honored by the people of Greece with a celebration at Corfu, including a procession in which the relic of the saint dressed in costly vestments is carried. 4.

Holidays and Civic Days

14 Alabama Admission Day. Alabama entered the Union as the twenty-second state on December 14, 1819. 268, 856, 862.

Anniversaries and Special Events Days

14 Birthday of John Mercer Langston (December 14, 1829–November 15, 1897). American lawyer and public official, probably the first black to be elected to public office in the United States; served as minister to Haiti and as a college president.

Holidays and Civic Days

15 Kingdom Day, or Statute Day, celebrated in the Netherlands Antilles to honor the autonomy granted on December 15, 1954, which provided for equal status with the Netherlands and Surinam. 868, 875.

Anniversaries and Special Events Days

15 Birthday of Marxwell Anderson (December 15, 1888–February 28, 1959). American playwright, famous for verse plays and such successful productions as *What Price Glory?* 864.

15 Bill of Rights Day, honoring the ratification of the first ten amendments to the United States Constitution; observed in the United States by presidential proclamation. 268, 269, 866.

15 Birthday of George Romney (December 15, 1734–November 15, 1802). English portrait painter whose celebrated model was Lady Hamilton. 864.

15 Zamenhof Day, sponsored by the Esperanto League for North America, commemorates the December 15, 1859, birthday of Dr. Ludwik Zamenhof, the founder of Esperanto, the international language. 857.

Holidays and Civic Days

16 Victory Day, a holiday in Bangladesh commemorating independence from Pakistan reached on December 16, 1971; the ceremonies include a citizen pilgrimage to the Mausoleum of the Martyrs to honor those who perished in the fight for liberation. 868, 875.

16 Nepal Constitution Day, a holiday in Nepal commemorating the inauguration of a constitution for the constitutional monarchial Hindu state on December 16, 1962. The constitution recognized towns and villages as basic units of democracy. 868, 875.

16 Day of the Covenant, a holiday in South Africa. The holiday was established on December 16, 1838, in commemoration of the victory of the Voortrekkers over Dingaan and his Zulus at the Battle of Blood River. The holiday was once called Dingaan's Day. 875.

Anniversaries and Special Events Days

16 Birthday of Jane Austen (December 16, 1775–July 18, 1817). English novelist, remembered for *Persuasion* and *Pride and Prejudice*. 783.

16 Birthday of Ludwig van Beethoven (December 16, 1770–March 26, 1827). German composer considered to be one of the foremost musicians of all time. 855.

16 Boston Tea Party Day, anniversary of the Boston Tea Party of December 16, 1773, when the colonists boarded a British vessel and dumped a shipload of tea into the Boston Harbor; a prelude to the American Revolution. 268, 295, 866.

16 Birthday of Noel Peirce Coward (December 16, 1899–March 26, 1973). British playwright, director, songwriter, and actor. His plays include *Blithe Spirit, Private Lives*, and *This Happy Breed*. His songs include "Mad Dogs and Englishmen" and "Someday I'll Find You." 864

16 Birthday of Ralph Adams Cram (December 16, 1863–September 22, 1942). American architect and authority on Gothic architecture whose firm designed the Cathedral of Saint John the Divine in New York City.

16 Misa de Gallo, the beginning of the Christmas season in the Philippines; each day begins with church bells breaking the night silence to call people to dawn masses; Misa de Gallow concludes with the midnight mass on Christmas eve.

16 Nine Days before Christmas, a religious custom observed by individuals and families in many Roman Catholic countries; each day represents one of the months Mary carried the Holy Infant. 74.

16 Posadas Days, or the "Lodgings," begins on December 16 in the cities and villages of Mexico with a procession that recalls the journey of Mary and Joseph to Bethlehem. Posadas lasts nine days and includes religious ceremonies, festivities, and the popular ceremony of the breaking of the piñata. Posadas is also celebrated on Olvera Street in Los Angeles. 85, 258, 261.

16 Birthday of George Santayana (December 16, 1863–September 26, 1952). Spanish poet and philosopher, author of the *Idea of Christ in the Gospels, Egotism in German Philosophy, The Last Puritan*, and an autobiography, *Persons and Places*. 864.

Holidays and Civic Days

17 Bhutan National Day, a public holiday, in the Kingdom of Bhutan where violent storms originating in the Himalayas give Bhutan the name "land of the thunder dragon." 868, 875.

Anniversaries and Special Events Days

17 Gdansk Food Riot Day, the anniversary of Polish riots of December 17, 1970, observed as a day of protest with remembrances of the Poles killed during the 1970 riots. 667.

17 Birthday of Joseph Henry (December 17, 1797–May 13, 1878). American physicist noted for research in electromagnetism. He was elected to the Hall of Fame for Great Americans in 1915. 864.

17 Birthday of Thomas Starr King .(December 17, 1824–March 4, 1864). American Unitarian clergyman and author. He represents the state of California in Statuary Hall in a sculpture done by Haig Patigian. 870.

17 Birthday of John Greenleaf Whittier (December 17, 1807–September 7, 1892). American poet, abolitionist, and journalist, known as "the Quaker poet." Elected to the Hall of Fame for Great Americans in 1905. 268.

17 Wright Brothers Day, observed in the United States by presidential proclamation to honor the Wrights' first flight on December 17, 1903; special observances near Kill Devil Hills and Kitty Hawk in North Carolina. December 17 is also Pan American Aviation Day. 268, 866.

Holy Days and Feast Days

18 The Fiesta of the Virgin of the Lonely, celebrated by thousands of pilgrims at Oaxaca, Mexico, to honor the patroness of muleteers and sailors.

Holiday and Civic Days

18 New Jersey Admission Day. New Jersey entered the Union on December 18, 1787, the third of the thirteen original United States to do so. 268, 856, 862.

18 Niger Republic Day, a civic holiday in the African nation named for the world's twelfth-largest river; commemorates the establishment of the constitutional government. 868, 875.

Anniversaries and Special Events Days

18 Birthday of William Allen (December 18, 1803–July 11, 1879). American politician, congressman, and governor of Ohio. Represents Ohio in Statuary Hall in a sculpture done by Charles Henry Niehaus. 870.

18 Anniversary of the orbiting of the United States *Atlas* satellite on December 18, 1958, which broadcast a message from the president of the United States, expressing "America's wish for peace on earth and good will . . . everywhere." 866.

18 Birthday of Edward Alexander MacDowell (December 18, 1861–January 24, 1908). American pianist and composer. He was elected to the Hall of Fame for Great Americans in 1960. An Edward MacDowell Medal is awarded annually by the Edward MacDowell Association to recognize individuals whose work has enriched the arts. 864.

18 Birthday of Charles Wesley (December 18, 1707–March 29, 1788). English Methodist preacher and famous hymn-writer of such hymns as "Jesus, Lover of My Soul" and "Love Divine, All Love Excelling." 864.

Anniversaries and Special Events Days

19 Birthday of Henry Clay Frick (December 19, 1849–December 2, 1919). American industrialist who left his priceless art collection and his mansion to the public as a museum, now known as the Frick Collection. 864.

19 Birthday of Albert Abraham Michelson (December 19, 1852–May 9, 1931). American physicist, the first American scientist to receive the Nobel prize; awarded the Nobel Prize in physics in 1907. Elected to the Hall of Fame for Great Americans in 1970. 864.

19 Princess Bernice Pauahi Bishop's birthday anniversary, observed in Hawaii on December 19, with ceremonies at the Kamehameha schools and at the Royal Mausoleum.

Anniversaries and Special Events Days

20 Birthday of Samuel Jordan Kirkwood (December 20, 1813–September 1, 1894). American politician; secretary of the interior under President Garfield; governor of Iowa. He represents Iowa in Statuary Hall in a sculpture by Vinnie Ream Hoxie. 870.

20 Anniversary of the transfer on December 20, 1803, of the Louisiana Territory from France to the United States. 268.

Holy Days and Feast Days

21 Feast of Peter Canisius, sixteenth-century Jesuit, leader in the Counter-Reformation; called the Second Apostle of Germany; a doctor of the church and one of the patron saints of Germany. 4.

21 Feast of Saint Thomas, the Doubting Thomas, one of the twelves apostles; celebrated by the Episcopal and Lutheran churches on December 21; by the Roman Catholics on July 3, and by the Eastern Orthodox Christians on October 6. 4.

Holidays and Civic Days

21 Independence Day, a holiday in Nepal honoring the change in status from British protectorate to independence on December 21, 1923. 868.

21 Transitional Government Day, a holiday in the Democratic Republic of São Tomé and Principe honoring December 21, 1974, when the transitional government took office. 868, 875.

21 Birthday of Jean Henri Fabre (December 21, 1823–October 11, 1915). French entomologist who devoted his life to studying and writing about the habits of insects. 864.

21 Forefather's Day, observed in Plymouth, Massachusetts, and by various New England societies to commemorate the landing of the Pilgrims on December 21, 1620. 268, 269, 866.

21 Birthday of Kemal Bey (December 21, 1840–December 2, 1888). Turkish poet and author whose writing influenced the Young Turk movement.

21 Birthday of Joseph Stalin (December 21, 1879–March 5, 1953). Russian dictator in power from 1929 until his death in 1953; credited with ruthless development of the USSR as a major world power. 864.

21 Birthday of Henrietta Szold (December 21, 1860–February 13, 1945). American teacher, Zionist leader, and founder of Hadassah; a founder of schools and hospitals in Palestine. 31.

Anniversaries and Special Events Days

22 International Arbor Day, established to encourage winter tree planting and the celebration of Arbor Day activities throughout the world. 857.

22 Anniversary of the death of Stephen Day on December 22, 1668. First printer in the British colonies in America; printed the *Bay Psalm Book* in 1640.

22 Anniversary of the death of John Newbery on December 22, 1767. English publisher and bookseller who made a specialty of children's books and in whose honor the annual Newbery Medal has been given since 1922 for the most distinguished contribution to children's literature published in the preceding year. 858, 863.

22 Birthday of Luca della Robbia (December 22, 1400–September 22, 1482). Italian sculptor who created the famous della Robbia reliefs in terra cotta. 864.

22 Birthday of James Edward Oglethorpe (December 22, 1696–July 1, 1785). English soldier and founder of the Georgia colony in the New World. 268.

22 Birthday of Giacomo Puccini (December 22, 1858–November 29, 1924). Italian operatic composer perhaps best known for *Madame Butterfly*. 864.

Anniversaries and Special Events Days

23 Birthday of Martin Opitz (December 23, 1597–August 20, 1639). German poet and critic known as "the father of modern German poetry."

23 Birthday of Joseph Smith (December 23, 1805–June 27, 1844). American Mormon leader, founder of the Church of Jesus Christ of Latter-Day Saints. 268.

Holidays and Civic Days

24 Christmas Eve Day, a full or partial holiday in twenty-nine countries and in thirty of the fifty states of the United States. 85, 875.

Anniversaries and Special Events Days

24 Birthday of Juan Ramón Jiménez (December 24, 1881–May 29, 1958). Spanish lyric poet who received the Nobel Prize in literature in 1956. 864.

24 Birthday of Benjamin Rush (December 24, 1745–April 19, 1813). American physician, signer of the Declaration of Independence, and medical pioneer for whom Rush University in Chicago was named.

Holy Days and Feast Days

25 Feast of the Nativity of Our Lord, or the Mass of Christ, commemorating the birth of Christ in a manger in Bethlehem; a day of rejoicing, prayer, and praise; a Solemnity in the Roman Catholic church. 5, 7, 35, 129, 138.

Holidays and Civic Days

25 Christmas Day, a holiday in 140 nations of the world, and in all of the fifty states of the United States. 33, 48–173, 269, 567, 572, 577, 582, 585, 588, 607, 624, 628, 631, 634, 641.

25 Family Day, a holiday in Angola and in the Democratic Republic of São Tomé and Principe. 875.

25 Congolese Children's Day, a holiday in the People's Republic of the Congo. 875.

25 Taiwan Constitution Day, a public holiday in Taiwan (Republic of China) honoring the adoption of the constitution on December 25, 1946. 868, 875.

Anniversaries and Special Events Days

25 Birthday of Clara Barton (December 25, 1821–April 12, 1912). American philanthropist, an organizer of the Red Cross. 268, 738, 799.

25 Birthday of Evangeline Cory Booth (December 25, 1865–July 17, 1950). International Salvation Army general serving in London, Canada, and the United States; author and composer of Salvation Army songs. 867.

25 PUSH Day, the anniversary of the founding of People United to Save Humanity (PUSH) on December 25, 1971; founded by the Reverend Jesse Jackson to fight for a better way of life for minority peoples and to encourage black children to excel.

Holy Days and Feast Days

26 Synaxis of the Most Holy Mother of God and Saint Joseph, her spouse; a holy day in the Byzantine calendar and celebrated in the Greek Orthodox church as the Day of Our Theotokos.

26 Feast of Saint Stephen, chosen by the apostles as the first of the seven deacons; stoned to death; the first Christian martyr; the patron saint of stonecutters and of Hungary. 4.

Holidays and Civic Days

26 Boxing Day, a holiday in forty-seven nations; the term is used for the second day of Christmas, which may have started with the opening of the church alms box for the poor or with the custom of distributing gratuities to trades people, mail carriers, and employees. 256.

26 Saint Stephen's Day, a religious and national holiday in Andorra, Austria, Italy, Liechtenstein, and Switzerland and in Barcelona, Spain. 74, 85, 875.

26 Sydney to Hobart Yacht race, begins on Boxing Day, a holiday in Australia; a spectacular race over 621 miles of water, lasting several days. 875.

26 Wren Day, a post-Christmas holiday event observed in the Dingle Peninsula of Ireland and on the Isle of Man on Saint Stephen's Day; a day for carrying out a modern version of hunting the wren without practicing the one-time custom of stoning the wrens in honor of Saint Stephen, the stoned martyr. 158, 256.

26 Family Day, a post-Christmas day holiday in Namibia located in southwest Africa. 875.

26 Day of Good Will, a holiday in the Republic of South Africa. 875.

Anniversaries and Special Events Days

26 Kwanza, a black-American seven-day spiritual festival, beginning on December 26, dedicated to the seven principles of blackness: unity, self-determination, collective work and responsibility, cooperative economics, purpose, creativity, and faith. *Kwanza* means "the first fruit," and the American celebration is related to the spirit and rituals of the harvest festivals of Africa. 610.

Holy Days and Feast Days

27 Feast of Saint John, the Beloved Disciple, an apostle and evangelist to whom Christ on the cross entrusted Mary; his feast is celebrated on May 8 by the Eastern Orthodox churches; patron saint of Asia Minor. 4.

Anniversaries and Special Events Days

27 Birthday of Louis Pasteur (December 27, 1822–September 28, 1895). French chemist and founder of microbiological sciences and of preventive medicine. 775.

Holy Days and Feast Days

28 Holy Innocents' Day, Feast of the Holy Innocents, or Childermas, commemorates the massacre of young children by Herod, who wished to be sure of killing the infant Jesus; celebrated by the Western churches on December 28 and by the Eastern churches on December 29. 5.

Holidays and Civic Days

28 Iowa Admission Day. Iowa entered the Union on December 28, 1846, as the twenty-ninth state. 268, 856, 862.

28 Proclamation Day, a holiday in South Australia, one of the federated states of the Commonwealth of Australia; commemorating the day in 1836 when the state was first proclaimed a colony. 875.

Anniversaries and Special Events Days

28 Cross Day, a folk-belief day in Ireland based on the old idea that anything begun on Holy Innocents' Day will come to a bad end.

28 Day of the Innocent Martyr Saints, Holy Innocents' Day, is observed in Belgium, Mexico, and Colombia with customs among children which are comparable to the tricks and hoaxes of April Fool's Day. 74, 85.

28 Birthday of Woodrow Wilson (December 28, 1856–February 3, 1924). Scotch-Irish ancestry; president of Princeton University; statesman; man of letters; advocate of the League of Nations; twenty-eighth president of the United States, 1913–21. Presbyterian. Awarded the Nobel Peace Prize in 1919. Buried in Washington Cathedral. Elected to the Hall of Fame for Great Americans in 1950. 359–66, 370–72, 374, 378, 379.

Holy Days and Feast Days

29 Feast of Saint Thomas of Canterbury, the anniversary of the day Thomas à Becket was murdered on the altar, December 29, 1170. His cathedral, Canterbury, became the mecca for pilgrims from all England and Europe. 4, 14.

Holidays and Civic Days

29 The King's Day, a holiday in the Kingdom of Nepal honoring the birth of His Majesty Birendra Bir Bikram Sha Dev, the supreme ruler of the nation. 875.

29 Texas Admission Day. Texas entered the Union as the twenty-eighth state on December 29, 1845. 268, 856, 862.

Anniversaries and Special Events Days

29 Battle of Wounded Knee, the anniversary of the last conflict between the American Indians and the United States army; fought in South Dakota on December 29, 1890.

29 Birthday of Pablo Casals (December 29, 1876–October 22, 1973). The greatest cellist of the twentieth century. Received the United Nations Peace Prize for his "Hymn to the United Nations." 864.

29 Birthday of John James Ingalls (December 29, 1833–August 16, 1900). American congressman from Kansas. He represents the state of Kansas in Statuary Hall in a sculpture by Charles Henry Niehaus. 870.

29 Birthday of Andrew Johnson (December 29, 1808–July 31, 1875). English ancestry; Tennessee politician; seventh president of the United States, 1865–69. No formal religious affiliation. Buried at Greenville, Tennessee. Elected to the Hall of Fame for Great Americans in 1910. 359–66, 370–72, 378, 379.

29 Paternoster Row Day, the anniversary of the Nazi bombing on December 29, 1940, of Paternoster Row, the historic center of British publishing. 691.

Holidays and Civic Days

30 Anniversary of the Democratic Republic of Madagascar, a holiday celebrating the establishment of the republic. The constitution went into effect on December 30, 1975. 868, 875.

30 Rizal Day, a holiday in the Philippines commemorating the death of José Mercado Rizal on December 30, 1896. Philippine doctor and author whose books denouncing the Spanish administration were an inspiration to the Philippine nationalist movement. 268, 875.

Anniversaries and Special Events Days

30 Birthday of Simon Guggenheim (December 30, 1867–November 2, 1941). American capitalist and philanthropist; founder, with his wife, of the John Simon Guggenheim Memorial Foundation, established as a memorial to their son. The Guggenheim Fellowships offer opportunities to further research and artistic creation for artists and scholars regardless of sex, color, creed, or marital status.

30 Birthday of Joseph Rudyard Kipling (December 30, 1865–January 18, 1936). English novelist, poet, and short-story writer famous for *Captains Courageous*, the Jungle Books, "Recessional," and many other titles. He was awarded the 1907 Nobel Prize in literature. 780.

30 Birthday of Stephen Butler Leacock (December 30, 1869–March 28, 1944). Canadian humorist and man of letters, political scientist, university professor, and lecturer, who ranked with Mark Twain in popular esteem. 864.

30 Romania Republic Day, a commemorative day, honoring the proclamation of the republic on December 30, 1947, following the abdication of King Michael. 868.

Holy Days and Feast Days

31 Feast of Saint Sylvester, the fourth-century pope who officiated at the consecration of the Basilica of the Most Holy Savior in 324, the first public consecration of a church. The basilica is now known as Saint John Lateran. 4.

Holidays and Civic Days

31 Independence Day, a holiday in the Federal Islamic Republic of the Comoros, consisting of three islands in the Indian Ocean between the African mainland and Madagascar. Comoros achieved independence on December 31, 1975. 868.

31 Congo Republic Day, a holiday in the People's Republic of Congo honoring both the proclamation of the establishment of Africa's first People's Republic in 1969, and the foundation of the Congolese Labor Party, the nation's sole legal party. 868, 875.

31 Evacuation Day, a public holiday in Lebanon celebrating the withdrawal of French troops on December 31, 1946.

31 New Year's Eve Day, a full or partial holiday in twenty of the nations of the world and in twenty-five of the fifty states of the United States. 875.

31 Saint Sylvester's Day, a holiday in Switzerland observed with the lighting of bonfires on the mountains and the ringing of church bells to signal the passing of the old year. 875.

Anniversaries and Special Events Days

31 Omisoka Day, the last day of the year, a traditional time for taking stock and paying debts in Japan.

31 Birthday of George Catlett Marshall (December 31, 1880–October 16, 1959). American soldier and statesman who developed the principles of the European Recovery Program implemented in 1948 and known as the Marshall Plan. 792.

31 Noche de Pedimento, a "wishing night," during which the Indians at Mitla, Oaxaca, gather around a cross to pray for their wishes for the coming year and present small miniatures of their wishes at the cross.

31 Hogmanay Day, observed in Scotland and northern England as a part of the New Year's festivities. The name comes from the Old French meaning "new year." 85.

31 Watch Night, or New Year's Eve, a traditional time of merrymaking in which people gather to watch the old year out and the new year in. 256.

31 Anniversary of the death of John Wycliffe on December 31, 1384. English religious reformer called "the morning star of the Reformation"; first to translate the Bible into English. 864.

Calendars of Movable Days

The term *movable days* has been used for generations to indicate the holy days and religious festivals that are determined by lunar and solar calculations and consequently occur at different times from year to year. The term also applies to secular festivities which have varying time schedules. The movable days do not fit into the Gregorian calendar, although the approximate time equivalents may be estimated.

This section on movable days includes the major movable days of the Christian, Islamic, and Jewish years, followed by a sampling of religious and secular festivals that are celebrated around the world.

The Christian Church Calendar

The focal point of the Christian church calendar is Easter, the day of the Resurrection of Christ. The death of Christ took place during the major Jewish feast, the Pesach, or Passover, which is celebrated at the full moon following the spring equinox. The Christians fixed the anniversary of the Resurrection on the first day of the week in which it took place. Consequently, Easter falls on the first day of the week after the first full moon following the spring equinox. It can be as early as March 22 and as late as April 25.

The Christian church calendar is thus dominated by the central event in Christianity and is regulated in part by the movement of the sun and the moon. It includes both fixed and movable feasts.

The first Christian church calendar was derived from the Hebrew calendar. At the beginning of the Christian era, many congregations developed their own calendars. The result was universal confusion. Finally, at the Council of Nicaea in A.D. 325, the Church accepted the Julian calendar as the basis for reckoning ecclesiastical dates. The inaccuracies in the Julian calendar led to the promulgation of calendar reform by Pope Gregory by 1582.

The Gregorian calendar, however, was not acceptable to all branches of the Christian church. The Orthodox church in the East continued to use the Julian calendar under the impact of the decisions at the Council of Nicaea. The sixteen-century Protestant Reformation contributed to the reluctance to adopt the Gregorian calendar in the West. A number of factors, not exclusively religious, led to the adoption of the Gregorian calendar by England and her colonies in 1752 and by Germany in 1775. From the middle of the eighteenth century, the Gregorian calendar supplemented the calendar of movable dates for Roman Catholic, Anglican, and Protestant observances. The Orthodox churches of the twentieth century still utilize the Julian calendar. In the 1980s, the major calendar negotiations between the Eastern and Western churches are concerned with the proposal to set a date for Easter on a permanent specific Sunday, an action that would simplify the ecclesiastical calendar for the entire Christian world.

The following are the major movable Christian holy days and feasts matched with the Gregorian timetable.

Gregorian Calendar Months	*Movable Christian days*
November–December	Advent Sunday, marks the beginning of the Christian church year, on the Sunday of or nearest to Saint Andrew's Day, November 30. The Advent season is a period of preparation for Christmas and includes four Sundays; varies in length from twenty-two to twenty-eight days. 1, 7, 49, 115, 133, 269.
February–March	Ash Wednesday, the first day of Lent, the period of Christian penance in preparation for Easter; derives its name from the ashes used to mark the sign of the cross on the forehead of the worshipper; observed forty-six days before Easter; a religious holiday in Brazil, the Cayman Islands, the French West Indies, Jamaica, and Panama. 7, 254, 268.
March–April	Palm Sunday, the Sunday before Easter, the beginning of Holy Week; the memorial of Christ's entrance into Jerusalem; named for the palms that were placed in his path by the multitude and for the palms that are distributed at the Palm Sunday services of many denominations. 7, 254, 269.
March–April	Maundy Thursday, or Holy Thursday, observed during Holy Week in commemoration of the day of the Last Supper; a religious holiday in twenty-four nations of the world. 7, 254, 269.
March–April	Good Friday, the Friday before Easter; the commemoration of the Passion and death by crucifixion of Jesus Christ; a day of fasting, abstinence, and penitence; a religious holiday in 105 nations of the world, and a legal or optional holiday in California, Connecticut, Delaware, Florida, Hawaii, Illinois, Indiana, Kentucky, Louisiana, Maryland, New Jersey, North Dakota, Pennsylvania, Tennessee, and Wisconsin. Lebanon is the one nation of the world which celebrates as religious holidays both the Good Friday of the Western rite and the Good Friday of the Eastern rite. 7, 254, 269, 875.
March–April	Easter Saturday, or Holy Saturday, the day before Easter, a holiday in Brunei, Samoa, Seychelles, Solomon Islands, Uruguay, Zambia, and Zimbabwe. 7.
March–April	Easter, the greatest day in the Christian calendar, celebrates the Resurrection of Jesus Christ; held on the first Sunday after the full moon following the vernal equinox. The date of Easter determines the dates of movable feasts, such as Ascension and Pentecost, and the number of Sundays after Epiphany and after Pentecost. 1, 235–48, 254, 256, 574, 588, 607, 624, 631, 831.
May–June	Ascension Day; the commemoration of the ascension of the Lord into heaven; a holy day of obligation observed forty days after Easter; a religious holiday in thirty-five nations. 7, 269.
May–June	Pentecost, or Whitsunday, the birthday of the church commemorating the coming of the Holy Spirit and the gift of faith to the apostles and disciples; observed on Sunday fifty days after Easter. 7, 254, 259.
May–June	Trinity Sunday, the first Sunday after Pentecost; a special commemoration in the name of the Father, Son, and Holy Spirit. 1.
May–June	Corpus Christi, the popular name for the Feast of the Most Holy Body of Christ; a festival in honor of the Holy Eucharist celebrated the Thursday after Trinity Sunday; also called Day of Wreaths in central Europe and France, in recognition of the wreaths that are carried in procession; a religious holiday in twenty-three nations. 5, 20.
November	Feast of Christ the King, observed in the Roman Catholic church on the last Sunday in November and by Protestant churches on the last Sunday in August to honor Christ as the ruler of all nations. 1, 5.

The Islamic Calendar

The Islamic, or Mohammedan, calendar is based on the moon's course, without regard to seasons. There are twelve lunar months totaling 354 or 355 days. Time is figured on a basis of cycles thirty years long. During each cycle, nineteen years have 354 days, and an extra day is added to each of the other eleven years.

Since the months and the seasons do not correspond in the Islamic calendar, the Moslem New Year and its related religious festivals occur in all seasons in the course of the overall time cycle. An unusual characteristic of the Islamic calendar is that these festivals move backward. The United Nations calendars, for example, show that the first month in the Islam year, Muharram, began on January 25 in the Gregorian year 1974, and on January 14 in 1975. The backward movement of the festivals

will continue until the thirty-year cycle is complete.

The Islamic calendar dates from the emigration, or hijrah, of the Prophet Mohammed from Mecca to Medina in A.D. 622. The weekly day of rest is Friday, Yawm al-Jum'ah. It is observed by all of the faithful of Islam who believe that Adam was born on Friday, and taken into paradise on Friday.

Some Islamic nations have adopted fixed dates for the commemoration of contemporary civil or national events. It is reported, however, that the orthodox recognize only the following festivals. No attempt has been made to indicate the Gregorian time equivalent, because of the continuing movement of the five important religious periods in the lunar Islamic calendar.

Movable Islamic Festivals

Variable Seasons   Muharram, the first month of the Islamic calendar year. The first ten days celebrate the beginning of the Moslem New Year. The first of Muharram is a holiday in Algeria, Bahrain, Bangladesh, Brunei, Djibouti, Egypt, Indonesia, Iraq, Kuwait, Lebanon, Libya, Malaysia, Mauritania, Oman, Sudan, Tunisia, United Arab Emirates, Yemen Arab Republic, and the Peoples' Democratic Republic of Yemen. 1, 261.

Ashura, the Mohammedan commemoration of Noah's leaving the ark on Mount Ararat, celebrated about the tenth day of the first moon month, Muharram; a holiday in Afghanistan, Algeria, Bahrain, Iran, Iraq, Lebanon, Pakistan, and Syria. 1.

Mawlid al-Nabi, the celebration of the birth of Muhammad, traditionally on the twelfth of Rabi the third month of the Moslem calendar. The founder of Islam is proclaimed as the last and greatest of the prophets and the intercessor with God for Muslims on Judgment day; a holiday in Afghanistan, Algeria, Bahrain, Bangladesh, Brunei, Chad, Cyprus, Djibouti, Egypt, Ethiopia, Fiji, Guinea, Guyana, Indonesia, Iran, Iraq, Jordan, Kuwait, Lebanon, Libya, Malaysia, Maldives, Mali, Mauritania, Mauritius, Niger, Nigeria, Oman, Pakistan, Senegal, Sierra Leone, Somali, Sri Lanka, Sudan, Syria, Tanzania, Tunisia, United Arab Emirates, Upper Volta, Yemen Arab Republic, and the People's Democratic Republic of Yemen. 1.

Lailat al Miraj, the commemoration of the ascension or night journey of Muhammad to heaven where he received instructions from Allah on the required number of times for daily prayer; observed on the evening of the twenty-seventh of Rajab the seventh month of the Moslem calendar; a holiday in Brunei, Djibouti, Jordan, Oman, United Arab Emirates, and the People's Democratic Republic of Yemen. 1, 18.

Ramadan, the ninth month of the Mohammedan calendar, commemorates the period during which Mohammed received divine revelations. Special observance of this month is one of the five great tenets of Islam and is marked by a strict fast from sunrise to sundown; the first day of Ramadan is a holiday in Afghanistan, Brunei, Malaysia, Maldives, Pakistan and Togo. 1.

Day of the Revelation of the Koran, or Qur'an, the sacred book of Islam, celebrated on the twenty-seventh of Ramadan, a holiday in Brunei and in Malaysia. 1.

'Id al-Fitr, a three-day celebration marking the end of the observance of the fast of Ramadan; begins on the first day of Shawwai, the tenth lunar month of the Moslem calendar; known as "the breaking of the fast"; a holiday in Afghanistan, Algeria, Bahrain, Bangladesh, Brunei, Chad, Cyprus, Djibouti, Egypt, Ethiopia, Gabon, Guinea, Indonesia, Iran, Iraq, Jordan, Kenya, Kuwait, Lebanon, Libya, Malaysia, Maldives, Mali, Mauritania, Mauritius, Niger, Nigeria, Oman, Pakistan, Qatar, Saudi Arabia, Senegal, Sierra Leone, Singapore, Somali, Sri Lanka, Sudan, Tanzania, Thailand, Togo, Tunisia, Turkey, Uganda, United Arab Emirates, Upper Volta, Yemen Arab Republic, and the People's Democratic Republic of Yemen. 1, 261.

Hajj, or Pilgrimage to Mecca; required once in each Muslim's lifetime, performed during the special pilgrimage season in the tenth, eleventh, and first ten days of the twelfth, month of the Islamic calendar. 1, 24.

Al-'id al-Kabir, the Great Festival, which concludes the Hajj is a period of feasting and celebrating in which Muslims throughout the world may join.

Tabaski, or 'Id al-Adha, a three-day festival of sacrifice celebrated on the twelfth day of Zu'lhijjah, the twelfth Moslem month, in tribute to Abraham's obedience to God in sending his son Ishmael into the desert. Ishmael is considered to be the forefather of the Arabs; a holiday in Afghanistan, Algeria, Bahrain, Bangladesh, Brunei, Chad, Cyprus, Djibouti, Egypt, Gabon, Guinea, Guyana, Indonesia, Iran, Iraq, Jordan, Kuwait, Lebanon, Libya, Malaysia, Maldives, Mali, Mauritania, Mauritius, Niger, Nigeria, Oman, Pakistan, Qatar, Saudi Arabia, Senegal, Sierra Leone, Singapore, Somali, Sri Lanka, Sudan, Syria, Tanzania, Togo, Tunisia, Turkey, United Arab Emirates, Upper Volta, Yemen Arab Republic and the People's Democratic Republic of Yemen.

The Jewish Calendar

The Jewish calendar is lunisolar. It is regulated by the positions of both the moon and the sun. Thus the day upon which an annual festival falls varies from year to year, even though that day may be fixed in the history of the Jews.

The Jewish calendar consists of twelve alternating months of twenty-nine and thirty days each. Adjustments are made in the calendar when necessary to reconcile the average lunar year of 355 days to the solar year of 365¼ days in order to assure that the major festivals fall into their proper season.

The great Jewish holy days are the heritage of all Jewish people. Reform, Orthodox, and Conservative congregations, however, may vary in the length of the observances and in the prescribed form of observance.

Gregorian Caldendar Months	*The Jewish Holy Days and Holidays*
September–October	Rosh Hashanah, the New Year of the Jewish people, which "ushers in the Days of Judgment for all mankind"; observed as the first day of the interlunar month of Tishri. 184, 193, 204, 208, 269, 628.

September–October	Yom Kippur, or Day of Atonement, the holiest day of the Jewish year, and the most solemn of the Jewish holy days; a day of fasting, penitence, and prayer observed on the tenth day of the month of Tishri. 184, 205, 208, 269, 628.
September–October	Sukkot, the Jewish Feast of the Tabernacles; originally a seasonal celebration of the ingathering of summer crops, it has a historical relationship to the Flight from Captivity, when the Israelites lived in sukkots, or booths; a joyous festival celebrated for seven days in the middle of the month of Tishri. 1, 184, 269, 628.
September–October	Shemini Atzeret, the eighth day of the Festival of Sukkot; observed on the twenty-second day of Tishri. 175.
September–October	Simhat Torah, a day of "rejoicing in the law" and completion of the Torah reading cycle; observed on the twenty-third day of Tishri. 1, 184, 261.
November–December	Chanukah, or Hanukkah, the Jewish Feast of Lights, also called the "feast of dedication"; commemorates the Maccabean victories but focuses on the re-lighting of the Temple Eternal Light; observed for eight days beginning with the twenty-fifth day of the month of Kislev. 183, 185, 187, 191, 198, 201, 206, 209, 210, 217, 219, 223, 225, 228, 230, 232, 588, 624, 628.
January–February	B'Shevat, the New Year of Trees, observed on the fifteenth of Shevat, is the Arbor Day of the Jewish people. 175.
February–March	Ta'anit Esther, the Fast of Esther, commemorates the memory of Queen Esther and the fast she proclaimed following the demands of Ahasuerus for the annihilation of her people; observed on the thirteenth of Adar. 234.
February–March	Purim, or the Feast of Lots, celebrates the deliverance of the Jews in Persia from the machinations of Haman; observed on the fourteenth day of Adar. 184, 198, 203, 269, 631.
March–April	Passover, or Pesah, the Jewish Feast of Unleavened Bread, instituted in commemoration of the deliverance of the Jews from Egypt; observed for eight days beginning with the fifteenth day of the month of Nisan. 174, 176, 192, 194, 197, 199, 202, 207, 212, 215, 221, 226, 229, 269, 628.
April–May	Holocaust Day, or Yom Hashoa, a memorial to the 6,000,000 Jews slaughtered by the Nazis between 1933 and 1945; observed on the twenty-seventh day of the month of Nisan; a commemoration in which many non-Jewish people participate around the world. 650, 669, 676, 682, 708.
April–May	Lag b'Omer, the thirty-third day of the forty-nine days between Passover and Shavout; its origin is attributed to the cessation of a plague that was decimating the student body of Akiba, a rabbinic sage in the second century; a semiholi-day celebrated in Israel with bonfires and dancing; Jewish communities in other nations plan programs for Lag b'Omer to express love of the Holy Land; observed on the eighteenth day of Iyar. 175.
May–June	Shavuot, or Feast of Weeks, marking the completion of seven weeks from the second day of Passover; celebrates the presentation of the Ten Commandments to Israel at Mount Sinai and the offering of the first fruits of the harvest at the Temple in Jerusalem; observed on the sixth and seventh days of the month of Sivan. 1, 184, 269.
July–August	Tishah Be'av, or Tisha B'Ab, a twenty-four hour day of fasting, lamentation and prayer; a day of mourning for the destruction of the first and the second Temples of Jerusalem which has been extended to include mourning for the destruction of all Jewish communities; observed on the ninth day of the month of Ab. 1, 184.

Feasts, Festivals, and Special Events Days

The lunar calendar in which each month starts with the new moon, the annual shift of dates for Easter, the seasons of the year, and local customs are the prime factors which regulate the time that movable feasts, festivals, and special events are celebrated in various parts of the world.

The following selection of movable occasions includes religious days that are associated with Lent or Easter in the Western world and with the traditions of the lunar months in the Eastern world. Many of these occasions are holidays or semiholidays. The special-events days which are listed are of a secular nature and generally are not official holidays but free-time attractions that are a part of the history of public enjoyment.

The movable feasts, festivals, and special events are arranged alphabetically with a corresponding column indicating the approximate relationship to the Gregorian calendar.

April	Feast of A-Ma, observed in Macao, an overseas province of Portugal off the China coast, honoring A-Ma, patroness of fishermen and seamen, with rituals in a 600-year-old temple.
August	American Indian Exposition, held annually at Anadarko, Oklahoma, the site of Indian City, U.S.A., where authentic reproductions of several Indian villages and murals by Kiowa artists in the intertribal Indian agency may be found; a six-day festival opening on the second Monday of August depicting through dances, ceremonies, and pageants the history of twelve Indian tribes of the Great Plains and the Southwest. 268.
February	Anchorage Fur Rendezvous, a ten-day annual celebration in Anchorage, Alaska, featuring championship sled dog races, parades, Eskimo dances, fur auctions, a miners and trappers' ball, sports, art shows, and exhibits. The festival has been described as the Mardi Gras of the North. 268.
April	Anjin Matsuri, observed in Yokosuka, Japan, as a memorial to William Adams, an Englishman who taught Western navigation, mathematics, and other technical subjects to the Japanese during the time of Shogun Tokugawa Ieyasu.
May	Apple Blossom Festival, celebrated annually at Wenatchee in the state of Washington since 1920, except during the years of World War II. The main attraction of the Washington State Apple Blossom Festival is the fragrant orchards in full bloom, but the festival lasts for more than a week and is packed with festivities and entertaining events. 268.
August	Awa Odori, the Fools' Dance, a Japanese holiday celebrated by all-night dancing in the streets.
February	Baika-sai, the Plum Blossom Festival, observed in Japan; commemorating Sugawara Michizane, the ninth-century patron saint of literature and school examinations; also a time for appreciating flowering trees.
April–May	Baisak, the Hindu New Year, celebrated with bathing in the Ganges and other holy waters, attendance at temple services, and gift exchanges. 1.
January–February	Basant Panchami, a Hindu festival honoring Sarasvati, goddess of learning, eloquence and the arts, commemorated in schools and universities. 1.
July	Battle of Flowers; celebrated on the Island of Jersey, usually in the fourth week of July; a spectacular floral carnival that began in 1902 as a part of the celebration honoring the coronation of Edward VII.
January	Black Nazarene Fiesta, observed in Manila, Philippine Islands, for eight days, honoring the patron saint of the Quiapo district of Manila.

July–August	Bon Festival, or Feast of the Dead, a Buddhist ceremonial observed by lighting lanterns for deceased ancestors, observed in mid-July in metropolitan areas and mid-August after the harvest in rural regions; a traditional festival in many parts of Asia. 1.
April	Boun Pimay, or the Festival of the Fifth Month, celebrated in Laos as the New Year, observed with prayers and the anointing of statues of the Buddha at the pagodas and with participation in the folk customs of the Laotian people. 1.
September	Braemar Gathering, an annual event in the village of Braemar in Scotland; a festive occasion with Highland dancing, games, and athletic competitions demanding skill and prowess. 844.
December	The Broken Needles Festival, or Hari-Kuyo, the Mass of the Broken Needles; at one time a Japanese religious festival honoring sewing needles which had outlived their usefulness; a twentieth-century neighborhood event in which broken needles are tied to an altar. 251.
April–May	Buart Nark, or Buat Nak, or the Admission to Priesthood, the Buddhist ordination day, usually observed in the spring when young men of Thailand are taken into the priesthood for varying periods of service. 1.
February–March	Bun Day, a children's festival of Iceland, held on the Monday before Shrove Tuesday, a traditional day for sharing whipped-cream buns with children.
July	Candy Festival, Seker Bayrami, a day of celebration in Turkey which follows Ramadan, the Islamic month of fasting. The Candy Festival is not only a time for buying candy but also for enjoying racing and dancing.
December	Caribbean Christmas Festival, begins on December 23 in Christiansted in St. Croix and lasts for two weeks, with wandering guitarists singing to the Christ Child. A unique feature of this festival is the jig-dance carried on since Elizabethan days, with the recitation of old poems and stories, such as Saint George and the Dragon.
February–March	Carnaval-Souvenir de Chicoutimi, celebrated in Chicoutimi, Quebec, from late February into early March to honor the history and the folkways of the region.
January–March	Carnival Days, the pre-Lenten festivals celebrated as holidays in thirteen nations of the world; a festive period of revelry and feasting lasting from one to three days; observed on varying dates from Epiphany to Ash Wednesday with major events held during the week before the beginning of Lent. 22.
January	Chalma Pilgrimage; observed at Chalma, Mexico, during the first week of January in veneration of the Chalma image of Christ; the last mile of the pilgrimage must be on foot or horseback.
February	Charro Days, a four-day pre-Lenten festival celebrated at Brownsville, Texas, and at Matamoros, Mexico, immediately across the Rio Grande; a border fiesta that features the costumes of the Spanish dons and other Mexican equestrian outfits, parades, costume dances in the streets, cultural exhibits, and brilliant balls. 268.
April–May	Cherry Blossom Festival, observed throughout Japan for about two weeks to celebrate the spring season and the blooming of the cherry blossoms.
March–April	The Cherry Blossom Festival in Washington, D.C., is held when the cherry trees that were presented to the United States by Japan and planted around the Potomac River Tidal Basin bloom; the season varies from approximately March 20 to April 15. 268.
July	Cherry Festival; held annually at Traverse City, Michigan, since 1928 in mid- or late July, with programs, festivities, and ceremonies attending the departure of the first loads to market. 268.

July	Cheyenne Frontier Days, an annual celebration held in Cheyenne, Wyoming, during the last full week of July; first organized in 1897, the festival re-creates the history and the customs of western America with pageants, rodeos, ceremonial Indian dances, and old-time vehicle parades. 268.
January–February	Chinese New Year, begins on the first day of the first month of the lunar calendar. This holiday is notable for its ten-day to two-week celebration which includes, among other traditional customs, the Ching Sen (or respect-for-ancestors) ceremony, the procession of lighted lanterns called the Feast of Lanterns, and the Parade of Dragons, featuring dragons as symbols of strength and goodness. The lunar New Year is a holiday with various names in the People's Republic of China, the Republic of China in Taiwan, Brunei, Hong Kong, Macao, Malaysia, Mauritius, and Singapore. Chinese New Year celebrations are major events in the major cities of the world where there are large populations of people with Chinese backgrounds. 253, 261, 269, 583.
August–September	Choosuk, or Moon Festival, observed in Korea at the end of the harvest period, a day of thanksgiving and a time to tend the graves of ancestors, hold hunting contests, and enjoy the year's biggest feast.
December	The Christmas Novena, the nine-day ritual preceding the celebration of Christ's birth, begins on December 16 in South America, and officially opens the Christmas season. The observance is a combination of religious fervor and fiesta, opening with the singing of traditional Christmas carols, prayers at the *pesebre*, and special prayers for the novena, followed by fireworks, dancing, and small parties. 74.
October	Chung Yeung, Festival of Ancestors, a Chinese festival to honor the dead by sweeping graves and tombs and by making sacrificial offerings to ancestors; a holiday in Hong Kong and in Macao. 249.
February–March	Collop Monday, the Monday before Shrove Tuesday; the traditional day for the faithful to stop eating meat; the day was once known as Poets' Monday because of the many poems that were written about this penitential day in England and Europe. 256.
April–May	Common Prayer Day, or Store Bededag, observed in Denmark on the fourth Friday after Easter; a nationwide day of prayer which has been observed since the eighteenth century when the king's prime minister decreed one great day of prayer to replace many penitential days; a religious holiday in Denmark.
June–July	Common Ridings Day, observed in June and July in the towns and villages of Scotland, commemorates "the riding of the borders of the town common" to retain royal charters; repeats ceremonies that were established four or five centuries ago. 844.
September	Confucius' birthday, a commemoration of the birth in 551 B.C. of the greatest sage of China whose teachings are recorded in *Lun Yii*, *The Analects*. The birthday of Confucius, called "grand perfection and teacher of ten thousand generations," is a holiday in the Republic of China on Taiwan. 1.
April	Daffodil Festival, the first Puyallup Valley Daffodil Festival, was held on April 6, 1926, near Sumner, Washington; now observed in Tacoma, Sumner, and Puyallup in April, with floral parades and picturesque coronation ceremonies for the daffodil queen. 268.
October	Dasain, a ten-day religious festival in the Kingdom of Nepal, commemorating the victory of Durga, the goddess of power, over the tyrant demons, Madhu and Kaitava, who ruled the earth. This festival which celebrates freedom includes prayers in homes and in temples, a Fulpati procession of flowers, and other ceremonials appealing for the continued protection of Durga. 1, 260.
August	David and Goliath Day, a re-creation of the biblical story, part of a centuries-old fall festival at Ath, Belgium; Goliath is vanquished but has the last line, "I'm not dead yet."

August	Days of '76, a three-day celebration held in Deadwood, South Dakota, during the first full weekend of August; a festival featuring rodeos and races, re-enactments of historic events of the area, and portrayals of such famous residents as Calamity Jane, Wild Bill Hickok, and Deadwood Dick in pageantry and parades. 268.
November	Deepavali, or Diwali, the Hindu Festival of Lights, the time when Lakshmi, the goddess of good fortune visits the homes of humans; a ceremonial festival observed throughout India, a holiday in Guyana, Mauritius, Singapore, and Sri Lanka. 22, 260, 261.
August	Doggett's Coat and Badge Race up the Thames River, an English event scheduled around August 1; originated as a tribute to the Company of Watermen of the River Thames; reported to be the world's oldest annually staged sporting event and the longest rowing race; now kept up under the supervision of the Fishmongers' Company. 256.
June	Dragon Boat Festival, or Tuan Wu, an old Chinese festival to honor the third-century Chinese poet and statesman, Ch'u Yuan, who committed suicide in Tungting Lake. The colorful dragon-boat racing contests re-create the search for his body. The Dragon Boat Festival is a holiday in the Republic of China on Taiwan and in Macao. 875.
October	Durga Puja, the festival of the Divine Mother, a ten-day holiday in India celebrating the creative force of the universe and honoring the ten-armed Durga, wife of Shiva. The day is also known as "the festival of victory" to commemorate the victory of the goddess Durga over the demon Mashishasura. 1.
September	Dussehra, the great autumn festival of India, celebrating the victory of good over evil; a commemoration of the ten-day struggle between Rama, the Prince of Ayodha, and Ravana, the king of the demons. The Rama's victory is re-enacted in puppet shows as well as by human actors and dancers. 1.
March–April	Easter Monday, the day after Easter Sunday is a holiday in eighty-two nations throughout the world, and in North Carolina. 1.
August	The Eisteddfod, or Royal National Eisteddfod of Wales; held annually in August in northern and southern Wales alternately, to encourage Welsh literature and music. Other Eisteddfodau are held in separate Welsh communities from May until early November for the preservation of the Welsh language and national customs.
August	Esala Perahera, a Buddhist festival celebrated in Sri Lanka, honoring the relic of the Lord Buddha, "the sacred tooth"; commemorated with pilgrimages to the Temple of the Tooth at Kandy and celebrated with processions of elaborately ornamented elephants, drummers, actors, and the famed Kandyan dancers. 1.
July	Ezra Meeker Days, presented at the end of July in Puyallup, Washington, to re-create the era of the pioneer who is credited with the marking of the Oregon Trail and whose work led to the establishment of the Oregon Trail Association and the American Trails Association.
March	Fallas de San José, the Bonfires of Saint Joseph, a week-long festival in Valencia, Spain; originated in medieval times when the carpenter's guild burned the annual accumulation of shop chips; a spectacular competition of ingenious bonfires and other events; honors Saint Joseph, father of Jesus and patron of carpenters.
February–March	Fasching, a Shrovetide festival observed in Austria and Germany on Rose Monday and Shrove Tuesday, between Fasching Sunday and Ash Wednesday; also called Fasnacht, Fasnet, or Feast of Fools; features processions of masked figures and customs observed for generations.

February– March	Fastelavn, a festive day for children observed in Denmark on the Monday preceding Ash Wednesday; a time of enjoying an old custom when children, armed with Lenten birches (twigs decorated with ribbons and colored paper flowers) pretend to beat their parents with demands for the traditional Shrovetide buns.
August	Feast of the Hungry Ghosts, observed in partsof Asia to honor ancestors, who, it is believed, return to earth to visit their descendants; a day of offering gifts at tombs and grave sites and of celebrating by burning joss sticks and fireworks. 22.
February	Festival du Voyageur, celebrated at St. Boniface, Manitoba, for five days in late February to honor the early *coureur-de-bois* and the founding of the French-speaking community in Manitoba.
March–April	Festival of States, a spring festival held in St. Petersburg, Florida, in late March and early April to welcome spring; a special feature is the band competition, with representatives from the various states vying for the Governor's Cup.
September– October	Gaelic Mod, observed in Scotland during the first two weeks in October, or occasionally beginning in the last week of September; a major cultural event since 1892, organized to promote the Gaelic language and the history and arts of the Highlands and the islands of Scotland. 844.
Variable	Galungan, the Bali New Year, observed in accordance with the Wauku calendar of 210 days a year; a ten-day celebration including a Feast of the Dead to honor departed ancestors. 1.
August– September	Ganesh Chaturthi, one of the liveliest festivals in the Bombay area of India; a week-long spectacular honoring Ganesh, the Hindu God of prosperity. The festival concludes with the immersion of a clay image of the elephant-god into the waters of Chowpatty Beach to ensure prosperity for both land and water. 1.
September	Gathering of the Fruits, a harvest festival in Albania celebrating the completion of the harvest of grapes, figs, and other fruits; a time of feasting and rejoicing.
July	Gion Matsuri, an ancient Japanese festival honoring the brother of Japan's sun goddess who responded to the petitions of the people and stopped a tenth-century plague; celebrated with ceremonials and processions of huge floats in the city of Kyoto. 251.
June	Good Neighbours Festival, observed at Dumfries, Scotland, in late June; commemorating an age-old custom to resolve complaints between neighbors; a week of festivities, including the Riding of the Marches. 844.
October	Green Squash Festival, or Wima'kwari, observed in Huichol, Mexico; a religious occasion when children carry wands with a woven design in the form of God's eye, a symbol of good health and long life. 628.
October	Han Lu, a Chinese festival marking the end of summer. Han Lu means "the dew grows cold" and on this day summer is treated as a departing guest.
August– September	The Highland Games of Scotland begin around the first of August and continue at varying dates and places into September; the most important features are competitions in bagpipe playing, Highland dancing, and caber (a fir tree) tossing, a competition that displays coordination. 844.
July–August	Hill Cumorah pageant, held annually at the time of the full moon in late July or early August at Cumorah Hill near Palmyra, New York, a drama re-creating the finding of the sacred book by Joseph Smith. The book, translated, became the Book of the Mormon. 869.

August	Hobo Days, a gathering of people with wanderlust; observed in late August in Britt, Iowa, with celebrations in the carnival manner and with the crowning of a king of the hoboes.
March–April	Holi, or Hola, a Hindu springtime festival commemorating the burning of Holika, a witch that once tormented all of India; observed throughout India on the fifteenth day of the light half of the moon of Phalguna; a celebration closing the old year with fire and ashes and welcoming the new with colorful water festivities, including the spraying of everyone with colored water from spray guns and bamboo blowpipes; a holiday in Malaysia and in Surinam. 1, 261.
July	Holy Queen Isabel Festival, observed in Coimbra, Portugal, during the first fortnight in July in even years; commemorates the memory of Queen Isabel, who saved Portugal's first capital from calamity and was canonized in 1625.
May–June	Immaculate Heart of Mary, celebrated on the second Sunday after Pentecost; an optional memorial on the calendar of the Roman Catholic church. 5.
December–January	John Canoe Days, a fiesta of Jamaica held between December 23 and January 23 with celebrations featuring costumed parades, fire dances, and other traditional rituals.
April	Kalpa Vruksha, a springtime festival in many villages of India welcoming Baisak, the Hindu new year, a celebration enjoyed by children who receive gifts around a tree just showing its leaves. The festival is also the occasion for tree planting in many parts of India. 261.
March	Kannon Festival, a two-day event observed in mid-March, at the Asakusa Kannon Temple in Japan; a festival of Chigo, or celestial children, honoring the better-behaved children of the parish.
September	Khordad'sal, commemoration of the birth of the Prophet Zoroaster, the founder of Zoroastrianism, an important day for the Parsis of India and the Parsi in other parts of the world. 1.
August	Krishna's Birthday, commemorated in India in honor of the Baby Kishna with ceremonials of prayer and anointment of an image of the infant god and stories of his life. 1.
December	Kriss Kringle's Fair; presented in Nuremberg, Germany, from early December until Christmas; reportedly began in the Middle Ages to display the arts of the Nuremberg craftsmen and specialty cooks.
July	Kutztown Fair, a Pennsylvania-Dutch festival in Kutztown, Pennsylvania, always held around the July 4 weekend, presenting authentic re-creations of early Pennsylvania-Dutch life, art, and handicrafts. 268.
July–August	Lantern-floating Festival, observed in rural Japan after the harvest with the floating of paper lanterns on the waters.
March–April	Lazarus Day, an ancient Slav festival observed in Bulgaria on the Saturday preceding Easter in honor of Saint Lazarus, raised from the dead by Jesus; a day for children to act out the biblical roles of Lazarus, Mary, and Martha.
February	Li Chum, a traditional Chinese seasonal observance celebrating the coming of spring. Li Chum means "spring is here." 22.
June–August	Lough Derg Pilgrimage, the greatest of the popular pilgrimages of Ireland, takes place between June 1 and August 15. During this season only the pilgrims may visit the island, and they must take only one meal a day, drink "pilgrim's wine," and go barefoot; also called the Pilgrimage of Saint Patrick's Purgatory. 34.
October–November	Loy Krathong, Thailand's Festival of Lights, an occasion when lighted candles are floated on banana leaves down rivers and waterways; a festival thought to have originated as a ceremony to appease water spirits, or as to worship Buddha's footprint left on the shores of the Nammada River. 260.

July	Magdalene Festival, La Fête de la Madeleine, observed in St. Baume, a region of Provence, by pilgrimages to the Holy Cave where the Magdalene reputedly lived in repentance of her sins. The shrine is visited at all times of the year, but July 22 is the day when many young girls visit the grotto to seek the help of Magdalene in finding husbands.
January	Magh Mela Fair, an annual purification pilgrimage to Allahabad, where devout Hindus bathe in the River Ganges. Allahabad is also the site for the Kumbh Mela Festival, which occurs every twelfth year. 1.
January–February	Mahashivarati, a religious ceremony observed by the Hindus of India by worshipping at temples dedicated to Shiva, one of the greatest of Hindu deities. 1.
April	Mahavira Jayanti, a festival celebrated by the followers of the Jain religion, observed on the thirteenth day of the bright half of the month of Chaitra; a pilgrimage day commemorating with eleborate ceremonies the birth of Lorol Vardhamana Mahavira, the great Jain teacher of the sixth and fifth centuries B.C. 1.
January	Makara Sankranti, a three-day festival in India celebrating the passing of the winter solstice, noted for its pilgrimages to the sacred river Ganges where people with strong faith in the power of moving water bathe. 1.
February–March	Mardi Gras, the most elaborate and joyous carnival in the United States; celebrated in New Orleans since 1827 between Twelfth Night and the beginning of Lent with parades, music, masqued balls, and pageantry. Mardi Gras day is Shrove Tuesday, a holiday in Alabama and Louisiana. 268.
February–March	Marfeh, meat-fare and cheese-fare days, observed in the Orthodox Catholic communities of Syria and Lebanon preceding the Lenten fast; observes old customs such as eating a boiled egg last at meals.
October	Mid-Autumn Festival, a Chinese festival marking the end of the harvest. The ceremonials center around the moon which influences crops, harvest, and humans. It is celebrated with the eating of round moon cakes and listening to music and poetry and is a holiday in the Republic of China on Taiwan, Hong Kong, and Macao.
May–July	Midnight Sun Days, observed at North Cape, Norway, beginning in mid-May and lasting two months; a series of festivals in honor of the round-the-clock sunshine.
October	Mop Fairs at Stratford-on-Avon in England; originally a harvest festival when the farmers picked their hired help for the next year; now a two-part carnival, including a time-honored ox-roasting ceremony during the first fair, and a traditional Runaway Mop Fair a few days later to recall early employment practices. 256.
April	Nagasaki Takoage, or Kite-flying Contest, features competing teams of costumed men and gaily decorated kites, observed in late April at Nagasaki, Japan. Comparable events are held on varying dates in other parts of Japan and in other nations of the East. 615.
August–September	Nanda Deven, a festival in the Kumaon region of India; honors the patron deity, Nanda Devi, the goddess who killed a demon disguised as a buffalo. The festival re-enacts the legend of the battle. 1.
September	Navajo Nation Fair, held during the second week of September at Window Rock, Arizona, the capital of the Navajo Nation; an exposition which presents Indian traditions through ceremonials and exhibits of art forms. A colorful demonstration of the contributions of Indians to American history and culture. 268.

September–October	Oktoberfest, one of Germany's most famous festivals, began on October 17, 1810, the wedding day of King Ludwig I; now held from mid-September into October and celebrated with best beers, foods, and entertainment of the season.
August	Old Spanish Days, a five-day fiesta in Santa Barbara, Califormia, held near the full moon of August. The festival begins with a fiesta blessing on the steps of Santa Barbara's mission and moves on to present historical parades and productions portraying California's Spanish and Mexican heritage. 268.
March	Omizutori, a two-week ascetic training ritual combining elements of the Shinto and Buddhist traditions; observed in Japan.
March	O-Mizutori Matsuri, or Water-drawing Ceremony, a fifteen-day festival at Nara in Japan; observed for twelve centuries in commemoration of ancient rites in which holy water is drawn from the Wakasa Well near the temple. 1.
August–September	Onam, a Hindu harvest festival in India's tropical Kerola, featuring the Valomkali musical boat races and elephant processions.
January	Our Lady of the Happy Ending, a religious festival held in Brazil which concludes with the purification of church stairs by a water-pouring ceremony.
August	Pajjusana, an eight-day period of penance observed by the followers of Jainism, commemorating the birth of Mahavira, founder of the Jain order and honoring Kalpa Sutra, the sacred scripture. 1.
February–March	Pancake Day, always observed on Shrove Tuesday; a day for eating pancakes; a special event is the International Pancake Race between the housewives of Liberal, Kansas, and Olney, England, in which they run a quarter mile while tossing pancakes in a skillet. 256.
November	Parliament Day, officially the State Opening of Parliament, a colorful British ritual dating back to Plantagenet times; observed in London after a general election and preceding the beginning of each parliamentary session; involves the queen in traditional royal ceremonies.
March	Parsi Remembrance of the Departed Days; commemorated during the last ten days of the Parsi year; commemorated within shrines in Parsi homes throughout the world with ceremonies and prayers centered around floral arrangements which are symbols of paradise.
October	Paung-daw-U Festival, observed in Yawnghe in the Shan states of Burma, a Buddhist festival featuring a water procession honoring three Buddha images.
September	The Pendleton Round-up, celebrated at Pendleton, Oregon, since pioneer days, and regularly since 1910, during the last four days of the second and third week in September. Its purpose is to recall and honor pioneer life. 268.
July	Pennsylvania-Dutch Days, celebrated at Hershey, Pennsylvania, during the last week of July; a festival which began in 1948 to demonstrate the richness of the customs and folklore of Pennsylvania's early German settlers as well as the creativity of their handicrafts and culinary arts. 268.
December	Philippine Christmas, held in the Philippine Islands from December 16 to January 6, with the observance of traditions and special Christmas-time events; reported to be one of the longest and gayest Christmas festivals in the world. 857.
August	Pilgrims' Progress, observed on five separate days in August and on November 2 in Plymouth, Massachusetts; an observance re-creating the Sabbath procession of the Pilgrims to church services.
April–May	Ploughing Ceremony, a holiday in Thailand, an agricultural ceremony to bless the seed and prepare for the planting season. The minister of agriculture officiates and plows circular furrows in a ceremonial field and then scatters the seed from gold and silver baskets to assure good crops. 250.

May–June	Poinciana Festival, celebrated in late May or early June in Miami, Florida; a festival centered around the royal poinciana trees planted throughout the Greater Miami area, art exhibits, and other festival events. 268.
Midsummer	Ragbrai, the annual Great Bicycle Ride Across Iowa, sponsored since 1973 by the *Des Moines Register*, an event that attracts bicyclists of all ages from all parts of the country for the sheer fun of the ride. There are no winners, no prizes.
July–August	Raksha Bandhaw, or Brother and Sister Day, or Salone, a festival of India observed on the day of the full moon of the Indian month of Savan; a family day dedicated to the observance of traditions which signify the sacred relationship between brothers and sisters.
July	Red Waistcoat Festival, or Festa de Colete Encarnado, celebrated in July at Vila Franca de Xira in Portugal; a festival honoring the bull herders in their red waistcoats and the chase of the black bulls down the streets.
August	Rokusai Nembutsu and O-Bon, observed in Japan with prayer and folk dancing combined with O-Bon, the Buddhist festival for the souls of the dead.
February–March	Rosemontag, or Rose Monday; the Monday before Lent, celebrated in Germany with processions, mummery, and masquerades.
March–April	Royal Maundy, observed in England on Maundy Thursday; a day when the queen of England, or her representative, distributes Royal Maundy gifts of coins to as many poor men and women as there are years in the sovereign's age. 256.
July	The Royal Tournament, an annual event in London providing a showcase for the British armed services, with mock battles, gymnastics, and precision marching.
May–June	Feast of the Sacred Heart of Jesus, a Solemnity in the Roman Catholic church celebrated on the Friday after Corpus Christi; a devotion dedicated to Christ whose heart is a symbol of his love for all humanity; a religious holiday in Colombia. 5.
January–February	St. Paul Winter Carnival, celebrated annually since 1886 in St. Paul, Minnesota, a winter festival of sleigh and cutter parades, ice capades, frolics, and sports, highlighted by happy events centered around Boreas, King of the Winds, the Queen of the Snows, and the King's enemy Vulcanus.
July–August	Salzburg Festival, a musical event of international fame scheduled annually for July and August in the colorful city of Salzburg, Austria.
May	Santa Cruz de Mayo, or the Santacruzan Festival, one of the most important traditions in the Philippines. An elaborate pageant lasting nine days, based on the account of Constantine's conversion to Christianity in A.D. 312, his vision of a fiery cross in the heavens on the eve of a battle, and the finding of the True Cross by Helena, his mother.
July–August	Santiago Fiesta, observed at Loize Aldea in Puerto Rico for ten days beginning in late July; combines a religious festival with a masquerade carnival in which citizens dress as Christian Spaniards or infidel Moors.
July–August	Schutzenfeste, a marksmen's festival that originated in Biberach, Germany; a traditional folk festival with the members of marksmen's societies as the principal participants; a popular event in other regions in Germany as well, observed on varying days in July or August.
April	Sinhala and Tamil New Year, a two-day holiday in Sri Lanka celebrating the solar New Year; observed by both Buddhists and Hindus through the recognition of ancient customs such as the selection of the new year's lucky color by an astrologer, the enjoyment of specially prepared dinners, and visits between families and friends.

June	Sitges Carnation Show, takes place in early June in Sitges, Spain, where carnations grow like weeds. The carnations are gathered by the community and woven into a decorated carpet a quarter of a mile long. At the close of the show, performers of the local Catalan dance crush the carpet into perfume.
January–February	The Snow Festival, celebrated annually in Sapporo, capital of Japan's northernmost main island, Hokkaido, the site of the 1972 Winter Olympic games; the festival originated in 1949 when school children built six immense snowmen. 251.
May	Soil Stewardship Sunday, or Rural Life Sunday, observed in the United States on Rogation Sunday which falls on the fifth Sunday after Easter; a day dedicated to the concept of prudent care of the soil and other natural resources by individuals and society, and to an understanding of environmental problems and their solutions. 268.
April	Songkran, the Buddhist New Year, commemorated with the bathing of the images of Buddha with libations of water, a three-day Asian water festival when everyone is splashed with water; a Thai way of blessing family and friends. 22.
July	Sunflower Festival, celebrated by the Mennonites, descendants of the nineteenth-century settlers of Manitoba; the festival honors more than a century of accomplishments, including the development of a successful process for extracting oil from sunflower plants. 857.
July	Tabuleiros Festival, or Festa dos Tabuleiros, observed in Tomar, in the province of Ribatejo, Portugal, for four days in mid-July every third year in odd years; a 600-year event celebrating a thanksgiving for the harvest and expressing Tomar's charity for the poor and the afflicted.
June–July	Teej, a festival celebrated in the month of Asadha in India; a festival of praise to the goddess Parvati, consort of the Lord Siva; a festival for girls and women during which a married woman may return for an annual visit to her parents' home. The festival of Teej also honors Krishna, a Hindu god, with ceremonials and plays re-acting events in Krishna's life. 1.
January–February	Tet, or Ten Nhat, the Vietnamese New Year, which occurs on the first day of the first month of the lunar calendar, a festival lasting several days which ushers out the old year and welcomes the new with playing ancient games, participating in rice-cooking contests, and watching the parade of the unicorn, a relative of the good-luck dragons of Asia. 261.
October	Full Moon of Thadingyut, the end of Buddhist Lent, observed in Burma and other Buddhist countries, a traditional time for engagements and weddings.
February	Thaipusam, a Hindu religious festival commemorating the birthday of Lord Subramian; a period of penitence, a holiday in Malaysia. 1.
April	Thingyan Festival, the three-day New Year festival in Burma observed just before the start of the monsoon rains to celebrate the end of the old year and the beginning of the new. *Thingyan* means "to change" and the festival ceremony includes washing statues and pouring water over people to wash away the sins of the past in order to be as pure as possible in the New Year; a holiday in Burma. 875.
July	Les Trois Glorieuses, A French celebration commemorating the three Glorious Days—July 27, 28, and 29, 1830—when a popular uprising in France replaced one king with another; special honors are given to Burgundy wine; the same fete is celebrated in the fall to mark the end of the grape harvest.
September–October	Trung-Thu, a Vietnamese mid-autumn festival occurring on the fifteenth day of the eighth month in the lunar calendar; a happy lantern-making occasion for people of all ages with music and dancing in the streets. 628.
January	Tsao Chun, Festival of the Kitchen God, observed by Chinese communities in preparation for the Chinese New Year. The custom is based on a traditional

farewell ceremony for Tsao Wang, Prince of the Oven, or Kitchen God, before he leaves on an annual trip to heaven to report on the family's behavior during the year.

November–
December

Vaikunth, a festival at Tiruchirapalli in Madras State in India; a twenty-day pilgrimage during which pilgrims pass through a celestial gateway to obtain the boon of paradise.

July–
October

Varsa, the Buddhist Lent, a period during which the monks may not leave their cloisters but people may bring gifts to the monks.

February

Vartanantz Day, commemorated by the Armenians in honor of Vartan, the Armenian national saint and patriot, and the 1,036 martyrs who fell in the A.D. 451 religious war between Armenia and Persia; observed by the Knights of St. Vartan and by Armenian communities around the world usually on the Thursday preceding Lent.

April–May

Vesak, or Buddha Visakha, a three-day (or more) holiday celebrated in all of the countries of the Near and Far East during the full month of Vishakha; commemorates the birthday, enlightenment, and death of Buddha; called the Full Moon of Waso in Burma; a holiday in Singapore, Sri Lanka, and Thailand. 23, 26, 37, 46.

May

Vijag, Festival of Fortune, an Armenian festival observed on Ascension Eve; celebrated with dancing, singing, and the telling of fortunes from tokens thrown into a bowl of water drawn from springs believed to be unusually pure on Ascension Eve.

September

Vintage Feast, or Fiesta de la Vendimia, celebrated in mid-September in Jerez de la Frontera, Spain; an annual thanksgiving for the grape harvest, honoring Saint Gines de la Jara, patron of vineyards; celebrated with religious services, cavalcades of Andalusian-bred horses, bullfights, and feasting.

October

Virgen del Pilar, Virgin of the Pillar, celebrated with a ten-day festival in Saragossa, Spain; honoring the legend of the Virgin revealing herself from a pillar to Saint James the Apostle when he was evangelizing Spain; the secular events include the famous parade of giants and dwarfs.

April

Virgin Islands Carnival, celebrated in the U.S. Virgin Islands after Easter; a tradition going back to slave days but held annually since 1952; features include calypso singers, limbo dancers, steel bands, continuous processions, water sports, a children's parade, a grand carnival parade, and other festivities.

March–April

White House Easter Egg Roll, a traditional event held annually on Easter Monday on the south lawn of the White House in Washington, D.C. 268.

May–June

Whitmonday, the day after Whitsunday, or Pentecost, is a holiday in thirty-five nations of the world.

July–August

Wild Horse Festival, or Nomaoi Matsuri, a festival recalling the achievements of the soldier-cowboy-knights in Japanese history; a spectacular display of horsemanship and archery lasting three days on the northeastern plains of Honshu in Japan. 251.

July

Wild Pony Round-up on Virginia's Chincoteague Island; also called Pony-penning Day. The wild ponies of the island are supposedly descendants of Arabian horses left by the pirates or early colonists. 268.

June

Xiquets de Valls, a part of the celebration of the Feast of Saint John at Valls in Spain; observed in June since 1633 with a gymnastic specialty forming human towers with musical accompaniment from a clarinet and a drum.

April

Yasukini Matsuri, observed in Tokyo at the Yasukini Shrine for four days to honor the deified spirits of the Japanese soldiers who died for their country in wars at home or abroad.

Books Related to Anniversaries and Holidays

Religious Days

1. Abingdon dictionary of living religions. Ed. by Keith Crum, Roger A. Ballard, and Larry D. Shinn. Nashville: Abingdon, 1981.

Comprehensive guide to religions of the twentieth century; broad in scope, with information on historical developments, beliefs, important religious leaders, traditions, and practices of active religions in every part of the world; topics arranged in dictionary format, with excellent cross-references to related topics.

2. Baha'i holy places at the world centre. Haifa: Baha'i World Centre, 1968.

Description of communities, gardens, and shrines associated with Baha'u'llah, the important sites of the Baha'i faith.

3. Bloch, Abraham P. The biblical and historical background of the Jewish holy days. New York: Ktav, 1978.

Thoughtful, readable study of socioreligious base for the Sabbath and historical background of the holy days as evidenced by sacred literary traditions, rituals, and customs. Indexed.

4. Butler, Alban. Lives of the saints. Rev. ed. by Herbert Thurston. 4 vols. Westminster, Md.: Christian Classic, 1981.

Standard source of information on lives of principal saints and *beati* venerated liturgically by the Christian church; arranged by calendar year. Indexed.

5. Catholic almanac. Ed. by Felician A. Foy. Huntington, Ind.: Our Sunday Visitor, annual.

Handbook of current information on Roman Catholic church; includes liturgical calendar; significant dates in U.S. Catholic chronology; list of saints, bishops, cardinals, popes, and other church dignitaries; summaries of church doctrine; news events and reports.

6. Child, Heather, and Colles, Dorothy. Christian symbols, ancient and modern. New York: Scribner, 1973.

Description of Christian symbols, correlating evolution of symbolism with developments in theology; well illustrated, with black-and-white plates and line drawings.

7. Cowie, L. W., and Gummer, John S. The Christian calendar; a complete guide to the seasons of the Christian year. Springfield, Mass.: Merriam-Webster, 1974.

Two-part interpretation of Christian calendar; part 1 focuses on feasts and festivals associated with life of Christ; part 2 lists saints for each day of the year and events in life of the Virgin.

8. Deems, Edward Mark. Holy-days and holidays. New York: Funk & Wagnalls, 1902; Detroit: Gale Research, 1968.

Source material on origin of church festivals and national holidays, originally published in 1902; excerpts from works of nineteenth-century writers on the meaning of holy days and holidays.

9. Delaney, John J. Dictionary of saints. Garden City, N.Y.: Doubleday, 1980.

One-volume coverage of major and minor saints of universal church; includes biographical sketches with feast dates; appendixes provide lists of saints as patrons and intercessors; symbols of saints in art, chronological chart of popes and world rulers, and the Roman and Byzantine calendars.

10. Donin, Hayim H. To be a Jew; a guide to Jewish observance in contemporary life. New York: Basic Books, 1972.

Introduction to laws and observances for all aspects of Jewish life, including special occasions; summaries of customs and ceremonies accompanied by biblical quotations.

11. Eisenstein, Judith Kaplan. Heritage of music; the music of the Jewish people. New York: Union of American Hebrew Congregations, 1972.

Survey of Jewish music through the ages, with examples of chants and folk tunes; examples arranged topically, and suggestions for use.

12. Encyclopaedia of religion and ethics. Ed. by James Hastings, with assistance of John A. Selbie and other scholars. 13 vols. New York: Scribner, 1908–27.

Old but basic encyclopedia on world religions, ethical systems, and movements; major source for ascertaining historic distinctions between sects of Oriental religions, for interpretation of founding beliefs, philosophical ideas, ceremonials, rites, and age-old customs of major and lesser-known faiths.

13. Farid al-Din 'Attar. Muslim saints and mystics. Chicago: Univ. of Chicago Press, 1966.

Translation of major thirteenth-century study of saints and mystics of Islam, their times, and deeds.

14. Farmer, David Hugh. The Oxford book of saints. Oxford: Clarendon, 1978.

Guide to English saints and most important representative saints of Ireland, Scotland, and Wales, including saints associated with notable cults; biographical sketches, with feast dates, arranged alphabetically.

15. Forsyth, Ilene H. The throne of wisdom; wood sculptures of the Madonna in Romanesque France. Princeton, N.J.: Princeton Univ. Press, 1972.

Study of origin, function, and character of carvings of enthroned Virgin and Child in Western Europe to the end of the twelfth century.

16. Gerhard, H. P. The world of icons. New York: Harper, 1972.

Introduction to creation and use of icons as religious symbols and art forms from time of Justinian to seventeenth century.

17. Gittelsohn, Roland Bertram. The meaning of Judaism. New York: World, 1970.

Interpretation of fundamentals of Judaism, including examination of origins of and traditions behind observances of holy days.

18. Glubb, Sir John Bagot. The life and times of Muhammad. New York: Stein & Day, 1970.

Biography of Mohammad, the founder of Islam, emphasizing impact of his teaching on Arabs; lists of notable dates.

19. Hansen, Klaus J. Mormonism and the American experience. Chicago: Univ. of Chicago Press, 1981.

Interpretation of Mormon faith from its nineteenth-century beginnings to its reconciliation with twentieth-century social and economic realities.

20. Harper, Howard V. Days and customs of all faiths. New York: Fleet, 1957.

Old but still useful collection of short essays on facts and legends about holy days, special days, religious folk beliefs, traditions, customs, and people of many faiths; arranged by calendar year. Indexed.

21. Haskins, James. Religions. Philadelphia: Lippincott, 1973.

Survey of Buddhism, Christianity, Hinduism, Islam, and Judaism which includes major holy days, ritual practices, and analysis of attitudes toward ethical behavior and mores.

22. Helfman, Elizabeth S. Celebrating nature; rites and ceremonies around the world. New York: Seabury, 1969.

Study of rites in honor of "Mother Earth" in Africa, East Indies, China, Japan, and among Hindus, Moslems, and some North American Indian tribes.

23. Hunter, Louise H. Buddhism in Hawaii; its impact on a Yankee community. Honolulu: Univ. Press of Hawaii, 1971.

Study of relationship of Japanese Buddhist and American Christian communities from 1868 through World War II, with evidence of contributions of Buddhist community to Hawaiian society.

24. Kamal, Ahmad. The sacred journey, being a pilgrimage to Makkah. New York: Duell, 1961.

Description of Mecca, holiest of cities of Islam, with explanation of significance of prescribed traditions in the "great pilgrimage."

25. **Kanof, Abram.** Jewish ceremonial art and religious observance. New York: Abrams, 1970.

History and role of ceremonial art in Jewish home and synagogue and its associations with such holy days as the Sabbath, Passover, Chanukah, and Purim.

26. **Kettelkamp, Larry.** Religions, East and West. New York: Morrow, 1972.

History and beliefs of Hinduism, Buddhism, Taoism, Confucianism, Zoroastrianism, Judaism, Christianity, and Islam; surveys their similarities and differences.

27. **King, Noel Q.** Religions of Africa; a pilgrimage into traditional religions. New York: Harper, 1970.

Interpretation of religious life of tribal groups in equatorial and tropical Africa, with examination of roles of leaders and "sacred persons."

28. **Kitov, Eliyahu.** The book of our heritage; the Jewish year and its days of significance. 3 vols. New York: Feldheim, 1970.

Comprehensive study of Jewish year, with interpretations of celebratory cycle and descriptions of rituals.

29. **Koller, John M.** Oriental philosophies. New York: Scribner, 1970.

Introduction to dominant characteristics and philosophies of Hinduism, Buddhism, Confucianism, Taoism, and neo-Confucianism.

30. **Laliberté, Norman, and West, Edward V.** The History of the cross. New York: Macmillan, 1960.

Illustrated history of the cross as a Christian symbol and important element in ecclesiastical observances, with identification of crosses of all periods of history; illustrated with line drawings.

31. **Levin, Marlin.** Balm in Gilead; the story of Hadassah. New York: Schocken, 1973.

Story of Hadassah in Israel, with accounts of Henrietta Szold and other leaders and their contributions to Jewish life.

32. **Long, Kenneth R.** The music of the English church. New York: St. Martin's, 1972.

History of Anglican liturgical music against religious, cultural, social, political backgrounds, and musical trends of 400 years.

33. **MacKay, Ruth.** They sang a new song; stories of great hymns. Nashville: Abingdon, 1959.

History of circumstances that inspired the writing of twenty hymns for Christmas, Thanksgiving, and various religious services.

34. **Madden, Daniel M.** A religious guide to Europe. New York: Macmillan, 1975.

Chatty, informal guide to pilgrimage places, village shrines, historic cathedrals, churches, and other sites that attract the faithful; limited to Great Britain, Ireland, and Europe. Indexed.

35. **Maus, Cynthia Pearl, comp.** Christ and the fine arts. Rev. ed. New York; Harper, 1959.

Classic anthology of pictures, poetry, stories, and music related to life of Christ.

36. **The message of the Qur'an,** presented in perspective by Hashim Amir-Ali. Rutland, Vt.: Tuttle, 1974.

English translation of the Koran, the holy book of Islam, with explanatory prefaces and appendixes.

37. **Mizuno, Kogen.** The beginnings of Buddhism. Livingston, N.J.: Kosei (dist. by Orient Book Distributors), 1980.

Life and teachings of the historical Buddha, with focus on how Buddha's use of supernatural powers led to acceptance of Buddhism. Indexed.

38. **Negev, Avraham, ed.** Archaeological encyclopedia of the Holy Land. New York: Putnam, 1972.

Commentary on the Bible, combined with survey of archeological discoveries in Holy Land that identify sites of biblical events associated with religious observances and studies.

39. **Parrinder, Geoffrey.** A dictionary of non-Christian religions. Philadelphia: Westminster, 1971.

Concise compilation of data, in dictionary form, on modern non-Christian faiths; religions of ancient Persia, Mesopotamia, Egypt, Greece, and Rome; faiths of ancient American cultures, such as Mayas, Aztecs, Incas; and beliefs and customs of Australasia and Africa.

40. **Patel, Satyavrata.** Hinduism; religion and way of life. London: Associated Publishing House, 1980.

Introduction to Hinduism as a faith and way of life; examines Hindu theology, customs, symbols, ceremonies, sacraments, values, philosophical schools. With overview of world's debt to Hinduism.

41. **Rice, Edward.** Ten religions of the East. New York: Four Winds, 1978.

Interpretive essays on origins, beliefs, and practices of ten religions that originated in the East: Jainism, Zoroastrianism, Sikhism, Taoism, Confucianism, Bonism, Shintoism, Cao Dai faith of Indochina, Baha'i faith, and "Theosophy" of Helena Blavatsky.

42. **Saddhatissa, H.** The Buddha's way. New York: Braziller, 1971.

Introduction to the Buddha's teachings; appendixes list Buddhist countries, shrines, historical events, and festivals.

43. **Seeger, Elizabeth.** Eastern religions. New York: Crowell, 1973.

Explanation of Buddhism, Confucianism, Hinduism, Shinto, and Taoism which interprets rituals, holidays, legends and discusses concepts, founders, and development of each faith.

44. **Silver, Daniel Jeremy and Martin, Bernard.** A history of Judaism. 2 vols. New York: Basic Books, 1974.

Comprehensive study of history, faith-culture, literature, values, world outlook, and customs of the Jewish people.

45. **Walsh, John Evangelist.** The bones of St. Peter; a full account of the search for the apostle's body. Garden City, N.Y.: Doubleday, 1982.

Intriguing review of archeological theories, research, and findings related to the belief that Saint Peter, first pope of the Roman Catholic church, was buried under site of St. Peter's Basilica in Rome. Indexed.

46. **Walsh, Michael J.** An illustrated history of the popes; Saint Peter to John Paul II. New York: St. Martin's, 1980.

Illustrated introduction to history of the popes, with personal data and commentary on policies of each pope; in addition, explains papal tradition in the context of church and world history. Indexed.

47. **Wray, Elizabeth,** and others. Ten lives of the Buddha; Siamese temple paintings and Jataka tales. New York: Weatherhill, 1972.

Account of Buddhism, including birth stories of the Buddha demonstrating the "ten virtues"; illustrated with fine reproductions.

Christmas

48. **Abisch, Roz.** 'Twas in the moon of wintertime; the first American Christmas carol. Englewood Cliffs, N.J.: Prentice-Hall, 1969.

Adaptation of a carol written for Huron Indians by Father Jean de Brebeuf in 1840s; musical accompaniment and words in both English and Huron.

49. **Anderson, Raymond, and Anderson, Georgene.** The Jesse tree; stories and symbols of Advent. Philadelphia: Fortress, 1966.

Guide to readings and prayers, to be correlated with symbolism of the Jesse tree during Advent, in preparation for Christmas.

50. **Auld, William Muir.** Christmas traditions. New York: Macmillan, 1931; Detroit: Gale Research, 1968.

Standard history of religious and secular aspects of Christmas traditions, origins, antecedents, and customs; with excerpts from literary and historical records.

51. **Barth, Edna.** A Christmas feast; poems, sayings, greetings and wishes. Boston: Houghton, 1979.

Interesting collection of Christmas poems, carols, rhymes, mottoes, sayings, and superstitions from literary and folk-lore sources; indexed by author, title, and first line.

52. ———. Holly, reindeer and colored lights: the story of Christmas symbols. New York: Seabury, 1971.

Explanation of origins and meaning of such Christmas symbols as the tree, Yule log, bells, ornaments, Santa Claus and his ancestors, cards and greetings, shepherds, angels, colors, and candles. Indexed.

53. **Belting, Natalia.** Christmas folk. New York: Holt, 1969.

Description in free verse of "hallow days of Yule" in Elizabethan England, with mummers starting revelries on Saint Andrews' Day (November 30) and closing on Twelfth Night, or January 5.

54. **Bernstrom, Virginia D.** "Collect for Christmas; some backlist favorites." *School Library Journal* 29 (September 1982): 42–43.

Pointers on "buried treasurers" of Christmas materials which are part of forty-one books available in most libraries. Annotations describe good Christmas "stories within stories" and cite chapters and pages.

55. **Better Homes and Gardens.** Treasury of Christmas crafts and foods. Des Moines: Meredith, 1980.

Craft handbook, packed with directions for making craft items and food specialties for the Christmas season. Separate craft and food indexes.

56. **Bishop, Claire Huchet, ed.** Happy Christmas! Tales for boys and girls. New York: Daye, 1956.

Anthology of tales about the First Christmas, Saint Nicholas and Santa Claus, Christmas Day, and Twelfth Night.

57. Bjorn, Thyra. Once upon a Christmas time. New York: Holt, 1964.
Reminiscence of Christmas season and customs in Swedish Lapland in early twentieth century, from Festival of Lights to Epiphany.

58. Boni, Margaret Bradford, ed. Favorite Christmas carols. New York: Simon & Schuster, 1957.
Fifty-nine Yuletide songs with piano arrangements and brief introductions on origins. Indexed.

59. The book of Christmas. Pleasantville, N.Y.: Reader's Digest, 1973.
Stories of the Nativity, history of Christmas by Rummer Godden, selections from traditional and modern literature, and color photographs of Christmas in Germany, Italy, Spain, Mexico, and other countries.

60. Braybrooke, Neville, comp. A partridge in a pear tree; a celebration for Christmas. Westminster, Md.: Newman, 1960.
Anthology of Christmas poems, stories, dramas, and devotional literature, ranging from Virgil to W. H. Auden.

61. Brewton, Sara, and Brewton, John E. Christmas bells are ringing. New York: Macmillan, 1951.
Anthology of merry and reverent poems for Christmas season; indexed by author, title, and first line.

62. Brown, Joan Winmill. Christmas joys. Garden City, N.Y.: Doubleday, 1982.
Attractive collection of Yuletide prose, poetry, selections from Scripture, excerpts from letters and speeches, and material on Christmas fare and traditions, centered on joy of the season. Authors range from Dickens to Presidents Washington and Coolidge.

63. Buday, George. The history of the Christmas card. London: Rockliff, 1954.
Its forerunners, influence of the valentine, and creators and card makers; with commentary on sentiments expressed in verse and types of cards.

64. Carr, Terry, ed. To follow a star; nine science fiction stories about Christmas. Nashville: Thomas Nelson, 1977.
Centered on Christmas and its meaning to creatures from other planets and speculations about Christmas celebrations in the world of the future.

65. Carroll, Gladys Hasty. Christmas through the years. Boston: Little, 1968.
Reminiscences of Christmas, reflecting moods and customs of fifteen periods from 1898 to 1968.

66. Chrisman, Irma. Christmas trees, decorations and ornaments. New York: Heartside, 1956.
Handbook on selection of trees and making artificial trees, ornaments, and decorations.

67. Christmas; an American annual of Christmas literature and art. Ed. by Randolph E. Haugan. Minneapolis: Augsburg, annual.
Yearly compilation of articles, stories, and pictures of religious and secular observance of Christmas.

68. The Christmas book, written by Robert Joseph; illus. by Maurice Hughes; musical arrangements by Donald Siegal; concept and art direction by Don McAfee. New York: McAfee, 1978.
Interesting Christmas mix: stories, legends, poems, party ideas, and a look at Christmas in twelve countries. Includes "cornucopia of carols: hymn-carols, lullaby-carols, carols of custom, carols of legend, and American carols."

69. The Christmas story in masterpieces, introd. by David Kossoff. New York: St. Martin's, 1981.
Fine reproductions of beautiful paintings which portray the Christmas story. Includes Kossoff's "First Donkey" story, an appealing tale of a donkey and a very special baby.

70. Clancy, John. John Clancy's Christmas cookbook. New York: Hearst, 1982.
Recipes and menus for the Christmas season. Section 1 deals with preparations for the holiday and traditional and contemporary recipes. Section 2 suggests menus for brunches, dinners, and parties.

71. Coffin, Tristram Potter. The book of Christmas lore. New York: Continuum-Seabury, 1973.
Scholarly study of development of Christmas lore and traditions in relation to older mythologies; topics include superstitions, mumming and folk drama, symbolism of food, drink, Christmas trees, and cards, transformation of Saint Nicholas into Santa Claus, and Christmas literature.

72. Cooke, Gillian, ed. A celebration of Christmas. New York: Putman, 1980.
Big book, packed with information on Advent and Christmas: customs, poems, carols, playlets, stories, foods, recipes, games. Many illustrations, no index.

73. Cooney, Barbara. The little juggler. New York: Hastings, 1961.
Adaptation of French legend of little juggler of Notre Dame, who had no gift for the Virgin Mary; illustrations are sites where the juggler might have wandered.

74. Coskey, Evelyn, Christmas crafts for everyone. Nashville: Abingdon, 1976.

European-researched account of Christmastime traditions and activities; includes directions for projects appropriate for Advent, for creating "living" Nativity scenes, making luminarios, decorations from paper or the sewing basket, and other traditional Christmas-related crafts.

75. Counted cross-stitch designs for Christmas. New York: Scribner, 1978.

Fifty religious and secular designs by Danish Handcraft Guide: ideas for designing table linens, wall hangings, and decorations for Christmas season.

76. Cutler, Katherine N., and Bogle, Kate Cutter. Crafts for Christmas. West Caldwell, N.J.: Lothrop, 1974.

Instructions for Christmas projects, including gifts and decorations made from commonly available materials.

77. Dalphin, Marcia. Light the candles; a list for Christmas reading. Rev. by Anne Thaxter Eaton. Boston: Horn Book, 1960.

Annotated list of stories, poems, legends, carols, and books about "family Christmas" in America and around the world, as reviewed in "Horn Book" to 1960; updated to 1960–72 by Sidney Long's "And the dark make bright like day."

78. Dawson, William Francis. Christmas; its origin and associations, together with historical events and festive celebrations during nineteen centuries. London: E. Stock, 1902; Detroit: Gale Research, 1968.

Origins, rituals, historical events, and celebrations from the first to the nineteenth century.

79. Dickens, Charles. A Christmas carol. Philadelphia: Lippincott, 1915.

The most famous of all Christmas stories; illustrated by Arthur Rackham.

80. Duncan, Edmonstoune. The story of the carol. New York: Scribner, 1911; Detroit: Singing Tree Press, 1968.

Standard history of carols, their antecedents, and forms, related to ecclesiastical days and seasonal celebrations.

81. Eaton, Anne Thaxter, comp. The animals' Christmas: poems, carols, and stories. New York: Viking, 1944.

Christmas legends and poems in which animals have the important roles.

82. Ehret, Walter. The international book of Christmas carols. Englewood Cliffs, N.J.: Prentice-Hall, 1963.

Carols in their original language, with translations and scores, from England, France, Germany, Scandinavia, the Slavic countries, Italy, Spain, and the United States; arranged by nationality, indexed by title and first line.

83. Engle, Paul. An old fashioned Christmas. New York: Dial, 1964.

Verses and sketches describing a midwestern Christmas in the United States of the early twentieth century.

84. Fields, Nora. New Ideas for Christmas decorations. New York: Hearthside, 1967.

Ideas and instructions for making wreaths, swags, mobiles, hanging ornaments, and corsages from greens, pods, cones, and scrap; includes a section for birds, with suggestions for pine-cone cookies and feeders.

85. Foley, Daniel J. Christmas the world over; how the season of joy and good will is observed and enjoyed by peoples here and everywhere. Philadelphia: Chilton, 1963.

Accounts of Christmas celebrations in Bethlehem. Australia, China, Japan, the United States, and parts of Europe and Latin America.

86. Forsyth, Frederick. The shepherd. New York: Viking, 1976.

Christmas "miracle" story of young RAF pilot and his crippled *Vampire* jet fighter, guided to safe landing by a flyer known to have been killed in a Christmas Eve 1943 patrol.

87. Gardner, Horace J. Let's celebrate Christmas. New York: Ronald, 1950.

"Idea book" on Christmas celebrations, including parties by age group, with "ice breakers," games, plays, poetry, quizzes, stories.

88. Gibson, George M. The story of the Christian year. Nashville: Abingdon, 1945.

The evolution of Christian festivals, from time of the primitive church to modern era.

89. The glory and pageantry of Christmas, by the editors of Time-Life books. Maplewood, N.J.: Hammond, 1974.

Anthology, centered on the significance of Christmas. Part 1 deals with the biblical story, from Isaiah's prophecy to the holy birth and the life of Christ; part 2 covers 2,000 years of observance, from ancient to modern times. Full-color art reproductions and photographs.

90. Goodall, John S. An Edwardian Christmas. New York: Atheneum, 1978.

Colorful, small-size pictorial record of English Christmas in the Edwardian period, centered on a family searching for holly, trimming the tree, serving carolers at the door, going to market and preparing Christmas dinner, and entertaining at home.

91. Hadfield, Miles, and Hadfield, John. The twelve days of Christmas. Boston: Little, 1961.

Historical survey of customs and traditions of the period Christmas Eve to Epiphany.

92. Harper, Wilhelmina, comp. Merry Christmas to you. Rev. ed. New York: Dutton, 1965.

Christmas stories from Poland, Australia, Denmark, Sweden, Germany, France, Bulgaria, and England.

93. Heath, Edward, comp. The joy of Christmas; a selection of carols. New York: Oxford, 1978.

Old favorites and some nice, lesser-known carols sung by an English club (of which Edward Heath, former British prime minister, is a member). Brief commentary, with a touch of history, accompanies the words and music of each carol, as well as suggestions on techniques of presentation.

94. Henderson, Yorke, and others. Parents' magazine's Christmas holiday book. Bergenfield, N.Y.: Parents' Magazine Press, 1972.

Time-tested ingredients for a reverent Christmas involving the entire family: seasonal lore, customs, selections for reading, recipes, and all-time favorite Christmas carols, with music. Indexed.

95. Hitchcock, Gordon, comp. Let joybells ring; carols for Christmas from many nations. North Pomfret, Vt.: David and Charles, 1975.

Carols from Christmas music of sixteen nations, with melodic lines and simple arrangements.

96. Hodges, Walter. Plain Lane Christmas. New York: Coward, McCann & Geoghegan, 1978.

Charming, illustrated Christmas tale with contemporary theme: English villagers save historic lane from bulldozers of urban renewal with a Christmas festival.

97. Horder, Mervyn. On Christmas day, first carols to play and sing. New York: Macmillan, 1969.

Welsh, French, and Old English carols are among the thirteen songs in this volume. For unison singing, with simple piano arrangements.

98. Hottes, Alfred Carl. 1001 Christmas facts and fancies. 2d ed. New York: Dodd, 1944.

Legends, stories, carols, toasts, superstitions, omens, and customs around the world, with ideas for making Christmas cards, decorating and cooking.

99. Ickis, Marguerite. The book of Christmas. New York: Dodd, 1960.

Christmas traditions in the United States, England, and Europe, with ideas for activities.

100. Irving, Washington. Old Christmas. Tarrytown, N.Y.: Sleepy Hollow, 1977.

Facsimile of first edition of Irving's famous stories of Christmas in Old New England, originally published in 1875.

101. Jackson, Kathryn. The joys of Christmas; Christmas customs and legends around the world. New York: Western, 1976.

Brightly illustrated look at the history behind Christmas markets and wares, wrappings, cards, stamps, Yule log, Christmas stockings and shoes, music and bells, and other Christmastime-only happenings.

102. Johnson, Lois S., ed. Christmas stories around the world. Chicago: Rand McNally, 1970.

Stories from many nations, including Colonial America; each story is prefaced by note on Christmas customs of the country.

103. Jupo, Frank. Christmas here, there, and everywhere. New York: Dodd Mead, 1977.

Simple explanation of how Christmas traditions came to be and how they differ in different lands; examples range from Newfoundland, where men go fishing for the church on Christmas morning, to the Netherlands, where there is an old custom of "candle jumping."

104. Kainen, Ruth Cole. America's Christmas heritage. New York: Funk & Wagnalls, 1969.

Compilation of observances and recipes brought to United States by the English, Dutch, Germans, Mexicans, Greeks, Orientals, and others; arranged by geographical regions and national groups. Indexed.

105. Kamerman, Sylvia E., ed. On stage at Christmas; a collection of royalty-free, one-act Christmas plays for young people. Boston: Plays, 1978.

Thirty-two Christmas plays, ranging from simple plays for children to more sophisticated plays for high school groups, with suggestions on costumes, properties, and sound effects.

106. Kane, Harnett T. The southern Christmas book; the full story from earliest times to present; people, customs, conviviality, carols, cooking. New York: McKay, 1958.

Christmas customs in the American South, from the first, genial season in Virginia through the years to the "Confederate Christmas," as well as a cowboy's Christmas ball and other festivities in the "many Souths," and such recipes as Martha Washington's "Great Cake."

107. Kurelek, William. A northern Nativity; Christmas dreams of a prairie boy. Plattsburg, N.Y.: Tundra, 1976.

Extraordinary paintings depicting the Holy Family as humble folk in various Canadian situations; each painting recalls the biblical account of no-room-at-the-inn. The twenty paintings are accompanied by appropriately lyrical text expressing the boy's dreams.

108. Langstaff, John, comp. American Christmas songs and carols. Garden City, N.Y.: Doubleday, 1974.

American carols with piano and guitar arrangements, grouped by such sections as folk, Shaker, Moravian, Indian, black traditional spirituals, shape-note hymns, and part songs.

109. ———, comp. On Christmas day in the morning. New York: Harcourt, 1959.

Carol verses from many places in the world supplement the familiar verses of four traditional carols, such as "On chris-i-mas day in the morning."

110. ———, adapter. Saint George and the dragon. New York: Athenenum, 1973.

Version of Saint George folk play performed at Christmastime in English communities by local actors and mummers; includes music, costume suggestions, and directions for a sword dance.

111. Lewis, Taylor. Christmas in New England. New York: Holt, 1972.

Full-color photographs and descriptive text on Christmas season throughout New England.

112. Listaite, Sister M. Gratia, and Hildebrand, Norbert A. A new look at Christmas decorations. Milwaukee: Bruce, 1957.

Directions for creating Christmas bells, wreaths, and other decorations that incorporate the art forms and customs of many lands. With color photographs of Christmas trees, featuring decorative specialties of nations in Europe, Asia, and North and South America.

113. Lohan, Robert, Ed. Christmas tales for reading aloud. Enl. ed. New York: Daye, 1966.

Legends and humorous, adventurous, and sentimental stories for reading aloud in the home, classroom, or club meeting; opens with the Nativity story and concludes with twelve great poems.

114. Long, Sidney. And the dark make bright like day; Christmas books, 1960–1972. Boston: Horn, 1972.

Annotated list of books on Christmas reviewed in "Horn Book" from 1960 to 1972; includes titles on the Nativity, miracles and legends, Christmas in America, and Christmas make-believe. Companion list to Dalphin's *Light the Candles*.

115. Luckhardt, Mildred C. Christmas comes once more. Nashville: Abingdon, 1962.

Collection of poems and stories to be used with lighting each candle on the Advent wreath in preparation for Christmas.

116. McCullough, Bonnie Runyan, and Cooper, Bev. 76 ways to get organized for Christmas and make it special too. New York: St. Martin's, 1982.

Yuletide planner's guide on organizing time and enjoying making gifts and decorations, preparing food, and carrying out unique traditions. Indexed.

117. McGinley, Phyllis. A wreath of Christmas legends. New York: Macmillan, 1967.

Retelling, in verse, of fifteen medieval legends of First Christmas, such as "Ballad of the Red Breast of the Robin" and "Canticle of the Bees."

118. Metcalfe, Edna, comp. The trees of Christmas. Nashville: Abingdon, 1969.

Instruction for making tree ornaments; illustrated with color photographs of decorated trees representative of European national decorative art forms. Indexed.

119. The Metropolitan Museum of Art. The Nativity; the Christmas creche at the Metropolitan Museum of Art. Garden City, N.Y.: Doubleday, 1969.

Superb photographs of figures from eighteenth-century Neapolitan creche recounting the Christmas story, with explanatory text.

120. Meyer, Carolyn. Christmas crafts; things to make the 24 days before Christmas. New York: Harper, 1974.

Guide to Advent crafts with unique projects for each day beginning December 1, correlated with customs; illustrated with project drawings and sketches.

121. Miles, Clement A. A Christmas in ritual and tradition, Christian and pagan. London: T. F. Unwin, 1912; Detroit: Gale Research, 1968.

Standard study of intermingling customs of Christmas and pagan festivals; cross-referenced index.

122. Moore, Clement Clarke. A visit from St. Nicholas; a facsimile of the 1848 edition. New York: Simon & Schuster, 1971.

Small volume with old-fashioned engravings and text of the 1848 edition of the all-time favorite among Christmas poems.

123. Muir, Frank. Christmas customs and traditions. New York: Taplinger, 1977.

Broad review of the evolution of Christmas customs; includes (among many topics) transformation of Saint Nicholas into Santa Claus, Christmas pudding, mummers' play, Lord of Misrule, dumb cakes, and wassailing. Illustrated with religious paintings, photographs, and engravings.

124. Newland, Mary Reed. The year and our children; planning the family activities for Christian feasts and seasons. New York: Kenedy, 1956.

Christian approach to family participation in activities for Christmas and other important days in the church calendar; ranges from Advent wreath and Jesse tree to preparing for Thanksgiving; concludes with list of liturgical symbols.

125. Oakley, Graham. The church mice at Christmas. New York: Atheneum, 1980.

Delightful, amusing story of Christmas party for church mice and their friend, Sampson, the church cat. Colorful drawings of kneeling pads, monuments, and ecclesiastical details add to the pleasure of joining the church mice.

126. The Oxford book of carols. New York: Oxford, 1964.

First published in 1928; a collection of traditional and twentieth-century carols. Well indexed.

127. Payne, Alma Smith. Jingle bells and pastry shells; holiday baking favorites for all year round. Cleveland: World, 1968.

Cookbook with international flavor, linking recipes for holiday breads, cakes, and cookies with customs in different lands; describes early American Christmas customs, traditional Christmas menus from Greece to West Indies, and some adaptations of recipes for dieters.

128. Perry, Margaret. Christmas card magic; the art of making decorations and ornaments with Christmas cards. Garden City, N.Y.: Doubleday, 1970.

Suggestions for keeping Christmas cards out of the wastepaper basket: ideas and decorations for transforming used cards into card trees, centerpieces, creches, mobiles, mats, candle ruffs, and even next summer's birthday party.

129. Petersham, Maud, and Petersham, Miska. The Christ Child as told by Matthew and Luke. Garden City, N.Y.: Doubleday, 1931.

The classic among picture books re-creating biblical record of the Nativity.

130. Pettit, Florence H. Christmas all around the house; traditional decorations you can make. New York: Crowell, 1976.

Ideas from different parts of the world on constructing Christmas decorations; handsome and useful guide. Indexed.

131. Pflug, Betsy. You can. New York: Van Nostrand, 1969.

Ideas and directions for making Christmas ornaments, lanterns, candleholders, and other items from tin or aluminum cans; for adept youngsters and group leaders.

132. Politi, Leo. The poinsettia. Palm Desert, Calif.: Best-West, 1967.

Picture book blending the legend of the moment the poinsettia became *the* Christmas flower with recollections of the mood of Christmas on Olvera Street, in representative churches in Los Angeles and Watts.

133. Powers, Mala. Follow the star. Millbrae, Calif.: Celestial Arts, 1980.

Anthology of stories, legends, and folk tales for storytelling for each of twenty-four days of Advent, with brief history of Advent season and its customs, and instructions for making Advent wreath.

134. Preston, Carol. A trilogy of Christmas plays for children. New York: Harcourt, 1967.

Three Christmas plays for school or club use, with list of appropriate music and its use for each play.

135. Purdy, Susan Gold. Christmas cookbook. New York: Watts, 1976.

Guide for young cooks interested in making edible Christmas trimmings, Santa Claus eggs, and similar holiday concoctions; has section on basic kitchen skills, such as level measurements and cooking safeguards.

136. ————. Christmas gifts for you to make. New York: Lippincott, 1976.
Handbook of instructions, including patterns, for creating simple, attractive Christmas gifts; useful craft book for children and adults.

137. ————. Christmas gifts good enough to eat! New York: Watts, 1981.
Festive, decorated book of recipes and instructions for making edible holiday gifts, with advice on such subjects as safety, measurement, and the decoration, packaging, and mailing of gifts of home-made treats.

138. Rand, Christopher. Christmas in Bethlehem; and Holy Week at Mount Athos. New York: Oxford, 1963.
Report on Latin, Greek, and Armenian Christmas services at Bethlehem, with description of Holy Week on Mt. Athos peninsula.

139. Reed, Will, comp. The second treasury of Christmas music. New York: Emerson, 1968.
Collection of traditional carols and spirituals of international origin, and modern compositions from Asia, Africa, Latin America, and Oceania.

140. Reeves, James, comp. The Christmas book. New York: Dutton, 1968.
Modern and traditional carols, stories, poems, legends, and verse representing wide variety of authors, from Dickens to Dylan Thomas.

141. Robinson, Jo, and Staeheli, Jean. Unplug the Christmas machine; how to recapture the simple joys of Christmas. New York: Morrow, 1982.
Practical handbook for Yuletide planning, designed to circumvent the pressures that undercut the values of Christmas. Text includes suggestions on entertaining, gift giving, budgeting, and charities. The ideas are of special value for large households and single-parent homes.

142. Rockwell, Anne. "El toro pinto" and other songs in Spanish. New York: Macmillan, 1971.
Christmas carols, folk songs, lullabies, and comic songs from Spain, Latin America, and southwestern United States, with translations.

143. Rollins, Charlemae, comp. Christmas gif'. Chicago: Follett, 1963.
Anthology of Christmas poems, stories, and songs by and about black people, with unique holiday recipes.

144. Sansom, William. A book of Christmas. New York: McGraw-Hill, 1968.
Informative essays on Christmas customs, literature, food, gifts, and special performances, such as Christmas pantomimes and shadow shows.

145. Sargent, Lucy. Tincraft for Christmas. New York: Morrow, 1969.
Manual on tools, materials, and techniques for using tin for Christmas stars, wreaths, wind chimes, and gift trinkets.

146. Sawyer, Ruth. Joy to the world; Christmas legends. Boston: Little, 1966.
Christmas legends and tales from ancient Arabia, Ireland, old and modern Spain; each is preceded by a Christmas carol. Companion volume to Sawyer's 1941 collection *The Long Christmas*.

147. Sayre, Eleanor, ed. A Christmas book; fifty carols and poems from the 14th to the 17th centuries. New York: Potter, 1966.
Multilingual collection of Christmas carols and poems with English translations; notes on history and source.

148. Schraffenberger, Nancy, ed. Woman's day celebrating Christmas; a complete family reference book for Christmas this year and ever after. New York: Columbia House, 1979.
Illustrated Christmas idea book compiled from over four decades of *Woman's Day*. Volume opens with history of Christmas as a national holiday in the United States. Chapters on organizing time and on entertaining; other sections on card, ornament, and gift making. Indexed.

149. Scovel, Myra. The gift of Christmas. New York: Harper, 1972.
Memoir of "Christmases past" in China, Thailand, India, and the United States; instructions for making partridge berry wreath and other decorations are interspersed with poems and recollections.

150. Sechrist, Elizabeth Hough, ed. Christmas everywhere; a book of Christmas customs of many lands. Rev. ed. Philadelphia: Macrae Smith, 1962.
Christmas customs as celebrated in a dozen European countries and in the United States. U.S. section tells customs of Alaskans, Moravians, Pennsylvania Dutch, Puerto Ricans, and Shakers.

151. Seeger, Ruth Crawford, comp. American folk songs for Christmas. Garden City, N.Y.: Doubleday, 1953.
Collection of carols and folk songs tell the Christmas story from song to song; simple accompaniments.

152. Seibel, Kathryn Holley. The joyful Christmas craft book. New York: Van Nostrand, 1963.
Guidebook to personal pleasures in making Christmas decorations with paper, foodstuffs, wood, baskets, straw, sea shells, cones, nuts, greens, clay, glass, plastics, sheet metal, and copper screen.

153. Seymour, William Kean, and Smith, John, comps. Happy Christmas. Philadelphia: Westminster, 1968.

Anthology for the Christmas season, with selections from English and American novels, autobiographies, and poetry; includes some carols with musical scores.

154. Shekerjian, Haig, and Shekerjian, Regina. A book of Christmas carols. New York: Harper, 1963.

Collection, with interpretive essays, of shepherd, dance, lullaby, Magi, Nativity, and legendary carols, carols of custom, and miscellaneous carols.

155. Sheraton, Mimi. Visions of sugarplums. Rev. and expanded ed. New York: Harper, 1981.

Traditional recipes for cakes, cookies, candies, and confections from all countries that celebrate Christmas. Notes on the origin of some dishes, such as plum pudding, said to have originated with Druids; one chapter records favorite recipes of author's friends.

156. Shoemaker, Kathryn E. Creative Christmas; simple crafts from many lands. Minneapolis: Winston, 1978.

Sampler of ideas for creating Christmas cards, tree and room decorations, wrapping paper and gifts from Latin America, Scandinavia, and early America.

157. Simon, Henry W., ed. A treasury of Christmas songs and carols. 2d ed. Boston: Houghton, 1973.

Collection of carols, hymns, chorales, solo songs, rounds, and canons from Britain, United States, and other parts of the world; indexed by title, first line, and musical and literary sources.

158. Spicer, Dorothy Gladys. 46 days of Christmas; a cycle of Old World songs, legends, and customs. New York: Coward-McCann, 1960.

Interpretation of celebration of Christmas in eighteen European and Asian countries; arranged in chronological order from Saint Barbara's Day to Old Twelfth Night. Indexed by countries.

159. Stevens, Patricia Bunning. Merry Christmas!; a history of the holiday. New York: Macmillan, 1979.

Covers such topics as ancient festivals, beginning of Christmas, gift bringers, music of Christmas, and Christmas in a changing world.

160. Thompson, Jean McKee, comp. Our own Christmas; an anthology. Boston: Beacon, 1967.

Collection of prose and poetry expresses the meaning of Christmas as light, love, and everlasting life; authors range from John Donne to Dick Gregory.

161. Thurman, Howard. The mood of Christmas. New York: Harper, 1973.

This book of Christmas meditations explores the quality and spiritual symbolism of the season.

162. Tudor, Tasha, ed. Take joy! Cleveland: World, 1966.

Anthology of Christmas thoughts, stories, poems, carols, lore and legends, with traditions of Advent calendars and wreaths, filling cornucopias, the "animal Christmas," marionette show, and other activities of Tudor's family in New England.

163. Uttley, Alison. Stories for Christmas, chosen by Kathleen Lines. London: Faber and Faber, 1977.

Twelve Christmas stories of magic and enchantment in which animals and plants talk to each other, and through which English customs are brought to life.

164. Walsh, William Shepard. The story of Santa Klaus; told for children of all ages from six to sixty, and illustrated by artists of all ages from Fra Angelico to Henry Hutt. Detroit: Gale Research, 1970.

Reprint of 1909 edition of history of the Santa Klaus legend and its relationship to Saint Nicholas, with account of Santa Claus traditions.

165. Wasner, Franz, ed. The Trapp family book of Christmas songs. New York: Pantheon, 1950.

Christmas songs from many lands and periods of Christian history, with English translations of foreign songs.

166. Watts, Franklin, ed. The complete Christmas book. Rev. ed. New York: Watts, 1961.

Manual of suggestions on celebrating Christmas, from home-made cards to recipes.

167. Weiser, Francis X. The Christmas book. New York: Harcourt, 1952.

Interpretation of origin and meaning of customs, ceremonies, and legends of Christmas.

168. Weiss, Ellen. Things to make and do for Christmas. New York: Watts, 1980.

Guide to easy projects for Christmas; directions for making cards, decorations, and things to eat; arranged by ideas to be carried out during the four weeks before Christmas.

169. Wernecke, Herbert H. Christmas customs around the world. Philadelphia: Westminster, 1962.
Record of Christmas customs, focused on geographical and cultural influences; arranged by continent and by country.

170. ———. Celebrating Christmas around the world. Philadelphia: Westminster, 1962.
Collection of material on Christmas customs, arranged alphabetically by continent and country.

171. ———. Christmas stories from many lands. Philadelphia: Westminster, 1961.
Reflects universal spirit of the Christmas season.

172. Wheeler, Opal. Sing for Christmas; a round of Christmas carols and stories of the carols. New York: Dutton, 1943.
Twenty-four Christmas carols with music and accounts of how most of them came to be written.

173. Wilson, Erica. Erica Wilson's Christmas world. New York: Scribners, 1980.
Illustrated idea book and guide to making Christmas ornaments and gifts by needlepoint, sewing, and embroidery; appendix includes instructions, "stitch dictionary," and list of suppliers.

Jewish Holidays

174. Adler, David A. Passover fun book; puzzles, riddles, magic, and more. New York: Hebrew Pub. Co., 1978.
Word and number games, puns, riddles, brain teasers, and magic tricks tied in with Passover themes.

175. ———. A picture book of Jewish holidays. New York: Holiday, 1981.
Picture book, with words and drawings, that evokes "warmth of the Sabbath, the solemnity of Yom Kippur, the joy of Purim, the awe of Shavuot, and more." Glossary of terms used in text, and a chart clarifies time relationships between Jewish and Julian calendars.

176. ———. A picture book of Passover. New York: Holiday, 1982.
Attractive picture book, retells events which led to liberation of children of Israel from slavery in Egypt and describes the customs of Passover (also called *Hag ha-Abib*, the "spring holiday") as a celebration of freedom.

177. Barish, Louis. High holiday liturgy. New York: Jonathan David, 1959.
Interpretation of the theology, history, and artistry of the Machzor, the prayer book of Rosh Hashanah and Yom Kippur.

178. Becker, Joyce. Hanukkah crafts. New York: Hebrew Pub. Co., 1978.
Handbook of simple directions for making menorahs, table decorations, party invitations, and other useful Hanukkah items; includes ideas for active and quiet games, and for production of plays and puppet shows.

179. ———. Jewish holiday crafts. New York: Hebrew Pub. Co., 1977.
Useful collection of ideas for craft projects for all Jewish holidays, from Israel's Independence Day to Yom Kippur. Indexed.

180. Birnbaum, Philip. The Birnbaum Haggadah. New York: Hebrew Pub. Co., 1976.
Well-illustrated version of a Haggadah, containing story of the exodus of Israelites from Egypt and a ritual for the seder (the commemorative meal), with music for seder songs.

181. Blau, Esther S. The spice and spirit of Kosher-Jewish cooking. New York: Bloch, 1977.
Collection of essays, prepared by Junior Division of Lubavitch Women's Organization, on Jewish culture and dietary laws, with interesting menus for festive and family occasions.

182. Bloch, Abraham P. The biblical and historical background of Jewish customs and ceremonies. New York: Ktav, 1980.
Detailed study of origins of Jewish customs and ceremonies in terms of the heritage of Jewish religious writings and records of historical developments; full explanation of ceremonies of major Jewish holidays, with brief commentaries on minor holidays. Indexed.

183. Burns, Marilyn. The Hanukkah book. New York: Four Winds, 1981.
Explanation of the traditions of Hanukkah, including effect of Christmas on Jewish children, with pointers on ways the two holidays may be interpreted and shared. Includes craft ideas for celebrations and for making Hanukkah gifts.

184. Cashman, Greer Fay. Jewish days and holidays. New York: SBS, 1979.
Colorful introduction for children to meaning of Rosh Hashanah, Yom Kippur, Sukkot, Simchat Torah, Chanukah, Purim, Pesach, Yom Ha-Atzmaut, Shavuot, Tisha B'Av, and the Sabbath.

185. Chaikin, Miriam. Light another candle; the story and meaning of Hanukkah. New York: Clarion Books, 1981.

Attractive book on background of the 2,000-year-old holiday, celebrated primarily in Jewish homes. Touches on universal and national Chanukah customs, and brief description of carrying the Torch of Freedom from Modin to the Western Wall in Jerusalem. Glossary and index.

186. ———. The seventh day; the story of the Jewish Sabbath. Garden City, N.Y.: Doubleday, 1980.

Fine interpretation of Jewish Sabbath as a spiritual experience and as a joyous occasion in keeping the covenant with the Lord; descriptions of preparation for Sabbath and prayers, hymns, and ceremonies used by Jewish families on Sabbath.

187. Chiel, Kinneret. The complete book of Hanukkah. New York: Friendly House, 1959.

Chanukah anthology, including history, traditions, legends, stories, songs, prayers, and typical recipes.

188. Cone, Molly. The Jewish New Year. New York: Crowell, 1966.

Explanation of origin and meaning of Jewish New Year, with description of traditional observance.

189. Cuyler, Margery. Jewish holidays. New York: Holt, Rinehart & Winston, 1978.

Religious significance, rich history, and interesting customs of major Jewish holidays; brief instructions for suitable crafts for each holiday. Indexed.

190. Donin, Hayim Halevy. To pray as a Jew. New York: Basic Books, 1980.

Guide to use of the Siddur, the Jewish prayer book, which includes prayers for the Sabbath, holy days, and personal spiritual needs. Of interest and value to people of all faiths.

191. Drucker, Malka. Hanukkah; eight nights, eight lights. New York: Holiday, 1980.

Fact-filled book about Chanukah, the Festival of Lights, as a commemoration of first great war of religious freedom and a happy celebration of lighting the Chanukah candles, signifying spirit, courage, justice, and hope. Chapters on crafts, food, and games such as the dreidel. Indexed.

192. ———. Passover, a season of freedom. New York: Holiday, 1981.

Interpretation of Passover (or *Pesach*, the festival of freedom), oldest of Jewish holidays. From account of exodus of Israelites from Egypt, with explanation of its meaning, to preparation for Passover and the seder meal. Includes recipes, craft ideas, and section on Passover fun. Appendix has prayers and a glossary. Indexed.

193. ———. Rosh Hashanah and Yom Kippur; sweet beginnings. New York: Holiday, 1981.

Interpretation of historical and spiritual significance of the two major, most solemn days of Jewish year. Includes recipes, games, and crafts suitable for wide range of ages and skills in observance of Rosh Hashanah and Yom Kippur. Appendix has high holy day prayers and glossary. Indexed.

194. Fredman, Ruth Gruber. The Passover seder; Afikoman in exile. Philadelphia: Univ. of Pennsylvania Press, 1981.

Analysis of continuing influence of Passover significance and symbolism on individual Jews and the Jewish community.

195. Freehof, Lillian S., and King, Bucky. Embroideries and fabrics for synagogue and home. New York: Hearthside, 1966.

Manual on hand-worked Jewish ceremonial art, with ideas, designs, and instructions.

196. Frucht, Phyllis, ed. The best of Jewish cooking. Ed. by Phyllis Frucht, Joy Rothschild, and Gertrude Katz, with the Ladies Auxiliary of Temple Beth Israel. New York: Dial, 1974.

Cookbook, beginning with recipes for Jewish holidays: Sabbath, Rosh Hashanah and Yom Kippur, Sukkot, Chanukah, Purim, Passover, Shavuot, and Thanksgiving, and concluding with other foods enjoyed by Jewish families around the world.

197. Gaster, Theodor Herzl. Passover; its history and traditions. New York: Schuman, 1949.

History, ceremonials, and significance of Passover in terms of tradition and twentieth-century research; includes seder and Passover songs.

198. ———. Purim and Hanukkah in custom and tradition. New York: Schuman, 1950.

History, development, and observance of Purim and Chanukah, with samples of Purim plays and mummeries.

199. Glatzer, Nahum N. The Passover Haggadah. 3d ed. New York: Schocken, 1979.

Guide to understanding a traditional seder, the feast commemorating exodus of the Israelites from Egypt, with suggestions for adaptation of historical and liturgical material to contemporary use.

200. Goodman, Hanna. Jewish cooking around the world. Philadelphia: Jewish Pub. Soc., 1974.

International variations of Jewish food from China, Europe, North Africa, and Middle East, with special menus for Sabbath, Passover, and other religious days correlated with Jewish traditions, dietary laws, and customs.

201. Goodman, Philip, comp. The Hanukkah anthology. Philadelphia: Jewish Pub. Soc., 1976.

Collection of writings on history and significance of Chanukah: includes stories, plays, and poems, with material on customs and activities.

202. ———, comp. Passover anthology. Rev. ed. Philadelphia: Jewish Pub. Soc., 1978.

Besides accounts of its origin and history of observance in many lands, chapters on Passover in literature, art, and music; ideas for programs and projects; and section on ceremonies of observance.

203. ———, comp. Purim anthology. Philadelphia: Jewish Pub. Soc., 1949.

Tells of Purim origin, identifies special Purims and observances by nations, considers Purim in literature, art, music, and Jewish law, and describes customs of commemoration; with supplement of appropriate music.

204. ———, comp. The Rosh Hashanah anthology. Philadelphia: Jewish Pub. Soc., 1970.

Material on the solemn Jewish New Year from biblical and postbiblical writings, medieval literature, and modern periods; covers law, music, culinary arts, and special programming for cycle known as Days of Awe.

205. ———, comp. Yom Kippur anthology. Philadelphia: Jewish Pub. Soc., 1971.

Demonstrates meaning of Yom Kippur through interpretations of biblical, talmudic, and midrashic selections; inspirational essays, prayers, modern literature, art, and music.

206. Greenfeld, Howard. Chanukah. New York: Holt, Rinehart and Winston, 1976.

Introduction to history of the great Jewish holiday, called Festival of Lights or Festival of Rededication, which commemorates heroism of the Maccabees, who fought for the right to exercise religious freedom.

207. ———. Passover. New York: Holt, Rinehart and Winston, 1978.

Focuses on Passover as a stirring festival of freedom, with precise explanations of its importance to Jewish people and clear descriptions of how it is celebrated.

208. ———. Rosh Hashanah and Yom Kippur. New York: Holt, Rinehart and Winston, 1979.

Introduction to these two high holy days in Jewish calendar. Clarifies meaning of these intensely religious holidays, which "embody the unique experience and values of being a Jew."

209. Hirsh, Marilyn. The Hanukkah story. New York: Hebrew Pub. Co., 1978.

Simple Chanukah narrative, in full-page illustrations with inserted texts, follows the tyranny of Antiochius IV, who desecrated the Temple, to rebellion of Mattathias and his sons and final victory of the Maccabees under Judah, with brief mention of one-day supply of oil that lasted eight days.

210. ———. Potato pancakes all around; a Hanukkah tale. New York: Hebrew Pub. Co., 1978.

Story of a peddler and his way of making potato pancakes from a crust of bread in celebration of first day of Chanukah; combines an amusing person with a recipe in a traditional setting.

211. Kimmel, Eric A. Nicanor's gate. Philadelphia: Jewish Pub. Soc., 1979.

Memorable story about Nicanor, a prosperous and pious Jew of Alexandria, who exhausted his great wealth to provide doors for Holy of Holies, most sacred part of the Temple in Jerusalem. One door was lost in storm at sea, but was washed ashore and installed (with its companion) in innermost court—known thereafter as Gate of Nicanor.

212. Kustanowitz, Shulamit E., and Foont, Ronnie C. A first Haggadah. New York: Bonim, 1979.

Attractive introduction for children to the Haggadah, which explains meaning of Passover and significance of rituals of the seder, the Passover meal observed by Jews all over the world.

213. Lazar, Wendy. The Jewish holiday book. Garden City, N.Y.: Doubleday, 1977.

Guide to easy handicraft and cooking projects and games appropriate for major Jewish holidays, Shabbat celebration, and Israel's Independence Day. Organized for use by children, with suggestions to parents on ways to adapt ideas recommended for one holiday to another.

214. Lesberg, Sandy. At the table of Israel; a unique collection of three hundred traditional and modern recipes. Indianapolis: Bobbs, 1973.

A cookbook reflecting diversity of Israeli "food culture"; arranged by types of dishes. Useful for planning special menus for Jewish holiday celebrations.

215. Levin, Meyer, adapter. An Israel Haggadah for Passover. Rev. Ed. New York: Abrams, 1977.

Service book in Hebrew (with English translation) designed to lift familiar words spoken at seder to pertinence for the individual and to encourage renewal of traditional spontaneity and joyousness in Passover celebration, with suggestions for enjoying the seder.

216. Metzger, Bruce M. The Oxford annotated Apocrypha. Rev. ed. New York: Oxford, 1977.

Source book for history and meaning of Chanukah, the Festival of Lights and Rededication. Contains all books of Maccabees I, II, III, and IV and Psalm 151, with commentaries.

217. Morrow, Betty. A great miracle; the story of Hanukkah. New York: Harvey House, 1968.

Narrative of overthrow of Syrians by Jewish people 2,000 years ago as background for modern observance of Chanukah.

218. ———, and Hartman, Louis. Jewish holidays. Champaign, Ill.: Garrard, 1966.

Examination of traditions and meaning of major Jewish holidays, demonstrating comparability of spirit of freedom in Jewish and American traditions.

219. Pearlman, Moshe. The Maccabees. New York: Macmillan, 1973.

Illustrated history of Maccabees and their role in firmly establishing identity of the Jewish people; retelling of Chanukah epic of great struggle for religious freedom.

220. Purdy, Susan Gold. Jewish holidays, facts, activities, and crafts. Philadelphia: Lippincott, 1969.

History of Jewish holidays, their origins, and traditional ways of celebration. Each holiday section is followed by suggestions for craft projects, such as greeting cards and decorations, and for preparing programs and food.

221. Raphael, Chaim. A feast of history; Passover through the ages as a key to Jewish experience. New York: Simon & Schuster, 1972.

History of Passover; its rituals, prayers, and songs, with contemporary translation of the Haggadah read at seder meal in commemoration of the exodus from Egypt. Section on preparations for seder. Illustrated in color.

222. Rockland, Mae Shafter. The Jewish party book; a contemporary guide to customs, crafts and foods. New York: Schocken, 1978.

Practical guide to celebration of Jewish holidays and family occasions, such as bar/bat mitzvahs. Variety of ideas and pointers on music, food, crafts, traditional ways and proper rituals. Appendix has Jewish holiday calendar for 5739–5761 (1978–2000), with brief explanations. Indexed.

223. Rosenblum, William F., and Rosenblum, Robert J. The story of Chanukah. Garden City, N.Y.: Doubleday, 1967.

Insights to be gained by people of all faiths in eight-day observance of Jewish Festival of Lights.

224. Rubin, Ruth, ed. Jewish folk songs in Yiddish and English. New York: Oak, 1965.

Wedding songs, ballads, love songs, lullabies, children's songs, work songs, and soldier songs, with English translations.

225. Scharfstein, Edythe, and Scharfstein, Sol. The book of Chanukah. 2d ed. New York: Ktav, 1959.

Short introduction to Chanukah, with "poems, riddles, stories, songs, and things to do."

226. Segal, J.B. The Hebrew Passover, from the earliest times to A.D. 70. London: Oxford, 1963.

Full examination of Passover up to the destruction of the Temple in A.D. 70, from viewpoint of twentieth-century religious research into historical documents and theories.

227. Silverman, Morris, comp. Passover Haggadah. Hartford, Conn.: Prayer Book Press, 1959.

Designed for adult study groups, Passover institutes, and home use; explanations and comments interpolated in text.

228. Simon, Norma. Hanukkah. New York: Crowell, 1966.

Simple interpretation of history, customs, and significance of Chanukah as the Festival of Lights, a symbol of religious freedom.

229. ———. Passover. New York: Crowell, 1955.

Passover explanation of events behind the first Passover and the traditions of commemoration which have been passed down from generation to generation.

230. Singer, Isaac Bashevis. The power of light; eight stories for Hanukkah. New York: Farrar, Straus & Giroux, 1980.
Excellent collection of stories about Chanukah by Singer, one of world's greatest storytellers. For individual enjoyment and/or reading aloud with groups.

231. Snaith, Norman H. The Jewish New Year festival. London: Soc. for Promoting Christian Knowledge, 1947.
A history including the pre-exilic New Year feast, a study of the exile and the change of calendar, and Tishri as the day of memorial, including an interpretation of the benedictions of New Year's Day and description of New Year festivals in Mesopotamia and Syria.

232. Solis-Cohen, Emily, Jr., comp. Hanukkah; the feast of lights. Philadelphia: Jewish Pub. Soc., 1937.
Articles on significance of Chanukah, with section on its commemoration from religious services to a candle drill and a Hanukkah party.

233. Steinkoler, Ronnie. A Jewish cookbook for children. New York: Messner, 1980.
Simple, practical guide to traditional Jewish foods, with explanations of cooking terms and recipes; arranged by holidays with brief introduction to each holiday, indicating special culinary arts and customs observed on a particular holiday.

234. Weil, Lisl. Esther. New York: Atheneum, 1980.
Excellent retelling of the courage of Queen Esther, who saved her people from the plots of Haman, cruel adviser to the king. Background story for feast of Purim, the joyous Jewish festival commemorating Esther's role in deliverance of the Jewish people.

Easter

235. Barth, Edna. Lilies, rabbits, and painted eggs; the story of the Easter symbols. New York: Seabury, 1970.
Explanation of Easter symbols: sunrise, flowers, fire and fireworks, hot cross buns, eggs, lambs, rabbits, colors, bells, chants, and rituals.

236. Benoit, Pierre; Leube, Konrad; and Hagolani, Elhanan, eds. Easter: a pictorial pilgrimage. Nashville: Abingdon, 1970.
Photographic record of holy places associated with Easter, with accompanying text and reproductions of religious art.

237. Coskey, Evelyn. Easter eggs for everyone. Nashville: Abingdon, 1973.
Comprehensive book on the Easter egg: lore, legend, customs, descriptions of dyed eggs, batik process and collage eggs, novelties; concludes with Easter entertainments and egg games. Indexed.

238. Harper, Wilhelmina, comp. Easter chimes; stories for Easter and the spring season. Rev. ed. New York: Dutton, 1965.
Anthology of legends, poems, and stories of Easter and springtime by such authors as Padraic Colum, Marchette Chute, and Hans Christian Andersen.

239. Hartman, Rachel. The joys of Easter. New York: Meredith, 1967.
Essays on significance of the customs of Easter season, concluding with commentary on spiritual values in typical celebrations and in communication through art, spirituals, and hymns. Indexed.

240. Hole, Christina. Easter and its customs. New York: Barrows, 1961.
Review of customs associated with Eastertide, Shrovetide, Mothering Sunday, Good Friday, Easter, Easter Monday, and Hocktide. Indexed.

241. Hopkins, Lee Bennett, sel. Easter buds are springing; poems for Easter. New York: Harcourt Brace Jovanovich, 1979.
Short poems about Easter by fourteen authors, illustrated by Tomie de Paola. Author and title indexes.

242. Lord, Priscilla Sawyer, and Foley, Daniel J. Easter garland. Philadelphia: Chilton, 1963.
Collection of Easter material, ranging from the biblical story and lore of Easter plants to winter demons and Mardi Gras.

243. ———. Easter the world over. Philadelphia: Chilton, 1971.
Comprehensive survey of Easter as it is celebrated from Austria to Wales, Bermuda, the Caribbean, Latin America, the United States, and the Orient, with sections on Easter music and Easter and the fine arts. Indexed.

244. Maier, Paul L. First Easter; the true and unfamiliar story in words and pictures. New York: Harper, 1973.
The scriptural events of Holy Week are examined in light of recent archeological and historical research on religious, social, and political situations during "week that changed the world."

245. Newall, Venetia. An egg at Easter; a folklore study. Bloomington: Indiana Univ. Press, 1971.
Study of folklore and symbolism of decorated eggs and concepts of their use.

246. Newsome, Arden J. Egg craft. New York: Lothrop, 1973.

Guide to becoming an "egger," with detailed advice on materials and tools, special instructions and diagrams for unique decorations, and sources of supply. Indexed.

247. Patterson, Lillie. Easter. Champaign, Ill.: Garrard, 1966.

Simply written account of "Sunday of joy" and traditions of eggs, rabbits, gifts, and greetings which are part of Easter season. Final chapter briefly covers Easter in legend, poetry, and song.

248. Sechrist, Elizabeth Hough, and Woolsey, Janette. It's time for Easter. Philadelphia: Macrae Smith, 1961.

Collection includes gospel story of Easter and sections on Easter customs around the world, as well as legends, music, and poetry. Indexed.

Religious Festivals

249. Ahern, Emily M. The cult of the dead in a Chinese village. Stanford, Calif.: Stanford Univ. Press, 1973.

Ethnographic study of relationships between social organization, religious beliefs, and behavior related to cult of the dead; background material on festivals of the dead.

250. Basche, James. "Phuket." *In his* Thailand; land of the free, pp. 236–45. New York: Taplinger, 1971.

Firsthand impressions of Thai New Year festival, "first plowing" ceremony, Buddhist religious celebrations, Loy Krathong and other religious days.

251. Buell, Hal. Festivals of Japan. New York: Dodd, 1965.

Descriptive sketches of religious and historical celebrations, athletic events, holidays for children, and other *matsuri* (festivals) of Japan. Photographs.

252. Casal, U. A. The five sacred festivals of ancient Japan. Rutland, Vt.: Tuttle, 1967.

Account of symbolism and historical development of five major festivals: New Year festival, girls' festival, boys' festival, star festival, and chrysanthemum festival.

253. Eberhard, Wolfgram. Chinese festivals. New York: Schuman, 1952.

Descriptions of Chinese New Year, dragon boat and seasonal festivals, religious feast of souls, and festivals of the dead.

254. Green, Victor J. Festivals and saints' days. Poole, Dorset, Eng.: Blanford, 1978.

A British review of festival days, religious and secular, including selected Christian, Jewish, Moslem, and Hindu holy days; saints are represented by David, Patrick, George, Cecilia, Andrew, Stephen, and John. Arranged by calendar year. Indexed.

255. Hogg, Garry. Customs and traditions of England. New York: Arco, 1971.

Brief descriptions of religious services and festivals, dances, sports, fairs, and military events; arranged alphabetically by county.

256. Hole, Christina. British folk customs. London: Hutchinson, 1976.

Describes old and new customs related to Candlemas, Plough Sunday (with its blessing of ploughs), Holy Week, Easter and Rogationtide, and Christmas Day and Twelve Days of Christmas. Religious and secular customs arranged alphabetically. Indexed.

257. Lu, Yu. The classic of tea; translated and introduced by Frances Ross Carpenter. Boston: Little, 1974.

First Western-language version of 1,000-year-old interpretation of ritual of tea drinking and its significance as a celebration of life.

258. Marcus, Rebecca B. Fiesta time in Mexico. Champaign, Ill.: Garrard, 1974.

Explanation of Mexican national and religious holidays, beginning with November's Day of the Dead, includes Day of Our Lady of Guadalupe, *posadas* and *piñatas* of Christmas season, Day of the Three Kings, Day of Saint Anthony the Abbot, Holy Week, and Saint John's Day.

259. Milne, Jean. Fiesta time in Latin America. Los Angeles: Ward Ritchie, 1965.

Month-by-month review of new and old religious, civic, and tribal fiestas (fetes) celebrated regularly or irregularly in urban and rural areas of Latin America.

260. More festivals in Asia. Tokyo and New York: Kodansha International, 1975.

Sponsored by Asian Cultural Centre for UNESCO, publication includes descriptions for children of such religious festivals as Eid-ul-Fitr in Pakistan, Lebaran in Indonesia, Hari Raya Puasa in Malaysia, Dasain in Nepal, Diwali Festival of Lights in India, and Loy Krathong in Thailand.

261. Nickerson, Betty. Celebrate the sun; a heritage of festivals interpreted through the art of children from many lands. Philadelphia: Lippincott, 1969.

Collection of children's paintings of seasonal and religious celebrations from thirty-two nations. Texts describe origin and nature of each festival.

262. Palmer, Geoffrey, and Lloyd, Noel. A year of festivals; a guide to British calendar customs. London: Frederick Warne, 1972.

Interpretation of origins of customs and religious rites in modern-day British Isles; begins with May and continues through calendar year. Special sections describe London customs and fairs; also calendar of events by counties.

263. Price, Christine. Talking drums of Africa. New York: Scribners, 1973.

How various drums are made and played in countries of West Africa; includes poems from Nigeria and Ghana to illustrate use of the drum for festivals and religious ceremonials.

264. Seaburg, Carl. Great occasions; readings for the celebration of birth, coming-of-age, marriage, and death. Boston: Beacon, 1968.

Anthology on four major life events: birth, adulthood, marriage, and death, for group or public observances; appendix includes ceremony for adoption, rite for divorce, and memorial service. Indexed by author, first line, and subject.

265. Sykes, Homer. Once a year; some traditional British customs. London: Gordon Fraser, 1977.

Brief descriptions of eighty-one British traditions, secular and religious, which include accounts of Tichborne Dole, Pax Cake Distribution, and other charities established by old wills and still honored by parish churches. Illustrated with black-and-white photographs and arranged by calendar year.

266. Thiselton-Dyer, Thomas Firminger. British popular customs, present and past; illustrating the social and domestic manners of the people. London: G. Bell, 1876; Detroit: Singing Tree Press, 1968.

Book of days, recording old English customs and commemorations; useful for descriptions of religious and secular events in the past.

National Holidays and Civic Days

267. Cordello, Becky Stevens. Celebrations; a unique treasury of holiday ideas featuring recipes, family games . . . . New York: Butterick, 1977.

Originally published in women's magazines from 1835 to 1935; suggestions for twenty-five special occasions, including national holidays, religious days, and traditional days of observance. Indexed.

268. Hatch, Jane M. The American book of days. 3d ed. New York: Wilson, 1978.

Expanded and revised edition of Douglas' *American book of days*. Comprehensive collection provides background material and current information on significant events associated with every day of the year. Excellent material on American national and civic holidays. Arranged by calendar year and indexed.

269. Myers, Robert J., and others. Celebrations; the complete book of American holidays. Garden City, N.Y.: Doubleday, 1972.

History, symbols, and special features of forty-two days celebrated in United States. Includes listing of selected state holidays, commentary on origin of holidays and past and present observances, holy days of major American faiths, federal legal holidays, and local or regional events. Indexed.

270. Quackenbush, Robert, sel. The holiday song book. New York: Lothrop, 1977.

Songs for twenty-seven days celebrated as holidays or days of observance, ranging from election day to Dr. Martin Luther King Jr.'s birthday. Indexed by first line, title, and holiday.

Columbus Day

271. Bradford, Ernie Dusgate Selby. Christopher Columbus. New York: Studio-Viking, 1973.
Re-creation of life of Columbus: his personality, efforts to obtain funds, voyages of discovery, colony administration, and eventual downfall.

272. Divine, David. The opening of the world; the great age of maritime exploration. New York: Putnam, 1973.
Survey of maritime explorations and discoveries from ancient times to sixteenth century, with focus on Prince Henry the Navigator and chronicles on Diaz, da Gama, Magellan, and Columbus.

273. Foster, Genevieve. The world of Columbus and sons. New York: Scribner, 1965.
Account of the world of Christopher Columbus and his sons, Ferdinand and Diego, in the time of Isabella, Gutenberg, Luther, Mohammed II, and other greats of history.

274. Fritz, Jean. Where do you think you're going, Christopher Columbus? New York: Putnam, 1980.
Introduction to Columbus, written for children. Good retelling of the story of his great dream of finding water route to the Indies and the problems stirred up by his enemies.

275. Frye, John. The search for the *Santa Maria*. New York: Dodd, 1973.
Account of underwater search off Cap-Haitien for the *Santa Maria*, in which Columbus voyaged to the New World.

276. Horizon Magazine. Ferdinand and Isabella; by the editors of Horizon Magazine. New York: American Heritage, 1965.
History of Spain of 1492 in the reign of Ferdinand and Isabella, with background material on the queen and her support of the ventures of Christopher Columbus.

277. Meredith, Robert, and Smith, E. Brooks, eds. The quest of Columbus. Boston: Little, 1966.
Account of the discovery of America, based on the writings of Ferdinand, son of Columbus.

278. Morison, Samuel Eliot. Christopher Columbus, mariner. Boston: Little, 1955.
Another version of Morison's *Admiral of the ocean sea*; a study of Columbus as seaman and navigator.

279. Sanderlin, George. Across the ocean sea; a journal of Columbus's voyage. New York: Harper, 1966.
The theories of early explorers about unknown worlds, with description of voyages of Columbus and other mariners; based primarily on journals of Columbus and his son Ferdinand.

Flag Day

280. Barraclough, E. M. C., and Crampton, W. G. Flags of the world. 3d ed. New York: Warne, 1978.
Comprehensive history of the flags that fly on every continent, rewritten to update political changes of the 1970s. Includes national flags and those of subdivisions, such as flags of the fifty states of United States. Separate chapters cover international code of signal flags, flags of merchant ships, and yacht flags. Illustrated in color. Indexed.

281. Furlong, William Rea, and McCandless, Byron. So proudly we hail; the history of the United States flag. Washington, D.C.: Smithsonian Institution Press, 1981.
Handsomely illustrated history of U.S. flag. Definitive study, beginning with flags of nations connected with the exploration and settlement of North America. Main text describes flags of the thirteen colonies and traces the changes in the Stars and Stripes. Appendixes include history of pledge of allegiance, explanation of flag's colors, American Creed, and laws and legal developments regarding the flag. Indexed.

282. Inglefield, Eric. Flags. New York: Arco, 1979.
Compact description of flags of Europe, Asia, Africa, Australia and Oceana, and North, Central, and South America. Brief statements on such topics as emotional power of flags, flags design, and purposes of flags. Illustrated in color. Indexed.

283. Krythe, Maymie R. What so proudly we hail; all about our American flag, monuments, and symbols. New York: Harper, 1968.
Study of such American symbols as the flag, presidential seal, great seal, American eagle, national motto, Liberty Bell, and Independence Hall.

284. Mastai, Boleslaw, and Mastai, Marie-Louise D'Otrange. The Stars and Stripes; the American flag as art and history from the birth of the republic to the present. New York: Knopf, 1973.
Comprehensive, illustrated history of U.S. flag, on land, sea, and on the moon. Descriptions of flag souvenirs, commemorative flags, decorative, political, and patriotic flag functions, and other historic data; also list of official American flags, with stars.

285. Neubecker, Ottfried. A guide to heraldry. New York: McGraw-Hill, 1979.
Interpretive guide to heraldry from age of crowns, helmets, and shields to contemporary use of coats of arms and other heraldic motifs on national flags and seals of governments and universities. Illustrated in full color and indexed.

286. Parrish, Thomas. The American flag. New York: Simon & Schuster, 1973.
History of U.S. flag beginning with placing of flag on the moon in 1969. Looks at the banners that have flown over American soil and discusses events and legends associated with the flag and its changes.

287. Smith, Whitney. Flags and arms across the world. New York: McGraw-Hill, 1980.
Beautifully illustrated guide to the flags and state arms of 174 modern nations, with explanations of significance of colors and symbols, dates of official adoption and hoisting. Includes flags of the fifty U.S. states, United Nations, Red Cross, international signal flags and pennants, and flag index.

288. Talocci, Mauro. Guide to the flags of the world. Rev. ed. New York: Morrow, 1982.
Handbook of flags of the world, geographically arranged to cover all continents and Oceania. Updated text (by Whitney Smith) includes national, state, provincial, and special governmental flags. Glossary defines terms in descriptions of flags. Index.

Fourth of July

289. Booth, Sally Smith. The women of '76. New York: Hastings, 1974.
Account of courage, ingenuity, and contributions of women participants in American Revolution.

290. Brand, Oscar. Songs of '76; a folksinger's history of the revolution. New York: Evans, 1973.
Words and music to Tory and Rebel songs of American Revolution, with commentary on historical and social background of each song.

291. Brewton, Sara Westbrook, and Brewton, John Edmund, comps. America forever new. New York: Crowell, 1968.
Collection of poems with patriotic themes, directed to United States of America. Indexed by author, title, and first line.

292. Cooke, Donald Ewin. Fathers of America's freedom; the story of the signers of the Declaration of Independence. Maplewood, N.J.: Hammond, 1969.
Insight into personal convictions and circumstances of the fifty-six men who signed the Declaration, with followup on their later lives.

293. Emerson, Ralph Waldo. The sound of trumpets. New York: Viking, 1971.
Selections from Emerson's work, illustrated by James Daugherty, expressing personal faith in the goodness of life and in America as the country of the future.

294. Ferris, Robert G., ed. Signers of the Declaration. Rev. ed. Washington, D.C.: U.S. Dept. of the Interior, National Park Service, 1975.
History of Declaration of Independence, with biographical sketches of signers, list of sites and homes associated with signers, and text of the Declaration.

295. Furneaux, Rupert. The pictorial history of the American Revolution as told by eyewitnesses and participants. Chicago: Ferguson, 1973.
Re-creation of events and locations of American Revolution, based on records of the experiences of soldiers and citizens, from Boston Tea Party (December 16, 1773) to Washington's farewell to his troops at Fraunces Tavern (December 4, 1783).

296. Handlin, Oscar. Statue of Liberty. New York: Newsweek, 1971.
Illustrated history of Auguste Bartholdi's Statue of Liberty, conceived as monument to Franco-American friendship and dedicated in New York Harbor July 4, 1886. Chronology of immigration and brief description of colossal statues through the ages.

297. Hatch, Eric. The little book of bells. New York: Duell, 1963.
Brief history of bells, inspired by broadcast of bells ringing across the United States in honor of July 4. A chapter on the Liberty Bell.

298. Hine, Al. This land is mine; an anthology of American verse. Philadelphia: Lippincott, 1965.
Collection of poetry for patriotic occasions that reflects the history of United States, beginning with Philip Frenau's "The Indian Burying Ground" and concluding with Phyllis McGinley's "Star-Spangled Ode." Indexed by author and first line.

299. Ickis, Marguerite. The book of patriotic holidays. New York: Dodd, 1962.

Ideas for patriotic holiday programs, from making a patriotic mural to displaying patriotic collections. Material for specific holidays, such as Flag Day, Fourth of July, and other patriotic days of the United States, and patriotic games and songs, symbols, and facts about the fifty American states.

300. Lomask, Milton. The first American revolution. New York: Farrar, 1974.

History of the American Revolution which challenges some legends and records contributions of blacks.

301. Mitchell, Broadus. The price of independence; a realistic view of the American Revolution. New York: Oxford, 1974.

Insights into civic, governmental-community problems, and alterations in social fabric that resulted from the Revolution.

302. Munves, James. Thomas Jefferson and the Declaration of Independence: the writing and editing of the document that marked the birth of the United States of America. New York: Scribner, 1978.

Account of the writing and editing of Declaration of Independence by Thomas Jefferson between June 18, 1776, and July 4, 1776; includes facsimiles of Jefferson's rough draft, showing changes and deletions. Text is based on Jefferson's notes, journals of Continental Congress, and letters of Jefferson, John Adams, and Benjamin Franklin. Indexed.

303. Murfin, James V. National Park Service guide to the historic places of the American Revolution. Washington, D.C.: U.S. Dept. of the Interior, 1974.

Illustrated guide to national, state, and local historic sites associated with the Revolution, with chronology of political and military events of the period.

304. Rabson, Carolyn. Songbook of the American Revolution. Peaks Island, Me.: NEO, 1974.

Ballads, national songs, and hymns of Rebels and Loyalists in early America: useful for patriotic programming.

305. Randel, William Peirce. The American revolution; mirror of a people. Maplewood, N.J.: Hammond, 1973.

Illustrated description of way of life in American cities and on farms in the year of the Declaration of Independence, combined with history of events that led to independence.

306. Reeder, Red. Bold leaders in the American Revolution. Boston: Little, 1973.

Biographical sketches of twelve men and women of the Revolution, including Thaddeus Kosciuszko, Polish patriot-soldier, whose major concern was freedom for all mankind.

307. Ross, George E. Know your Declaration of Independence and the 56 signers. Chicago: Rand McNally, 1963.

Summary of events that led to signing the Declaration, with concise biographies of signers.

308. Silber, Irwin, ed. Songs of independence. Harrisburg, Pa.: Stackpole, 1973.

Study of earliest patriotic music in United States; ninety-seven songs reflecting the revolutionary spirit in words and tunes of Colonial times.

309. Wright, Esmond. A time for courage; the story of the Declaration of Independence. New York: Putnam, 1971.

Examination of American Revolution from positions of independence taken by Jefferson, Patrick Henry, George Washington, Sam and John Adams, John Hancock, and others.

Martin Luther King Jr.'s Birthday

310. Bennett, Lerone. What manner of man. 3rd rev. ed. Chicago: Johnson, 1968.

Biography of Martin Luther King Jr. points to factors which influenced his development as a leader in civil rights movement and the nation.

311. Brooks, Thomas R. Walls come tumbling down; a history of the civil rights movement—1940–70. Englewood Cliffs, N.J.: Prentice-Hall, 1974.

Thirty years of civil rights movement in United States, including studies of A. Philip Randolph, Martin Luther King Jr., and other leaders.

312. Clayton, Ed. Martin Luther King; the peaceful warrior. 3d ed. Englewood Cliffs, N.J.: Prentice-Hall, 1968.

Short biography, focused on Martin Luther King Jr.'s efforts to achieve equality through nonviolent methods.

313. Faber, Doris, and Faber, Harold. The assassination of Martin Luther King, Jr. New York: Watts, 1978.

Account of life and death of Martin Luther King Jr. (for young readers) begins on assassination day, April 4, 1968. Reviews King's role in civil rights movement and reports on investigations of the assassination. Illustrated with black-and-white photographs. Indexed.

314. Fager, Charles. Selma 1965; the town where the South was changed. New York: Scribners, 1974.

Report on civil rights confrontations in Selma in 1965 and leadership of Martin Luther King, Jr.

315. Haskins, James. The life and death of Martin Luther King, Jr. New York: Lothrop, 1977.

Two-part study of the civil rights leader and Nobel Peace Prize winner. Part 1 covers his early years, preparation for ministry, and his nonviolent leadership role. Part 2 deals with his assassination, its aftermath, and still unanswered questions about the senseless tragedy.

316. King, Coretta Scott. My life with Martin Luther King, Jr. New York: Holt, 1969.

Autobiography of King's widow, with reminiscences and reflections on her marriage to the great black leader.

317. King, Martin Luther, Jr. Strength to love. New York: Harper, 1963.

Collection of King's sermons, concluding with his personal credo, which explains his understanding of Christian faith and way of life.

318. Lincoln, C. Eric, ed. Martin Luther King, Jr.: a profile. New York: Hill & Wang, 1970.

Essays assessing King's philosophy of nonviolence, his response to social problems, and his leadership role.

319. Oates, Stephen B. Let the trumpet sound; the life of Martin Luther King, Jr. New York: Harper, 1982.

Detailed record of King's home background, educational experiences, relationships with associates, and events which molded his philosophy of service to his people and dedication to nonviolence.

320. Schulke, Flip, ed. Martin Luther King, Jr.; a documentary . . . Montgomery to Memphis. New York: Norton, 1976.

Documented material on life and work of Martin Luther King, Jr., with introduction by Coretta Scott King. Includes chronology of important dates in King's life and career and reprints of important speeches and sermons, such as his 1964 Nobel Peace Prize acceptance speech and 1963 "I have a dream" speech at Lincoln Memorial in Washington, D.C.

321. Smith, Kenneth L. and Zepp, Ira G., Jr. Search for the beloved community; the thinking of Martin Luther King, Jr. Valley Forge, Pa.: Judson, 1974.

Examination of King's concepts of social justice and nonviolence, based on theology and ethics of his Christian faith.

322. Wilson, Beth P. Giants for justice; Bethune, Randolph, and King. New York: Harcourt Brace Jovanovich, 1978.

Study of interrelated missions of Mary McLeod Bethune, A. Philip Randolph, and Martin Luther King, Jr., and how they supported each other in a commitment to quality education, job opportunities, and human rights legislation for black America.

Labor Day

323. Biddle, Marcia McKenna. Labor. Minneapolis: Dillon, 1979.

Biographical sketches of five women leaders in labor movement in United States: Mother Jones, union organizer and "miners' angel"; Mary Heaton Vorse, labor reporter; Frances Perkins, U.S. secretary of labor; Addie Wyatt, union spokesperson for blacks and women; and Dolores Huerta, champion of migrant farm workers.

324. Bornstein, Jerry. Union in transition. New York: Messner, 1981.

Account of structures and function of trade unions in United States, beginning with May 26, 1937, conflict between United Auto Workers' Union and guards at Ford Motor Company; includes brief description of unions in other countries. Indexed.

325. Coffin, Tristram Potter, and Cohen, Hennig, ed. and introd. Folklore from the working folk of America. Garden City, N.Y.: Doubleday, 1973.

Anthology of folklore about workers, selected from archives and journals and including tales, proverbs, songs, riddles, and verse.

326. Davis, Daniel S. Mr. Black Labor; the story of A. Philip Randolph, father of the civil rights movement. New York: Dutton, 1972.

Biography of A. Philip Randolph, focused on his lifelong campaign to bring black workers into American trade unions and on his strategy for civil rights action.

327. Haskins, James. The long struggle; the story of American labor. Philadelphia: Westminster, 1976.

History of labor in the United States from Colonial days, when economic situation favored independent laborer, to late twentieth century, characterized by power and problems for organized labor movement. Glossary of labor and union terms, and chronology of events, beginning with 1768 strike of New York Journeyman Tailors. Indexed.

328. Labor on the march; the story of America's unions; by the editors of American Heritage magazine; narrated by Joseph L. Gardner. New York: American Heritage, 1969.

Illustrated history of American labor, beginning with Homestead Strike of 1842, describes earlier and later struggles for fair working conditions and such leaders as Debs, Gompers, and Lewis.

329. Lens, Sidney. The labor wars; from the Molly Maguires to the sitdowns. Garden City, N.Y.: Doubleday, 1973.

Account of battles, issues, and leaders in first three generations of labor movement in United States.

330. Lingenfelter, Richard E. The hardrock miners; a history of the mining labor movement in the American West, 1863–1893. Berkeley: Univ. of California Press, 1974.

History of labor movement, centered on lives, aspirations, and problems of hardrock miners of American West from establishment of first union in 1863 to the federation of hardrock unions in 1893.

331. Lomax, Alan, comp. Hard-hitting songs for hard-hit people; notes on the songs by Woody Guthrie. New York: Oak, 1967.

Ballads and folk songs of longshoremen, miners, farmers, and other groups of American laborers.

332. Meltzer, Milton. Bread—and roses; the struggle of American labor, 1865–1915. New York: Knopf, 1967.

Illustrated history of era of child labor, sweatshops, and company towns, which led to strikes, strikebreakers, and successful labor movement.

333. Myers, Robert J. "Labor day." *In his* Celebrations; the complete book of American holidays, pp. 209–212. Garden City, N.Y.: Doubleday, 1972.

Brief history of Labor Day in United States and of Peter J. McGuire, its founder, with short paragraphs contrasting first Labor Days with modern observances.

334. Pflug, Warner. The U.A.W. in pictures. Detroit: Wayne State Univ. Press, 1971.

Pictorial history of growth and development of automobile workers' union and its leaders.

335. Sandler, Martin W. The way we lived; a photographic record of work in a vanished America. Boston: Little, 1977.

Collection of photographs between 1880 and 1920, when photographers used glass negatives. Visual record, with background text, illustrates jobs and tools of miners, draymen, coopers, stone crushers, firemen, farmers, and other laborers a century ago.

336. Scott, Goeffrey. Labor Day. Minneapolis: Carolrhoda, 1982.

Book for young reader which tells of planning for and celebration of "monster labor festival" on September 5, 1882, in New York City, which sparked the movement to establish Labor Day as national holiday honoring American workers.

337. Schnapper, M. B. American labor; a pictorial social history. Washington, D.C.: Public Affairs, 1972.

Illustrated history of American labor, beginning with typical indenture contract of 1726, through the years to 1972 election. Indexed.

338. Taft, Philip. Defending freedom; American labor and foreign affairs. Los Angeles: Nash, 1974.

Influence of American labor on foreign affairs from World War II to 1971, with focus on labor's opposition to totalitarianism.

Lincoln's Birthday

339. Bullard, Frederic L. Lincoln in marble and bronze. New Brunswick, N.J.: Rutgers Univ. Press, 1952.

Publication of Abraham Lincoln Association, describes sixty-seven Lincoln statues and sites, with details on sponsorship, dedication services, sculptors, and locations of replicas.

340. Davis, Michael. The image of Lincoln in the South. Knoxville: Univ. of Tennessee Press, 1971.

Study of changes in attitudes toward Lincoln from the period preceding Civil War to early twentieth century.

341. Findley, Paul. A. Lincoln, the crucible of Congress. New York: Crown, 1979.

Illustrated study of Lincoln as a congressman in the 1840s, a two-year term during which he formulated his principles on such issues as slavery, economic policies, national entanglement in foreign affairs, and presidential leadership. Indexed.

342. Hamilton, Charles, and Ostendorf, Lloyd. Lincoln in photographs; an album of every known pose. Norman: Univ. of Oklahoma Press, 1963.

One of the most comprehensive compilations of photographs of Lincoln, with informative captions and documentation.

343. Horgan, Paul. Citizen of New Salem. New York: Farrar, 1961.

Biographical essay on Lincoln's young manhood; retelling of the familiar story of the example of Mentor Graham, of reading books, and of life in New Salem.

344. Johnson, James Weldon, and Johnson, J. Rosamond. Lift every voice and sing. New York: Hawthorn, 1970.

Words and music of a song written in 1900 to celebrate Lincoln's birthday; considered to be "black national anthem."

345. Kerner, Fred, comp. A treasury of Lincoln quotations. Garden City, N.Y.: Doubleday, 1965.

Authenticated quotations from Lincoln's writings and self-edited speeches; arranged alphabetically by topics, from abolition to youth. Indexed.

346. Mearns, David Chambers. Largely Lincoln. New York: St. Martin's, 1961.

Collection of essays, nine of which deal with such topics as Lincoln as an inexhaustible story, Lincoln and the image of America, and the "great day in Ottaway" when Douglas and Lincoln met face to face.

347. Miller, Edward, and Mueller, Betty Jean. The halls of Lincoln's greatness. New York: Meredith, 1968.

Photographs, with brief essays, of residences, places, and memorials associated with Lincoln, from Hodgenville, Kentucky, to New Salem and Springfield, Illinois, and Ford's Theatre and Lincoln Memorial in Washington, D.C.

348. Mitgang, Herbert. The fiery trial; a life of Lincoln. New York: Viking, 1974.

Lincoln as a president who found in the Constitution his solutions to problems of states' rights and other issues; text is preceded by a Lincoln chronology and concludes with analysis of Lincoln's image in the world.

349. Neely, Mark E. The Abraham Lincoln encyclopedia. New York: McGraw-Hill, 1982.

Valuable addition to Lincolniana of articles on people, issues, places, and happenings of significance in personal, social, and political life of the sixteenth president.

350. Nevins, Allan, ed. Lincoln and the Gettysburg Address; commemorative papers. Urbana: Univ. of Illinois Press, 1964.

Addresses by specialists on such subjects as Lincoln's religion, Lincoln and the law, and significance of Gettysburg address; authors include Nevins, John Dos Passos, Arthur Goodhart, Reinhold Niebuhr, Robert Lowell, Paul H. Douglas, and David C. Mearns.

351. Sandburg, Carl. Lincoln; the prairie years and the war years. New York: Harcourt, 1970.

Condensation of two-volume *The Prairie Years* and six-volume *The War Years*, biographical studies of Lincoln that achieved great popular acclaim.

352. Sigelschiffer, Saul. The American conscience; the drama of the Lincoln-Douglas debates. New York: Horizon, 1973.

Study of Lincoln–Douglas debates of 1858.

353. Van Doren, Mark. Last days of Lincoln. New York: Hill & Wang, 1959.

Verse play, in six scenes, covering last weeks of Lincoln's life and centered on Civil War president's thinking about such issues as surrender terms for defeated South.

354. Zell, P. M., ed. Abe Lincoln laughing; humorous anecdotes from original sources by and about Abraham Lincoln. Berkeley: Univ. of California Press, 1982.

Reflects wit, humor and down-to-earth wisdom of Lincoln; material by and about the sixteenth president, from the time of an 1835 speech by Lincoln to articles published about Lincoln in 1980. Arranged chronologically with topical and subject indexes.

Memorial Day

355. Goudge, Elizabeth, ed. A book of comfort; an anthology. New York: Coward-McCann, 1964.

Treasury of British and American poetry and prose, selected for inspiration and consolation; sections on the comfort of faith and comfort in tribulation.

356. Greenberg, Sidney, ed. A treasury of comfort. New York: Crown, 1954.

Prose and poetry reflecting heritage of Jewish thought and wisdom on such themes as time as healer, memory as life's afterglow, and faith as strength for the living.

357. Hatch, Jane M. "Memorial day." *In her* The American book of days, pp. 501–4. New York: Wilson, 1978.

Succinct history of Memorial Day in United States, citing several places which have reasonable claim to be "birthplace" of Memorial Day. Text describes first national Memorial Day, May 30, 1868, and subsequent observances on land and at sea, at national cemeteries, in large cities and small towns.

358. Mary Immaculate, Sister, ed. The Cry of Rachel; an anthology of elegies on children. New York: Random House, 1966.
Poems mourning and memorializing children, from sixth century B.C. to 1960s; poets represent six continents and twenty-six nations.

Presidents' Day

359. American Heritage. The American Heritage pictorial history of the presidents of the United States. 2 vols. New York: American Heritage, 1968.
Picture portfolio, with narrative essays on presidents from Washington through Johnson, with brief biographical sketches of their associates. Indexed.

360. Armbruster, Maxim Ethan. The presidents of the United States, and their administrations from Washington to Nixon. 5th ed. New York: Horizon, 1973.
Study of American presidents as individuals and leaders.

361. Boller, Paul F., Jr. Presidential anecdotes. New York: Oxford, 1981.
Entertaining but substantial contribution to American history, with anecdotes, both light and profound, about thirty-nine presidents, beginning with aristocratic Virginian, George Washington, and ending with Ronald Reagan. Arranged chronologically, with presidential anecdotes preceded by personal background resumes. Indexed.

362. Bonnell, John Sutherland. Presidential profiles; religion in the life of American presidents. Philadelphia: Westminster, 1971.
Brief background information on religion in lives and careers of American presidents.

363. Collins, Herbert Ridgeway. Presidents on wheels. Washington, D.C.: Acropolis, 1971.
Illustrated history of vehicles used by American presidents, from Washington's horse-drawn coach to armored cars of contemporary times.

364. Cunliffe, Marcus. American presidents and the presidency. New York: American Heritage, 1972.
Presidency of United States from time of Washington, showing how politics, events, and social fabric affected conduct of the office.

365. Faber, Doris. The presidents' mothers. Rev. ed. New York: St. Martin's, 1978.
Thirty-eight women—mothers of men who became presidents of United States; collective biography with human-interest approach, based on thesis that these women had to be "exceptionally strong characters."

366. Freidel, Frank. Our country's presidents. 14th ed. Washington, D.C.: Nat. Geographic Soc., 1972.
Biographical sketches of the presidents: their contributions, leadership style, and families.

367. Goldberg, Richard Thayer. The making of Franklin D. Roosevelt; triumph over disability. Cambridge, Mass.: Abt, 1982.
Psychotherapist's study of effect of extreme disability (resulting from polio) on Franklin Roosevelt's personality, philosophy, and decisions as governor of New York and president of United States. Also points to Roosevelt's influence on polio research. Indexed.

368. Greenstein, Fred I. The hidden-hand presidency: Eisenhower as leader. New York: Basic Books, 1982.
Interesting analysis of Eisenhower's leadership style; examines his seemingly artless strategies, use of language, refusal to engage in personalities, and selective delegation.

369. Johnson, Richard T. Managing the White House; an intimate study of six presidents. New York: Harper, 1974.
Managerial styles of Presidents Roosevelt, Truman, Eisenhower, Kennedy, Johnson, and Nixon.

370. Jones, Olga. Churches of the presidents in Washington. New York: Exposition, 1961.
Sixteen churches in nation's capital in which presidents have worshiped, from Friends' meeting house to Washington Cathedral.

371. Kane, Joseph Nathan. Facts about the presidents; a compilation of biographical and historical information. 4th ed. New York: Wilson, 1981.
Prime source of information about thirty-nine presidents, from Washington to Reagan. Data on backgrounds, families, elections, important dates in their lives and terms of office. Includes facts about vice presidents, Congress, presidential appointments in each administration, and comparative statistics on presidents. Indexed.

372. Klapthor, Margaret Brown. The first ladies' cook book; favorite recipes of all of the presidents of the United States. Rev. ed. New York: Parents, 1982.

Favorite meals of presidents and their wives from George and Martha Washington to Ronald and Nancy Reagan. Includes recipes, as well as details of "meal functions" and domestic life in the White House during each administration. Indexed.

373. Leish, Kenneth W. The White House. New York: Newsweek, 1972.

History of White House as a symbol of the presidency and home of America's chief executive, with chapters on selected periods, such as Lincoln Years and Teddy Roosevelt era.

374. MacNeil, Neil. The presidents' medal, 1789–1977. New York: Clarkson & Potter, 1977.

Information-packed history of design and production of presidential inaugural medals, from Washington to Jimmy Carter. Published in association with National Portrait Gallery, Smithsonian Institution. Accounts of ceremonies associated with medals. Indexed.

375. Malone, Dumas. Jefferson and his time. Vol. 6: The sage of Monticello. Boston: Little, 1981.

Final volume of a six-volume biography of Thomas Jefferson. *The Sage of Monticello* deals with Jefferson's last years, 1809 to 1826, when he devoted himself to architectural and educational projects, planning the University of Virginia and seeing his private library become nucleus of Library of Congress.

376. Ryan, William, and Guinness, Desmond. The White House; an architectural history. New York: McGraw-Hill, 1980.

Examines documents related to planning, design, construction, and subsequent interior and exterior changes. Illustrated with drawings and period photographs. Indexed.

377. Sinkler, George. The racial attitudes of American presidents, from Abraham Lincoln to Theodore Roosevelt. Garden City, N.Y.: Doubleday, 1971.

Examines writings of ten American presidents (between 1860 and 1908) to determine their attitudes toward southern blacks and other minority groups.

378. Taylor, John M. From the White House inkwell. Rutland, Vt.: Tuttle, 1968.

Black-and-white reproductions of letters and documents signed by presidents from Washington through Johnson.

379. Taylor, Tim. The book of presidents. New York: Arno, 1972.

Facts about presidents of United States, from Washington through Nixon, listing significant events and decisions associated with each; data on vice presidents, cabinets, Supreme Courts, governmental agencies, and families. Arranged chronologically.

380. Truman, Harry. Strictly personal and confidential; the unmailed letters of Harry Truman, Boston: Little, 1982.

Collection of letters drafted by President Truman between 1945 and 1972 but never mailed; letters range from indignant responses to critics to thoughtful opinions on such controversies as use of atomic bomb. Background notes on situations which sparked the letter writing provided by the editor, Monte Poen. Indexed.

Revolution/Independence Days

381. Archer, Jules. African firebrand; Kenyatta of Kenya. New York: Messner, 1969.

Account of Kenya's freedom from British dominion, coupled with biography of Kenyatta, hero of the independence movement.

382. ———. The Philippines' fight for freedom. New York: Crowell, 1970.

Review of Filipinos' struggle to throw off (successively) Spanish, American, and Japanese rule to establish independent nation.

383. Bebler, Anton, ed. Military rule in Africa; Dahomey, Ghana, Sierra Leone, and Mali. New York: Praeger, 1973.

Study of coups d'etats in four West African states and effect of military intervention on life and freedom in each nation.

384. Cornwall, Barbara. The bush rebels; a personal account of black revolt in Africa. New York: Holt, 1972.

Journalist's report on struggle for independence in Mozambique and Portuguese Guinea.

385. Dakin, Douglas. The Greek struggle for independence, 1821–1833. Berkeley; Univ. of California Press, 1973.

Short history of Greek independence movement and events leading to establishment of modern Greek state.

386. Eyck, Frank, comp. The revolutions of 1848–49. New York: Harper, 1972.

Collection of documents on relationships of European revolutions of 1848–49, with focus on France, Germany, Austria, and Italy.

387. Franke, Wolfgang. A century of Chinese revolution. Columbia: Univ. of South Carolina Press, 1970.
Description of Taiping Rebellion, reform movement, Boxer uprising, Republican Revolution of 1911, May 4 movement of 1919, victory and ultimate collapse of Kuomintang, and victory of Chinese Communists.

388. Godechot, Jacques. The taking of the Bastille, July 14th, 1789. New York: Scribner, 1970.
Interpretation of significance of revolutionary movement that resulted in fall of the Bastille, honored each year by French citizens.

389. Goldston, Robert. The Cuban revolution. Indianapolis: Bobbs, 1970.
Chronological history of Cuba, focused on Twenty-sixth of July movement.

390. Hall, Linda B. Alvaro Obregon, power and revolution in Mexico, 1911–1920. College Station: Texas A&M Univ. Press, 1981.
Biography of Obregon, Mexican soldier-hero in 1911 revolution against Diaz; focuses on nine years preceding his presidency and his vision of implementing revolutionary ideal written into the constitution.

391. McFarland, Milton C. Cudjoe of Jamaica; pioneer for black freedom in the New World. Short Hills, N.J.: Ridley Enslow, 1977.
Biography of brilliant eighteenth-century Jamaican leader of fugitive slaves, most important strategist in Maroon wars in West Indies.

392. Merriam, Allen Hayes, Gandhi vs. Jinnah; the debate over the partition of India. Columbia, Mo.: South Asia Books, 1980.
Analysis of 1937–47 debates between Gandhi and Jinnah over Partition issues and problems for establishment of Islamic Republic of Pakistan, which occurred in 1947.

393. Niemeyer, E. V., Jr. Revolution at Queretaro; the Mexican Constitutional Convention of 1916–1917. Austin: Univ. of Texas Press, 1974.
Study of personalities, issues, and developments of convention that gave Mexico the base for its present constitution.

394. Ott, Thomas O. The Haitian revolution, 1789–1804. Knoxville, University of Tennessee Press, 1973.
Concise history of Haitian revolution, 1789 through 1804, and its consequences for the independent nation.

395. Perez-Benero, Alex. Before the five frontiers; Panama from 1821–1903. New York: AMS, 1978.
History of Panama, covering period from the end of colonial era (1821) to independence (1903); provides background for understanding Panama's separation from Colombia. Indexed.

396. Postal, Bernard, and Levy, Henry. And the hills shouted for joy; the day Israel was born. New York: McKay, 1973.
History of events leading to creation of state of Israel. Appendix has biographical sketches of signers of Israel's declaration of independence.

397. Prago, Albert. The revolutions in Spanish America; the independence movements of 1808–1825. New York: Macmillan, 1970.
Independence movements of early 1800s in Latin America.

398. Sterne, Emma Gelders. Benito Juarez; builder of a nation. New York: Knopf, 1967.
History of Mexican struggle for independence, combined with life story of Juarez, "leader of the common man."

399. Wilson, Duncan. Tito's Yugoslavia. New York: Cambridge, 1980.
Introduction to history of Yugoslavia under Tito, with events during World War II and Yugoslavian revolution.

See also: Fourth of July

Thanksgiving Day

400. Barth, Edna. Turkey, Pilgrims, and Indian corn; the story of the Thanksgiving symbols. New York: Seabury, 1975.
History of American Thanksgiving, beginning with Pilgrims and their 1621 harvest festival now called the first Thanksgiving. Easy text that features the symbols of the day: turkey, "Indian Three Sisters: corn, beans, and pumpkins," the crane berry (which became the cranberry), and the "Horn of Plenty." Indexed.

401. Bartlett, Robert Merrill. Thanksgiving day. New York: Crowell, 1965.
Simple explanation of the custom of giving thanks at harvest time, with special attention to Pilgrims and their Thanksgiving celebrations of 1621 and 1623.

402. Colby, Jean Poindexter. Plimouth plantation, then and now. New York: Hastings, 1970.
Background material on Pilgrims, correlated with information on Plimouth Plantation (recreation of original Pilgrim settlement), and brief statement on the First Thanksgiving. Indexed.

403. Cowie, Leonard W. The Pilgrim fathers. New York: Putnam, 1972.
Brief notes on first harvest and thanksgiving in a history of the Pilgrims in England, Holland, and Plymouth colony.

404. Dalgliesh, Alice. The Thanksgiving story. New York: Scribner 1954.
Classic interpretation of the meaning of Thanksgiving through a story of first Thanksgiving in America. Illustrated in "autumn colors."

405. Harper, Wilhelmina, comp. The Harvest feast; stories of Thanksgiving, yesterday and today. Rev. ed. New York: Dutton, 1965.
Stories of the First Thanksgiving and Thanksgivings of twentieth century, from books by Dorothy Canfield Fisher, Carl Sandburg, Elizabeth Coatsworth, and others.

406. Hopkins, Lee Bennett, sel. Merrily comes our harvest in; poems for Thanksgiving. New York: Harcourt Brace Jovanovich, 1978.
Collection of poems about Thanksgiving by well-known writers and poets, including (among others) Dorothy Aldis, Marchette Chute, Robert Graves, Ivy Eastwick, and Myra Cohen Livingston. Indexed.

407. Luckhardt, Mildred C., comp. Thanksgiving; feast and festival. Nashville; Abingdon, 1966.
Anthology of poetry, stories, and essays about Thanksgiving and harvest festival observances, with information on customs.

408. Sechrist, Elizabeth H., ed. It's time for Thanksgiving. Philadelphia: Macrae Smith, 1957.
Stories, poems, plays, recipes, and games for Thanksgiving season, and history of Thanksgiving Day.

409. Weisgard, Leonard. The first Thanksgiving. Garden City, N.Y.: Doubleday, 1967.
Attractively illustrated interpretation of Pilgrims and events leading to First Thanksgiving; based on old-style calendar dates and William Bradford's diary.

Veterans' Day

410. Berry, Henry. Semper fi, Mac; living memories of the U.S. marines in World War II. New York: Arbor, 1982.
Experiences of U.S. marines in Pacific during World War II, based on interviews. Book proves "there is no such thing as a ex-marine."

411. Essame, H. The battle for Europe, 1918. New York: Scribners, 1972.
British view of last year of first World War; credits Allied victory to courage and spirit of the ordinary soldier, who is honored on Veterans' Day.

412. Greene, Robert E. Black defenders of America, 1775–1973; a reference and pictorial history. Chicago: Johnson, 1974.
Biographical sketches of blacks who fought in wars, from Revolution to Vietnam; arranged by war. Indexed.

413. Herring, George C. America's longest war; the United States and Vietnam, 1950–1975. New York: Wiley, 1975.
History of U.S. involvement in Vietnam, the most unpopular war in American history. The killed and missing in action are honored, with veterans of other wars, on Veterans' Day.

414. MacCloskey, Monro. Hallowed ground; our national cemeteries. New York: Richards Rosen, 1968.
Development of National Cemetery system from 1862; national and overseas cemeteries and memorials, with separate chapters on Arlington and the Tomb of Unknowns.

415. Meyer, Frank S., ed. Breathes there the man; heroic ballads of the English-speaking peoples. La Salle, Ill.: Open Court, 1973.
Ballads and lyrics chosen from four centuries of English verse. Section on American poetry includes McCrae's "In Flanders Fields" and other poems appropriate for Veterans' Day.

416. Middlebrook, Martin. The first day on the Somme, 1 July 1916. New York: Norton, 1972.
History of tragic battle of Somme evokes courage of the ordinary soldier in World War I.

417. Prange, Gordon W.; Goldstein, Donald M.; Dillon, Katherine V. Miracle at Midway. New York: McGraw-Hill, 1982.
Outstanding history of June 1942 battle of Midway analyzes American strategies and Japanese weaknesses which led to humiliating defeat of Japanese fleet and to end of war in Pacific. Based on official documents and interviews with American and Japanese survivors.

418. Sulzberger, C. L. World War II. New York: American Heritage, 1970.
Abridged version of American Heritage picture history of World War II, providing overview of war from Hitler era to Japanese surrender in 1945.

Washington's Birthday

419. Billias, George A. George Washington's generals. New York: Morrow, 1964.
Essays examine careers of most important Continental Army commanders (including Lafayette) who were associated with Washington in major capacities or campaigns.

420. Bourne, Miriam Anne. First family; George Washington and his intimate relations. New York: Norton, 1982.
A look at George Washington, concerned with welfare of his mother, wife, siblings, nieces and nephews, stepchildren and grandchildren. This popular study is based on, and includes, excerpts from family correspondence and memoirs.

421. Busch, Noel P. Winter quarters; Washington and the Continental Army at Valley Forge. New York: Liveright, 1974.
Account of winter of 1777–78 at Washington's quarters.

422. Callahan, North. George Washington; soldier and man. New York: Morrow, 1971.
Concise biography of Washington, with major focus on his years as commander in chief of Revolutionary forces.

423. Fleming, Thomas J. First in their hearts; a biography of George Washington. New York: Norton, 1968.
Washington as young man, surveyor, soldier, husband, businessman, and president.

424. Flexner, James Thomas. George Washington; anguish and farewell. Boston: Little, 1972.
Last in a four-volume biography, examines Washington's second term in office and his retirement. Definitive biography of America's first president.

425. Freidel, Frank, and Aikman, Lonnelle. George Washington; man and monument. Washington, D.C.: Washington National Monument Association, 1965.
Brief review of life of Washington and history of Washington Monument and events associated with it since laying of cornerstone July 4, 1848.

426. Heusser, Albert H. George Washington's map maker. New Brunswick, N.J.: Rutgers Univ. Press, 1966.
Study of Robert Erskine, surveyor-general of Continental Army whose knowledge and maps helped Washington outmaneuver the British.

427. Ketchum, Richard M. The winter soldiers. Garden City, N.Y.: Doubleday, 1973.
Washington's army from autumn of 1776 to spring of 1777, with brief accounts of his generals, their shortcomings, and talents.

428. McDonald, Forrest. The presidency of George Washington. Lawrence: Univ. Press of Kansas, 1974.
Study of the first president, his influence on symbolic qualities of the office, and achievements of his administration.

429. Wright, Esmond. Washington; the man and the myth. Edinburgh: Oliver & Boyd, 1967.
British view of Washington as a leader of men and assessment of the legends that surround him.

Days of Observance

Arbor Day

430. Cowle, Jerry. Discover the trees. New York: Sterling, 1977.
Children's introduction to trees; facts about trees, suggestions on things to look for and do in the woods, and seven trees which live in history, such as Washington elm (where Washington took command of Continental Army). Indexed.

431. Droze, Wilmon Henry. Trees, prairies and people; a history of tree planting in the Plains States. Denton: Texas Woman's Univ. Bookstore, 1977.
History of Prairie States forestry project, initiated by President Franklin Roosevelt as a scientific program of tree planting to alleviate effects of dust storms in Midwest and to aid states suffering from drought and the Depression.

432. Earle, Olive L. State trees. rev. ed. New York: Morrow, 1973.
Account and description of trees which have been chosen as "official trees" by U.S. states.

433. Hora, Bayard, ed. The Oxford encyclopedia of trees of the world. New York: Oxford, 1981.
Outstanding encyclopedia; illustrated with art work and color photographs, and descriptions and information on trees of every kind. World map indicates distribution of trees. Indexes of common and Latin names.

434. Jackson, James P. Pulse of the forest; a guide to the vitality and variety of life in our broadleaf woodlands. Washington, D.C.: American Forestry Association, 1980.
Attributes of hardwoods of eastern and central United States within forest community; color photography underscores characteristics and beauty of hardwoods and forest life in each of the four seasons.

435. Leathart, Scott. Trees of the world. New York: A&W, 1977.
Comprehensive study of trees of the world, illustrated with photographs. Indexed.

436. Menninger, Karl. "Trees are forever— we hope." Morton Arboretum Quarterly 9, no. 1 (Spring 1973): 7–9.
Statement by well-known psychiatrist and author on the meaning of Arbor Day and its significance for all mankind.

437. Phillips, Roger. Trees of North America and Europe. New York: Random House, 1978.
Guide to identification of native trees, hybrids, and cultivars of North America and Europe, illustrated with beautiful color plates of leaves, bark, details of flowers and fruits, and habitat drawings; leaf-key index, information on common and scientific names, native countries, and other details of interest to laypersons.

438. Randall, Janet. To save a tree; the story of the coast redwoods. New York: McKay, 1971.
The California redwoods from prehistoric times to creation of Redwood National Park in 1968, and subsequent efforts to preserve additional redwood acreage.

439. Roberts, Martha McMillan. Public gardens and arboretums of the United States. New York: Holt, 1962.
Illustrated introduction, including Morton Arboretum at Lisle, Illinois, established by J. Sterling Morton, originator of Arbor Day.

440. Stone, Christopher D. Should trees have standing? Toward legal rights for natural objects. Los Altos, Calif.: William Kaufmann, 1974.
Development of a concept that trees and other natural resources might be legally represented in court by organizations or groups; based on a California court case involving the Sierra Club.

Armed Forces Day

441. American Medal of Honor recipients; complete official citations. Golden Valley, Minn.: Higland, 1980.
Historical background and documentation of awards, arranged by war, campaign, conflict, or era, beginning with Vietnam and going back to the Civil War. Lists recipients by state (as well as foreign-born recipients), and alphabetical list of recipients.

442. Berg, Fred Anderson. Encyclopedia of Continental Army units—battalions, regiments, and independent corps. Harrisburg, Pa.: Stackpole, 1972.
Concise history of each unit in Continental Army, militia, and state troops.

443. Casewit, Curtis W. The saga of the mountain soldiers; the story of the 10th Mountain Division. New York: Messner, 1981.

Account of division's mission to destroy units of German army in Italy in World War II, as well as training in Colorado mountains, military skills and mountaineering, and battlefield experiences.

444. Dupuy, R. Ernest. The compact history of the United States Army. 2d ed. rev. New York: Hawthorn, 1973.

History, organization, administration, and development of U.S. army, with short accounts of important battles.

445. Greene, Robert Ewell. Black defenders of America, 1775–1973. Chicago: Johnson, 1974.

Pictorial history documents service records of black men and women in armed forces in ten wars, from American Revolution to Vietnam. Appendix notes contributions and "milestones" in black military history.

446. Gurney, Gene. The United States Coast Guard. New York: Crown, 1973.

Illustrated history from its beginning in 1790 (as revenue fleet) to current global responsibilities as guardian of maritime safety, ocean stations, and pollution control. Reproductions of insignia and cap devices.

447. Heinl, Robert Debs, Jr. Dictionary of military and naval quotations. Annapolis, Md.: U.S. Naval Institute, 1966.

On traditions, personalities, and participants in military and naval services, and modes of war on land, sea, and in air. Arranged alphabetically by topic.

448. Huston, James A. Out of the blue; U.S. Army airborne operations in World War II. West Lafayette, Ind.: Purdue Univ. Studies, 1972.

Comprehensive study of army parachute and glider experience from late 1930s to 1945 and contributions of airborne operations to allied victory.

449. Kerrigan, Evans E. American war medals and decorations. New York: Viking, 1971.

Military award insignia from Revolution to Vietnam; includes NASA awards.

450. McKay, Ernest A. Carrier strike force; Pacific air combat in World War II. New York: Messner, 1981.

History of U.S. aircraft carriers from Pearl Harbor to end of World War II, with primary focus on 1943–45, when highly trained pilots, military strategy, and skilled maneuvers made carriers one of most important assets in Pacific war.

451. Martin, Tyrone G. A most fortunate ship; a narrative history of "Old Ironsides." Chester, Conn.: Globe Pequot, 1980.

History of "Old Ironsides," symbol of spirit of Navy, recounts frigate's days of action as man-of-war, service as training vessel, and status national treasure.

452. Miller, Nathan. Sea of glory; the Continental Navy fights for independence. New York: McKay, 1974.

All aspects of naval war, with eighteenth-century shipbuilding, privateering, life of seamen, and roles of John Paul Jones, John Barry, and other "naval patriots."

453. ———. The U.S. navy; an illustrated history. New York: American Heritage/Naval Institute Press, 1977.

Well-illustrated history covers 200 years of duty in war and peace, from establishment of navy in 1776 through 1976.

454. Millett, Allan Reed. Semper fidelis; history of the United States Marine Corps. New York: Free Press, 1980.

History of corps from establishment as guardian of navy ships during American Revolution to twentieth-century status as assault force and "ready unit"; includes accounts of corps in action and those who made marine history. Indexed.

455. Mollo, Andrew. The armed forces of World War II; uniforms, insignia and organization. New York: Crown, 1981.

Descriptions of design and detail of uniforms and insignia of various units of armed forces of all nations, large and small, in World War II; 350 full-color illustrations.

456. North, Rene. Military uniforms, 1686–1918. New York: Grosset, 1970.

Illustrated guide to campaign and dress uniforms of American and European soldiers.

457. Reynolds, Clark G. The fast carriers; the forging of an air navy. New York: McGraw-Hill, 1968.

Establishment of fleet of aircraft carriers in U.S. navy, carriers' record in World War II; appendixes include dates of commissioning.

458. Robles, Philip K. Unites States military medals and ribbons. Rutland, Vt.: Tuttle, 1971.

History and description, with data on origin, purpose, rank.

459. Sweetman, Jack. The U.S. naval academy; an illustrated history. Annapolis, Md.: U.S. Naval Institute, 1979.
Popular history from time of its establishment (1845); developments and changes recorded in blend of historic facts and anecdotes.

460. Tunney, Christopher. Biographical dictionary of World War II. New York: St. Martin's, 1972.
Brief biographies of soldiers, sailors, airmen, secret agents, politicians, propagandists, entertainers, journalists, and poets in World War II. Arranged alphabetically.

461. United States. Navy. U.S. Navy war photographs: Pearl Harbor to Tokyo Bay. Ed. by Edward Steichen, text by Tom Maloney. New York: Crown, 1980.
Remarkable photographs, taken from aircraft carriers, battleships, and beaches. Includes tribute to Steichen, who directed navy's photography unit.

462. Utley, Robert M. Frontier regulars; the United States Army. New York: Macmillan, 1974.
Army's contribution to national expansion, centered on life of frontier soldier, military leadership, and Indian problems in post–Civil War period.

463. Walsh, John E. Night on fire, the first complete account of John Paul Jones's greatest battle. New York: McGraw-Hill, 1978.
Decisive sea battle between Revolutionary naval vessel, *Bonhomme Richard*, and British frigate, *Serapis*; based on log entries and documents to underscore Jones's successful battle strategy.

Aviation Day

464. Angelucci, Enzo. Airplanes; from the dawn of flight to the present date. New York: McGraw-Hill, 1973.
Well-illustrated survey of historic and contemporary aircraft, with important dates, designers, and data on size, characteristics, and performance.

465. Freudenthal, Elsbeth Estelle. Flight into history; the Wright brothers and the air age. Norman; Univ. of Oklahoma Press, 1949.
Study of Orville and Wilbur Wright evaluates their major contribution to aviation history and their debt to Octave Chanute, pioneer glider experimenter.

466. Glines, Carroll V., Jr. The compact history of the United States Air Force, ed. by James Gilbert. New York: Arno, 1979.
From first successful balloon ascension (1783) to sophisticated aircraft of today's air force.

467. Green, William. The warplanes of the Third Reich. Garden City, N.Y.: Doubleday, 1970.
Appraises each type of warplane developed in Germany between 1933 and 1945 and relates them to rise and fall of Luftwaffe.

468. Harris, Sherwood. The first to fly; aviation's pioneer days. New York: Simon & Schuster, 1970.
Experiences of pioneer pilots, beginning with Dr. Samuel Langley in 1900 and concluding with death of Lincoln Beachey in 1915.

469. Hart, Clive. The dream of flight; aeronautics from classical times to the Renaissance. New York: Winchester, 1973.
Man's initial concepts of flight and early experiments with kites, windmills, rockets, ornithopters, and other devices; covers period 400 B.C.–A.D. 1600.

470. Hayman, LeRoy. Aces, heroes and daredevils of the air. New York: Messner, 1981.
Introduction to aviation heroes: Charles Lindbergh, Eddie Rickenbacker, Wiley Post, Amelia Earhart, Pappy Boyington, Billy Mitchell, Red Baron, and others; biographical sketches point to courage and skill of individuals who made aviation history from time of Wright brothers' flight in 1903 to dropping of atomic bomb in Japan in 1945.

471. Holliday, Joe. Mosquito! The wooden wonder aircraft of World War II. Garden City, N.Y.: Doubleday, 1970.
History of "most versatile" aircraft of World War II, including its achievements, anecdotes, and biographies of pilots and technicians.

472. King, Horace Frederick. Milestones of the air. New York: McGraw-Hill, 1969.
Descriptions of 100 significant aircraft representing important steps in aviation since "Wright Flyer" flew on December 17, 1903; honors diamond jubilee of Jane's *All the World's Aircraft*.

473. Lindbergh, Charles A. The spirit of St. Louis. New York: Scribner, 1953.
Lindbergh's story of first solo transatlantic flight, New York to Paris; appendix includes log of the flight and reproductions of headlines from world press.

474. Smith, Elinor. Aviatrix. New York: Harcourt Brace Jovanovich, 1981.

Memoirs of Elinor Smith, named "best woman pilot" in 1930; personal record of testing 158 models of aircraft and setting altitude and endurance records. Includes commentaries on great flyers: Lindbergh, Bert Acosta, Amelia Earhart, Lady Mary Heath, Louise Thaden.

475. Taylor, Michael J. H., and Taylor, John W. R., eds. Encyclopedia of aircraft. New York: Putnam, 1978.

Comprehensive encyclopedia (with descriptions) of 244 of more than 35,000 aircraft during enterprising periods of aviation history; focus is on most significant aircraft (many illustrations in color). Indexed.

476. Wright, Wilbur, and Wright, Orville. Miracle at Kitty Hawk. Ed. by Fred C. Kelly. New York: Farrar, 1951.

Selections from letters of Wright brothers (1881–1946) reveal their personalities and tell of their experiments with aeronautical problems, achievements, litigations, and commercial negotiations. Arranged chronologically.

Bird Day

477. Anderson, John M. The changing world of birds. New York: Hold, 1973.

Environmental approach to ornithology; covers adaptability of birds, their life cycles, and mortality rates.

478. Berger, Andrew. Hawaiian birdlife. Honolulu: Univ. Press of Hawaii, 1972.

Survey of birds of Hawaiian Islands, including Leeward Islands, with emphasis on conservation.

479. Choate, Ernest A. A dictionary of American bird names. Boston: Gambit, 1973.

Common and scientific names for birds, with essays on origin and meaning. Appendix has information on European and American namers of birds.

480. Gruson, Edward S. Words for birds; a lexicon of North American birds with biographical notes. Chicago: Quadrangle, 1972.

Scholarly study provides etymologies of common names of birds in North America, translates scientific names, and tells of people for whom birds are named.

481. Haley, Neale. Birds for pets and pleasure. New York: Delacorte, 1981.

Practical guide on care and feeding of birds and advice on traveling *with* birds, based on personal experience and observations. Appendix has instructions for building an aviary.

482. Halliday, Tim. Vanishing birds; their natural history and conservation. New York: Holt, Rinehart and Winston, 1978.

Book for conservationists, examines problem of endangered birds; also, study of natural history of birds, relationship of birds and humans, tragedy of extinct species, and importance of conserving endangered birds. Indexed.

483. Hartshorne, Charles. Born to sing; an interpretation and world survey of bird song. Bloomington: Indiana Univ. Press, 1973.

Comprehensive study of function and significance of bird songs of species from all over the world. Indexed.

484. Kress, Stephen W. The Audubon Society handbook for birders. New York: Scribner, 1981.

Practical guide for bird watchers, with recommendations on observation techniques, suggestions on notetaking for personal records, photography, sketching, and recording bird songs and sounds. Appendixes list sources of birder equipment and publications from natural resource agencies.

485. Leahy, Christopher. The birdwatcher's companion, an encyclopedic handbook of North American birdlife. New York: Hill & Wang, 1982.

Comprehensive handbook of North American birds. In addition to essays on birds and their habits, lists common names, explains terms in bird watching, and provides information on good bird-watching localities and ornithological organizations. Alphabetically arranged.

486. McElroy, Thomas P. The habitat guide to birding. New York: Knopf, 1974.

Bird watcher's guide to species and field techniques, and nature lore which relates birds to environments.

487. Murton, R. K. Man and birds. New York: Taplinger, 1974.

Study of interrelationships between humans and birds in technological society, with analysis of wildlife management.

488. Peterson, Roger Tory. The birds. New York: Time, 1967.

Overview of bird life: migration, conservation, habits and protective devices, language of birds, oddities, and adaptations.

489. Richert, Jon E., ed. A guide to North American bird clubs. Elizabethtown, Ky.: Avian, 1978.
Handbook on bird clubs in fifty states of United States and provinces of Canada; location of clubs in each area, meeting schedules, and individuals to contact for reports, publications, or information on field trips.

490. Schutz, Walter E. How to attract, house, and feed birds. Rev. ed. Milwaukee: Bruce, 1970.
Bird watching as hobby, with information on feeds, nesting accommodations, water supplies, and shelters.

491. Simon, Hilda. Bird and flower emblems of the United States. New York: Dodd, 1978.
Alphabetically arranged summary for young readers of birds and flowers selected as state emblems in United States; includes reasons for selections. Introduction reviews use of bird and flower symbols throughout history.

492. Terres, John K. The Audubon Society encyclopedia of North American birds. New York: Knopf, 1980.
Beautifully illustrated encyclopedia of birds of North America, including Alaska, Canada, Greenland, contiguous forty-eight states, Baja California, and Bermuda. Defines ornithological terms, provides information on seventy-eight bird families, and brief biographies of 126 naturalists. Arranged alphabetically.

Halloween/Houdini Day

493. Barth, Edna. Witches, pumpkins, and grinning ghosts; the story of the Halloween symbols. New York: Seabury, 1972.
Symbols of Halloween from ancient Britain to modern times; for young readers.

494. Brewton, John E., comp. In the witch's kitchen; poems for Halloween. New York: Crowell, 1980.
Traditional and modern verses for the ghoulish season. Rhythmic lines and twisted words in modern poems enhance the fun of such Halloween images as ghosts, skeletons, jack-o-lanterns, and witches.

495. Christian, Roy. Ghosts and legends. North Pomfret, Vt.: David & Charles, 1973.
British historical legends and ghostly tales connected with places such as Glastonbury and people like Ann Boleyn.

496. Christopher, Milbourne. Houdini; the untold story. New York: Crowell, 1969.
Character, personality, and career of the celebrated magician whose birthday is observed on Halloween.

497. ———. The illustrated history of magic. New York: Crowell, 1973.
From time of Egyptian sorcerer-priests to Houdini, Blackstone, and Dunninger; includes chapter on American Indian magic.

498. Cox, Marcia Lynn. Creature costumes. New York: Grosset, 1977.
For making monster costumes for children out of inexpensive and accessible materials; imaginative aid for preparing for Halloween.

499. Coxe, Antony H. Haunted Britain; a guide to supernatural sites frequented by ghosts, witches, poltergeists, and other mysterious beings. New York: McGraw-Hill, 1973.
Guide to places in England, Scotland, Wales, and Isle of Man where ghostly and other supernatural manifestations occur.

500. Cuyler, Margery. The all-around pumpkin book. New York: Holt, Rinehart & Winston, 1980.
Introduction to pumpkin: its uses throughout history, pumpkin festivals in Illinois, and folk yarn about origin of jack-o-lantern; direction for carving and painting pumpkins, recipes and directions for "pumpkin cooks," and party ideas for Halloween (including pumpkin jokes).

501. Dobrin, Arnold. Make a witch, make a goblin; a book of Halloween crafts. Englewood Cliffs, N.J.: Four Winds, 1977.
Craft book, with directions for making Halloween costumes, disguises, scarecrows, jack-o-lanterns, trick-and-treat bags, black-cat bookmarks, and party decorations. Also a section on preparing Halloween party food.

502. Fitzsimmons, Raymund. Death and the magician; the mystery of Houdini. New York: Atheneum, 1981.
Explains some tricks made famous by the master escape artist and examines his interest in supernatural.

503. Gresham, William Lindsay. Houdini, the man who walked through the walls. New York: Holt, 1959.
Houdini's career as magician and crusader against fakery, and explanation of some of his magic.

504. Harper, Wilhelmina, comp. Ghosts and goblins; stories for Halloween. Rev. ed. New York: Dutton, 1965.
Folklore from different countries.

505. Hoffman, Phyllis. Happy Halloween! New York: Atheneum Aladdin, 1982.
Idea book for Halloween, directed toward interests of small children; includes short history of Halloween and directions for making costumes and masks and preparing Halloween fare. Encourages adult involvement and emphasizes safety.

506. Hoke, Helen, sel. Horrors, horrors, horrors. New York: Watts, 1978.
Anthology of chilling tales, of particular interest at Halloween, by such authors as Ray Bradbury, August Derleth, E. F. Benson, Betty Ren Wright, Mary Barrett, Mary Danbury, and Theodore Sturgeon.

507. ———, comp. Sinister, strange and supernatural. New York: Elsevier/Nelson, 1981.
Ten tales of the macabre, the strange, and the suspenseful for personal reading and sophisticated Halloween storytelling; authors range from H. P. Lovecraft and Algeron Blackwood to Jean Stubbs and Ray Bradbury.

508. Hopkins, Lee Bennett, comp. Hey-how for Halloween! Poems. New York: Harcourt, 1974.
Halloween poems for personal reading, storytelling hours, and reading aloud.

509. ———, sel. Witching time; mischievous stories and poems. Chicago: Whitman, 1977.
Short stories and poems about witches for young readers; classical and modern selections, concluding with Shakespeare's "witches chant."

510. Kaye, Marvin. The Stein and Day handbook of magic. New York: Stein & Day, 1973.
For beginning magic entertainer, with descriptions and instructions for over eighty tricks. Has section on entertaining children, the hospitalized, and others.

511. Leach, Maria. Whistle in the graveyard; folktales to chill your bones. New York: Viking, 1974.
Tales for Halloween; includes White House ghosts, Anne Boleyn, treasure ghosts, bogeys and bugaboos, ghostly things, witch lore, and fakes.

512. Linton, Ralph, and Linton, Adeline. Halloween through twenty centuries. New York: Schuman, 1950.
Halloween in relation to All Hallows' and All Souls' days, folk beliefs, witchcraft in Europe and New England, and the custom of trick or treat.

513. Marks, Burton, and Marks, Rita. The spook book. New York: Lothrop, 1981.
Halloween idea book suggests building "vampire's castle" for a party; directions for making a haunted house, props and special sound effects, and devilish decorations, ghoulish goodies, and eerie entertainment.

514. Purdy, Susan Gold. Halloween cookbook. New York: Watts, 1977.
Colorfully illustrated guide for young cooks interested in Halloween meals, treats, and sweets. Book of recipes and directions, with standard and metric measurements, for planning and producing lunch, brunch, and edible decorations. Indexed.

515. Roach, Marilynne K. Encounters with the invisible world; being ten tales of ghosts, witches, and the devil himself in New England. New York: Crowell, 1977.
Ghost stories based on New England folk tales with legends linked to historical events. Several stories in this excellent collection are called "literary inventions."

516. Roberts, Nancy. Appalachian ghosts. Garden City, N.Y.: Doubleday, 1978.
Ghost stories from Applachian mountain country; interest-holding tales whose settings range from haunted copper mine to lonely road used by phantom wagon train.

517. Schwartz, Alvin, comp. Scary stories to tell in the dark; collected from American folklore. New York: Lippincott, 1981.
Appropriately illustrated collection of scary tales for personal reading and storytelling sessions. Grouped by traditional ghost stories, modern tales, and "chillers." Selections are documented as to source in American folklore.

518. Wallace, Daisy, ed. Witch poems. New York: Holiday, 1976.
Eighteen poems about witches; authors range from William Shakespeare to E. E. Cummings, Eleanor Farjeon, and other twentieth-century writers. Illustrated with black-and-white drawings by Trina Schart Hyman.

Mother's Day

519. Fremantle, Anne, ed. Mothers; a Catholic treasury of great stories. New York: Daye, 1951.
Anthology of prose, with some poems, in tribute to mothers. Authors are representative of various nations and range in time from Saint Augustine to W. H. Auden and Charles Peguy.

520. Hatch, Jane M., ed. "Mother's day." *In her* The American book of days, pp. 439–40. New York: Wilson, 1978.
Details origin of Mother's Day, with material on Anna Jarvis, the person most responsible for establishment of the day. Brief descriptions of contemporary observances.

521. Lifshin, Lyn, ed. Tangled vines; a collection of mother and daughter poems. Boston: Beacon, 1978
Poems from forty contributors, selected for range of feelings that characterize relationship of mother and daughter.

522. Phelan, Mary Kay. Mother's day. New York: Crowell, 1965.
Simply written, short introduction to history of Mother's Day, from myths and festivities of ancient world to spread of the idea from the United States to other parts of the world.

523. Phelps, William Lyon. The mother's anthology. Garden City, N.Y.: Doubleday, 1940.
Prose and poetry expressing sentiments for and memories of mothers; authors range through generations, from William Blake to Pearl Buck.

524. Spellman, John W., ed. "Mother's day." *In his* The beautiful blue jay and other tales of India, pp. 26–27. Boston: Little, 1967.
Explains the fast observed by many mothers in Maharashtra State on the last day of the month of Shravana.

Native American Day

525. Belting, Natalia. Our fathers had powerful songs. New York: Dutton, 1974.
Anthology of free-verse poems expressing beliefs of several western and southwestern tribes of United States; poems are related to ceremonials of mourning, healing, and communal activities.

526. Bierhorst, John, ed. In the trail of the wind; American Indian poems and ritual orations. New York: Farrar, 1971.
Collection of prayers, incantations, song texts, myths, and legends reflecting tribal beliefs of American Indians. Arranged by theme.

527. ———, comp. Songs of the Chippewa, adapted from the collections of Frances Densmore and Henry Rowe Schoolcraft, New York: Farrar, 1974.
Ritual chants, dream songs, medicine charms, and lullabies of Chippewa Indians; translated for solo or group singing, with piano and guitar arrangements.

528. Broder, Patricia Janis. Hopi painting; the world of the Hopis. New York: Dutton, 1978.
Study of traditional and contemporary art of Hopi Indians of America's Southwest, with biographical detail and fine plates and illustrations.

529. Feest, Christian F. Native arts of North America. New York: Oxford, 1980.
North American Indian arts and crafts "categorized into tribal, ethnic, pan-Indian and Indian mainstream"; includes interpretation of regional styles of art forms, such as textiles, paintings, and sculpture. Indexed.

530. Frederickson, Joye N., and Gibb, Sandra. The covenant chain; Indian ceremonial and trade silver. Chicago: Univ. of Chicago Press, 1980.
Study of Indian trade and ceremonial silver as part of North American cultural heritage; includes bargaining by white men with silver or silver ornaments for Indian furs during fur-trade period.

531. Grainger, Sylvia. How to make your own moccasins. New York: Lippincott, 1977.
Craft handbook with directions for making soft leather footwear, with styling based on designs of Eastern Woodland, Plains, Northwest, and Southwest Indian tribes; suggestions on sources of materials and equipment.

532. Highwater, Jamake. Many smokes, many moons. Philadelphia: Lippincott, 1978.
History of American Indians, with focus on Indian art and artifacts which illustrate viewpoints of Indians toward major cultural, political, and military events in United States.

533. ———. The sweet grass lives on; fifty contemporary North American Indian artists. New York: Lippincott & Crowell, 1980.
Introduction to work of modern American Indian artists; brief history of Indian art and biographies and quotations from fifty artists. Illustrated with black-and-white and brilliant color reproductions of paintings and sculpture.

534. Kubiak, William J. Great Lakes Indians. Grand Rapids, Mich.: Baker, 1970.
Illustrated study of Indian tribes of the Great Lakes area of the United States; text and drawings illustrate their physical characteristics, weapons, tools, ceremonial dress; lists of synonymous names.

535. Lavine, Sigmund A. The games the Indians played. New York: Dodd, 1974.
Ceremonial origins of games of Eskimos and Indians of North America, with chapters on types of games and tribal variations.

536. Minor, Marz, and Minor, Nono. The American Indian craft book. Lincoln: Univ. of Nebraska Press, 1878.

Introduction to American Indian culture and crafts reflecting their lifestyles; instructions for making moccasins, clothing, pouches, bead work, tepees, fish traps, war clubs, and directions for preparing food.

537. Nabokov, Peter, ed. Native American testimony; an anthology of Indian and white relations, first encounter to dispossession. New York: Crowell, 1978.

Narratives, from primary sources, through which native Americans expressed their feelings about the land which was their heritage and about Indian culture, their way of life.

538. Niethammer, Carolyn. American Indian food and lore. New York: Macmillan, 1974.

Traditional Indian recipes with ethnic information: plant identification, tribal lore, festival dishes.

539. Oswalt, Wendell H. This land was theirs; a study of the North American Indian. 2d ed. New York: Wiley, 1973.

Look at twelve native American groups in United States and Canada which examines "who is an Indian?" digs into history, and analyzes past mid-century status and circumstances of each tribe.

540. Sanders, Thomas E., and Peek, Walter W. Literature of the American Indian. New York: Glencoe, 1973.

Myths, poems, oratory, laws, rituals, and memoirs of American Indian tribes, Mexican and South American aborigines, and Eskimos; arranged chronologically and by literary form.

541. Taxay, Don. Money of the American Indian and other primitive currencies of the Americas. Flushing, N.Y.: Nummus, 1971.

History of currency of American Indians in pre-Columbian and early colonial America; organized geographically. Indexed.

542. Turner, Frederick W., III, ed. The portable North American Indian reader. New York: Viking, 1974.

Literature by and about American Indian; divided into "Myths and Tales," "Poetry and Oratory," "Culture Contact," and "Image and Anti-Image."

543. Wright, James Leitch. The only land they knew; the tragic story of the American Indians in the old South. New York: Free Press, 1981.

History of Deep South Indians, including such tribes as Catawbas, Creeks, Cherokees, and Seminoles, from Ponce de Leon exploration of Florida in 1513 to forced removal of Indians by white men in 1830s; includes relationship between Indians and black and white men of the period. Indexed.

Pearl Harbor Day

544. Farago, Ladislas. The broken seal; the story of "Operation Magic" and the Pearl Harbor disaster, New York: Random House, 1967.

Record of Japanese and American code breaking between 1921 and 1941 in relation to attack on Pearl Harbor.

545. Feis, Herbert. The road to Pearl Harbor, the coming of the war between the United States and Japan. Princeton, N.J.: Princeton Univ. Press, 1950.

Well-balanced account of negotiations and diplomatic maneuvering which resulted in the attack on Pearl Harbor.

546. Goldston, Robert. Pearl Harbor! December 7, 1941; the road to Japanese aggression in the Pacific. New York: Watts, 1972.

Concise review of militarism in Japanese history, which culminated in the attack on Pearl Harbor in 1941.

547. Lord, Walter. Day of infamy. New York: Holt, 1957.

Detailed account of the action and human drama in the attack on Pearl Harbor, Sunday, December 7, 1941.

548. Prange, Gordon W. At dawn we slept; the untold story of Pearl Harbor. New York: McGraw-Hill, 1981.

The Japanese attack on Pearl Harbor on December 7, 1941, based on research into American and Japanese sources; account of the results of Japanese preparedness and American unpreparedness. Also examines speculations and theories about failure at high levels of government to prevent the attack.

549. Taylor, Theodore. Air raid—Pearl Harbor! The story of December 7, 1941. New York: Crowell, 1971.

History of events which culminated with attack on Pearl Harbor; written from both the American and Japanese points of view.

Saint Patrick's Day

550. Barth, Edna. Shamrocks, harps and shillelaghs: the story of St. Patrick's Day symbols. New York: Seabury, 1977.
Account of Saint Patrick (once called Old Shaved Head) and history of symbols of the day celebrated in his honor. Excellent material on shamrock, shillelagh, leprechauns, Irish harps, food, parades, and the singing of "Saint Patrick's Breastplate."

551. Farjeon, Eleanor. Ten saints. New York: Oxford, 1936.
Includes story about Saint Patrick and "A Rhyme for Patrick" in honor of March 17.

552. Gallico, Paul. The steadfast man; a biography of St. Patrick. Garden City, N.Y.: Doubleday, 1958.
Study of Patrick, Ireland's patron saint, beginning with brief reference to Saint Patrick's Day and the wearin' of the green and proceeding to Patrick's life and work. Appendix includes translations of "Confession of St. Patrick" and his letter to the soldiers of Coroticus.

553. Gogarty, Oliver St. John. I follow Saint Patrick. New York: Reynal & Hitchcock, 1938.
A pilgrimage in 1930s to the places in Wales and Ireland which legend or history has associated with Saint Patrick.

554. Irvine, John. A treasury of Irish saints; a book of poems. New York: Walck, 1964.
A little book about Saint Patrick and other Irish saints, with brief explanatory and biographical notes.

555. Reynolds, Quentin. The life of Saint Patrick. New York: Random House, 1955.
Blends facts, folk beliefs, and legends as reconstruction of life and adventures of Saint Patrick.

556. Scherman, Katharine. "St. Patrick." *In her* The flowering of Ireland; saints, scholars and kings, pp. 83–100. Boston: Little, 1981.
Excellent retelling of the story of Saint Patrick, the traditions and legends. "Attempts to discern something of the character behind the myth."

557. Ward, Maisie. Saints who made history; the first five centuries. New York: Sheed, 1959.
Contributions of saints of the early centuries of Christian church, with chapter on Saint Patrick, his boyhood, preparation for apostolate, and as bishop of Ireland.

Valentine's Day

558. Barth, Edna. Hearts, cupids, and red roses; the story of Valentine symbols. New York: Seabury, 1974.
Origin, development, symbols, and customs of world's most sentimental holiday; named for third-century Saint Valentine, but goes back to Roman festival of Lupercalia.

559. De Paola, Tomie. Things to make and do for Valentine's Day. New York: Watts, 1976.
Attractive craft book for children with easy directions for making valentines and envelopes, mailbags, and other items for Valentine's Day. Recipes, games, jokes, riddles, and tongue twisters with Valentine touch.

560. Guilfoile, Elizabeth. Valentine's Day. Champaign, Ill.: Garrard, 1965.
Simply written account of origins of Saint Valentine's Day, with old customs, symbols, first paper valentines, and brief history of valentines in America.

561. Kessel, Joyce. Valentine's Day. Minneapolis: Carolrhoda, 1981.
Young reader's introduction to tales of Roman origins of Saint Valentine's Day, with brief description of (possible) first valentine and samples of plain, fancy, and "penny dreadful" Valentine's Day cards of recent times.

562. Lee, Ruth Webb. A history of valentines. Wellesley Hills, Mass.: Lee, 1952.
From Roman times, with illustrations of collectors' items and commentaries on their artists and publishers.

563. Quinn, Gardner. Valentine crafts and cookbook. New York: Harvey House, 1977.
Book of ideas for Valentine's Day parties, with hints for messages and instructions for making paper flowers and forget-me-not candy, lollipops, and valentine boxes. Section on valentine superstitions and customs.

564. Sandak, Cass R. Valentine's Day. New York: Watts, 1980.
Book for young readers, tells of origin and customs of Valentine's Day; with simple instructions for making a valentine.

565. Staff, Frank. The valentine and its origin. New York: Praeger, 1969.
History and customs of exchange of valentines from the time of Chaucer to the mid-twentieth century; appendix notes on the legend, love tokens, and information for collectors.

Holiday Preparations

566. Aaberg, Jean, and Bolduc, Judith H. Classics in the kitchen; an edible anthology for the literary gourmet. Los Angeles: Ward Ritchie, 1969.
Menu for each month of year, correlated with quotation from famous authors.

567. Alexander, Sue. Small plays for special days. New York: Seabury, 1977.
Seven children's plays for two actors; includes April Fool's Day, first day of spring, and such traditional days as Valentine's, Fourth of July, Thanksgiving, and Christmas. Notes on staging and costumes, and list of plays for wide range of ages.

568. Barron, Cheryl Carter, and Scherzer, Cathy Carmichael. Great parties for young children. New York: Walker, 1981.
Ideas for children's parties, ranging from birthdays, holidays, and special-observance day events to parties for handicapped children. Basic concept, underlying suggestions and instructions, is that every party should be unique and "unforgettable." Pointers on party themes, decorations, games, activities, and food. Indexed.

569. Bennett, Charles; Taylor, Gerald; and Yatabe, Peggy. The year-round, all-occasion make your own greeting card book. Los Angeles: Tarcher, 1977.
Handbook on card making for holidays, days of observance, and special events; includes design ideas and basic instructions for creating all kinds of cards, from paper doily to stained-glass-look cards. Illustrated with detailed instructional drawings. Types of cards are indexed by occasion.

570. Born, Wina. Famous dishes of the world. New York: Macmillan, 1973.
Introduction to international cooking; recipes correlated with brief information on history of each dish.

571. Boyles, Margaret. Margaret Boyles' needlework gifts for special occasions. New York: Simon & Schuster, 1981.
Craft book for making stitched gifts, with modern or traditional motifs, for birthdays, wedding days, holidays, and general or special occasions. Ideas, with instructions, range from holiday ornaments to sophisticated tote bags.

572. Bradley, Virginia. Holidays on stage; a festival of special-occasion plays. New York: Dodd, Mead, 1981.
Ten plays for young people, for such occasions as New Year's, Groundhog, April Fool's, Halloween, and Valentine's Day. Traditional holidays represented with plays for Lincoln's and Washington's birthdays, Thanksgiving, Chanukah, and Christmas.

573. Capon, Robert Farrar. Party spirit; some entertaining principles. New York: Morrow, 1979.
Philosophical approach to entertaining, dedicated to refreshment of the party spirit. Recipes blend into the narrative, and include Armenian Easter dinner menu and some Caribbean and Thai recipes, with paragraph on Armenian custom of dyeing Easter Eggs with onion skins.

574. Chernoff, Goldie Taub. Easy costumes you don't have to sew. Costumes designed and illustrated by Margaret A. Hartelius. New York: Four Winds, 1975.
Party or celebration-planning aid with easy instructions for making costumes and disguises from paper bags, cardboard, cartons, garbage bags, and other inexpensive materials, which do not require sewing. Useful for all kinds of holiday parties and special occasions.

575. Christian, Mary Blount. April fool. New York: Macmillan, 1981.
Amusing tale for young readers about a day of deliberate foolishness which, according to legend, is associated with the beginning of April Fool's Day. In well-chosen words and clever illustrations, tells of the people of Gotham, England, who duped thirteenth-century King John into believing that Gotham was a village of fools—and not an acceptable neighborhood for a new hunting lodge.

576. Comins, Jeremy. Eskimo crafts and their cultural backgrounds. New York: Lothrop, 1975.
Introduction to Eskimo crafts, with suggestions and instructions on application of Eskimo designs and techniques to making dolls, masks, leather appliques, and other useful objects. List of supply sources. Indexed.

577. Conaway, Judith. Manos; South American crafts for children. Chicago: Follett, 1978.
How South Americans use crafts in everyday lives. Lists tools and materials, with instructions, for making negrito mask (worn during fiestas) and building a *pesebre* (manger scene) for Christmas. All projects illustrated with instructive drawings and photographs.

578. Corrigan, Adeline, sel. Holiday ring; festival stories and poems. Chicago: Whitman, 1975.
Material for national holidays, such as Dominion Day (in Canada) and Fourth of July and such special days as Arbor Day. Arranged by calendar year. Index of titles, first lines of poems, and holiday references.

579. Cummings, Richard. 101 costumes for all ages, all occasions. New York: McKay, 1970.
Suggestions for making historical, ethnic, and unusual costumes, from impromptu costume to Civil War uniform.

580. D'Amato, Alex, and D'Amato, Janet. African crafts for you to make. New York: Messner, 1969.
Guide to African craftwork, with explanation of symbols and functions. Directions and illustrations.

581. De Wit, Dorothy. Children's faces looking up. Chicago: ALA, 1979.
Informative examination of art of storytelling; looks at evolution of storytelling, defines a tellable tale, and suggests story programs with motifs such as holidays, magic, animals, and feasting. Annotated lists of stories for popular holidays.

582. Drehman, Verna L. Holiday ornaments from paper scraps. New York: Hearthside, 1970.
Patterns and directions for paper-scrap ornaments for Christmas, New Year's, Valentine's, Mother's and Father's days, Halloween, Thanksgiving, and birthdays, with suggestions for wrapping presents. Indexed.

583. Eisner, Vivienne. Quick and easy holiday costumes. Illus. by Carolyn Bentley. New York: Lothrop, 1977.
Directions for producing instant costumes from common household supplies for all traditional holidays and special occasions, such as Chinese New Year, Earth Day, May Day, and United Nations Day. Costumes for historical figures range from Johnny Appleseed to Mary Todd Lincoln. Arranged by calendar year. Indexed.

584. Elicker, Virginia Wilk. Biblical costumes for church and school. New York: Ronald, 1953.
Ideas, principles, and directions for costuming biblical plays, particularly for eras of Abraham, Joseph, David, Esther, the Nativity, and Jesus in his ministry.

585. Ellison, Virginia H. The Pooh cook book; inspired by Winnie-the-Pooh and The house at Pooh Corner. New York: Dutton, 1969.
A cookbook for all ages and many occasions, with section of Christmas specialties; all recipes accompanied by quotation from A. A. Milne.

586. ———. The Pooh party book. New York: Dutton, 1971.
Party book inspired by the works of Milne. Options for five parties, such as spring party correlated with Easter or May Day; sequel to *Pooh Cook Book.*

587. Emmens, Carol A. An audio-visual guide to American holidays. Metuchen, N.J.: Scarecrow, 1977.
Source book on films, videotapes, filmstrips, prints, slide sets, transparencies, multimedia kits, and relia related to holidays and seasons of year; bibliographic information indicates age levels and summarizes content.

588. Fiarotta, Phyllis, and Fiarotta, Noel. Confetti, the kids' make-it-yourself, do-it-yourself party book. New York: Workman, 1978.
Handicraft book for young people with ideas and instructions for preparing for twenty-two events. Crafts relate to Valentine's Day, Saint Patrick's Day, Easter, Halloween, Chanukah, and Christmas. Special occasions include Mother's Day, Father's Day, and anniversaries.

589. Fitzgibbon, Theodora. A taste of Ireland; Irish traditional food. Boston: Houghton, 1969.
Recipes from rural and urban Ireland, including colcannon (traditionally eaten at Halloween), spiced beef for Christmas, dulse, sloke, and willicks for Easter Monday, and goose for Michaelmas Day.

590. Ford, James Lauren. Every day in the year; a poetical epitome of the world's history. New York: Dodd, 1902. Detroit: Gale Research, 1969.
Turn-of-the-century collection on memorable events and people, from assassination of Julius Caesar to sinking of the *Maine*; arranged by days in calendar. Of value in locating elusive material from nineteenth century.

591. Fujioka, Ryoichi, and others. Tea ceremony utensils. New York: Weatherhill, 1973.
Brief explanation of Japanese tea ceremony, with major focus on each category of utensil used in the ceremonial; beautifully illustrated.

592. Gilbreath, Alice. Making costumes for parties, plays, and holidays. New York: Morrow, 1974.

Instructions for making ghost, valentine, firecracker, and other kinds of costumes for special days; arranged in order of difficulty.

593. Greenhowe, Jean. Making costume dolls. New York: Watson-Guptill, 1973.

Instructions for making dolls for dioramas and displays; ideas for representing historical periods, fairy tale characters, and imaginative scenes.

594. Gupta, Pranati Sen. The art of Indian cuisine; everyday menus, feasts, and holiday banquets. New York: Hawthorn, 1974.

Recipes from India adapted for American use; brief introduction correlates food with special events; wedding feast, holy festival of Durga Puja, and others.

595. Holz, Loretta. The how-to book of international dolls; a comprehensive guide to making, costuming, and collecting dolls. New York: Crown, 1980.

Describes dolls of Africa, Near East, Asia, Pacific, Europe, Latin America, and North America. Lists supply and doll sources. Indexed.

596. In praise of hands; contemporary crafts of the world. Published in association with the World Crafts Council. New York: Graphic, 1974.

Illustrated study of primitive, traditional, and innovative crafts of fifty-four nations; based on first World's Crafts Exhibition in Toronto in summer of 1974.

597. Ives, Suzy. Children's costumes in paper and card. New York: Taplinger, 1973.

British costume manual on making children's costumes from inexpensive materials; instructions for creating masks, disguises, Halloween guises, theatrical costumes, and fun extravaganzas.

598. Jervey, Phyllis. A world of parties; the busy gourmet's guide to exciting entertaining. Rutland, Vt.: Tuttle, 1964.

Round-the-world dishes representing many nations, from Spanish gypsy outing and North African banquet to an American Thanksgiving and a New Year's Eve in Germany.

599. John, Sue. The special days cookbook. New York: Philomel, 1982.

Illustrated cookbook for youngsters, with recipes and instructions for preparing dishes for birthdays, seasonal days, outdoor days, and special days.

600. Johnson, Lois S. Happy birthdays around the world. Chicago: Rand McNally, 1968.

Birthday and name-day customs of twenty-four nations, from Belgium to Venezuela. Translations of birthday or saints' songs, descriptions of parties, gifts, and special foods. Indexed.

601. Joseph, Joan. Folk toys around the world and how to make them. New York: Parents' Magazine Press, 1972.

Guidebook, published with UNICEF, on making toys of various nations; geographical and historical information and directions for making twenty-three toys, from Russian bear to cymbal-clacking Egyptian clown.

602. Kaufman, William I. The Catholic cookbook. New York: Citadel, 1965.

Foods for Catholic feast days, holidays, and days of fast and abstinence. Indexed by category and country of origin.

603. Kolba, St. Tamara. Asian crafts. New York: Lion, 1972.

Craft book on holiday-related activities in Asia. Instructions for making the kites which are colorful feature of many special occasions in Japan and other Asian countries.

604. Korty, Carol. Plays from African folktales. New York: Scribner, 1975.

Dramatization of four African folk tales about animals for presentation by children, with suggestions on costumes, masks, scenery, and rehearsing and performing.

605. Lane-Palagyi, Addyse. Successful school assembly programs. West Nyack, N.Y.: Parker, 1971.

Guidelines for planning, organizing, and producing assembly programs for elementary and secondary schools; includes sample-tested program ideas, such as Colonial Thanksgiving tableaus and Labor Day dramatizations.

606. Langseth-Christensen, Lillian. The holiday cook. New York: Lion, 1969.

Cookbook for young people and their parents, with recipes for holidays from Happy New Year Beans to plum pudding for Christmas; arranged by calendar year.

607. Larrick, Nancy, sel. Poetry for holidays. Champaign, Ill.: Garrard, 1966.

Little poems for little people for Halloween, Thanksgiving, Christmas, New Year's Day, Saint Valentine's and Saint Patrick's Days, Easter, May Day, Fourth of July, and their birthdays.

608. Leisy, James. The good times songbook; 160 songs for informal singing, with resources for song leaders, accompanists, and singers. Nashville; Abingdon, 1974.

Collection of folk, camp, cumulative songs, ballads, hymns, and carols, with notes on their origins or idioms. Suggestions on performance techniques. Useful for observance of patriotic days, Christmas, Thanksgiving, and for opening and closing songs for all kinds of observances. Indexed by song categories.

609. Livingston, Myra Cohn, ed. O frabjous day! Poetry for holidays and special occasions. New York: Atheneum, 1977.

Anthology for holidays, religious days, and special days of observation (with title from Lewis Carroll). Poems arranged in three sections: celebrating, honoring, remembering. Indexed by author, title, first line, and translator.

610. Madhubuti, Safisha L. The story of Kwanza. Chicago: Third World, 1977.

Brief explanation of Kwanza, festival of thanksgiving and love celebrated by black communities. Clear, supporting illustrations by Murry N. DePillars.

611. Manning-Saunders, Ruth, comp. Festivals. New York: Dutton, 1973.

Anthology of poems, stories, and songs for major and minor festivals; international in scope, with brief introductions for selected days. Arranged by calendar year.

612. Mazda, Maideh. In a Persian kitchen; favorite recipes from the Near East. Rutland, Vt.: Tuttle, 1960.

Introduction to Persian culinary arts and hospitality, with commentaries on special foods and recipes, with sample menu for New Year's dinner and seasonal lunches or dinners. Indexed.

613. Meyer, Carolyn. The bread book: all about bread and how to make it. New York: Harcourt, 1971.

A history of bread and instructions for making it, with references to holy day and holiday use by various faiths and to once-a-year traditions, such as barmbrack for Irish Halloween.

614. Moore, Eva. The cookie book. New York: Seabury, 1973.

Cookie recipes for celebrating one special day of each month, such as coconut drops for Valentine's Day and molasses cookies for April Fool's Day.

615. Newman, Lee Scott, and Newman, Jay Hartley. Kite craft; the history and processes of kitemaking throughout the world. New York: Crown, 1974.

History of kites, with special chapters on Oriental kites and their symbolism and kites of twentieth century. Basic construction techniques and decorating ideas. Useful for seasonal observances and kite competitions. Indexed.

616. Newmann, Dana. The teacher's almanack: practical ideas for every day of the school year. West Nyack, N.Y.: Center for Applied Research in Education, 1973.

Almanac for teachers, organized by school year. Each school month has calendar of important dates, including holidays, anniversaries of important events, and birthdays of famous people. Monthly calendar is followed by quotations from outstanding men and women born in the month, notations on historical facts related to events of the month, and bulletin board suggestions featuring holidays and seasonal projects. Index of activities.

617. Nightingale, Marie. Out of old Nova Scotia kitchens; a collection of traditional recipes of Nova Scotia and stories of people who cooked them. New York: Scribner, 1971.

History of table traditions of Micmac Indians, French, English, Scots, Irish, blacks of Nova Scotia: their food beliefs, traditional festivals, pie socials, and other events.

618. Opie, Iona, and Opie, Peter. Children's games in street and playground; chasing, catching, seeking, hunting, racing, duelling, exerting, daring, guessing, acting, pretending. New York: Oxford, 1969.

Survey of "games that children, aged about 6–12, play on their own accord when out-of-doors, and usually out of sight."

619. Parish, Peggy. Costumes to make. New York: Macmillan, 1970.

Simple directions for making story-book, animal, historical, and national costumes for holidays and special events.

620. Pellowski, Anne. The world of storytelling. New York: Bowker, 1977.

Scholarly but readable book on types and styles of storytelling. Suggestions for authentic storytelling, multilingual dictionary of storytelling terms, comprehensive bibliography, and index.

621. Perl, Lila. Foods and festivals of the Danube lands. Cleveland: World, 1969.
Overview of traditional menus and food customs associated with German and Austrian festivals, celebrations of Hungarian gypsies, Yugoslav saints' days, and major festivities of Bulgaria, Romania, and Russia.

622. ———. Red flannel hash and shoo-fly pie. Cleveland World, 1965.
Good eating for 400 years in all parts of United States: food of Indians, Pilgrims, pioneers, Cornish, and other national groups. Recipes arranged by regions of mainland, Alaska, and Hawaii.

623. ———. Rice, spice and bitter oranges; Mediterranean foods and festivals. Cleveland: World, 1967.
Cuisines and dining customs of Portugal, Spain, Syria, Lebanon, Israel, and North Africa, correlated with feast days, festivals, weddings, and funerals.

624. Polette, Nancy, and Hamlin, Marjorie. Celebrating with books. Metuchen, N.J.: Scarecrow, 1977.
Guide for teachers to use of books in developing lesson plans on significance of holidays and special days of observance. Suggests book titles and outlines related activities for Columbus Day, United Nations Day, Halloween, Thanksgiving, Christmas, Chanukah, the February birthdays, Valentine's Day, Saint Patrick's Day, and Easter. Index to titles, authors, illustrators.

625. Poston, Elizabeth. The baby's song book. New York: Crowell, 1972.
Traditional English-language nursery songs with basic piano accompaniment; also songs in French, German, Italian, and Spanish with English translations.

626. Price, Christine. Happy days; a UNICEF book of birthdays, name days, and growing days. New York: U.S. Committee for UNICEF, 1969.
Descriptions of landmark days of children throughout world: when a baby is named, birthday anniversary, and day of initiation into adulthood. Appendix includes music and words, with English translations, of birthday songs from Egypt, Holland, Japan, Mexico, and Venezuela.

627. Purdy, Susan. Costumes for you to make. Philadelphia: Lippincott, 1971.
Ideas and instructions for designing and making costumes, hats, masks, disguises, suits of armor, and two- or more-person animals for theatrical productions and parties on special days of observance.

628. ———. Festivals for you to celebrate. Philadelphia: Lippincott, 1969.
Activity-craft book on American nonpatriotic holidays and festivals, with directions for projects. Arranged by seasons. Entries in the subject index key level of difficulty to such activities as making costumes and puppets.

629. ———. Holiday cards for you to make. Philadelphia: Lippincott, 1967.
Suggestions and directions for creating hand-made marbleized, collage, pressed flower, cutout, and boxed cards, with ideas on use of old greeting cards.

630. Roden, Claudia. A book of Middle Eastern food. New York: Knopf, 1972.
Culinary traditions and recipes from Syria, Lebanon, Egypt, Iran, Turkey, Greece, Iraq, Saudi Arabia, Yemen, Sudan, Algeria, Tunisia, Morocco, and Israel; includes interpretations of origins of foods, rules for being a host or guest, superstitions, and dietary laws.

631. Ross, Laura. Holiday puppets. New York: Lothrop, 1974.
Suggestions for puppet shows for Lincoln's birthday, Saint Valentine's, Washington's birthday, Saint Patrick's, Purim, Easter, Columbus Day, Halloween, Thanksgiving, and Christmas.

632. Sattler, Helen Roney. Holiday gifts, favors, and decorations. New York: Lothrop, 1971.
Idea and instruction book for making table decorations, party favors, and gifts for major holidays, mother-daughter or father-son banquets for club, school, or home festivities; arranged by seasons of the year.

633. Sayer, Chloe. Crafts of Mexico. Garden City, N.Y.: Doubleday, 1977.
Colorful introduction to contemporary customs and crafts in cities and villages of Mexico. Step-by-step instructions for making "toy made to be broken" (holiday *piñata*) and other craft items.

634. Shannon, Alice, and Shirrod, Barbara. Decorative treasures from papier-mache. Great Neck, N.Y.: Hearthside, 1970.
Suggestions and instructions for making Christmas ornaments and objects for other purposes from papier-mache.

635. Shapiro, Rebecca. A whole world of cooking. Boston: Little, 1972.
Recipes from around the world, beginning with Canadian fish cakes. Table of contents arranged alphabetically by country. Indexed by type of dish.

636. Slivka, Rose, ed. The crafts of the modern world. New York: Horizon, 1968.
Pictorial compendium of over 400 objects of contemporary craft from over 70 countries; useful as idea book for holiday crafts.

637. Stephan, Barbara B. Decorations for holidays and celebrations: ideas, inspiration, and techniques for making festival objects from natural materials. New York: Crown, 1978.
Manual, illustrated with black-and-white photographs, of suggestions and directions for making decorations and objects for holidays and special celebration days. Concentrates on craft materials from nature: pods, cones, and grasses; straw and corn; wood and wood shavings. Additional chapters on decorated eggs and paper, kitchen, and other crafts. Indexed.

638. Temko, Florence. Folk crafts for world friendship. Garden City, N.Y.: Doubleday, 1976.
Customs and crafts of twenty-four countries with directions for unusual games and making costumes, masks, toys, and decorations enjoyed by children throughout the world.

639. ——, and Takahama, Toshie. The magic of kirigami; happenings with paper and scissors. Elmsford, N.Y.: Japan Pubns., 1978.
On the art of making holiday decorations, birthday cards, May baskets, gift-package ornaments, and many other objects with paper and scissors. Clear, concise directions, illustrated with black-and-white diagrams, photographs, and drawings.

640. Turgeon, Charlotte Snyder. Cooking for many on holidays and other festive occasions. New York: Crown, 1962.
Holiday recipes and menus for club, church, and home functions; includes Christian and Jewish holidays.

641. Van Zandt, Eleanor. Crafts for fun and profit. Garden City, N.Y.: Doubleday, 1974.
Manual on craft projects, ranging from candle making to polished stones; special section on Christmas ideas.

642. Waltner, Willard, and Waltner, Elma. Holiday hobbycraft. New York: Lantern, 1964.
Craft book with directions for making favors, gifts, and decorations for thirty special-events days from traditional holidays to ideas for April Fool's day and a witch's den for Halloween.

643. Wendorff, Ruth. How to make cornhusk dolls. New York: Arco, 1973.
Basic instructions for making cornhusk dolls for Thanksgiving, Nativity scenes, decorations, and holiday souvenirs.

644. Wilcox, R. Turner. Folk and festival costumes of the world. New York: Scribner, 1965.
Description of folk costumes around the world, from Afghanistan to Yugoslavia, including selected American states, such as Alaska and Wisconsin. Illustrations are black-and-white line drawings.

645. Wilson, Ellen Gibson. A West African cookbook. New York: Evans, 1972.
Recipes from Ghana, Liberia, Sierra Leone, and Nigeria, with chapter on Awoojah, a feast of thanksgiving, and customs involving foods at funerals, weddings, baptisms, and harvest festivals.

646. Wolfsohn, Reeta Bochner. Successful children's parties. New York: Arco, 1979.
By mother and party expert who is convinced that children's birthday parties are fun. Text shares secrets of successful party formula and advice on every aspect of party giving, from preplanning to ending the perfect party. List of do's and don'ts to cancel out party problems.

Historic Events Days

647. Andrews, Ralph W. Historic fires of the West. Seattle: Superior, 1966.
Pictorial history of volunteer firemen, bucket brigades, early pumping stations, and historic fires of early days in western American states, Alaska, and British Columbia. A book for display on Fire Prevention Day, October 9.

648. Baker, David. Space shuttle. New York: Crown, 1979.
Pictorial interpretation of American space shuttle, with fine photographs, detailed drawings, and artists' sketches. Text reviews concept of re-usable space transport and facts about its development. Indexed.

649. Bills, Scott. Kent State/May 4; echoes through a decade. Kent, Ohio: Kent State Univ. Press, 1982.
Review of events that culminated in shooting of students on Kent State campus May 4, 1970; essays and reports on interviews related to tragedy and its aftermath.

650. Blatter, Janet, and Milton, Sybil. Art of the Holocaust. New York: Rutledge, 1981.
Collection of Holocaust art, the work of Hitler's victims in concentration camps and ghettos from 1939 to 1945, ranging from landscapes and portraits to particular events. Book includes essays, biographical directory of the artists, and list of Holocaust museums and memorials.

651. Bodechtel, Johann, and Gierloff-Emden, Hans-Gunter. The earth from space. New York: Arco, 1974.
Maps and photographs from the Gemini and Apollo flights and lunar and meteorological satellites, with narrative texts. Shows Earth crust movements, landscapes, and Earth's environment in relation to surroundings and the moon.

652. Boly, William. Fire mountain; the eruptions of Mount St. Helens. Beaverton, Ore.: Graphics Arts, 1980.
Photographic record of May 18, 1981, explosion. Indian tales of fiery temper of "Fire Mountain," and photographer's work substantiates the legend. Explanatory diagrams and a clear text aid in understanding cause and processes in a volcanic eruption.

653. Bradford, Ernie. The story of the *Mary Rose*. New York: Norton, 1982.
Contribution to history of nautical archeology focuses on recovery of *Mary Rose,* pride of the fleet of King Henry VIII of England, which sank in British waters in 1545. Text chronicles history of the vessel and planning and salvage process, and describes recovered artifacts and anticipation of new knowledge about Tudor period from the raising.

654. Brown, John Russell. Shakespeare and his theatre. New York: Lothrop, 1982.
Colorfully illustrated introduction to long-vanished Globe Theatre and Elizabethan society for whom Shakespeare wrote and produced his plays. Text, based on historic manuscripts and documents, describes architectual features of Globe, actors and their onstage and backstage business, and audiences, which took the theater very seriously in Shakespeare's day.

655. Caffrey, Kate. The *Mayflower*. New York: Stein & Day, 1974.
Chronicle of the Pilgrims in America: doctrines, leaders, and settlement decisions. Appendix includes passenger list, "Mayflower Compact," representative Pilgrim letters, and other historic materials.

656. Carson, Gerald. Man, beasts, and gods; a history of cruelty and kindness to animals. New York: Scribner, 1972.
Survey of animal treatment in Europe from Stone Age to Victorian England, followed by examination of practices in United States from colonial period to present. Concludes with plea for animal rights.

657. Carter, Samuel, III. Blaze of glory; the fight for New Orleans, 1814–1815. New York; St. Martin's, 1971.
Popular history of issues, strategies, and personalities in Battle of New Orleans, which ended January 8, 1815.

658. Cate, Curtis. The ides of August; the Berlin Wall crisis, 1961. New York: Evans, 1978;.
Account of construction of Berlin Wall by East Germans, creating physical and psychological barrier between East and West Berlin—a permanent symbol of the loss of freedom.

659. Catton, Bruce. Gettysburg; the final fury. Garden City, N.Y.: Doubleday, 1974.
Civil War history that interprets Lee's strategy at Battle of Gettysburg and throws light on his fight against a man who did not wear a uniform, Abraham Lincoln.

660. Chandler, David G. Waterloo; the hundred days. New York: Macmillan, 1981.
Account of nineteenth-century Battle of Waterloo, personalities of opposing military geniuses, and strategies and decisions that brought an end to Napoleon's dreams.

661. Chew, Peter. The Kentucky Derby; the first 100 years. Boston: Houghton, 1974.
Historical tribute, with facts about horses, tracks, and jockeys.

662. Clark, Patrick. Sports firsts. New York: Facts on File, 1981.
Compilation of record-establishing "firsts" in sports and origins of athletic events. In addition, text gathers facts on where teams originated and when matches and tournaments began. Covers all kinds of sports. Illustrated with photographs and indexed.

663. Colby, Jean Poindexter. Lexington and Concord, 1775—what really happened. New York: Hastings, 1974.

First battles of American Revolution, combined with tour of sites of major events. Based on diaries, letters, and eyewitness accounts.

664. Curry-Lindhahl, Kai. Let them live; a worldwide survey of animals threatened with extinction. New York: Morrow, 1972.

Facts about 982 mammals, birds, reptiles, amphibians, and fishes in danger of extinction on land masses and waters of world. Indexed.

665. Davis, William C. Battle at Bull Run; a history of the first major campaign of the Civil war. Garden City N.Y.: Doubleday, 1977.

Full-scale history of battle at Manassas examines the situation, analyzes roles of commanding officers of opposing sides, and reports on men in the ranks. Indexed.

666. Deighton, Len. Battle of Britain. New York: Coward, 1980.

Lively day-by-day record of 1940 aerial battles known in World War II history as "Battle of Britain." Based on firsthand accounts and official documents. Illustrated with paintings, drawings, maps, and diagrams. Indexed.

667. Dobbs, Michael; Karol, K. S.; and Trevisan, Dessa. Poland; Solidarity; Walesa. New York: McGraw-Hill, 1981.

Report centered around August 1980 in Poland. Text includes three essays: Poland, background to crisis; the peaceful revolution and emergence of Solidarity movement; and Lech Walesa, "the symbol of the Polish August." Illustrated with color and black-and-white photographs. Indexed.

668. Earnest, Ernest Penny. The volunteer fire company; past and present. New York: Stein & Day, 1979.

History of volunteer fire fighters in United States from Colonial times into twentieth century—of individuals whose concern for community has been a major contribution in saving lives and property where professional fire fighters were not available or affordable.

669. Eisenberg, Azriel. Witness to the Holocaust. New York: Pilgrim, 1981.

First-hand accounts of horrors of the Holocaust, gathered from diaries, letters, journals, and newspaper reports, that document the misery experienced by young and old, known and unknown, and reflect human views of the Holocaust and its aftermath.

670. Eisenhower Foundation. D-day; the Normandy invasion in retrospect. Lawrence: Univ. Press of Kansas, 1971.

Retrospective articles on planning for D-day (June 6, 1944) and after; prepared in commemoration of the twenty-fifth anniversary.

671. Ervin, Samuel James. The whole truth; the Watergate conspiracy. New York: Random House, 1980.

Evaluation of 1973 findings of U.S. Senate Select Committee charged with investigation of Watergate; written by chairman of committee, a central figure in hearings.

672. First on the moon; a voyage with Neil Armstrong, Michael Collins, and Edwin Aldrin, Jr. Boston: Little, 1970.

Journalistic, authorized report of flight of *Apollo II*, the astronauts, and their families; concludes with rationale for space program by Arthur Clarke.

673. Fisher, Leonard Everett. Two if by sea. New York: Random House, 1970.

Account of events during evening of April 18, 1775, and actions of the patriots, Joseph Warren, Paul Revere, and Robert Newman, and British general, Thomas Gage.

674. Flexner, Eleanor. Century of struggle; the woman's rights movement in the United States. Cambridge, Mass.: Harvard Univ. Press, 1959.

History of women's rights movement from 1820s to adoption of woman's suffrage amendment (1919).

675. Frassanito, William A. Antietam; the photographic legacy of America's bloodiest day. New York: Scribner, 1978.

A look at bloodiest day of Civil War through photographs taken at Antietam shortly after the battle, modern views of same locations, and sketches of soldiers who were in the battle.

676. Friedman, Ina R. Escape or die; true stories of young people who survived the Holocaust. Reading, Mass.: Addison-Wesley, 1982.

Firsthand accounts, based on interviews with twelve survivors who were children or teenagers during the period. Accounts range from memories of a beating on Crystal Night to experimentations at Auschwitz. Accounts arranged by country, and each national section is prefaced by summaries of Jewish history in land where horrors occurred.

677. Gilbo, Patrick F. The American Red Cross; the first century. New York: Harper, 1981.

Pictorial history and account of organization's founders, contemporary leaders, and long history of practical service in times of war, peace, and disasters. Written in honor of centennial of its founding (May 21, 1881).

678. Goodrum, Charles A. Treasures of the Library of Congress. New York: Abrams, 1980.

Handsome volume describes vast holdings of Library, from books, manuscripts, and musical instruments to computer tapes and microforms. Reflects philosophy behind growth of Library as a national institution and goals of preservation and usefulness. Foreword by Daniel J. Boorstin, Librarian of Congress.

679. Gray, Tony. Champions of peace; the story of Alfred Nobel and the peace prize and the laureates. New York: Paddington, 1976.

Two-part history. Section 1 deals with Alfred Nobel, Swedish "dynamite king," whose will established peace prize. Part 2 summarizes achievements of winners in chronological order, beginning with Henri Dunant and Frederic Passy in 1901 and concluding with Andrei Sakharov in 1975. Indexed.

680. Hahn, Emily. Once upon a pedestal; an informal history of women's lib. New York: Crowell, 1974.

Popular account of women in America, from arrival of Anne Forrest at Jamestown in 1607 to 1970s. Commentaries on authors who wrote about women, books women read, and various movements that influenced women.

681. Haines, Aubrey L. The Yellowstone story; a history of our first national park. 2 vols. Boulder: Colorado Associated Univ. Press, 1977.

History of Yellowstone Park, established March 1, 1872, first of great national parks of United States. Comprehensive chronicle sponsored by Yellowstone Library and Museum Association. Illustrated with maps, charts, and historic photographs. Indexed.

682. Hellman, Peter, and Meier, Lili. The Auschwitz album; a book based upon an album discovered by a concentration camp survivor, Lili Meier. New York: Random House, 1982.

Impressive documentary on horror of Auschwitz with 185 pictures of doomed Hungarian Jews, forced into German death factory. Meier, only surviving member of her family, found the album, which speaks louder than words.

683. Hickey, Des, and Smith, Gus. Seven days to disaster; the sinking of the *Lusitania.* New York: Putnam, 1982.

Chronicle of tragedy on high seas following German U-boat torpedoeing off coast of Ireland on May 7, 1915. Based on reports of survivors and eyewitnesses.

684. Hiroshima and Nagasaki; the physical and social effects of the atomic bombings. By the committee for the compilation of materials on damage caused by the atomic bomb in Hiroshima and Nagasaki. New York: Basic Books, 1981.

Painstaking audit of 1945 atomic bombings. Facts, figures, maps, photographs, and firsthand accounts document immediate and delayed effects of the bombings and sufferings of first victims of nuclear war.

685. Hohenburg, John, ed. The Pulitzer Prize story II: 1959–1980. New York: Columbia Univ. Press, 1980.

Review of awards between 1959 and 1980 for distinguished contributions of reporters, columnists, editorialists, news photographers, and cartoonists to American journalism.

686. Holliday, J. S. The world rushed in; the California gold rush experience. New York: Simon & Schuster, 1981.

Firsthand view of gold rush of 1849, based on a two-year diary of William Swain and his (and other gold seekers') letters to and from their families. Illustrated with maps and contemporary drawings. Indexed.

687. Howarth, David. D day, the sixth of June 1944. New York: McGraw-Hill, 1959.

Chronicle of planning, strategy, and military movements in invasion of Normandy, June 6, 1944, called "the greatest day of World War II."

688. Hubbard, Freeman. 150 years of railroading in the United States and Canada. New York: McGraw-Hill, 1981.

Browsing book and reference resource. Comprehensive coverage, ranging from railroad achievements, disasters, and anecdotes to accounts of railroad companies and labor unions. "Lingo of the rails" glossary. Indexed by subject.

689. Hughes, David. The star of Bethlehem; an astronomer's confirmation. New York: Walker, 1979.

Analysis of astronomical events associated with birth of Christ. Based on historical and astronomical studies documenting theory that Christ was born in August or September, 7 B.C.

690. An introduction to the Hirshhorn Museum and sculpture garden. New York: Abrams, 1974.

Plates and photographs of holdings presented to nation by Joseph H. Hirshhorn in 1966. Introduction by Abram Lerner, director of museum.

691. Johnson, David. The London Blitz, the city ablaze, December 29, 1940. New York: Stein & Day, 1981.

Portrayal of inferno in London on night of December 29, 1940, caused by German incendiary bombs on City of London area. Based on official records, interviews with eyewitnesses, and statements from both British and Germans.

692. Kennedy, David M. Over here; the first World War and American society. New York: Oxford, 1980.

Comprehensive study of United States in World War I examines change in national attitudes, with analysis of American overseas military and diplomatic strategies. Indexed.

693. Kent, Peter C. The pope and the duce: the international impact of the Lateran agreements. New York: St. Martin's, 1981.

Summary of diplomacy between Vatican and Italian government from 1929 to 1935 and diplomatic concerns of the period.

694. Key, Francis Scott. The star-spangled banner. Garden City, N.Y.: Doubleday, 1973.

Pictorial interpretation of national anthem, illustrated by Peter Spier, with historical note on event that inspired its writing. Reproduction of Key's manuscript.

695. Kingston, Jeremy, and Lambert, David. Catastrophe and crisis. New York: Facts on file, 1979.

Illustrated survey of natural disasters and man-made catastrophes: storms, floods, drought, famine, fire, volcanic eruptions, plagues, pestilences, accidents, wars, and assassinations. Indexed.

696. Kogan, Herman, and Cromie, Robert. The great fire; Chicago, 1871. New York: Putnam, 1971.

Pictorial history of Chicago's great fire, October 8–10, 1871, which is commemorated annually by fire-prevention days and weeks.

697. Kornhaber, Arthur, and Woodward, Kenneth L. Grandparents/grandchildren; the vital connection. New York: Anchor/Doubleday, 1981.

Study of emotional attachment between grandparents and grandchildren. Quotes viewpoints of various writers on role of grandparents and discusses meaning (in children's drawings of grandparents) of intimacy of their relationship.

698. Lord, Walter. The miracle of Dunkirk. New York: Viking, 1982.

Detailed account of rescue of over 338,000 Allied troops from Dunkirk in 1940. True story of "weekend sailors" repeatedly crossing English Channel in amazing ferrying venture. Based on interviews and official records.

699. McKinley, Edward H. Marching to glory; the history of the Salvation Army in the United States of America, 1880–1980. New York: Harper, 1980.

History of first 100 years of Salvation Army in United States, beginning with its arrival on March 10, 1880. Describes years of hard work and expansion into national institution dedicated to serving outcasts and unfortunates.

700. Maruki, Toshi. Hiroshima no pika. New York: Lothrop, 1982.

Extremely moving recall of Hiroshima on August 6, 1945. Picture book based on struggle for survival by Japanese mother and her seven-year-old child. Portrayed through paintings and words.

701. Moynihan, Maurice, ed. Speeches and statements by Eamon de Valera, 1917–73. New York: St. Martin's, 1980.

Speeches and statements of the president of Irish Republic; contribution to the history of problems of twentieth-century Ireland.

702. Naden, Corinne J. The Chicago Fire—1871; the blaze that nearly destroyed a city. New York: Watts, 1969.

Detailed account of Chicago Fire, with maps to assist reader follow the spread of one of nation's most dramatic fires.

703. Palmer, Alan, and Palmer, Veronica. Who's who in Shakespeare's England. New York: St. Martin's, 1981.

Book for a Shakespeare birthday observance: "verbal portrait gallery" of prominent men and women living between 1590 and 1623, an important period in Shakespeare's creative life. Includes writers, printers, merchants, musicians, actors, church and state dignitaries, and leading persons in society.

704. Palmer, Leonard. Mt. St. Helens; the volcano explodes! Portland, Ore.: Northwest Illustrated, 1980.

Collection of photographs with explanatory notes and brief text documenting eruption. From warnings of March 1980 through eruption of May 18, 1980, to beginning of the lava dome in June 1980.

705. Pohl, Frederick J. The Viking settlements of North America. New York: Potter, 1972.

Contribution to research on Viking settlements, with descriptions of Leif Ericson's three landings and voyage home from Vinland. Indexed.

706. Quackenbush, Robert. The boy who dreamed of rockets; how Robert H. Goddard became the father of the space age. New York: Parents, 1979.

A book for Goddard Day: compact biography for young readers highlights significant details of Goddard's life and entry into rocketry.

707. Revere, Paul. Paul Revere's three accounts of his famous ride. 2d ed. Boston: Massachusetts Historical Society, 1968.

Facsimiles of Revere's accounts of events of April 18, 1775.

708. Rossel, Seymour. The Holocaust. New York: Watts, 1981.

Introduction to the Holocaust for young readers. Examines questions about nature of prejudice, causes for German anti-Semitism, leadership of Hitler, concentration camps, and extermination of millions of Jews, gypsies, Slavs, and handicapped people. Notes "echoes" of Holocaust in present-day terrorism and violence. Indexed.

709. Russell, Francis. Lexington, Concord, and Bunker Hill. New York: American Heritage, 1963

History of last days of British rule in Colonial America. Beginning with Paul Revere's report of night of April 18, 1775, interprets first events of Revolution.

710. Salinger, Pierre. America held hostage; the secret negotiations. Garden City, N.Y.; Doubleday, 1981.

Contribution to record of American hostage crisis in Iran, which ended January 20, 1980, with release of fifty-three hostages after 444 days. Examines secret diplomatic negotiations during crises and presents background on Iranian politics.

711. Saul, Eric, and DeNevi, Don. The great San Francisco earthquake and fire, 1906. Millbrae, Calif.: Celestial Arts, 1981.

Pictorial history of 1906 earthquake and fire, highlighting physical destruction and human misery. Photos are supplemented with photographs of city before earthquake and following the rebuilding. Eyewitness reports and observations.

712. Schackburg, Richard, Yankee doodle. Englewood Cliffs, N.J.: Prentice-Hall, 1965.

Illustrated account of song "Yankee Doodle," written by British surgeon, sung by British soldiers as they marched to Lexington, and taken over by Americans as they drove British back to Boston.

713. Schiffrin, Harold Z. Sun Yat-sen; reluctant revolutionary. Boston: Little, 1980.

Biographical study of Sun Yat-sen, enigmatic twentieth-century revolutionary hero and first president of Chinese republic. Revered in Chinese communities throughout world, his birthday is a holiday on Taiwan.

714. Schwartz, Alvin. To be a father; stories, letters, essays, poems, comments, and proverbs on the delights and despairs of fatherhood. New York: Crown, 1967.

Writings about fathers as proud parents, friends, protectors, teachers, and disciplinarians, including address by Adlai E. Stevenson to National Father's Day Committee on May 25, 1961.

715. Shachtman, Tom. The day America crashed. New York: Putnam, 1979.

History of October 24, 1929, blackest day in stock market collapse of 1929. Account of individual and corporate financial tragedies of the day and aftermath of devastation in human lives and depressed economy.

716. Smith, Richard K. First across! The U.S. Navy's transatlantic flight of 1919. Annapolis, Md.: Naval Institute Press, 1973.

Record of history-making 1919 flight of navy's NC-4 flying boat, first aircraft to carry men over the Atlantic.

717. Stubenrauch, Bob. Where freedom grew. New York: Dodd, 1970.

Photographs and word sketches of buildings and sites associated with Revolutionary War, including Paul Revere's house and Old North Church in Boston, Hancock-Clarke house and the green in Lexington, and *Minuteman* and bridge at Concord.

718. Tremain, Rose. The fight for freedom for women. New York: Random House, 1973.

Comparison of woman's suffrage movements in Britain and United States, with lessons learned by American leaders from British suffragettes.

719. Turnbull, Patrick. Dunkirk; anatomy of disaster. New York: Holmes and Meier, 1978.

Firsthand report of gallant rescue of British Expeditionary Force and European allies from Dunkirk, French village across English Channel from Britain. One of great human-interest stories of World War II, involving not only British navy but seafaring citizens and their little boats, who evacuated over 300,000 men.

720. Tute, Warren, and others. D-day, New York: Macmillan, 1974.

British view of planning, organization, and execution of 1944 Normandy invasion, based on eyewitness reports. Photographs, maps, and diagrams.

721. Wheeler, Richard. Sherman's march. New York: Crowell, 1978.

General William Tecumseh Sherman's devastating but militarily successful march through the South during the Civil War; based on eyewitness accounts recorded in diaries, letters, documents, and reports by wide variety of soldiers, journalists, and citizens of the Confederacy.

722. William, Paul, ed. The international bill of human rights. Glen Ellen, Calif.: Entwhistle, 1981.

Source book on human rights, containing brief histories and texts of "Universal Declaration of Human Rights" and "Covenant on Economic, Social and Cultural Rights."

People Related to the Calendar

723. Abodaher, David J. Freedom fighter; Casimir Pulaski. New York: Messner, 1969.

Biography of Pulaski, leader of Pulaski Legion in American Revolutionary War, who is honored annually by Polish Americans on October 11, Pulaski Memorial Day.

724. Alexander, Lloyd. Fifty years in the doghouse. New York: Putnam, 1964.

Adventures of William Michael Ryan, special agent for American Society for the Prevention of Cruelty to Animals, oldest humane society in Western Hemisphere.

725. Allen, Gay Wilson. Waldo Emerson; a biography. New York: Viking, 1981.

Major biography of Emerson combines study of his personal life (including preference of Waldo as Christian name) with analysis of his intellectual development and interpretation of his work as foremost American essayist, poet, and philosopher of nineteenth century.

726. Anderson, David D. William Jennings Bryan, Boston: Twayne, 1981.

Analysis of speeches, essays, articles, and books of William Jennings Bryan, American politician, whose "cross of gold" speech led to Democratic presidential nomination in 1896. Book concludes with 1925 prosecution of John Scopes (Dayton, Tenn.) for teaching Darwinian theory, contrary to state statute.

727. Archer, Jules. Famous young rebels. New York: Messner, 1973.

Short sketches of early lives of famous people considered radicals in their day: Jawaharal Nehru, Elizabeth Gurley Flynn, Marcus Garvey, Robert La Follette, Margaret Sanger, Leon Blum, Lazara Cardenas, Samuel Gompers, Mussolini, Elizabeth Cody Stanton, and Sam Adams.

728. Ayre, Leslie. The Gilbert and Sullivan companion. New York: Dodd, 1972.

Encyclopedic study of partnership between W. S. Gilbert and Arthur Sullivan, summaries of their operettas, major artists, and text of their songs. Arranged alphabetically.

729. Bar-Zehar, Michael. Ben-Gurion; a biography. New York: Delacorte, 1978.

Biography of David Ben-Gurion, "principal architect of Israel" and its first prime minister. Focuses on his personality and interprets his achievements.

730. Barth, Alan. Prophets with honor; great dissents and great dissenters in the Supreme Court. New York: Knopf, 1974.
Circumstances, philosophy, and issues behind six historic "dissents" in Supreme Court involving individual rights and liberties. Dissenters are Harlan, Brandeis, Black, Stone, and Douglas.

731. Bickel, Lennard. Facing starvation; Norman Borlaug and the fight against hunger. New York: Reader's Digest Press, 1974.
Study of Norman Borlaug, Nobel Prize-winning agronomist, and his effort to increase world's food supply to alleviate threats of starvation.

732. Bober, Natalie. A restless spirit; the story of Robert Frost. New York: Atheneum, 1981.
Biography of prize-winning New England bard, poet-in-residence at colleges, universities, and Library of Congress, and poetry-reading participant in John Kennedy's inauguration. Narrative of personal experiences and poetic accomplishments, with introduction by Frost's granddaughter Robin Hudnut. Indexed.

733. Bond, Creina, and Siegried, Roy. Antarctica; no single country—no single sea. New York: Mayflower, 1979.
History of exploration of Antarctica. Includes accounts of explorers: Ross, Amundsen, Shackleton, David, Scott, and others, with descriptions of emperor penguins, albatrosses, and other wondrous creatures of area. Illustrated with beautiful photography. Indexed.

734. Brodie, Fawn McKay. Thomas Jefferson, an intimate history. New York: Norton, 1974.
Focused on philosophy, experiences, and personality which molded his career. Appendix includes reminiscences by his sons.

735. Brooks, Paul. The house of life; Rachel Carson at work. Boston: Houghton, 1972.
Her work as biologist and author whose books inspired conservation-minded Americans and laid foundation for the ecological movement.

736. Calder, Jenni. Robert Louis Stevenson; a life study. New York: Oxford, 1980.
Study of ever-fascinating personality and career of this nineteenth-century novelist, poet, and essayist from Scotland, whose writings ended at Vailima (Samoa) with his death in 1894.

737. Cassidy, Robert. Margaret Mead; a voice for the century. New York: Universe, 1982.
Engrossing study of productive life of American anthropologist. Traces influences that led her into anthropology, documents her accomplishments, and pays tribute to her courageous stand on major issues facing contemporary society, from environmental problems and Third World development to the family and changing role of modern women.

738. Chicago, Judy. The dinner party; a symbol of our heritage. Garden City, N.Y.: Anchor/Doubleday, 1979.
Record of five-year project involving hundreds of artists and artisans in creation of *The Dinner Party*, documenting contributions of women to world history. Brief biographies of 999 women selected for their accomplishments or spiritual or legendary influence.

739. Clark, Ella Elizabeth, and Edmunds, Margot. Sacagawea of the Lewis and Clark expedition. Berkeley: Univ. of California Press, 1980.
Assessment of Shoshone Indian woman who served as interpreter during Lewis and Clark expedition. Traces spread of Sacagawea legends and tells of her later life on Wind River Reservation. Indexed.

740. Clarke, Elizabeth. Bloomers and ballots; Elizabeth Cady Stanton and women's rights. New York: Viking, 1972.
Portrayal of Stanton as seeker for her own individuality and leader in nineteenth-century suffragette movement.

741. Clarke, James Mitchell. The life and adventures of John Muir. San Francisco: Sierra, 1980.
Biography of American naturalist, inventor, explorer, and discoverer of Muir Glacier in Alaska. Examines his many capabilities and intellectual pursuits, including his theory of valley formation by glacial action in Yosemite area.

742. Clifford, Deborah Pickman. Mine eyes have seen the glory; Julia Ward Howe, 1819–1910. Boston: Little, 1979.
Life story of author of "Battle Hymn of the Republic." Interesting account of gifted woman who was abolitionist, suffragist, and leader in cultural reform movements of nineteenth century.

743. Collins, Philip, ed. Dickens; interviews and recollections. 2 vols. New York: Barnes & Noble, 1981.
Collection of observations from family, friends, professional associates, journalists, and other observers. Touches all aspects of life and career of this nineteenth-century English novelist: appearance, personality, philosophy, acting ability, work habits, and relationships with people.

744. Cooke, Jacob Ernest. Alexander Hamilton. New York: Scribner, 1982.
In-depth biography of first secretary of treasury of United States. Traces his life from West Indies boyhood to his death in duel with Aaron Burr, and his contributions to new nation.

745. Croy, Homer. Our Will Rogers. Boston: Little, 1953.
Based on personal friendship, interviews with cowboy friends and neighbors, and examination of scrapbooks and documents at Will Rogers Memorial.

746. Curtis, Bruce. Justice William O. Douglas. New York: Twayne, 1981.
Study of Supreme Court justice as author of autobiographies, travel books, and essays on intellectual freedom, conservation, court decisions, and law. Examines his writings to determine Douglas's place in American literary history.

747. Davies, Hunter, William Wordsworth, a biography. New York: Atheneum, 1980.
Biography of romantic poet of late eighteenth and early nineteenth centuries, associated with England's Lake District. Makes good use of unpublished letters in interpreting his personal life.

748. de Paola, Tomie. Francis, the poor man of Assisi. New York: Holiday, 1982.
Beautifully illustrated biography of Saint Francis for young readers and family sharing. Retells familiar story of conversion of wealthy young man, founding of Friars Minor, and kinship of Saint Francis with all of God's creation, from Saint Clare to birds, wolves, and other wild creatures. Reprint of his "Song of the Sun" and brief listing of facts about Saint Francis and Saint Clare.

749. Douglas, Emily Taft. Remember the ladies; the story of great women who helped shape America. New York: Putnam, 1966.
Narrative history of leaders in advancement of social, economic, and intellectual life of women in United States. Includes Anne Hutchinson, Abigail Adams, Anne Royal, Margaret Fuller, Dorothy Dix, civil rights and suffrage crusaders, Jane Addams, and Eleanor Roosevelt.

750. Drake, Stillman. Galileo at work; his scientific biography. Chicago: Univ. of Chicago Press, 1978.
Galileo's professional life, based on his collected works, correspondence, account books, letters, and court proceedings. Presents Galileo as complete scientist and examines his theories in religious, intellectual, and scientific environment of his time.

751. Durant, Mary, and Harwood, Michael. On the road with John James Audubon. New York: Dodd, Mead, 1980.
Biography, history, and travelogue linked to life and times of Audubon. Text tells of a year's journeys to trace Audubon's travels; quotations from his writings set conversational mood and correlate his findings with contemporary conditions. Illustrated with woodcuts, portraits, and photographs.

752. Earhart, Amelia. Letters from Amelia; an intimate portrait of Amelia Earhart. Ed. by Jean L. Backus. Boston: Beacon, 1982.
Collection of letters by Earhart to her mother, with background commentary by editor. Letters of a daughter concerned about her family reveal much about personality of the aviatrix in terms of family relationships. Chart of her record-breaking flying achievements.

753. Eber, Dorothy Harley. Genuis at work; images of Alexander Graham Bell. New York: Viking, 1982.
A look at Bell, his supportive wife and family, and laboratory assistants on vacation in Nova Scotia. Based on interviews and Bell Papers, this account of work and play over thirty-seven summers (beginning in 1885) reveals much about Bell's many interests, from sheep shearing to hydrofoil propulsion.

754. Eichelberger, Clark Mell. Organizing for peace; a personal history of the founding of the United Nations. New York: Harper & Row, 1977.
Contribution to history of founding United Nations in 1945; firsthand account of long efforts to establish an organization to maintain world peace. Insight into failure of League of Nations, preparations for drafting UN charter, and decisions on establishing UN headquarters in New York.

755. Ellis, Jack D. The early life of Georges Clemenceau, 1841–1893. Lawrence: Regents Press of Kansas, 1980.
Formative period in life of Clemenceau, who became prime minister of France and was regarded as the country's "savior" at end of World War I.

756. Engen, Rodney. Kate Greenaway; a biography. New York: Schocken, 1981.
Study of nineteenth-century English illustrator of children's books—her solitary life, relationship with John Ruskin (English art critic), and work. Based on correspondence and on interviews with her descendants. Color plates and black-and-white illustrations.

757. Fisher, Richard B. Joseph Lister, 1827–1912. New York: Stein & Day, 1977.
Biography of English surgeon, honored by medical profession as founder of antiseptic surgery. Study of Lister's career relates his operative techniques and innovations to medical world of his day.

758. Flood, Charles Bracelon. Lee; the last years. Boston: Houghton, 1981.
Study of Lee's productive years following his surrender at Appomattox at end of Civil War; Lee's advocacy of healing process between North and South and contributions as president of Washington College (later named Washington and Lee University).

759. Franklin, John Hope, and Meier, August. Black leaders of the twentieth century. Champaign: Univ. of Illinois Press, 1982.
Well-written essays document and interpret careers and contributions of fifteen blacks who dedicated their lives to elimination of racism, such as Booker T. Washington, W. E. B. Dubois, Mary McLeod Bethune, Martin Luther King Jr., and Malcolm X.

760. Fraser, Nicholas, and Navarro, Marysa. Eva Peron. New York: Norton, 1981.
Biography of the activist wife of Argentina's dictator Juan Domingo Peron. Traces her life from childhood poverty to years of immense political influence and achievements on behalf of urban and rural poor, who regarded her as a heroine.

761. Frommer, Harvey. Rickey and Robinson; the men who broke baseball's color barrier. New York: Macmillan, 1982.
A look at Branch Rickey, general manager of Brooklyn Dodgers, and Jackie Robinson, first black to play in major leagues, and their combined roles in breaking down discrimination against blacks in professional sports.

762. Garbarini, Vi, and others. "Strawberry fields forever"; John Lennon remembered. Special introduction by Dave Marsh. New York: Bantam, 1980.
Profile by journalists; includes in-depth interview with Lennon and Yoko Ono and tributes to his musical career.

763. Gasnick, Roy M., ed. The Francis book; 800 years with the saint from Assisi. New York: Macmillan, 1980.
Collection of writings about life, teachings, and influence of Saint Francis. Authors range from Matthew Arnold to Dorothy Day.

764. Gies, Frances. Joan of Arc; the legend and the reality. New York: Harper, 1981.
Chronological biography, including examination of legends that surround her. Concluding chapter looks at treatment of Joan in literature and art from the fifteenth century to modern times.

765. Gopal, Sarvepalli, ed. Jawaharial Nehru; an anthology. New York: 1981.
Nehru's thoughts and ideas, selected from statesman's autobiography, historical writings, and letters. Topics range from India's struggle for independence to reflections on world of nature.

766. Grigg, John. Lloyd George; the people's champion, 1902–1911. Berkeley: Univ. of California Press. 1979.
Study of famous Welsh patriot and British statesman when he was strongest leader in Liberal party and articulate anti-imperialist member of parliament.

767. Gross, David C. Pride of our people; the stories of one hundred outstanding Jewish men and women. Garden City, N.Y.: Doubleday, 1979.
Jewish men and women who have made contributions to science, government, education, politics, art, entertainment, industry, scholarship, literature, religion, medicine, and social service. Book opens with sketch of Jonas Salk, conqueror of polio, and closes with Uriah P. Levy, commodore in U.S. navy.

768. Guinness, Desmond, and Sadler, Julius T. Mr. Jefferson, architect. New York: Studio-Viking, 1973.
Jefferson's interests and talents as architect, from first plans for Monticello to design of University of Virginia, with record of his influence on architecture of Colonial America.

769. Harlow, Alvin F. Henry Bergh; founder of the A.S.P.C.A. New York: Messner, 1957.
The life of Bergh and his twenty-two years of leadership in American Society for Prevention of Cruelty to Animals and organization of Society for Prevention of Cruelty to Children.

770. Heckscher, August, and Robinson, Phyllis. When LaGuardia was mayor; New York's legendary years. New York: Norton, 1978.
Account of the flamboyant mayor of New York City during tumultuous years 1934 through 1945; based largely upon contemporary newspaper reports.

771. Heinz, Thomas A. Frank Lloyd Wright. New York: St. Martin's, 1982.
Illustrated introduction to work of Wright interprets his architectural philosophy and style and points to his achievements in architectural design.

772. Hemmings, Frederick William John. The life and times of Emile Zola. New York: Scribner, 1977.

Biography of nineteenth-century French novelist centered on his many interests, from Dreyfus Affair to associations with Impressionist painters. Illustrated with black-and-white photographs, some the work of Zola.

773. Hendrickson, Robert A. The rise and fall of Alexander Hamilton. New York: Van Nostrand, 1981.

Introduction to Hamilton: his role in Revolutionary War, leadership in Federalist party, government service as secretary of treasury, and theories of strength in government at national level.

774. Hirst, Wolf Z. John Keats. New York: Twayne, 1981.

Biography of English Romantic poet considers effect of illness and other human factors on his writing and analyzes his creative philosophy. Based upon Keats letters and related sources.

775. Holmes, Edward, and Maynard, Christopher, with Jennifer L. Justice, ed. Great men of science. New York: Watts, 1979.

Introduction to history of science and scientific concepts, from ancient Egypt to modern genetics. Brief biographies of such scientists as the Curies, Copernicus, Newton, and Pasteur. Illustrated with color and black-and-white photographs. Indexed.

776. Hough, Richard Alexander. Mountbatten. New York: Random House, 1981.

Biography of Earl Mountbatten of Burma, godson of Queen Victoria, First Sea Lord of Britain, last viceroy of India; a central figure in historic events of first half of twentieth century. Victim of IRA bomb in 1979.

777. Howarth, William, ed. Thoreau in the mountains. New York: Farrar, Straus & Giroux, 1982.

Retracing of Thoreau's walks in mountains of New England. Captivating text includes excerpts from his writings, with commentary on Thoreau as naturalist and comparison of landscapes of Thoreau's time with today's. Also, recommendations on how hikers can duplicate Thoreau's walking experiences.

778. Kemp, Martin. Leonardo da Vinci; the marvelous works of nature and man. Cambridge, Mass.: Harvard Univ. Press, 1981.

Illuminating study of da Vinci as artist, scientist, anatomist, inventor, and greatest example of Renaissance genius.

779. Ketchum, Richard M. Will Rogers; his life and times. New York: American Heritage, 1973.

Illustrated biography of quotable (and unforgettable) commentator on American scene of 1920s and 1930s. Developed in cooperation with Will Rogers Memorial at Claremore, Okla.

780. Kidd, Walter E. British winners of the Nobel literary prize. Norman: Univ. of Oklahoma Press, 1973.

Essays on selected Nobel Prize winners: Kipling, Yeats, Shaw, Galsworthy, Russell, Churchill, and Beckett, with biographical notes and unique qualities of each author.

781. Kingman, Russ. A pictorial life of Jack London. New York: Crown, 1981.

Pictorial biography of American novelist, short-story writer, and gold seeker in the Klondike. Over 250 unusual or rare photographs, with supporting text.

782. Kronenberger, Louis. The last word: portraits of fourteen master aphorists. New York: Macmillan, 1972.

Introduction to careers and talents of such aphorists as Shaw, Chesterton, Butler, Johnson, Goethe, and Emerson.

783. Landon, H. C. Robbins. Haydn; a documentary study. New York: Rizzoli, 1981.

Introduction to life and work of Franz Joseph Haydn, eighteenth-century Austrian composer, taken in part from Landon's five-volume biography of Haydn. 220 illustrations, some in color.

784. Laubach, Frank C. Thirty years with the silent billion. Westwood, N.J.: Revell, 1960.

Account of worldwide "each one teach one" career of Frank Laubach, literacy crusader. Covers period 1929 to 1957.

785. Longford, Elizabeth. Eminent Victorian women. New York: Knopf, 1981.

Illustrated biographical sketches of Annie Besant, Brontes, James Barry, Josephine Butler, George Eliot, Mary Kingsley, Florence Nightingale, Harriet Beecher Stowe, and Ellen Terry. Chapter 1 reviews social and legal status of nineteenth-century women.

786. Longford, Lord. Pope John Paul II, an authorized biography. New York: Morrow, 1982.

Beautifully illustrated biography of Karl Wojtyla, elected pope in 1978 (the first with origins in Eastern Europe). Well-balanced text provides background on his early life, career in church, and first three years in the Vatican.

787. McCarthy, Harold T. The expatriate perspective; American novelists and the idea of America. Cranbury, N.J.: Fairleigh-Dickinson Univ. Press, 1974.

Essays on ten Americans—Cooper, Hawthorne, Melville, James, Twain, Cummings, Hemingway, Miller, Wright, and Baldwin—examine use of expatriate experiences to assess American values. Indexed.

788. Marks, Geoffrey, and Beatty, William K. Women in white. New York: Scribner, 1972.

Study of the role of women in the healing arts, from Stone and Bronze ages to 1970s. Recalls years of struggle for women's rights in medicine and reviews achievements of Elizabeth Blackwell, Florence Nightingale, Dorothea Lynde Dix, Marie Curie, and others in medicine, nursing, and research. Indexed.

789. Mayes, Stanley, Markarios; a biography. New York: St. Martin's, 1981.

Biography of Archbishop Makarios, Greek Orthodox prelate, Cypriot statesman, and president of Cyprus. Traces his life from childhood to his death in 1977 and reveals much about his personality and qualities of leadership.

790. Millgate, Michael. Thomas Hardy; a biography. New York: Random House, 1982.

Contribution to literature on Hardy, British novelist and poet. Traces his life from rural beginnings, examines his creative years as a leading British writer, and discusses his major work.

791. Morris, Richard B. Seven who shaped our destiny; the founding fathers as revolutionaries. New York: Harper, 1973.

Interpretations of Franklin, Jay, Washington, Jefferson, John Adams, Madison, and Hamilton, with insight into their positions on independence from England and their contributions to unique character of American Revolution.

792. Mosley, Leonard. Marshall; hero for our times. New York: Hearst, 1982.

Full-scale biography of America's great soldier-diplomat, George C. Marshall. Facts and anecdotes related to his roles in World Wars I and II and his contributions as secretary of state. Absorbing portrait of a man of war and architect of peace.

793. Noble, Iris. Emmeline and her daughters; the Pankhurst suffragettes. New York: Messner, 1971.

Study of Emmeline Pankhurst and her three daughters, and their thirty-year struggle for equality for women.

794. Phillips, Elizabeth. Marianne Moore. New York: Ungar, 1982.

Study of American poet whose style and innovations with images and forms assure her a leading position in history of American writing.

795. Rice, Edward. Margaret Mead; a portrait. New York: Harper & Row, 1979.

Study of Mead's many accomplishments as anthropologist with broad interest in human relations. Photographs of Mead and her associates, from time of her childhood to shortly before her death in 1978.

796. Richardson, Ben Albert, and Fahey, William A. Great black Americans. 2d ed. New York: Crowell, 1976.

Sketches of thirty-one black American leaders in music, theater, art, literature, education, public affairs, science, and sports (such as Marian Anderson, Paul Robeson, Jacob Lawrence, James Baldwin, Ralph Bunche, George Washington Carver, Althea Gibson, Mohammad Ali).

797. Rogers, Will. A Will Rogers treasury; reflections and observations. Comp. and ed. by Bryan B. Sterling and Francis N. Sterling. New York: Crown, 1982.

Collection of articles written by Will Rogers, perceptive and quotable observer of national and international events in twentieth century. Selections, written from 1922 through 1935, supplemented with background on happenings that were subject to Rogers's sharp analysis and wit. Indexed.

798. Rosenberg, Jakob. Rembrandt; Life and work. Rev. ed. Ithaca, N.Y.: Cornell Univ. Press, 1980.

Distinguished study of life and work of Rembrandt van Rijn, celebrated Dutch painter and etcher of seventeenth century.

799. Ross, Ishbel. Angel of the battlefield. New York: Harper, 1956.

Clara Barton on battlefields of the Civil War and inspiration for establishment of American Red Cross.

800. Sadat, Anwar. In search of identity. New York: Harper, 1978.

Autobiography of Anwar el-Sadat, peasant-born president of Egypt, assassinated in 1981. Written from point of view of an Egyptian whose career was intimately linked to modern-day Egypt and whose aims were to serve cause of liberty and peace.

801. Samuels, Ernest. Bernard Berenson; the making of a connoisseur. Cambridge, Mass.: Harvard Univ. Press, 1979.

In-depth study of American art critic and authority on Italian art. Examines his early life, maturing of intellectual interests, and contributions as critic and interpreter of art to 1904.

802. Sayers, Isabelle S. Annie Oakley and Buffalo Bill's Wild West. New York: Dover, 1981.
Review of career of Annie Oakley, American sharp-shooter and entertainer, follows her through seventeen years with Buffalo Bill's Wild West Show. Reproductions of old photographs, handbills, and posters.

803. Slater, Robert. Golda; the uncrowned queen of Israel; a pictorial biography. New York: Jonathan David, 1981.
Biography of Golda Meir, distinguished stateswoman and world leader, covers her personal life as well as her public career as ambassador, Israeli prime minister, and exponent of Zionism and Israel's search for peace.

804. Spink, Kathryn. The miracle of love; Mother Teresa of Calcutta, her Missionaries of Charity, and her co-workers. New York: Harper, 1982.
Study of Mother Teresa, founder of Missionary Sisters of Charity, and her years of dedication to alleviating suffering of poor and dying, which brought her Nobel Peace Prize in 1979 and admiration of the world. Her Nobel lecture and Templeton Award speech are included.

805. Stites, Francis N. John Marshall, defender of the Constitution. Boston: Little, 1981.
Study of first chief justice of United States covers his early years, devotion to his wife, dedication to principles of the Constitution, and such landmark cases as Burr treason trial.

806. Stoddard, Hope. Famous American women. New York: Crowell, 1970.
Collective biography of such distinguished American women as Jane Addams and Harriet Tubman who made contributions to American life in nineteenth and twentieth centuries.

807. Sullivan, George. Sadat; the man who changed Mid-East history. New York: Walker, 1981.
Introduction to career of Anwar el-Sadat assassinated October 6, 1981. Brief biography deals with Sadat's concern with building a modern army, relationship with his countrymen, role in 1973 Arab-Israeli conflict, and signing peace treaty with Israel.

808. Taylor, Hilary. James McNeill Whistler. New York: Putnam, 1978.
Examination of Whistler's reputation and career reveals him as maverick artist who contradicted the art establishment while maintaining his own standards. Text also explores factors that influenced Whistler's concepts of art, and his influence on contemporaries.

809. Teichmann, Howard. Alice; the life and times of Alice Roosevelt Longworth. Englewood Cliffs. N.J.: Prentice-Hall, 1979.
American legend, Alice Roosevelt Longworth, daughter of President Theodore Roosevelt; keen-eyed, articulate observer of fourteen U.S. presidencies; noted for her nonconforming approach to political scene, sharp wit, and longevity.

810. Treece, Patricia. A man for others; Maximilian Kolbe; Saint of Auschwitz; in the words of those who know him. San Francisco: Harper & Row, 1982.
Moving testimony to brotherly love of Father Kolbe, martyred at Auschwitz (1941) when he volunteered to die in place of fellow prisoner. Kolbe was beatified in 1971 and proclaimed a saint in 1982. Based on interviews, written reminiscences, and records from beatification process.

811. Tregaskis, Richard William. The warrior king; Hawaii's Kamehameha the great. New York: Macmillan, 1973.
Life and achievements of Polynesian warrior who unified Hawaiian Islands in 1810 and reigned until his death in 1819.

812. Urofsky, Melvin I. A voice that spoke for justice; the life and times of Stephen S. Wise. Albany: State Univ. of New York Press, 1982.
In-depth study of one of most articulate rabbis of twentieth century, spokesman for Jewish community, leader in founding American Jewish Congress, supporter of rights of women and blacks, and adviser to American presidents. Indexed.

813. Wagenknecht, Edward. Ambassadors for Christ; seven American preachers. New York: Oxford, 1972.
Biographical sketches of seven influential preachers of nineteenth century, such as Phillips Brooks, D. L. Moody, and Henry Ward Beecher, with commentaries on their interest in literature and the arts, science and nature, social-economic climate, and religion.

814. ———. Henry David Thoreau; what manner of man? Amherst: Univ. of Massachusetts Press, 1981.
Character study links Thoreau's personality, friendships, schooling, life style, and creative techniques to his work as naturalist, poet, essayist, and social critic.

815. Wagner, Jean. Black poets of the United States from Paul Laurence Dunbar to Langston Hughes. Urbana: Univ. of Illinois Press, 1973.
Survey of lives and works of major black poets in United States from days of slavery to Langston Hughes; looks at social conditions revealed by major and minor poets. Bibliography.

816. Washington, Ida. H. Dorothy Canfield Fisher; a biography. New York: New England Press, 1982.
Life and career of author, champion of books and reading, supporter of adult education movement, and member of first selection committee of Book of the Month Club. Indexed.

817. Watson, Derek. Richard Wagner; a biography. New York: Schirmer-Macmillan, 1981.
Compact review of nineteenth-century German composer, with new material (such as Wagner's letters and Cosima Wagner's diaries). Photographs.

818. Weymouth, Lally, comp. Thomas Jefferson; the man, his world, his influence. New York: Putnam, 1974.
Scholarly studies of Jefferson's relationship to Enlightenment and Renaissance, his interpretation of political scene, and his contributions to architecture and libertarian thought.

819. White, Hilda. Truth is my country; portraits of eight New England authors. Garden City, N.Y.: Doubleday, 1971.
Emerson, Dickinson, Frost, Hawthorne, Millay, Robinson, Stowe, and Thoreau, presented in light of times that affected their work.

820. Wilder, Alec. American popular song; the great innovators, 1900–1950. New York: Oxford, 1972.
History of distinctive contributions in United States; separate chapters deal with Kern, Berlin, Gershwin, Rodgers, and Arlen.

821. Wilkins, Roy, with Tom Mathews. Standing fast; the autobiography of Roy Wilkins. New York: Viking, 1982.
Personal account of private and public life of Roy Wilkins, former executive director of NAACP. Major contribution to long and continuing struggle for equality and justice for minorities from perspective of black leader, convinced that "the only master race is the human race." Indexed.

822. Williams, George Huntston. The mind of John Paul II; origins of his thought and action. New York: Seabury;, 1981.
Study of factors which have influenced his thinking: traditions in Polish church, themism, World War II and the spread of communism, contemporary Roman Catholic scholarship, and Vatican II.

823. Wilson, Derek. The world encompassed; Francis Drake and his great voyage. New York: Harper, 1977.
Account of great figure in English maritime history, first Englishman to circumnavigate world. This history of Drake's 1577–80 voyage is linked to England, Elizabeth I, and her people, who needed the "lift" of Drake's achievement.

824. Yost, Nellie Snyder. Buffalo Bill; his family, friends, fame, failures, and fortunes. Athens: Ohio Univ. Press, 1980.
Full-length study of William Frederick Cody, American plainsman and showman known as Buffalo Bill; separates facts and legends.

825. Zamoyski, Adam. Paderewski. New York: Atheneum, 1982.
Full-scale biography of famed Polish pianist and composer covers his musical career and post–World War I contributions to Poland as articulate spokesman for national independence. Also as premier of coalition ministry in new nation and representative of Poland at Versailles.

Background Readings

826. Asimov, Isaac. The clock we live on. Rev. ed. New York: Abelard-Schuman, 1965.
Study of complexities of measuring time, numbering years, naming days, and problems of calendar reform.

827. Beijer, Agne. Court theatres of Drottningholm and Gripsholm. New York: Benjamin Blom, 1972.
Description of eighteenth-century Swedish court theaters at Gripsholm Castle and Drottningholm Palace (sites of contemporary theatrical revivals).

828. Brody, Alan. The English mummers and their plays; traces of ancient mystery. Philadelphia: Univ. of Pennsylvania Press, 1970.

Examination of three types of mummer play: hero combat, sword play, and wooing ceremony. Indexed.

829. Cabral, Olga. So proudly she sailed; tales of Old Ironsides. Boston: Houghton, 1981.

Action-packed stories from 100-year service of *U.S. Constitution*, revered naval treasure known as Old Ironsides. Action in foreign waters, battle conditions, seaboard life, and other interesting details.

830. Coleman, Lesley. A book of time. New York: Nelson, 1971.

Calendars, sundials, sand glasses, clocks, clock makers, time zones, and international date lines, from Sumerian priests to atomic clocks at Greenwich.

831. Cosman, Madeleine Pelner. Medieval holidays and festivals; a calendar of celebrations. New York: Scribner, 1981.

Beginning with description of medieval feast, history of celebrations of each month includes foods, games, theatricals, and other customs; also recipes and craft instruction. Illustrated with prints and reproductions of medieval manuscript artwork.

832. Couzens, Reginald C. The stories of the months and days. London: Blackie and Son, 1922; Detroit: Gale, 1970.

Reprint of history of myths and legends connected with names of days of week and months.

833. Delaney, Frank. James Joyce's odyssey; a guide to the Dublin of *Ulysses*. New York: Holt, 1982.

Lively introduction to Dublin of "Bloomsday," June 16, 1904. Chapters correspond to chapters of *Ulysses* in providing historical detail and literary anecdotes and insights into Dublin setting of Joyce's time and today. Period photographs. Indexed.

834. Doherty, Jim. "Bald eagle thrives as our symbol, survives in the wild." Smithsonian 13 (May 1982): 105–13.

Illustrated article, reviews 1782 selection of bald eagle as emblem of United States in design of nation's great seal and use on official stationery, coins, stamps, doorway of American embassies abroad, and in arts and crafts.

835. Emrich, Duncan, comp. The hodgepodge book; an almanac of American folklore. New York: Four Winds, 1972.

Curious fancies and information about seasons, months, and special days from American folklore.

836. Frazer, James George. The illustrated golden bough. General editor, Mary Douglas; abridged and illus. by Sabine MacCormack. Garden City, N.Y.: Doubleday, 1978.

Abridgment of *Golden Bough*, originally published in thirteen volumes. Classic study of magic, origins of religious rituals, and primitive customs that live on in twentieth century, such as Maypole dances of England, fire festivals of midsummer, and sprinkling of rice on newlywed.

837. Greene, Theodore P. America's heroes. New York: Oxford, 1970.

American hero as reflected in periodical literature in four major historical periods, 1787 to 1918. Provides insight into continuing public interest in days of recognition for popular heroes.

838. Howse, Derek. Greenwich time and the discovery of longitude. New York: Oxford, 1980.

Historic facts behind "Greenwich mean time," used to time and date events. History, going back to 300 B.C., gives reasons for selection of Royal Greenwich Observatory for international time standard and zero longitude. Appendixes include material on determining longitude, precision clocks, and men who chose Greenwich (in 1884). Indexed.

839. Irwin, Keith Gordon. The 365 days. New York: Crowell, 1963.

Evolution from Egyptian calendar (based on cycles of flooding of Nile) to Gregorian calendar; explains variable months, progression of dates for days of week, tree-ring records, temperature studies, and radiocarbon dating.

840. Jones, Charles Williams. Saint Nicholas of Myra, Bari, and Manhattan; biography of a legend. Chicago: Univ. of Chicago Press, 1978.

Study of one of oldest legends in history, linked to figure of Saint Nicholas (fourth-century bishop of Myra), traces story from early Christian observances to secularized customs of twentieth century.

841. Jones, William, Crowns and coronations; a history of regalia. London: Chatto & Windus, 1902; Detroit: Singing Tree Press, 1968.

Royal coronation days, regalia, rituals, and pageantry in various ages and countries; primarily British.

842. Lewis, Linda Rannells. Birthdays; their delights & disappointments, past and present, worldly, astrological, and infamous. Boston: Little, 1976.

How birthdays have been celebrated from time of ancient Greeks to twentieth century; describes birthday customs in different lands and records reactions, as well as eccentricities of some of famous on their birthday.

843. Llewellyn, Robert. Washington; the capital. Charlottesville, Va.: Thomasson-Grant, 1981.

Photographic description of Washington, capital of United States; a book chosen by State Department as "official diplomatic gift."

844. MacGregor, Geddes. Scotland forever home. New York: Dodd, 1980.

Introduction to Scotland as "homeland for American and other Scots." Text describes many aspects of life in Scotland, including grouse season, golf, Highland games, and kilts, tartans, and bagpipes.

845. McPhee, Carol, and Fitzgerald, Ann, comps. Feminist quotations. New York: Crowell, 1979.

Quotations from American and English women leaders in women's rights movement, covering 200 years; grouped by issue themes and presented chronologically within theme chapters. Indexed.

846. Michael, George. George Michael's treasury of Federal antiques. New York: Hawthorn, 1972.

American craftsmanship between 1770 and 1830, last era of "hand creativity" and manufacture in United States; background material for commemorative programs.

847. Morrison, Theodore. Chautauqua; a center for education, religion, and the arts in America. Chicago: Univ. of Chicago Press, 1974.

History of seasonal offerings and experimental programs of Chautauqua, most popular out-of-school educational movement of nineteenth-century United States.

848. Murphy, Brian. The world of weddings; an illustrated celebration. New York: Paddington, 1978.

Handsome volume on marriage ceremonies around the world; examines origins of bridal veil, ring, wedding cake, showers, and points to ancient customs and superstitions that touch modern marriage services and events.

849. Rajanen, Aini. Of Finnish ways. Minneapolis: Dillon, 1981.

Introduction to present-day Finland reviews Finnish history, culture, language, folkways, and food. One chapter describes contemporary holidays and celebrations. Indexed.

850. Shenker, Israel. In the footsteps of Johnson and Boswell. Boston: Houghton, 1982.

Retracing of 1773 route by Johnson and Boswell from Edinburgh to western islands of Scotland. Fascinating view of situations which attracted Johnson and Boswell, contrasted with changes the years have wrought. Text is enlivened by Shenker's reports of conversations with present-day Scots, on subjects from flora and fauna to life on contemporary Iona.

851. Steiner, George. "Books; ladies' day." New Yorker: 57 (August 17, 1981): 104–6.

On induction of Marguerite Yourcenar, novelist, essayist, and translator, into French Academy (January 22, 1981). Brief commentary on election of first woman since 1635 to very select body of "Immortals," with observations on her major and minor writings.

852. Strong, Roy. Splendour at court; Renaissance spectacle and the theater of power. Boston: Houghton, 1973.

History of Renaissance court fetes; impact of celebrations in sixteenth- and seventeenth-century society and their influence on later creative forms.

853. West, Richard. Back to Africa; a history of Sierra Leone and Liberia. New York: Holt, 1970.

Account of black repatriation movement on African continent in terms of people behind back-to-Africa idea and events that formed modern-day nations of Sierra Leone and Liberia. Indexed.

Source Materials

854. Baha'i Calendar. Wilmette, Ill.: Baha'i Publishing Trust, annual.
Calendar of Baha'i year, with charts of nineteen-day feasts: month of observance, Arabic name and translations, and dates of first days. Chart also lists Baha'i holy days (on which work should be suspended) and anniversaries.

855. Biography almanac. Ed. by Annie Brewer. Detroit: Gale, 1981.
Guide to identification of over 20,000 people who have left imprint on history, from biblical times into twentieth century. Entries identify individuals by complete names, dates, and places of birth and death (when applicable), nationality, occupations, and achievements. Listings include citations to biographical material in 325 source books.

856. Book of the states. Lexington, Ky.: Council of State Governments, biennial.
Authoritative source of information on government of individual states of United States. Historical data on each state, such as source of state lands, date admitted to Union, and Nickname, motto, flower, bird, and song.

857. Chase, William D., and Chase, Helen M. Chases' calendar of annual events. Flint, Mich.: Apple Tree Press, annual.
Resource for quick information on traditional holidays, ethnic days, anniversaries, festivals, fairs, "sponsored weeks," and month-long observances, in one-year time frame. Includes such special features as presidential proclamations related to important observances.

858. Children's books; awards and prizes. New York: Children's Book Council, biennial.
Three-part compilation of awards and prizes in children's book field: U.S. awards, British Commonwealth awards, international awards. Brief background information on each name award prefaces chronological list of honored books. Indexed by title and person.

859. Granger's index to poetry. Ed. by William James Smith. 6th ed. New York: Columbia Univ. Press, 1973; supplement 1970–77, 1978.
Index to anthologies of poetry published through 1977. Source for locating poems suitable for traditional holidays and such special occasions as Arbor or commencement days.

860. Ireland, Norma Olin. Index to fairy tales, 1949–1972, including folklore, legends and myths in collections. Westwood, Mass.: Faxon, 1973.
Reference tool for locating fairy tales, folklore, legends, myths. Continuation of index and supplements compiled by Mary Huse Eastman. Includes an analyzed list of collections, followed by alphabetically arranged subject index to the stories and tales.

861. Kane, Joseph Nathan. Famous first facts. 4th ed. New York: Wilson, 1981.
Comprehensive record of over 9,000 "American firsts"; major source for confirmation of facts about first happenings, discoveries, inventions, and memorable achievements or occasions in American history. Arranged alphabetically by subject. Quick access to data through four indexes: years, days of month, personal names, geographical location.

862. ———. and Alexander, Gerald L. Nicknames and sobriquets of U.S. cities and states. 2d ed. Metuchen, N.J.: Scarecrow, 1970.
Index to well- and little-known nicknames of states, cities, and towns, organized into four sections: geographical by city, with nicknames; nicknames for cities; geographical by state; and nicknames for states.

863. Kingman, Lee, ed. Newbery and Caldecott medal books, 1966–1975. Boston: Horn, 1975.
Collection of acceptance papers from Newbery and Caldecott award winners, with biographical notes and evaluating essays. Successor to Newbery medal books, 1922–55; Caldecott medal books, 1938–57; and Newbery and Caldecott medal books, 1956–65

864. Nicholsen, Margaret E. People in books; a selective guide to biographical literature arranged by vocations and other fields of reader interest. New York: Wilson, 1969; first supplement, 1977.
"The purpose of this reference tool is to identify by vocation or field of activity, by country, and by century the subjects of biographies and other biographical writings which are recommended for libraries serving children, young adults, and adults" (preface).

865. Parise, Frank, ed. The book of calendars. New York: Facts on File, 1982.
Informative handbook on world calendars developed from time of ancient world. Includes historic data on each calendar and excellent conversion tables relating calendars to the Julian or the Gregorian.

866. Peter, Lawrence J. Peter's almanac. New York: Morrow, 1982.

Amusing book of days, chronologically arranged. Lists traditional days, along with days "christened" by author in the name of event that happened on that day. Each entry supplemented with typical Peter principles, laws, and one-liners. Indexed.

867. Silverman, Judith. Index to collective biographies for young readers. 3d ed. New York: Bowker, 1979.

Guide to contents of 942 collective biographies, totaling 7,245 notable men and women. Organized through alphabetical section of biographees, with pertinent data on birth, death, nationality, activity, and section listing biographees under fields of activity. Indexed books listed by title and arranged alphabetically.

868. The statesman's year-book; statistical and historical annual of the states of the world. New York: St. Martin's, annual.

Major source for confirmation of dates in history of nations throughout the world, such as achievement of independence and adoption of constitution. Concise information on national flags and anthems, makeup of populations, and governmental statistics. Arranged alphabetically by country. Indexed.

869. UNICEF wall calendar. New York: U.S. Committee for UNICEF, annual.

Records national, religious, and special days celebrated by member nations of United Nations. Illustrated with reproductions of art by children around the world. Special feature describes unique holidays.

870. United States Architect of the Capitol. Compilation of works of art and other objects in the United States Capitol. Washington, D.C.: U.S. Printing Office, 1965.

Introduction to art forms in U.S. Capitol, including sketches of famous Americans represented in Statuary Hall.

871. Wasserman, Paul, ed. Awards, honors, and prizes. 4th ed. 2 vols. Detroit: Gale, 1978.

Compilation of awards in all fields, from academic honors to sports prizes. Vol. 1 covers awards in United States and Canada; vol. 2 describes awards, honors, and prizes of countries in other parts of world. Indexed by subject and award title.

872. ———. and Herman, Esther, eds. Festivals sourcebook. Detroit: Gale, 1977.

Information on over 3,800 events celebrated throughout North America: location, official names, schedules, description, and year of origin. Celebrations range from agricultureal to cultural and historical events (excluding traditional holidays and religious festivals). Access to information through four indexes: chronological, event name, geographical, subject.

873. Whitaker, Joseph. An almanack. London: Whitaker, annual.

British compilation of current information, including dates for bank holidays in England, Wales, Northern Ireland, Scotland, and Channel Islands; a table of Easter days and Sunday letters from 1500 to 2000; table of movable religious feasts; and other quick-reference calendar tables.

874. World almanac and book of facts. New York: N.Y. Newspaper Enterprise Association, annual.

Comprehensive compilation of statistics and information on current and preceding years; data on holidays and holy days includes legal or public holidays, selected days of observance, Jewish and Islamic religious days (with Gregorian calendar equivalents), Greek Orthodox calendar, and date of Paschal full moon.

875. World holiday and time guide. New York: Morgan Guaranty Trust Company. Annual.

Listing of holidays observed by world's principal countries and fifty American states. Notes provide data on half-day observances and regional or local exceptions.

Index

FOR REFERENCE

NOT TO BE TAKEN FROM THE ROOM

CAT. NO. 23 012

PRINTED
IN
U.S.A.